JOHN TAFFIN'S BOOK OF THE .45 CALIBER

JOHN TAFFIN'S BOOK OF THE 45 CALIBER

by

John Taffin

Wolfe Publishing Company
2180 Gulfstream, Suite A
Prescott, Arizona 86301-6182

Printed in the United States of America

23 22 21 20 19   5 4 3 2 1

First Edition

Published October 2019

ISBN: 978-0-935632-59-0

This Book Is Dedicated to
ROGER BISSELL
Friend, Brother, Hunting Partner

---

*"Well Done, Thy Good
And Faithful Servant"*

TABLE OF CONTENTS

PART 1

SIXGUNS AND THEIR CARTRIDGES

PART 2

SEMIAUTO PISTOLS AND THEIR CARTRIDGES

THE CARTRIDGES

THE SEMIAUTOMATICS

PART 3

LONG GUNS AND THEIR CARTRIDGES

FOREWORD

Clichés become clichés because they are, by and large, truths repeated over and over. The reputation of America's various .45-caliber pistol cartridges has been built on such repetition to the point where everyone has taken up the idea this caliber is just slightly less powerful than a tactical nuke. This is part of the cliché.

Years ago I got a phone call from a fellow on his way to an Alaskan bear hunt. He obviously wanted me to tell him his .45 ACP 1911 pistol was up to the task and the bears stood not a chance in mortal combat with it. My answer?

"The .45 ACP is the *least* powerful of all the .45s, a weak-kneed sister compared to many other pistol cartridges of .45 — even .44 — caliber."

Well, he erupted in a volcano of anger and vindictive comments. Evidently all the clichés were still true in his eyes. Finally he calmed down after I told him the .45 ACP was designed to whack two-legged varmints, not big, mean, huge-clawed ones. What really got his attention was when I told him I knew a fellow who had a .45 ACP hardball bounce off his head at a distance of 50 feet.

Make no mistake though. All, and I do mean *all* of the .45-caliber cartridges from the .45 Colt, the .45 Smith & Wesson, and all the rest throughout history have done their jobs in fine style, taking care of those aforementioned two-legged varmints. In John's new book, you're going to see how the .45-caliber pistol cartridges served in many tasks for which they were not originally designed.

Now we have many light rifles and carbines chambered in .45 Colt that are a delightful addition to the levergun arsenals of many shooters. In some of those same guns you can even opt for a .454 Casull chambering, which will give as much — or more — power as many .45-70 loads from heavier leverguns. Mine is a jewel that easily shot up the .454 Casull seconds from the ammunition company I worked for at the time, making me a wee bit punch-drunk from the joy of the experience. (There's no .45-caliber cartridge anywhere that has the panache of the .454 Casull.)

As you read this book, you might stop and ponder the last remaining Peters-designed cartridge remaining in production — the .45 Auto Rim. This one-of-a-kind cartridge was designed for use in .45 ACP sixguns left over from two world wars and several U.S. government agencies (including the United States Postal Service!). In my 1955 Smith & Wesson 6½-inch heavy-barreled .45, it gave me the smallest 25-yard group I ever shot with open sights, ¼-inch center-to-center with my own cast-bullet handloads. The delightful .45 Auto Rim is still available today for those of us shooting .45 ACP sixguns (don't miss out on it).

And the .45 S&W is again available. It is a wonderful "sub-load" for most .45 Colt revolvers and also shoots to beat the band because of its short powder column.

All the rest of the goodies in John's book you're going to have to dig out for yourself. I am sure this work will be standard pistolero reading fare for decades to come.

Terry Murbach
Dakota Territory

INTRODUCTION

Forty-four or .45? That's the age-old question facing sixgunners. It all began in 1869 when Smith & Wesson introduced the first truly workable big-bore, centerfire single action. It was the American Model No. 3 and was chambered in .44 S&W American. Two years later Colt was offering the 1871-72 Open Top in .44 Colt.

When the U.S. Army announced tests to select a new revolver, Colt entered Open Top and was told in no uncertain terms that the army not only wanted a revolver with a topstrap, but it would also have to be a .45. From those early years, the paths of Smith & Wesson and Colt were set.

S&W would mostly produce .44s, beginning with the American, then such excellent sixguns as the Model No. 3 Russian, the New Model No. 3, the Triple-Lock, the 2nd Model Hand Ejector, the 1926 Model, the 1950 Target and the original .44 Magnum. From 1869 until the last decade of the 20th century, S&W was synonymous with .44.

On the other hand, Colt, beginning in 1873, offered mostly .45s beginning with the Single Action Army and then going on to the New Service and the 1911. As this is written, they are still producing both the Single Action Army and the 1911. During this span, of course, S&W did produce some .45s and Colt also offered .44s, although the first number that came to mind when Colt was mentioned was definitely .45. But S&W's .45s will be covered in depth beginning with the Schofield Model of 1875 right up to its current double-action sixguns and 1911s.

When my *Book of the .44* arrived in 2006, most folks probably thought I'd settled the ".44 or .45?" question for myself. However, as soon as I finished my .44 book, I started outlining *The Book of the .45*. I've always had a difficult time choosing between them. Elmer Keith started his career using a .45 Colt before switching to the .44 Special and spending nearly 30 years touting the .44 as the all-around cartridge. Of course, when the .44 Magnum arrived, that's what he packed daily until his debilitating stroke in 1981. As a member of the Elmer Keith Museum Foundation, it was my privilege to go through all of Elmer's sixguns. It should come as no surprise that I found several of them loaded. One was a .45 Colt Single Action Army with five black-powder rounds in the cylinder. So Keith never totally gave

Circa 1957: John with Government Model .45 ACP.

A young John Taffin with a pair of 7½-inch .45 Colt Single Actions.

up on the .45. In fact, long after the .357 Magnum had arrived – and 30 years after he discovered the .44 Special – he still said if he had only factory rounds to choose from, he would take the .45. I also find it quite interesting that the dust jacket of his book *Sixguns By Keith* from that same year has a print of Charlie Russell's *Smoke of the .45*.

Skeeter Skelton had a very large soft spot in his six-gunning soul for the .44 Special; however, he also had room in there for the .45 Colt. Even the most ardent proponents of one or the other cartridge cross over from time to time. Mention Jeff Cooper and one immediately thinks of the .45 ACP, however, Col. Cooper also appreciated and shot the S&W .44 Magnum.

Dick Casull started the experiments with the .45 Colt which eventually led to the .454 Casull way back in the 1950s, however, I have personally fired his custom-cylindered Colt Single Action .44 Magnum. John Linebaugh has produced some very powerful sixguns chambered in .475 and .500 Linebaugh, but he started with heavy-duty .45 Colts, and his everyday packing gun for all the years I've known him has been first a 4-inch Model 25-5 S&W and now an S&W .45 Colt Mountain Gun. John may choose to carry an S&W sixgun, but he goes with the Colt cartridge. The difficult decision is still ".44 or .45?" The only reasonable answer remains "Buy 'em both."

I was 17 years old when the Ruger .44 Magnum Flat-Top Blackhawk arrived. At about the same time, Colt began offering the Single Action Army .45 once again. I bought both of them, although I am not a collector by any means. Collectors normally try to come up with every possible variation of a particular firearm. I simply accumulate the things I like. Although I've written before how .44s probably saved

me — and my family — from possible serious harm, the .45s have not been left out.

Shortly after I acquired my 7½-inch .45 Colt Single Action, the very first one to arrive in my area, I was driving my beautiful 1953 Mercury. It was yellow with a black top and yellow leather upholstery. Four guys in another car started harassing me by cutting in front of me, coming awfully close to the side of my Merc. I laid my 7½-inch .45 on the dashboard, and they disappeared as quickly as if they'd vaporized. A 17-year-old with a Mercury was no threat to them; the .45 was a different story.

In 1966 I attached a U-Haul trailer to the bumper of our 1965 Ford station wagon, put the back seat down and added a mattress for our three small kids to spend the next four days on as Diamond Dot and I headed from Ohio to Idaho.

All set up: John with his prize 7½" .45 Colt SAA and Arvo Ojala fast-draw rig.

In a military flap holster under the front seat was a World War II surplus 1911, chambered in .45 ACP, of course.

Beginning in 1969, I spent three summers attending graduate school in Missoula, Montana. I made the 400-mile trip home most weekends and that 1911 rode in the center of my back, stuffed in my belt on every trip. No, I never needed to fire either the .45 SAA or the 1911 Government Model in self-defense, but their presence was very comforting.

This book consists of a lifetime of experiences with .45-caliber firearms — sixguns, semiautos, single shots and leverguns. It is not even close to being the *Complete Book of the .45* for several reasons. I have not experienced every type of .45 ever made, and although I've seen several books with the word "complete" in their title, they were far

from it. It is simply impossible to write a complete book of anything.

Since I mainly cover firearms I've had personal experience with, there are some notable missing examples. I have shot the .458 Winchester but certainly not enough to write about it. I've never experienced, nor at this stage of my life do I ever *intend* to experience, the .460 Weatherby or .458 Lott. My body is long past the stage of handling such rifles, so I draw the line at the .45-110 Sharps.

You will also find a few, a very few, .45 handgun cartridges missing, such as the .451 Detonics and the .45 Super. I simply have no experience with them. However, the .45 Colt, .45 Schofield, .45 Auto Rim, .45 ACP, .45 GAP, .45 Win Mag, .454 Casull, .460 Rowland, .460 S&W, .45-70, .45-90 and .45-110 will all be found here, along with many of the firearms in which they are chambered (as well as specially selected loads). I can't cover every cartridge in a book this size, nor can I cover every sixgun, semiauto, single shot and levergun. What you'll find here are those cartridges and guns I pretty much favor.

I'll close this introduction with the same paragraph found in my last book: We are told "Many are called, few are chosen." In my life I've been both called — and chosen — to be a teacher. This, of course, means I approach everything with a teacher's mentality. I've tried to arrange everything chronologically whenever possible, while at the same time making it possible to read any chapter individually. Review is a constant part of teaching, and you'll find a running review as you progress. It may sound like repetition in some cases (the scourge of my later years!). Every writer repeats himself. Every older writer repeats himself repeatedly. I prefer to call it a "continual reviewing process." May you enjoy reading this book as much as I enjoyed writing — and living — it. ◉

Most of you reading this book will think of the work the author has put in,
and yes it was monumental to say the least.
But without the editors, proofreaders, layout artist, caption writer and staff,
it would never have come together — it has also been a monumental task for them.
It's impossible to thank Roy Huntington (Editor, American Handgunner Magazine)
Payton Miller, Mike Humphries and especially Lisa Tsonetokoy —
the world's greatest layout artist — for all they have done.
GOOD SHOOTIN' AND GOD BLESS, JOHN TAFFIN.

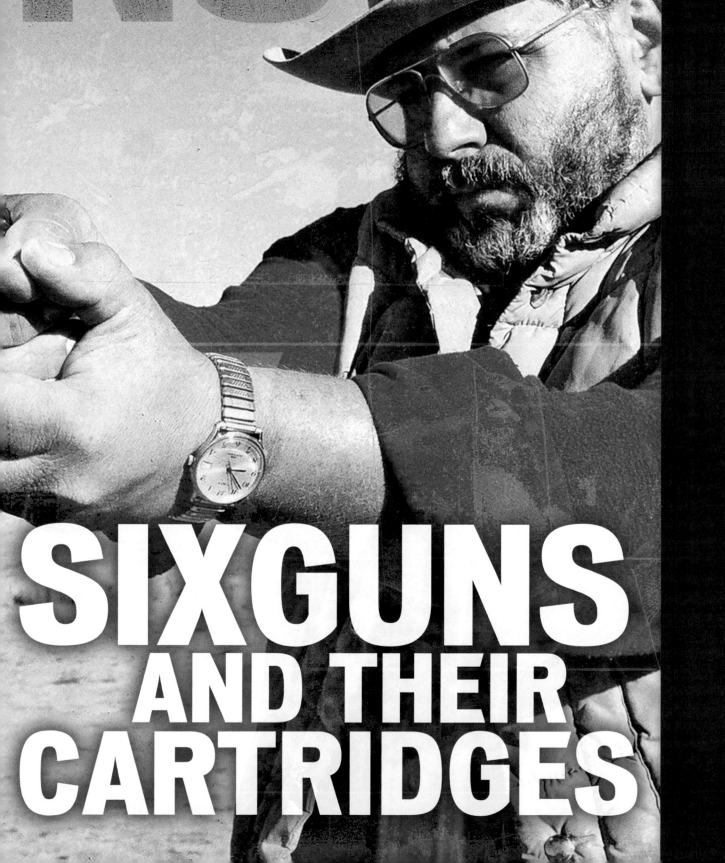

SIXGUNS
AND THEIR
CARTRIDGES

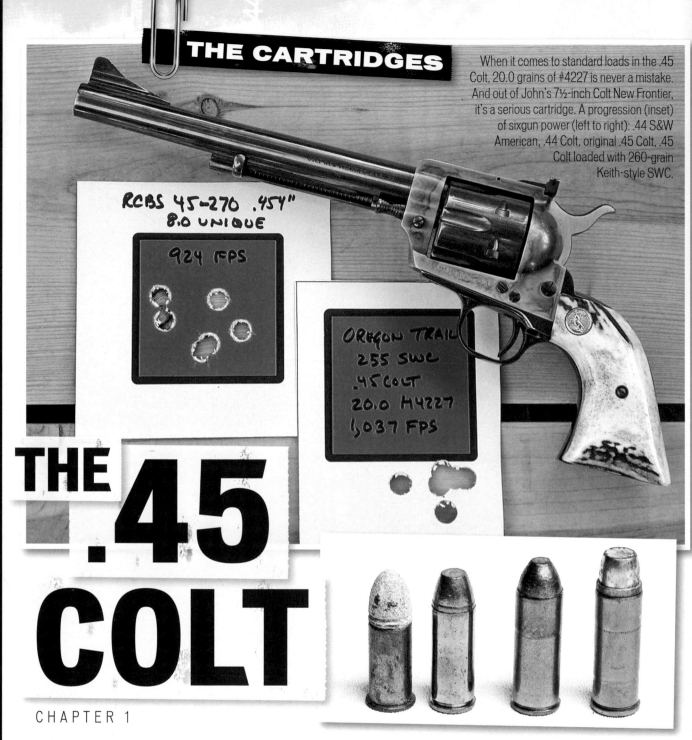

THE CARTRIDGES

When it comes to standard loads in the .45 Colt, 20.0 grains of #4227 is never a mistake. And out of John's 7½-inch Colt New Frontier, it's a serious cartridge. A progression (inset) of sixgun power (left to right): .44 S&W American, .44 Colt, original .45 Colt, .45 Colt loaded with 260-grain Keith-style SWC.

RCBS 45-270 .454"
8.0 UNIQUE
924 FPS

OREGON TRAIL
255 SWC
.45 COLT
20.0 H4227
1,037 FPS

THE .45 COLT

CHAPTER 1

The road of .45s we are about to travel is a long one, not necessarily straight, with a lot of turnoffs and even some dead ends. History is like that.

Sam Colt began the dynasty that would become Colt Firearms in 1836 with the introduction of the Paterson. As groundbreaking as this first successful revolver was, Colt's original foray into firearms failed and he went bankrupt, only to re-emerge in 1847 when he and Sam Walker put their heads together to come up with the Walker Colt.

Both the Paterson and the Walker, of course, were cap-and-ball revolvers. Even when Smith & Wesson introduced the first successful cartridge revolver with the Model 1 (a 7-shot .22 Short) in 1857, Sam Colt proclaimed shooters would always want to load their own ammunition percussion-style. During the Civil War, Colt's success was assured with the production of the .44 Model 1860 for the Union forces. Sam Colt died in 1862, but not before setting the company's future production path to be a "percussion only" one.

BIG BORE, BIG BUSINESS

However, in 1869 Smith & Wesson brought forth the .44 American sixgun using fixed ammunition. The day of the percussion revolver would soon be over. Even the management at Colt could see the future, and began converting the Model

Some of John's favorite .45 Colt bullets are (left to right) the Lyman/Keith #454424, the RCBS #45-270SAA, the Lyman/Thompson #452490 GC, the NEI #310.451 and #325.454 and the Lyman/Casull #454629 GC.

1860 to the .44 Colt cartridge. When the military called for tests to select a new sidearm, Colt produced the 1871-72 Open Top. This revolver looks much like the original 1860 and, as the name suggests, lacked a top strap. As cartridges go, both the S&W .44 American and the .44 Colt were not very powerful — using bullets of approximately 210 grains at a muzzle velocity of 700-750 fps. The military panel was not satisfied with the Open Top and requested Colt come up with a new revolver chambered for a more powerful cartridge.

William Mason of Colt designed the Single Action Army, and those first Peacemakers were chambered not in .44 Colt, but rather .45 Colt. A new era in firearms had begun.

POWER FROM THE GET-GO

By any standard, the .45 Colt was and is a powerful cartridge. The original loading was a bullet of approximately 255 grains with a muzzle velocity of somewhere between 850 and 900 fps. This was achieved with 40 grains of black powder. Up until around 1950, cartridges such as .38-40, .44-40, .44 Special, and .45 Colt utilized the balloonhead brass cartridge case. The primer pocket protruded above the base of the case into the interior. This was changed at mid-century by surrounding the primer pocket with solid brass, resulting in what is now known as "solid head" cases. They are much stronger but also reduce case capacity. When I have tried to duplicate the old loading of the .45 Colt using balloonhead brass with today's black powder and primers, it is not unusual to achieve more than 900 fps from a 7½-inch barrel. Who can say how many buffalo and grizzlies were killed by frontiersmen using the original .45 Colt load?

The United States military adopted the Single Action Army along with the .45 Colt cartridge with delivery begin-

ning in late 1873. The .45 Colt soon proved too powerful for military use, so it was reduced by cutting the powder charge from 40 grains back to 30-34 grains.

However, by the 1890s the military began looking for something more modern and went from the tried-and-true SAA .45 Colt to a new double-action with a swing-out cylinder chambered in the anemic .38 Long Colt. This proved a disaster when used in the Philippines, and the .45 Colt was resurrected. However, the SAA was now felt to be obsolete, and the search for a new handgun began.

RESURRECTION BY WESTERN MOVIES

Colt stopped production of its .45 Colt sixguns just prior to World War II. Sales were very slow by then, and shooters were more interested in such modern cartridges as the .357 Magnum chambered in double-action revolvers. But after television arrived in the late 1940s, all those old westerns being shown spurred the demand for sixguns again. But the real turning point for the .45 Colt cartridge was the introduction

Big-bore sixgun cartridges (left to right) began with the .44 S&W American in 1869, then Colt countered with the .44 Colt and finally came out with the .45 Colt in 1873.

Favorites all (left to right): original 255-grain conical, 260-grain Keith and the 310- and 325-grain Keith-style SWCs from NEI.

of Ruger's .45 Colt Blackhawk in the early 1970s, giving shooters a stronger platform.

Some time in the winter of 1956/1957, I purchased one of the brand-new 2nd Generation Colt SAAs chambered in .45 Colt with a 7½-inch barrel. I learned to reload for that sixgun with a Lyman #310 nutcracker tong tool. It didn't take me long to realize that more modern reloading equipment was needed, but I will always have a warm spot in my heart for those early reloading days.

Bigger is better! There were actually some folks who thought the .38 Long Colt could replace the .45 Colt!

A myth grew up early around the .45 Colt, namely that the brass was weak and the cartridge itself was inaccurate. But I can attest to the fact with proper loads, .45 Colt sixguns will shoot right alongside any other big-bore sixgun, and the brass is no weaker than the cylinder holding it. Yes, the old balloonhead brass should be relegated to collections. However, modern brass is strong enough. I've run .45 Colt loads to 1,700 fps with 260-grain bullets, but *only* in properly chambered, heavy-duty revolvers.

POWER LEVELS

There are several "levels" of revolvers chambered for the .45 Colt, necessitating at least five levels of loading. This makes the .45 Colt the most versatile of sixgun cartridges. I have never had any problems loading for it, but I am careful to stay within the proper parameters. Although there may be some overlapping in the five levels, here are the basic ones I adhere to:

Level I is for the Colt SAA and replicas thereof. These

are standard-duty sixguns, and I normally use 260-grain bullets at 850-950 fps. For these loads, bullets are of the original conical style or the Keith semiwadcutter. Even at these velocities, the .45 Colt is powerful enough for most uses, including deer-size game at reasonable ranges.

Moving up to the next level, Level II brings us to the Colt New Frontier with its adjustable sights and heavy top strap, as well as the Smith & Wesson Model 25/625 double actions. Both of these are slightly stronger than Level I sixguns, so I go with the same bullets at 1,000-1,100 fps (and sometimes creep carefully up on 1,200 fps).

Most loading manuals have a separate section for Level III loads, often referred to as "Ruger loads."

The Ruger Blackhawk and Bisley models, along with the original Vaqueros, really stretched the performance envelope of the .45 Colt. At this level, instead of increasing the velocity, I mostly go instead with 300-grain bullets at around 1,200 fps. On those rare occasions when I want a really heavy-duty 260-grain load using one of my Rugers, I will go up to 1,400-1,450 fps — or .44 Magnum level. With these first three levels, brass will last virtually forever, at least until necks wear out from expanding and crimping.

For most of us, these three levels cover everything we will ever need. However, there are two more.

THE OUTER LIMITS

I am fortunate to include among my close friends two

custom gunsmiths, Hamilton Bowen and John Linebaugh, both of whom specialize in converting smaller-caliber, large-frame Rugers to .45 Colt. Now we're talking 260-grain bullets at 1,600-1,700 fps and 300-330-grain cast bullets at 1,500-1,600 fps. However, these loads are for *custom .45 Colt sixguns only*. Any attempts to reach these levels in factory-chambered .45 Colts would most assuredly result in disaster.

The final level of loading for the .45 Colt is for use in the .454 Casull from Freedom Arms. All of the experimental loading which resulted in the .454 was done with .45 Colt brass. (Dick Casull was getting 2,000 fps in the late 1950s with 230-grain bullets.)

I often use .45 Colt brass in my .454s so I can use longer 325-grain Keith-style bullets crimped in the crimping groove and not exceeding the length the Freedom Arms .454 Casull cylinder will accept.

There are some beautiful cast-bullet designs available for the .45 Colt. One of the oldest, but still one of the best, is an Elmer Keith design from the 1920s, namely Lyman's now-out-of-production #454424, which casts out at around 260 grains. From RCBS we have the #45-255KT, also around 260 grains, and the heavier #45-270SAA, which weighs around 280 grains from my normal alloy. Some .45 Colt cylinders will be found to be too short to accept the original Keith bullet; however, the other two have slightly shorter noses and have fitted fine in every cylinder I've tried them in. For high-performance loading in the Ruger Blackhawk, I often go with two other excellent Keith-style bullets — NEI's 310-grain #451.310 and 325-grain #454.325. These heavier bullets seem to shoot even more accurately than the 260-grain bullets, while still having the large frontal area for maximum shock along with the extra weight for penetration. My standard load for these bullets in the Ruger Blackhawk (and also in the .454 Casull when using .45 Colt brass) is 21.5 grains of H110 or WW296 for right around 1,200 fps. Dick Casull also designed a 300-grain gas-checked flat-nose Lyman #454629GC for use in his .454. I have used the same bullet with this same powder charge out to 700-800 yards with exceptional accuracy.

More than 30 years ago, I received a call on the Fourth of July from a fellow I had never heard of before. His name was John Linebaugh and he made some incredible claims about his test gun, which happened to be chambered in .45 Colt. What he sent me was an El Dorado with a 10½-inch barrel. I took him at his word and loaded 260- and 310-grain bullets to his specifications. With these loads hitting 1,700 and 1,600 fps, respectively, a whole new era of the .45 Colt opened up to me. I would never look at the old cartridge in the same way again.

TWO POTENTIAL PROBLEMS

There is very little you can't accomplish with the .45 Colt, but there are two problems associated with it, namely case capacity and cylinder-throat diameters. At least until the arrival of the .475 and .500 Linebaugh cartridges, the .45 Colt was considered huge, and trying to produce lighter loads with slow-burning powders can give very poor results. Such powders as Unique, Universal and W231 work very well for standard loads, while #4227 bulks up nicely in .45 Colt brass, with 19.0-20.0 grains giving approximately 900-1,000 fps. Any time I have a .45 Colt that doesn't shoot the way I think it should, I don't give up on it until I try this load, and it has never failed me.

The cylinder throat diameter problem is common. For several years Smith & Wesson cut its throats at .455 inch or even larger. Now, however, they seem to be running at a more proper .451 to .452 inch.

Instead of being overly large, Ruger throats have been way too tight – some measuring around .449 inch. But now Ruger is cutting them at .451 to .452 inch. Colt Single Actions are right around .454 inch. The key for the best results is to size cast bullets accordingly, or even open the throats if necessary.

The .45 Colt is still a good choice for self-defense, hunting, long-range shooting, big-bore plinking or as an everyday working gun caliber.

It is never a mistake. ◉

Manstoppers of the 1870s (left to right): S&W .44 American, S&W .44 Russian, .45 Colt, .45 S&W.

The Smith & Wesson Schofield wheelgun and .45 Schofield round are a classic combo. While some reproductions are designed to accept .45 Colt, the S&W Model 2000 "reissue" shown only accepts the .45 Schofield round. Properly headstamped Schofield brass (inset) is now available from Starline.

THE .45 S&W SCHOFIELD

CHAPTER 2

The arrival of the Smith & Wesson .44 American in 1869 resulted in major changes in the revolver world. When the U.S. military ordered 1,000 of them in 1870, this first successful cartridge-firing sixgun affected one of S&W's rivals. Colt – which had been making percussion revolvers – changed its plan of action by first offering cartridge conversions, then the 1871-72 Open Top. And finally, in 1873, the .45 Single Action Army.

THE RUSSIAN EFFECT

The Russians were also paying attention, and they placed an order for Smith & Wesson revolvers that eventually totaled 150,000 units. However, the Russians made a change for which we have been grateful ever since.

The original .44 American cartridge used a bullet whose base diameter was smaller than the balance of the bullet. This smaller diameter fit inside the case much like found on .22 Long Rifle cartridges today. The Russians wanted a bullet of uniform diameter. The result was the .44 Russian, which is the template for the way cartridges are still made today. Of course, the .44 Russian eventually evolved into the .44 Special in late 1907, which was lengthened to become the .44 Magnum in late 1955. All this happened because of Russian influence.

Military authorities liked the convenience and quick loading of the .44 American compared to the percussion 1860 Colt Army. However, they preferred something more powerful than the .44 American's 210-grain bullet at 700 fps. This resulted in the 1873 adoption of the Colt Single Action Army .45, with its 255-grain bullet at nearly 900 fps.

Big-bore revolver cartridges surfacing from 1869 to 1875 included (from left) .44 S&W American, .44 S&W Russian, .45 Colt and the .45 S&W Schofield.

All of this was not lost on one Col. George Schofield. Not only did he look at the larger chambering, but also at an improvement in the top-break S&W. The .44 American and .44 Russian required two hands to operate. The locking mechanism was on the top strap, and it required holding the sixgun in one hand and operating the latch with the other. Once the action was opened, all cartridges extracted simultaneously. Although it took two hands to operate the Smith & Wesson, three hands would've been very handy with the Colt!

Col. Schofield redesigned the latch on the Smith & Wesson placing it on the frame. Now, the shooter only had to press with the thumb of the shooting hand and the barrel would unlatch and could be pressed against the leg, or any other stationary object, and pushed downward to open. The empties were still ejected simultaneously, and once the cylinder was reloaded, the barrel could be moved up and latched into place. The operation was now simplified.

A NEW CARTRIDGE

Changing cartridges, however, created problems. The .45 Colt used a cartridge case which was 1.28 inch in length — too long for use in the shorter cylinder of

the Smith & Wesson. The obvious solution would be to lengthen the frame and cylinder of the S&W. Instead the cartridge case was shortened to 1.10 inch in length and the .45 S&W — also known as the .45 Schofield — arrived. One doesn't have to be too smart to see a problem on the horizon. The military, which had already purchased 23,000 Colt SAAs, now ordered 3,000 Schofield Models in 1875, followed by 5,000 more shortly thereafter, along with a large supply of the new cartridges.

Remington, Peters and UMC all offered the .45 Schofield loaded with the original 255-grain .45 Colt bullet. Remember, the original .45 Colt loading was 40 grains of black powder, however this was soon reduced to 30 grains for military use and 35 grains for ammunition destined for civilians. The military had found the cartridge was too powerful; however, it is hard for me to believe lawmen, outlaws, frontiersmen and wilderness wanderers were tougher than those men serving in the military. There must be another reason somewhere.

I have seen powder charges for the .45 Schofield listed at 27-30 grains with the original 255-grain bullet, which was soon reduced to 230 grains. So apparently the military now had a choice of the .45 Colt/255/30 grains in the full-length

SIXGUNS AND THEIR CARTRIDGES

case, or the .45 Schofield/230/28 grains in the shorter case. But things were not so simple. The military now had two .45 revolvers and two types of ammo. And therein lies the problem. The .45 Schofield worked fine in both revolvers; the .45 Colt would only work in the Colt SAA. If troops received .45 Schofield ammunition, it didn't make any difference which revolver they were issued. However, if .45 Colt ammunition wound up with Schofield-armed troopers, the ammo was useless.

It didn't take long for this to result in the .45 Schofield revolvers being dropped by the military with many of the barrels cut from 7 to 5 inches and sold off — many to Wells Fargo. With the passing of the Schofield, the military still had a large stock of .45 Schofield cartridges, which worked just fine in the Colt sixguns.

Had this been the end of the story, the .45 Schofield cartridge would have eventually gone off into oblivion. But things didn't work out that way. The rise of modern Cowboy Action Shooting fueled a demand for period-correct firearms and ammunition, so high-quality, Italian-made replicas of the .45 Schofield Model 3 (in .45 Colt) began coming in from Navy

> *The S&W .45 Schofield was originally designed for black powder use, and I get even better results with black powder in my Schofields using the same 230-grain bullet.*

Arms and Cimarron. Then in 2000, Smith & Wesson resurrected the Schofield, chambered in .45 Schofield.

Now, thanks to Starline, we have all the brass necessary to load any of the frontier cartridges, including the .45 Schofield. This brass, like the original, is 1.10 inches in length. Also like the original, it has a slightly larger diameter rim for positive ejection. The star on the S&W ejector does not mate up well with the smaller rim of .45 Colt brass.

MIX AND MATCH?

So, what happens when we go the other way? Will .45 Schofield brass/ammunition work in firearms chambered in .45 Colt? It normally works in Colt replicas as well as the Schofield replicas chambered in .45 Colt; however, it will not work in my older Ruger Blackhawks with recessed chambers. Leverguns? My Winchester 94AE not only accepts the .45 Schofield rounds, but it also shoots them very accurately. An added bonus is the fact the shorter Schofield case is more efficient when used with the faster-burning powders.

Reloading the .45 Schofield can be accomplished with .45 Colt dies — almost. The problem is the crimping operation. Most .45 Colt dies are too long to crimp the shorter case. The solution is to remove enough metal from the bottom of the seating/crimping die to work on the shorter case. This won't interfere when this same die is used with Colt brass. Crimping can also be accomplished with a .45 Auto Rim seating die or, if it has the crimping feature, a .45 ACP seating die.

Thanks to such companies as Black Hills, we have

The .45 Schofield (left) is shorter and less potent than the .45 Colt (right). Whereas the Colt Single Action Army could fire the S&W Schofield round, the Schofield would not accept the Colt round.

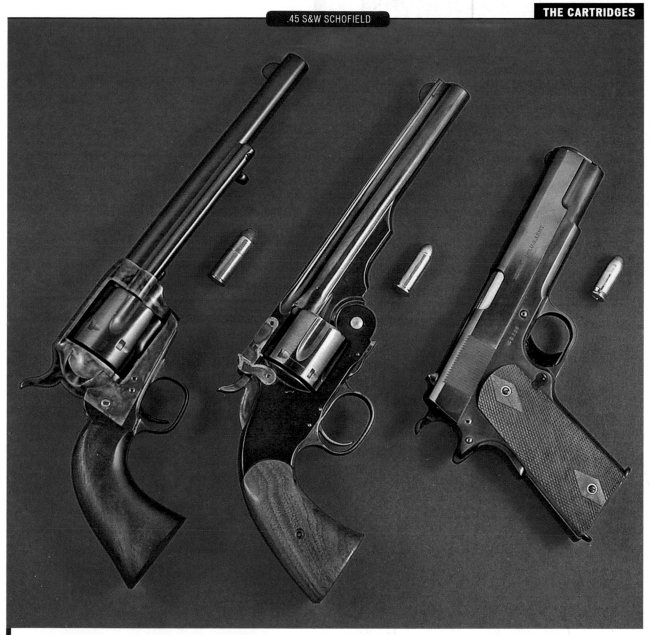

Three handguns, three .45 cartridges (from left): Colt SAA .45 Colt, S&W .45 Schofield, Government Model 1911 .45 ACP.

access to .45 Schofield ammo. Its mild-shooting factory load consists of a 230-grain bullet at 750-800 fps, depending upon barrel length. It also feeds through and chambers in .45 Colt lever actions such as the Marlin 1894, Winchester 1894, Rossi Model 92 and the Cimarron Model 1866. From such rifles, the velocity gets boosted to around 950-1,000 fps.

For most of my loading of the .45 Schofield, I use the Oregon Trail 230-grain RN bullet intended for the .45 ACP. There is no crimp on this bullet, but my loads are so mild it has never been a problem. For use in my Cimarron Schofield, 5 grains of Red Dot results in a muzzle velocity of around 650 fps with groups just over one-inch. A charge of 5 grains of

TiteGroup gives the best results with this bullet in my Navy Arms Schofield with a muzzle velocity of around 725 fps.

The S&W .45 Schofield was originally designed for black powder use, and I get even better results with black powder in my Schofields using the same 230-grain bullet. With 30 grains of FFg or Pyrodex P, muzzle velocities are around 850-900 fps, but as you approach these velocities, it's necessary to crimp the case into the bullet ogive.

Is there any real use for the .45 Schofield today? Many Cowboy Action Shooters have gravitated to the lesser .32 and .38 cartridges because of the milder recoil. However, the .45 Schofield, for me at least, remains an excellent understudy for my .45 Colt loads. ◉

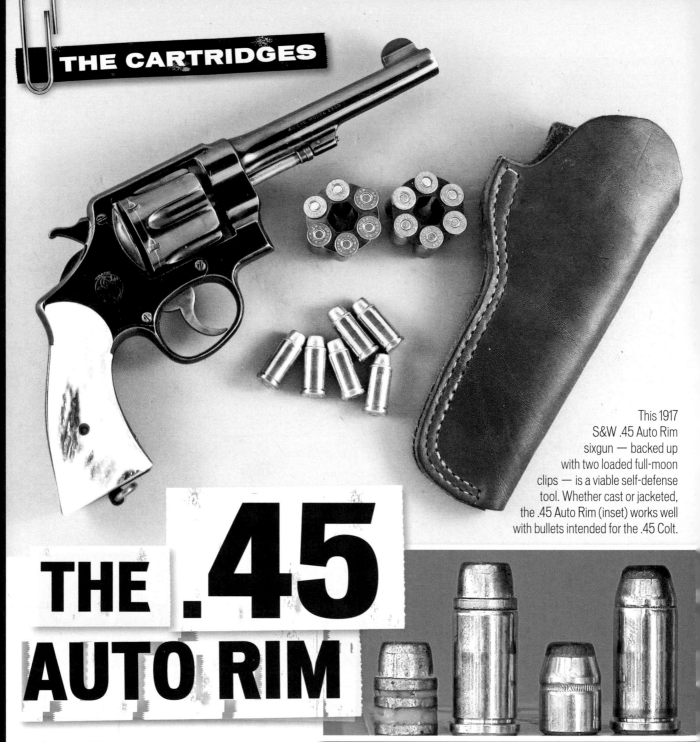

This 1917 S&W .45 Auto Rim sixgun — backed up with two loaded full-moon clips — is a viable self-defense tool. Whether cast or jacketed, the .45 Auto Rim (inset) works well with bullets intended for the .45 Colt.

THE .45 AUTO RIM

CHAPTER 3

Even though World War I had been raging for three years before the United States entered the fray, we were still not as prepared as we should have been. There were not enough 1903 Springfields to go around, so the 1917 Enfield — chambered in .30-06 — was also pressed into service.

The same problem existed when it came to sidearms. The .45 ACP Model 1911 had been adopted six years before our declaration of war, but there weren't enough of them and they couldn't be produced fast enough. Fortunately, an engineer at Smith & Wesson came up with a "revolver solution."

A SIMPLE STOPGAP

Because the .45 ACP is rimless, there's nothing to catch on the rear of a cylinder for headspacing – nor for the ejector star to engage for extraction. But the engineer came up with the ingenious idea that would allow S&W's N-frame 2nd Model Hand Ejector to handle the cartridge – the three-round half-moon clip. When placed in the cylinder, it provided proper headspacing and prevented the cartridge from moving forward in the cylinder. Placing two of these loaded clips in the cylinder not only permitted the use of rimless ammo in a revolver, but it also facilitated quick reloads. Thus the problem

The strange-looking sixgun John is shooting is a .455 Webley Top-Break converted to .45 Auto Rim.

Cast bullets made for the .45 Colt (left to right) are equally at home in the .45 Auto Rim: Lyman 260-grain Keith #454424, the "improved" #452424 and the Thompson #452490GC.

someone killed in a gunfight. Military handguns were available in abundance (as late as the mid-1950s we could still buy them at a very reasonable price) but ammunition remained a problem.

It was time for someone else to come up with a good idea.

was solved and many soldiers of the American Expeditionary Force were armed not with Colt 1911s, but with either a Colt 1917 New Service in .45 ACP or S&W's big N-frame.

After the war, as usually happens, these new Colt and S&W sixguns became popular with civilians as well as law officers, but those troublesome clips could be bent or lost. Wouldn't it be great if they weren't needed? It was discovered the S&W and most of the Colts had a shoulder in the front of the chamber which prevented the .45 ACP rounds from dropping straight through. The .45 ACP could actually be used without the clips! Well, they could be if all the brass was the same length — which was not always the case. Short brass would allow the case to move forward just enough to cushion the blow of the firing pin, resulting in misfires. The same thing could happen if the shoulder was not cut sharp enough.

Then there was the problem of empties — each .45 ACP case had to be picked out with the fingernails or poked out from the front with a pencil or rod of some sort. This was no great problem in a plinking session, but it could get

A SIMPLE RIM

This time it was a worker at Peters Ammunition (now part of Remington) who came up with a logical solution in the early 1920s. The simple answer was to put a rim on the rimless .45 ACP brass. The .45 Auto Rim was born.

Most revolver cartridges have a rim thickness of .060-065 inch, but the .45 Auto Rim required a rim of .090 inch to take up the headspace provided by the half-moon clips.

These 1917s from Colt and Smith & Wesson may be nearly a century old, but they still shoot well. They are definitely not to be used with John's hotter .45 Auto Rim loads.

Fine factory stuff: Black Hills offers an excellent .45 Auto Rim load with a SWC bullet.

The .45 Auto Rim is quite an interesting looking cartridge with its stubby length and thick rim. Smith & Wesson has always taken the cartridge seriously — offering numerous models over the past 90-plus years for it. The 1917 Model was not only offered in military versions, but commercial models as well. After World War II it was upgraded to the 1950 Military and the 1950 Target, and then the 1955 Target followed. Later, the 1955 Target became the Model 25-2,

which has since been joined by the 625 series of stainless steel sixguns.

Although the .45 Auto Rim is no longer in demand as a target cartridge, it is excellent for Action Shooting, self-defense, even close-range hunting.

BRASS, BULLETS AND RELOADING

When I first started using the .45 Auto Rim, it was in an extra cylinder from Christy Gunworks for a .45 Colt Single Action. Brass was exceptionally hard to come by, and the only loaded ammo available was Remington's 230-grain RN. Today there are several companies — including Black Hills and Buffalo Bore — offering excellent .45 Auto Rim loads, and Starline also has great brass.

Reloading the .45 Auto Rim is about as easy as it gets. There are probably as many excellent .45 bullets available — jacketed and cast — as for any other handgun. If you already have a set of .45 ACP dies, all you need for the .45

After World War II, 1917 S&W and Colt sixguns found their way into the hands of returning doughboys, civilians and lawmen.

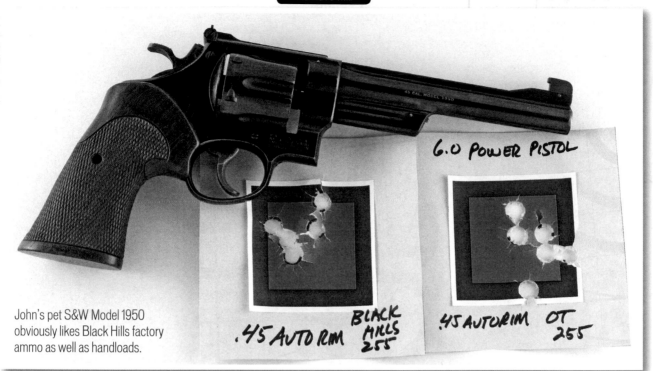

John's pet S&W Model 1950 obviously likes Black Hills factory ammo as well as handloads.

Auto Rim is a shellholder and possibly a seating die, if your .45 ACP dies aren't set up for crimping.

Some of my favorite bullets for the .45 ACP also work well for the .45 Auto Rim. This includes two old standbys, the Lyman #452460 and the RCBS #45-201KT. These are both SWCs in the 200-grain weight range and are best when cast hard for the rifling in most .45 Auto Rim sixguns. My favorite load for both is 7 grains of Unique or Universal for right around 975 fps.

Bullets originally designed for the .45 Colt also work well. Lyman's 260-grain #454424 is a fine one. In strong modern guns, I load 15.0 grains of #2400 for a very powerful 1,100 fps. This should be approached with great caution. A milder loading of 6 grains of Unique gives a more sedate 800 fps – not all that far behind the standard factory loading for the .45 Colt.

I've actually had better results with the 260-grain Keith — either the Lyman or the RCBS version — in .45 Auto Rim guns than in some .45 Colt revolvers. Although the big bullet has to make a long journey from the stubby rimmed case to the barrel, it seems to manage without any major problems.

One of my favorites was designed by Ray Thompson in the early 1950s. The semiwadcutter gas-check #452490 was intended for his S&W 1950 Target .45 Auto Rim. It weighs 254 grains with my alloy and also works well with the .45

Colt. (I use it for hunting loads in a Ruger Blackhawk.) With this heavy bullet in the .45 Auto Rim, 13 grains of #2400 gives me just under 1,000 fps, while going up another grain gets me right under 1,100 fps. Again, caution! These two loads should only be used in modern revolvers in excellent shape.

The .45 Auto Rim is more efficient than the .45 Colt with most loads because of its reduced case capacity. The .45 Colt is, of course, the cartridge of choice when heavy-duty loads are desired and the sixgun is strong enough to take advantage of the large case capacity. The .45 Auto Rim is better in standard size cylinders, and heavy loads mentioned here for it must never be used in 1917 Smith & Wesson or Colt revolvers. These are good, old sixguns with the emphasis on "old." They should be treated as such.

An added bonus for the .45 Auto Rim is the fact it works quite well with the range of jacketed bullets designed for the .45 ACP. The lightweight 185-grain JHPs can easily be loaded to over 1,000 fps with 8.5 grains of Unique. With a typical 230-grain FMJ, 7 grains of Unique gives about 860 fps — plenty powerful for most uses.

One final bonus. We can always go right back to the beginning and use any of the revolvers chambered for the .45 Auto Rim with .45 ACP brass in half-moon or full-moon clips.

Now *that's* versatility. ◎

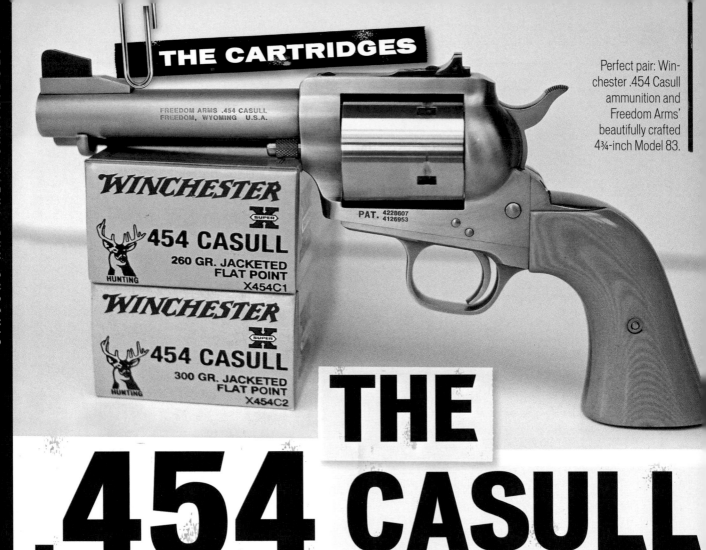

THE CARTRIDGES

Perfect pair: Winchester .454 Casull ammunition and Freedom Arms' beautifully crafted 4¾-inch Model 83.

THE .454 CASULL

Power pioneer: Dick Casull with his 12-inch Freedom Arms .454.

CHAPTER 4

No sixgun cartridge in history has had more experimentation behind it than the .454 Casull. As a young man, Dick Casull often rode the hills around his home in Utah packing a Colt Single Action Army. Like so many of the rest of us, the Colt SAA had a special spot in his sixgunnin' soul. But the Colt is not what you'd call a very strong sixgun.

Casull's first efforts at developing the .454 used the Colt, but it was obvious it was more than the old Peacemaker could handle. The Colt would definitely have to be beefed up, made stronger. New firing pins were developed to withstand the pressure and frames were re-heat treated. However, with his loads, Casull still blew cylinders. And his loads were not all that accurate. So he began using barrels of a higher-strength steel. The results were the same — disastrous.

Casull's initial goal was a 230-grain bullet at 1,800 fps. This was at a time when factory loads for both the .45 ACP

and the .45 Colt achieved less than half of that velocity. This was also at a time before H110/WW296 had been developed — the best powder available was 2400. Casull also had ignition problems, so he developed a special tool to ream the primer pockets of the solid-head .45 Colt brass to

Freedom Arms' .45 Colt Model 97 cylinder (left) and .454 Casull Model 83 cylinder (right) help dramatically to illustrate the difference between the two cartridges.

accept rifle primers. Even so, he *still* had problems with ignition. So he began experimenting with duplex loads — two layers of powder in the same case. But even if that worked, he still needed a sixgun strong enough to hold it. Something would have to be done to alter the Colt Single Action to give it more strength.

A STRONGER PLATFORM

Casull turned to five-shot cylinders — as this would provide more steel between the chambers as well as place the locking bolt notches in between the chambers. Today there are several custom sixgunsmiths who can build five-chamber cylinders to replace a six-cylinder one, but in the early 1950s Casull may have been the first one to actually do it. In addition, he had to redesign the ratchet at the back of the cylinder and also alter the hand. When you go from six to five shots the geometry changes.

The next step was to make an oversize cylinder as large as the Colt SAA frame would accept, and to make them from 4140 steel and heat-treated to Rockwell 42C. Now he was getting somewhere. No more blown frames or top straps. At last he felt he was on the right path, and using the Custom Colt with an oversize five-shot cylinder and a 7½-inch barrel, a 230-grain bullet achieved 1,825 fps. The load? One grain of Unique and 28 grains of #2400. Casull also found that 26 grains of #2400 would drive a 250-grain bullet at 1,650 fps, while a 300-grain bullet over 25 grains of #2400 achieved

1,500 fps. Remember, all this was in 1954 — before the advent of the .44 Magnum.

A STEP FARTHER

Casull's next step was to totally hand-build a single action. Using a 10-inch barrel with a 1:24-inch twist and a muzzle brake to help tame the recoil, Casull now arrived at 2,000 fps with a 230-grain bullet. Casull's recipe for the load was a triplex charge of 2 grains of Unique, 25 grains of #2400 and 3 grains of Bullseye. Switching to a 300-grain bullet using 25 grains of #2400 grains gave him 1,700 fps. The .454 Casull had arrived.

NEW DIRECTIONS

Once Ruger introduced the Super Blackhawk, Casull and his partner Jack Fullmer offered five-shot conversions chambered for the .454. Through all of the experimentation with custom guns, the brass was nothing more than standard .45 Colt. So even today when I hear someone claim .45 Colt brass is weak, I remember how Casull proved that to be a myth 50 years ago.

But if the .454 Casull was to have a future, it would have to be offered in a factory-built sixgun with available factory-loaded ammunition. But with all the old .45 Colt Single Actions around, the possibility of someone dropping a ".454-loaded" .45 Colt cartridge into one of those old guns would have been unthinkable. However, just as Smith & Wesson had lengthened the .44 Special case to create the

Evolution of an idea (from bottom up):
Custom Colt .454 Magnum, Custom Single Action
.454 Magnum, Dick Casull's personal .454 Casull.

> *I've tried about every load level there is in the .454 Casull using both Freedom Arms factory brass and Starline brass.*

.44 Magnum to prevent such a catastrophe, it was obvious the .45 Colt case would also have to be lengthened.

AMMO, COMPONENTS

Since 1983, the .454 Casull revolver has been made by Freedom Arms. Originally, Freedom Arms also offered bullets, brass and loaded ammunition but no longer. Several manufacturers now offer components as well as loaded ammunition. The .454 is a straight-walled case which is ¹⁄₁₀ inch longer than standard .45 Colt brass. Original brass used Large Rifle primers, however this was soon changed to Small Rifle primers to allow more room for brass in the head of the case. Personally, I prefer to use Starline brass and Remington #7½ Small Rifle primers.

The Model 83 Freedom Arms revolver itself is built to exacting tolerances. It has to be to accept the pressures we're talking about here and will not normally accept casually assembled reloads. Reloads must be specifically tailored to fit the chambers or you may find yourself with a large quantity of ammunition that won't fit the precisely line-bored chambers. There is simply no slop built into a Freedom Arms revolver, so brass must fit perfectly. Trying to resize with .45

Left to right: .45 Colt brass, .454 brass and the Dick Casull-designed 300-grain gas check bullet.

The .454 is a reloading dream come true. In the Freedom Arms Model 83 you can come up with loads which will deliver outstanding accuracy with both cast and jacketed bullets at velocities from 800 to 2,000 fps, even beyond. No longer are reloaders limited to #2400, but now we have H110, WW296, AA9 and several others. Ruger and Taurus both offer .454 revolvers, and there are several custom gunsmiths also building five-shot .454s on Ruger single-action and double-action revolvers.

One final cautionary note: Trying to build duplex or triplex loads can be dangerous, and with today's powders, there is no need to even consider it. Dick Casull himself would tell any of us to stay away from mixing powders, as H110 or WW296 can do anything we need to accomplish with the .454 Casull. ◎

Colt dies may or may not work, but .454 Casull-labeled dies will normally size brass tighter than standard .45 Colt ones.

With the .454, primers must be seated exactly flush — or even slightly below — or the cylinder won't rotate. I recommend a priming tool separate from the reloading press itself. When it comes to bullets, it is best to make a couple dummy rounds first and make sure they will fit the tight chambers of the Model 83.

THE BULLET QUESTION

Jacketed bullets designed for the .45 Colt should be held to 1,600 fps or less, or there is a possibility of them coming apart under high pressures. When I was shooting long-range silhouettes regularly with the .454, my bullet of choice was the Speer 260-grain .45 Colt JHP at 1,600 fps from the 10-inch barrel of my Model 83. I also found very quickly the Lyman #454424 Keith bullet, which works so well in the .45 Colt, would not shoot well when driven at .454 speeds.

I've tried about every load level there is in the .454 Casull using both Freedom Arms factory brass and Starline brass. SSK's 340-grain truncated cone cast bullet can be driven over 1,800 fps, but I prefer to stay down around 1,200 to 1,500 fps for comfortable shooting. Dick Casull, incidentally, also designed Lyman's excellent #454629GC mold for a 300-grain, flat-nosed, gas-check bullet that can be driven to a full 1,800 fps with excellent accuracy. It can also be used in the .45 Colt at around 1,200 fps, again with great accuracy.

Both Hornady and Black Hills have offered .454 ammunition.

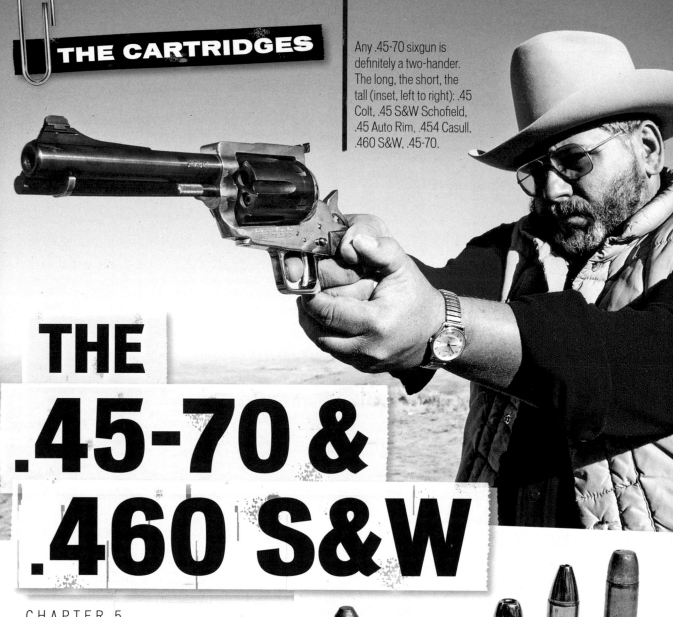

THE CARTRIDGES

Any .45-70 sixgun is definitely a two-hander. The long, the short, the tall (inset, left to right): .45 Colt, .45 S&W Schofield, .45 Auto Rim, .454 Casull, .460 S&W, .45-70.

THE .45-70 & .460 S&W

CHAPTER 5

For more than 100 years, from the introduction of the .45 Colt in 1873 to the spread of long-range silhouette shooting in the 1980s, sixgun cartridge cases were pretty much maximized at a length of 1.3 inches (.45 Colt, .44 Magnum) to 1.4 inches (.454 Casull, .475 and .500 Linebaugh). Long-range silhouette shooting definitely affected most major handgun manufacturers. Most of them produced specialized silhouette models, some excellent, others not so good.

Elgin Gates was the head of IHMSA, the governing body of silhouette shooting, and he had some definite ideas on new cartridges that were needed for competition. In fact, Gates had worked up prototype cases of 1.6 inches in length in several calibers from .357 all the way up to .600 inch. The first one to surface was the .357 SuperMag as

it was called in Dan Wesson revolvers and .357 Maximum when chambered in the Ruger Blackhawk. Both companies had to stretch the frame and cylinder of their respective revolvers to be able to chamber the new cartridges.

STRETCHING THINGS OUT

Once the .357 SuperMag was established we soon had the .375 SuperMag, the .445 SuperMag and then later the .414 Super Magnum. Meanwhile out in Cody, Wyoming, John Linebaugh was working on his own ultra-potent .44, .475 and .500 Linebaugh cartridges. The Linebaugh .475

.45-70 & .460 S&W   **THE CARTRIDGES**

The X-Factor illustrated: Smith & Wesson's .500 (introduced 2003) and .460 (introduced 2005).

and .500, built on the relatively lightweight Ruger Bisley, exhibited recoil one had to experience to actually believe.

Eventually, the silhouette game faded. Elgin Gates passed away. Dan Wesson closed its doors (although it has since reopened twice to produce mostly 1911s today). Now it is difficult to find any of these cartridges in currently produced factory or custom sixguns.

"X" MEANS EXTRA

Then in the early years of this new century, Smith & Wesson moved up from the N-frame revolver size to what it calls the "X-frame." For this huge revolver, it introduced a new cartridge, the .500 Smith & Wesson in 2003. With a case of approximately 1.600 inches in length, it was without a doubt the most powerful factory-produced revolver/cartridge combination ever. Even with its large frame and excessive weight, recoil is still substantial. With a 440-grain bullet at nearly 1,700 fps from an 8⅜-inch barrel, all arguments as to what was "the world's most powerful revolver" suddenly became moot.

Then, just as the company did in 1964 with the .41 Magnum coming 10 years after the .44 Magnum, Smith & Wesson backed up. This time it only took two years to take a step *down* the

ladder. Using the basic X-frame of the Model 500, S&W introduced the Model 460 XVR (Extreme Velocity Revolver) chambered in .460 S&W Magnum. This new cartridge had a case just under 1.8 inches in length.

With it, S&W claimed the high-velocity record for a revolver — perhaps for all time. A .460 factory round from Cor-Bon using the 200-grain Barnes XPB bullet is rated at 2,300 fps. When you consider the fact there are many rifles out there in the same velocity neighborhood with lighter bullets, you'll appreciate what S&W has accomplished. To me, the .460 is a whole lot more "practical" and pleasant than the .500. The Model 460 XVR weighs 73 ounces with an 8⅜-inch barrel. Felt recoil is much less than the .500, tra-

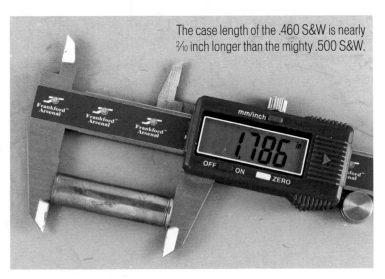

The case length of the .460 S&W is nearly 2⁄10 inch longer than the mighty .500 S&W.

.45-70 & .460 S&W

Hunting revolver/cartridge combos of two eras: The .460 S&W (top) and the Ruger Blackhawk in .45 Colt (bottom).

jectory is flatter, and it is superbly accurate with either the Barnes 200-grain or 250-grain XPB bullets. In the hands of a competent pistolero, it will definitely handle anything that walks on this planet.

If Elgin Gates had not passed, and if Dan Wesson had not closed, and if silhouetting had continued to flourish, Smith & Wesson would probably have been beaten to the finish line as Gates already had a prototype ".45 Maximum" made up. However it never did come to pass,

so it remained for S&W to give us a ".45 Maximum." Even thought it's called a ".460," it takes the same diameter bullets as the .45 Colt and .454 Casull.

.45-70 SIXGUN

As we come to the end of this section on sixgun cartridges, we wind up right back where we started in 1873. At the same time the military adopted the .45 Colt, it also took on a new rifle, the Trapdoor Springfield, chambered in .45-70. And just as with the .45 Colt, the .45-70 is probably at its height of popularity here in the 21st century. It was chambered in the 1873 and 1884 Trapdoors, the Sharps and Remington single-shot rifles, the 1886 Winchester, 1881 and 1895 Marlins, and today can be found in Winchester and Marlin lever actions as well as Italian replicas of the 1886, the Browning 1885, Shiloh and C. Sharps rifles and the Ruger No. 1. However, over the years, some pistoleros looked at it and asked "Why not build a .45-70 revolver?"

In the 1950s Elmer Keith reported on just such a revolver, but it was poorly timed and not very accurate. In the 1960s the late Stu Brainard

The Century .45-70 dwarfs the Ruger .44 Super Blackhawk.

The .45-70 BFR from Magnum Research has been the only commercially successful .45-70 production revolver.

got together with Clarence Bates to build at least two quality .45-70 revolvers. I saw the one Stu had many times. A fellow in Indiana produced the bronze-framed Century .45-70 revolvers, and these were quality pieces. (I waited eight years to get mine and then later sold it to a collector.) Elmer Keith held on to his and had the barrel cut flush with the ejector rod housing. (It was on display in the Elmer Keith Museum.) There have been a few other attempts to produce a .45-70 revolver, not all of which have been successful. However, one that is remains today — the BFR from Magnum Research.

THE QUESTION OF PRACTICALITY

With a case length of 2.105 inches, the .45-70 dwarfs even the .460 Smith & Wesson. And sixguns chambered for it are even larger than the S&W X-frame. Then there's the bullet weight factor. The .460 S&W generally uses bullets in the same weight range as the .45 Colt and .454 Casull. With the .45-70, bullet weights start at 300 grains and go up to 500 grains.

Both .460 S&W and .45-70 sixguns are fun to shoot and definitely attract a crowd. But for hunting, is it practical to carry a revolver weighing anywhere from 4½ to 6 pounds? For most folks the whole point of handgun hunting is to travel lighter (most magnum sixguns weigh around three pounds). If you're willing to carry the extra bulk and weight, there's no question the .460 S&W and the .45-70 will deliver plenty of power for big, tough game animals. But would a carbine chambered in either cartridge be more practical? We have now covered the six .45 sixgun cartridges — .45 Colt, .45 S&W Schofield, .45 Auto Rim, .454 Casull, .460 S&W and .45-70. As we go through the various sixguns chambered for those cartridges, we'll take a greater look at them and also share loading data. ◎

Hard-cast hunting with the Big Boys: Double Tap's .454 360-grain (1,500 fps), Cor-Bon's .460 395-grain (1,550 fps).

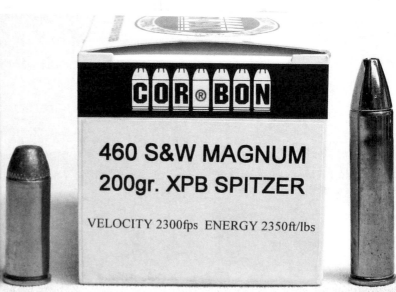

COR·BON

460 S&W MAGNUM 200gr. XPB SPITZER

VELOCITY 2300fps ENERGY 2350ft/lbs

It has been a long road of development from the .45 S&W Schofield of 1875 to the .460 S&W Magnum of today.

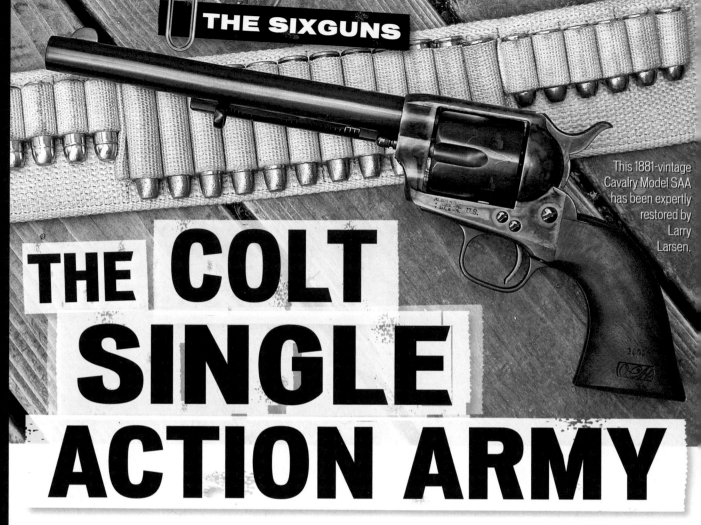

This 1881-vintage Cavalry Model SAA has been expertly restored by Larry Larsen.

THE COLT SINGLE ACTION ARMY

CHAPTER 6

Author's note: If it didn't happen this way, it should have. ↓

I t's late 1869. The Board of Directors for Colt Patent Firearms is meeting and the president is speaking. He is laying out production goals for the next year, planning how many 1860 Army and 1861 Navy percussion pistols to produce. Suddenly he is interrupted. A messenger stoops down and whispers in his ear. The president's face registers surprise and shock. Something momentous has happened.

A METALLIC MESSAGE

What was the message? Something like this: Smith & Wesson had just *totally* changed the revolver playing field. Sam Colt, who had died in 1862, felt shooters would always want to load their own ammunition — powder, ball and percussion cap. He had ignored the appeal of S&W's tip-up Model 1 which had been introduced the previous decade. After all, the Model 1 had been chambered in .22 Short. Even though many officers in the Civil War had carried one

under their tunic, the main sidearm in that struggle had been the Colt 1860 Army .44.

But in 1869 Smith & Wesson did something they'd been planning to do before the Civil War, namely bring out a *big-bore* cartridge revolver in the equally new .44 S&W American. Suddenly, everything Colt had produced up to then was obsolete.

The military — which had been buying 1860 Colts for nearly 10 years — had ordered 1,000 of the new S&W's. To make matters worse for Colt, S&W held the Rollin White patent on producing revolvers with bored-through cylinders to accept metallic cartridges. Fortunately for Colt, however, the patent would soon run out. To counter this challenge, Colt began converting its 1860s to cartridges by replacing the cylinders, using both the Richards and Richards-Mason configuration. The military was about to call for testing to adopt a new revolver, and to this end Colt produced its first big-bore cartridge sixgun — the 1871-72 Open-Top.

However, the military board was not impressed. They disliked the open-top frame and instead wanted a "top strap"

Who says a 7½" .45 Colt SAA isn't a target pistol? Certainly not John!

design like the one on the Remington percussion revolvers of the period. They felt this would offer a significant increase in strength, not only to make the gun more rugged, but also to handle the cartridge they *really* wanted — a .45.

So Colt went back to the drawing board. The chambering, mainframe and grip frame were all changed. The result was the Colt Single Action Army.

The new Colt SAA incorporated the solid top strap of the Remington, the grip frame Sam Colt had first designed for his 1851 Navy .36 percussion revolver, and a new chambering, the .45 Colt. While the previous .44 Colt had used a bullet of approximately 210 grains at around 750 fps, the new .45 employed a bullet of 250-255 grains over 40 grains of black powder for a muzzle velocity well over 850 fps. The barrel length of the 1860 Army had been 8 inches, the new SAA .45 had what I consider a perfectly balanced 7½-inch barrel.

Although the Smith & Wesson was much easier to load and unload than the Colt SAA, which called for single-loading and single-ejecting each cartridge through a loading

gate, the U.S. Army liked the ruggedness and the power the new Colt SAA afforded. Although the SAA held six rounds, it didn't take long for both the military and civilians to learn the only safe way to carry it was with an empty chamber under the hammer. The so-called safety notch was not strong enough to keep the firing pin from hitting the primer should the hammer receive a sharp blow. This was true in 1873 and it is still true today. All SAA-pattern sixguns should only be carried with an empty chamber under the hammer.

The new Colt was officially referred to by the factory as the "Model P." Unofficially it was called the "Peacemaker." It was just what the army was looking for. The first order was for 8,000 of the 7½-inch Cavalry Models being purchased in 1874, followed by 6,400 the following year, with the last order for 3,000 in 1891. The total number of Cavalry Model SAAs purchased by the U.S. government was just over 37,000.

By the time of the Battle of the Little Big Horn in 1876, Custer's troops were equipped with a Cavalry Model Colt and 18 rounds of ammunition, along with a single-shot Trapdoor .45-70 Springfield with 50 rounds. Most of them got separated from their horses, so all they had was their Colt and not enough ammo for the battle which ended so tragically for the Seventh Cavalry. Interestingly enough, Custer, who had been issued a Colt, was probably not carrying it at the time.

In 1895, 2,000 of the guns were returned to Colt for inspection and repair. Approximately 25 percent were con-

Taffin's 1917-vintage .45 Colt may be well-worn on the outside, but it's in perfect mechanical condition inside. The grips are carved fleur-de-lis ivory.

demned, and most of the rest had their barrels cut to 5½ inches ("Artillery Model" length). In 1901, 2,600 5½-inch Artillery Models were inspected and repaired by Colt, with 550 being shipped to the Philippines immediately. By this time someone had made the foolish decision to mothball the .45 SAA in favor of the new double action New Model Army/Navy in .38 Long Colt. When this cartridge proved entirely inadequate against the Moro tribesmen, the old .45 Colt was taken out of mothballs and shipped to the troops. This decision probably saved more than a few lives.

THE NUMBERS GAME

Another barrel length option, the 4¾-inch version was dubbed the "Civilian Model." There is a letter surviving from Bat Masterson in 1881 written on saloon stationary ordering

Hard lessons learned in the Philippines: Someone actually thought the double-action .38 Long Colt could replace the .45 Colt Single Action!

a Colt .45 from the factory with the barrel cut even with the ejector rod housing. This may have been the first ordered from the West, however there were already some with this barrel length in England. But the three barrel lengths, 7½, 5½ and 4¾ inches had become standardized.

From 1873 to the end of production in 1940, there were a grand total of 356, 629 Colt SAAs produced. The greatest year of production was 1902 (18,000 units). But by 1935 and 1936, only 100 left the factory for each of those years. We were in the midst of a depression, the machinery was wearing out, and there would soon be a great demand for wartime production. It was time to end the Colt SAA. Collectors now refer to the guns from 1873 to 1940 as "1st Generation."

Although there were at least 30 different caliber variants, the .45 Colt was way out in front of all the rest with 150, 683 units so chambered being produced (plus 100 more as Target Models), 8,005 Bisleys and 97 Bisley Target Models. To make the Colt Single Action Army even more conducive to target shooting, Colt drastically changed the grip frame and gave the Target Model Bisley adjustable sights and a wide trigger. Whereas the standard SAA grip frame was designed to roll in the hand, the Bisley was made more vertical to the bore axis and made to ride up higher along the backstrap. In fact, Bisley mainframes are also higher along the back edge to gain the needed height. The front strap also came up higher behind the trigger guard to allow the grip frame to really set back into the shooting hand. The Bisley was also given what is now normally referred to as a target hammer for easier cocking, and the trigger was made wider and also curved to fit the trigger finger.

After the introduction of the Target Model Bisley, there was enough of a demand for a standard model Bisley for Colt to begin producing one. While the Bisley is nowhere near as fast from leather as the SAA, it's easier for most shooters to operate once it is nestled in the hand. Both Target Models (SAA and Bisley) had target sights, but these were very crude when compared to today's offerings. The rear sight was adjustable by moving it back and forth in a dovetail and locking it in place with a screw. The front sight

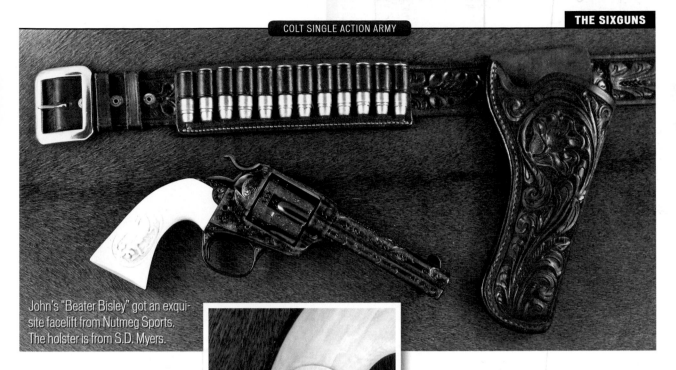

John's "Beater Bisley" got an exquisite facelift from Nutmeg Sports. The holster is from S.D. Myers.

blade could be raised or lowered and then locked in place. No click adjustments here.

COLT PROJECTS

I have several 1st Generation SAAs, including three chambered in .45 Colt. About 10 years ago, a friend called to let me know he had been selling guns for the widow of a friend. But by the time I heard about it, there was only one left. No one else wanted it.

What I found was a .45 with a 7½-inch barrel with very little finish and shrunken one-piece walnut grips. The barrel had what appeared to be several pipe wrench marks. As I turned it over in my hands and caught the light I saw something on the frame. What caught my eye was "US." It appeared I had an original Cavalry Model.

There was no caliber marking on the barrel, and it appeared to have a reblue of sorts mixed in with a little bit of rust. It seemed to function okay. The top of the loading gate, where it met the frame, shared one-half of a circular dent with the frame itself. I tried to envision it as a mark made by a 19th-century bullet. Whatever the cause, it would require extensive welding to fix (so much for my bargain frame!). All early SAAs had the serial number marked on the mainframe, trigger guard and butt. However, these were mismatched.

The last three digits of the mainframe number were all zeros.

It was a good candidate for restoration, so I turned it over to Larry Larsen, a local fellow who just happens to specialize in restoring old Colts. Larry removed the rust damage from the cylinder, a small spot weld had to be repaired, and the original hammer and trigger were welded and recut to allow perfect timing and lockup. He installed and fire-blued a new black powder-style base pin and fire-blued all the screws as well. Larry then removed all rust from the trigger guard without removing the serial number or inspector's mark and properly beveled both sides of the trigger guard to meet the frame sharply.

The butt had become rounded and worn, so Larry flat-sanded and contoured it correctly. He cut a new serial number for it, one that would ensure I had no intention to fake it as an authentic, all-original US Colt. New one-piece walnut stocks were installed with the correct cartouches and inspector's marks. The cylinder flutes were polished and beveled, and the barrel was polished to remove rust and scratches while still maintaining all original markings. The tip of the ejector housing was beveled, and then an ejector rod was installed, complete with a round bullseye head. The entire sixgun, except for the mainframe and hammer, which were re-case hardened by Color Case Company, was "period-correctly" reblued. The necessary restamping was performed by Dave

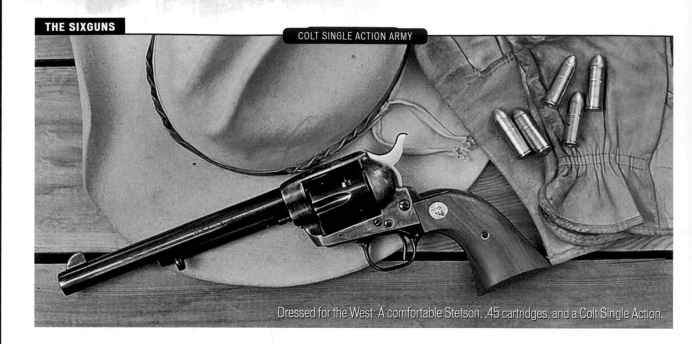

Dressed for the West: A comfortable Stetson, .45 cartridges, and a Colt Single Action.

Lanara. When we were all finished, I had a US Cavalry Colt as beautiful as it was the day in 1881 when it left the Hartford factory. Naturally, it is for black-powder loads only.

A BEATER BISLEY

Ten years ago I came into a Bisley Model chambered in .45 Colt with a 4¾-inch barrel. It was basically what one would call a "beater" with no finish left, markings very faint and some pitting on the outside. The upside is it shot relatively well; it just showed its age even more than I do. Born 100 years earlier, it had been heavily used but not abused. It was worth being brought back to life.

A resurrection project is too big of a job for one person, but Jim Alaimo was the ideal one to head it up. When Jim returned home from Vietnam in 1969, he managed to hire on at Colt as a supervisor on the night shift overseeing the polishing department, where he learned all about bluing, plating and color-casehardening as well. Then he switched to a position which allowed him to spend time with the old school assemblers. From there he became supervisor of the assembler's training school. Over the next 20 years he served in many capacities, notably as head of the Colt Custom Shop. In 1993 Jim left Colt and struck out on his own and started Nutmeg Sports in Connecticut.

I sent my Bisley to Jim and was absolutely stunned when he sent it back. There is no way I could have expected anything so beautiful. Before performing any finish work on the Bisley, Jim installed a new bolt, hand and bolt spring

and totally retimed the old Colt. The cylinder notches were too shallow and the metal too thin to be recut, so a new cylinder was installed. One of Jim's subcontractors then went to work on the metal by using draw files, sandpaper and emery cloth to bring the metal back to original perfection. Virtually all the lettering and serial numbers had to be recut. All the screwheads had to be recut and polished.

The next step was fitting the ivory grips. Jim says: "I selected what I thought would be the very best ivory for this Colt. I had to make sure first that the color was strong and it matched from side to side. The plan was to carve the right grip panel. The configuration of the Bisley grip lends itself perfectly to the Mexican eagle. The bird's wings are folded down, so I decided to tell the carver to place the eagle with it in a cameo style frame. I left the right grip panel very heavy to accommodate the high relief carving. I was still faced with what to do with the right panel screw. Not wanting the screw end to protrude through the carving, I configured the grip assembly with what is referred to as a blind screw hole. This means that I mechanically embedded the threaded screw into the inside of the right grip panel. That way the screw is not visible when viewing the carved side."

The next step was to do the actual carving of the right grip. For this it was sent off to Dennis Holland in Lubbock, Texas. Dennis has been chosen in the past to carve many grips for the Colt Collector's Annual Meeting and Gun Show. His efforts resulted in one of the finest renditions of the Mexican eagle Jim or I had ever seen.

The Bisley was thought by many to be a superior target gun to the standard SAA. John's old one makes a strong case for that line of reasoning.

While the grips were being carved, Jerome Harper of Tennessee, and former professor at UCLA, began the actual engraving. Jerry is under contract with Nutmeg Sports and one of his major clients is the Colt Custom Shop. For my Bisley, he followed the style of two well-known masters — Cuno Helfricht and L.D. Nimschke.

The mainframe, loading gate and hammer were given the color-casehardening treatment by Doug Turnbull, while the rest of the gun was finished in Carbona blue. The Bisley was then returned to Nutmeg Sports for final assembly and tuning.

There is no way words can express how beautiful my Bisley is and how much I appreciate all the work by all of these talented artisans. It is the most beautiful sixgun I have ever actually experienced and certainly the most magnificent piece of artwork I will ever call my own.

LEGENDARY SAA'S

Although Colt had the three standardized barrel lengths, shooters could have any length they wanted from short-barreled Sheriff's Models (without ejector rod housings) to extra long barrels. Edward Zane Carroll Judson, known by the pen name of "Ned Buntline" was an author of dime novels toward the end of the 19th century. He created long-standing myths about western heroes. He is also known as having presented five "Buntline Specials" to five lawmen in Dodge City in the late 1870s — Charlie Bassett, Neal Brown, Bat Masterson, Bill Tilghman and Wyatt Earp.

Research has shown long-barreled SAAs (which the Colt factory did *not* refer to as Buntline Specials) were produced in a serial number range from 1876 to 1884. To date, 22 have been uncovered — 19 chambered in .45 Colt. Usually, they were fitted with a wire stock and a long-range rear sight which lifted out of its mortise on the topstrap. Is the original presenting of the five Buntline Specials reality or myth? There are no factory records to confirm the shipping of five long-barreled Buntline revolvers. Records, however, are not always complete.

In Stuart Lake's 1931 book *Wyatt Earp Frontier Marshall*, we may or may not have an authentic life of Wyatt Earp. Many contend there were more lies and myths told to Lake by Earp than true stories. Lake says of the Buntline Specials:

"Buntline was so grateful to the Dodge City peace officers for the color they supplied that he set about arming them as befitted their accomplishments. He sent to the Colt

COLT SINGLE ACTION ARMY

Colt originally submitted an 1871-72 Open-Top to the military (top), which was then redesigned and "recalibrated" to become the Single Action Army .45.

factory for five special forty-five-caliber six-guns of regulation single-action style, but with barrels four inches longer than standard, a foot in length, making them eighteen inches over all. Each gun had a demountable walnut rifle stock, with a thumbscrew arrangement to fit the weapon for a shoulder-piece in long-range shooting. A buckskin thong slung the stock to belt or saddle-horn when not in use. The walnut butt of each gun had the word 'Ned' carved deeply in the wood and each was accompanied by a hand-tooled holster modeled for the weapon."

Lake records Wyatt saying:

"There was a lot of talk in Dodge about the Specials slowing us on the draw. Bat and Bill Tilghman cut off the bar-

Elmer Keith's King Gun Sight custom 7½-inch .44 Special and his No. 5 .44 Special flank his custom .45 Colt.

rels to make them standard length. But Bassett, Brown, and I kept ours as they came. Mine was my favorite over any other gun. I could jerk it as fast as I could my old one and I carried it at my right hip throughout my career as marshal. With it I did most of the six-gun work I had to do. My second gun, which I carried at my left hip, was a standard Colt frontier model 45-caliber, single-action six-shooter with the seven-and-one-half-inch barrel, the gun we called the Peacemaker."

Is Wyatt being truthful here or is he pulling Stuart Lake's leg? Holsters in those days were mainly the Mexican loop style that rode high on the belt. Drawing a 7½-inch Colt from one is not an easy task, let alone one with a 12-inch barrel. We may never know the truth about the original so-called Buntline Specials.

Probably the most famous of the 1st Generation SAA .45s was delivered to the Shelton Payne Arms Company in El Paso, Texas, on March 4, 1916. Serial number 332088 has a 4¾-inch barrel, is fully engraved and fitted with ivory grips with a "Screaming Eagle" and the initials "GSP" intertwined. This beautiful sixgun cost Lt. George S. Patton, Jr. a grand total of $50. Five days after Lt. Patton received his Colt, bandits shouting "Viva Villa" raided Columbus, New Mexico.

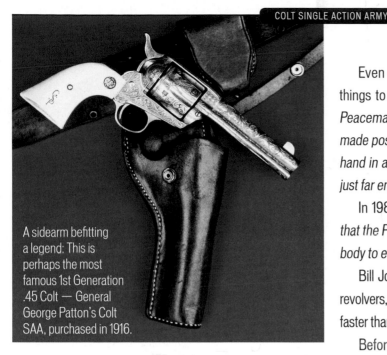

A sidearm befitting a legend: This is perhaps the most famous 1st Generation .45 Colt — General George Patton's Colt SAA, purchased in 1916.

At the time Patton was stationed at Fort Bliss as an aide to Brig. Gen. John J. "Black Jack" Pershing who commanded the 8th Cavalry. On March 14, General Order No. 1 set up the Punitive Expedition. The Punitive Expedition was no great success and Pancho Villa was never captured, but Patton and a caravan of three Dodge touring cars jumped a group of bandits, Patton jumped out of the car with his Colt in hand, killing two of the bandits and returned to camp with the bodies strapped over the hoods of the Dodges. During World War II, General Patton carried that same Colt SAA in an S. D. Myers Border Patrol holster. It became his trademark, complete with two notches in the grip.

My third old Colt is not too far removed from Patton's Single Action (as it was made in 1917). Mine also has a 4¾-inch barrel and beautiful one-piece ivory stocks with the checkered fleur-de-lis pattern; however, it is not even close to being engraved. Most of the finish is gone and it has some light pitting. But it has been tuned and tightened by Eddie Janis of Peacemaker Specialists, who also supplied the stocks. It oozes nearly 100 years' worth of character. I wouldn't even think of having it refinished.

SHOOTISTS ALL

In 1955 Elmer Keith said: *"For the man who was raised on the Colt single action, nothing is faster for the first shot, draw and hit. Even the latest double action is no faster for that first shot ..."*

Even Col. Jeff Cooper, *the* 1911 proponent had good things to say about the SAA: *"The striking thing about the Peacemaker is its wonderful balance — the balance that made possible the art of the gunslinger. It snuggles into your hand in a way that is essentially comforting. Its weight rides just far enough forward to let you feel where it's pointing ..."*

In 1980 Skeeter Skelton said: *"Almost everyone agrees that the Peacemaker grip is the nearest thing to fitting everybody to ever come down the pike ..."*

Bill Jordan, while completely committed to double-action revolvers, once privately acknowledged to me that no gun is faster than the single action for the draw and the first shot.

Before I was 18, I had a pair of 7½-inch Colt SAA .45s. I've used 7½-inch SAAs in Fast Draw and later in Cowboy Action. At the time I was the only one using such a long barrel. Now they have a "Shootist Category" in my honor which requires the use of a 7½-inch gun. To this day I haven't found a sixgun which balances in my hand as perfectly as a 7½-inch Colt SAA. And a lot of old timers agreed with me.

Since I've lived long enough to become an old timer myself, I feel comfortable quoting from something I wrote 20 years ago: *"Pick up a seashell and it is said one can hear the sea as the shell is placed over the ear. Pick up a Colt Single Action Army and you can hear the tinkling of the ivories in the saloon on Main Street in Dodge City. You can smell wet cattle as they are driven north through the wind and rain and dust. You can taste fresh cooked bacon and beans over a campfire in the mountains of Montana. And you can see the history of our country stretching over a century."* ◎

This Artillery Model .45 Colt is still in service.

THE SIXGUNS

John draws down on a distant target with his New Service chambered in .45 Colt.

THE COLT MODEL 1878 & NEW SERVICE

CHAPTER 7

When Smith & Wesson pushed Colt's percussion revolvers into obsolescence in 1869, it began a competition between the two companies. By way of one-upmanship, Colt became the first to offer truly workable double-action sixguns with the 1877 Lightning and Thunderer chambered in .38 Long Colt and .41 Long Colt, respectively. These were somewhat fragile mechanically, and certainly not the most powerful, even though they were popular with men on both sides of the law, including Billy the Kid.

In 1878 Colt took the next step in DA progression with the Model 1878, mainly chambered in .45 Colt. S&W would follow in 1881 with its DA .44 Russian.

The Colt Model 1878 is basically a Colt SAA with a DA trigger. A look at both sixguns side by side shows great similarities. In fact, the Model 1878 loads and unloads through a loading gate one cartridge at a time, just as with the SAA. The grip is different and shaped to stay in place in the hand

Early Colt New Services have a straight barrel (bottom). Later versions (top) have a barrel with a collar at the frame.

when firing double action, unlike the SAA which rolls in the hand to put the shooter's thumb in the proper place to easily recock the hammer.

Those first Model 1877s — the Lightning and Thunderer — were so named by a Colt distributor, who also named the Peacemaker. For the Model 1878, they came up with the name "Omnipotent." None were official Colt company designations, but rather advertising gimmicks. However, the Model 1878 went one step farther than the other three, with some special-order specimens featuring the inscription "Omniponent" on the barrel.

Once in a very great while — if you're paying attention — you'll spot a Model 1878 in one of the old "B" Westerns. It also shows up in one of the early scenes of *Tombstone* as Wyatt Earp (Kurt Russell) places the barrel of a cocked, nickel-plated Model 1878 against the forehead of the actor playing Ike Clanton. In recent years, United States Fire Arms made a very few "Omnipotent" repros, which were actually single actions fitted with a Model 1878-type grip frame.

Anyone who has ever tried to fire a sixgun while wearing heavy gloves knows the problem of trying to get your trigger finger into the trigger guard. To solve this problem, Colt offered a Model 1878 with an enlarged bow. This version is known as the Philippine and/or Alaskan Model. But regardless of the version, the most prevalent caliber for the Model 1878 was the .45 Colt.

A Model 1878 Diamond Dot brought home is well-worn on the outside with what appears to be an old reblue. The 4¾-inch barrel is unmarked, and the front sight appears to be a replacement made of brass. When you look at a Model 1878, you'll notice there are no bolt slots on the cylinder because Colt's early double actions locked from the back.

ARMY/NAVY

In the late 1880s, Colt introduced what would become the basic "swing-out" DA revolver we still use today. Their Army Model and Navy Models were chambered mainly in .38 Long Colt and .41 Long Colt. Eventually, the powers that be decided the Colt SAA .45 and the double-action Model 1878 .45 were obsolete, so the double-action .38 Long Colt was selected to replace them.

Colt New Service Revolver

SIX SHOTS, DOUBLE ACTION

Jointless Solid Frame Simultaneous Ejection Swing-out Cylinder

CALIBERS:
.38 Special. (Using in the same arm .38 Short Colt; .38 Long Colt; .38 Colt Special Hi-Speed; .38 S. & W. Special (full and mid-range loads); .38-44 S. & W. Special High Velocity; .38-44 S. & W. Special.)
.357 Magnum.
.38-40 (.38 Winchester).
.44 Special.
.44-40 (.44 Winchester).
.45 Colt.
.45 Automatic.
.455 Eley (English).

Colt Forged One Piece Frame

The strength, the rigidity and the perfect balance of Colt Revolvers is due in no small part to the care with which the frame is designed and forged. From a bar of solid steel, Colt frames are formed, red hot, under the thudding blows of a giant drop hammer. Over and over it is turned until it has been hammered into the rough shape of a revolver frame—tough, strong and unbreakable. There are no castings in Colt Arms—the hammer, trigger, etc., being machined from solid bars of steel—each type of steel laboratory tested and carefully inspected before finally accepted.

The New Service is essentially a holster Revolver for the man in the open — Mounted, Motorcycle and State Police; the Hunter, Explorer and Pioneer. It is the Arm adopted as Standard by the Royal Canadian Mounted Police, and hundreds of city and state Police Organizations throughout the world. This Arm has the well known COLT GRIP, ample for the brawniest hand yet so formed that it is easily grasped by the smaller hand. Light reflection is eliminated by non-reflecting sights and matting along the entire top of the frame.

General Specifications

LENGTHS OF BARREL: calibers .38 and .357 Magnum, 4, 5, 6 inches, other calibers 4½, 5½ or 7½ inches.
LENGTH OVER ALL: With 4½ inch barrel, 9¾ inches; with 6 inch barrel, 11¼ inches.
STOCKS: Checked Walnut, either round or square. Lanyard loop furnished at no extra cost.
TRIGGER: Checked.

SIGHTS: Fixed, Non-reflecting, giving "Patridge" effect in sighting.
FINISH: Full Blued (or Full Nickel Plated), top of frame matted to eliminate reflection and glare.
WEIGHT: With 4½ inch barrel, (.45 caliber) 39 ounces; with 6 inch barrel (.38 caliber) 43 ounces.

The New Service Revolver was designed for those requiring an especially sturdy Fire Arm of sufficiently large caliber for the most serious service without excessive weight. It withstands the rigors of heat, cold, rain or snow as well as excessive use, as many as 250,000 rounds having been fired from a New Service Revolver without noticeable impairment of accuracy.
It is the Model chosen by men who frequently find themselves far from gunsmiths and whose lives may depend upon the reliability of their Fire Arms, for it is capable of stopping any animal on the American Continent. Absolute safety is assured by the COLT POSITIVE LOCK which prevents accidental discharge.

Special Features

.45 COLT

26

Colt "Shooting Master"

DE LUXE TARGET REVOLVER

Jointless Solid Frame Simultaneous Ejection Swing-out Cylinder

CALIBERS:
.38 Special. (Using in the same arm .38 Short Colt; .38 Long Colt; .38 Colt Special; .38 Colt Special Hi-Speed; .38 S. & W. Special (full and mid-range loads); .38 S. & W. Special High Velocity; .38-44 S. & W. Special).
.357 Magnum
.44 Special
.45 Colt
.45 Automatic

Special "Non-Reflecting" Shooting Master Frame.

Features designed to eliminate sun glare and reflection are always of importance to the target shooter. Special care has been taken in designing the "Shooting Master" to provide non-reflecting sights and a frame carefully stippled on top and rear in such a way as to make light reflection impossible. Even the top of the hammer has been dulled in order that no light may be reflected when the hammer is in the cocked position.

General Specifications

LENGTH OF BARREL: 6 inches.
LENGTH OVER ALL: 11¼ inches.
STOCKS: Selected Checked Walnut, Rounded Butt. Square Butt if desired, at no extra charge.
TRIGGER: Checked.
STRAPS: Deeply Checked.
BARREL: Super-precisioned. Tapered to insure perfect balance.

SIGHTS: "Patridge" (regularly furnished) or "Bead." Both non-reflecting; Front Sight adjustable for elevation; Rear Sight adjustable for windage.
FINISH: Full Blued; top and back of frame stippled to eliminate reflection and glare.
ACTION: Velvet-smooth hand finished target action.
WEIGHT: (.38 Caliber) 44 ounces.

The Colt "Shooting Master" is a man's gun — produced to meet the exacting requirements of those shooters who are satisfied with nothing less than the ultimate in a target arm. It is a de luxe product of Colt ingenuity and Colt craftsmanship — and stands out as the finest and most accurate target Revolver yet produced.
The heavy frame, full grip and perfect balance of the "Shooting Master" lend confidence and steadiness to the shooter — and the velvet smoothness of its action makes higher scores a certainty. A gun-among-guns, the "Shooting Master" is destined to blaze a trail of records from one end of the country to the other.

Special Features

The perfectly distributed weight of the "Shooting Master," is such as to reduce recoil to a point where it is scarcely noticeable.
A special feature of this Arm is its rounded, palm-fitting grip. Both back and front straps are deeply checked, providing a firm, full grip for large as well as small hands. The velvet-smooth action of the "Shooting Master" will prove a delight in the hands of experienced and novice shooters alike.

.38 COLT SPECIAL

Vintage 1940 ads for the Colt New Service and Shooting Master.

The Model 1878 loads through a loading gate like the Colt SAA. Swing out cylinders were still a ways off.

Anyone who knows anything about firearms history knows what a mistake this was, as the cartridge proved totally inadequate in the Philippines. Old Cavalry Model .45 Colt SAAs were taken out of mothballs and their barrels cut to 5½ inches. Then they were shipped to the troops in the Philippines where they proved to be just as effective as ever.

THE NEW SERVICE

Just before the dawn of the 20th century, Colt took the next step in double-action evolution with the New Service, which holds the distinction of being the largest revolver ever offered by Colt. In fact, it was the largest cartridge revolver period until the coming of Ruger's Redhawk and Dan Wesson's Model 44 in the 1980s. Ten years after the introduction of the New Service, Smith & Wesson would counter with the first N-frame, the 1st Model Hand Ejector. For the first 40 years of the 20th century, Colt's New Service and Smith & Wesson's Hand Ejectors would be worthy rivals. I've considerable experience with both and have found the S&W grip frame is better suited to my large but short-fingered hand.

My experience with the New Service began as a teenager with a Model 1917 chambered in .45 ACP. I wasn't smart enough to hold on to that one; however, over the years I have acquired several others in .44 Special, .44-40, .38-40, .38 Special and, of course, .45 Colt. My 5½-inch Colt New Service .45 Colt may be several years older than me, but it is still a viable choice for self-defense work. Loaded with six rounds with 260-grain bullets at 900 fps, it is definitely something to be reckoned with.

NEW SERVICE VARIANTS

While the S&W Hand Ejectors were going through the process of 1st, 2nd, 3rd, and 4th Models that would eventually lead to the .44 Magnum in 1955, Colt was also following an evolutionary path of standard models and several variations thereof.

Collectors now apply special terms to distinguish the various models of New Services from 1898 to 1941. The "Old Model" name applies to the first 21,000 units. These were rather ungainly looking with a straight stovepipe shaped barrel and a trigger guard that looked like it was added on as an afterthought. After the Old Model, approximately 2,000 Transitional Models were offered with (mainly) interior improvements including a hammer-block safety. Next came the Improved Model, which would go to serial number 328,000; it is, of course, the New Service most often encountered.

The barrel was given a larger collar where it screwed into the frame and the trigger guard was also larger and better shaped. We can thank the United States Army for the collar on the barrel, as all Model 1917 military models were ordered in this configuration to provide a snug fit of barrel to frame. Designed for better function, it also resulted in a better form. Sometime around 1928, the Late Model New Service arrived with a reshaped top strap resulting in a more flattened appearance. At the same time, the rear sight had been milled to a square notch.

In its 1940 catalog Colt offered three versions of the New Service with barrel lengths of 4½, 5½ and 7½ inches

The Colt Model 1878 .45 (top) was challenged in the marketplace by S&W's double-action .44 Russian (bottom), introduced in 1881.

(blue or nickel finish). It was definitely a sixgun for both outdoor and duty use and was adopted as the official sidearm of both the RCMP and the United States Border Patrol. The Mounties chose the .45 Colt, while our officers on the southern border opted for .38 Special.

One variant — the New Service Target Revolver — was one of the fincst double-action revolvers ever offered by any manufacturer at any time. This beautiful version of the standard model was available in a choice of either a 6- or 7½-inch barrel. Stocks were checkered walnut, the trigger was checkered, as were the front and back straps. The finish was a deep blue, and sights were adjustable with a choice of a Patridge or bead front.

The final version of the New Service was the Shooting Master. It featured a velvet-smooth hand-finished action and sights and a top strap that were finished to eliminate glare. The Shooting Master represented the highest quality revolver that Colt could build.

THE FITZ SPECIAL

The last time I saw the late Col. Rex Applegate, I took a personally guided tour through his private museum. It held many sixguns which had formerly belonged to friends of his like Col. Doug Wesson, Col. Charles Askins, Elmer Keith and Bill Jordan.

Texas Ranger Clint Peoples' .45 ACP Model 1917 got the full-bore "Fitz Special" custom treatment. *Photo: Timothy Mullin*

However, the Colonel's favorite may have started life as a standard Colt New Service .45 Colt, probably with a 5½-inch barrel. But considering Col. Applegate's friendship with Colt's John Henry FitzGerald, this revolver was probably one of the very few specially manufactured "Fitz Specials." On the side plate were the words "To Rex from Fitz."

Colonel Applegate was one of the original members of the O.S.S. during World War II. Until the day he died he stayed with his original theory of point shooting which was definitely not hip shooting, but rather required the gun to be brought up, arm straight and "pointed" at the target.

John Henry Fitzgerald was "Mr. Colt" between the two world wars, traveling to all the large pistol matches, shooting and fixing Colts, and being a genuinely good ambassador for the company. Before Clint Smith, Mas Ayoob, Jeff Cooper, even before Colonel Applegate himself, there was Fitzgerald, teaching principles of quick shooting with a revolver. Not only was he a top shooter, he was also the designer of the Fitz Special.

I first became aware of the Fitz Special through the writings of Col. Charles Askins. Askins said:

"The grandest defense gun I have ever had was a Colt New Service with the barrel cut down to two inches ... The hammer had been dehorned ... the trigger guard was cut entirely away in the front ... the grip was shortened ... it was a whiz for the purpose intended."

Actually the Fitz Special started more than 40 years earlier as Fitz started experimenting with the then new Colt New Service. It was common knowledge among his contemporaries that Fitz always carried a pair of .45 Colt Fitz Specials in his two front pockets. He definitely knew how to use them.

I've wanted to have a Fitz Special ever since I was the kid learning to shoot big-bore sixguns of the 1950s. There was very little hope of ever having an original, which would be very rare and very expensive, and definitely a collector's item. I would be happy simply to have a top gunsmith build one for me on a Colt New Service. Earlier I found what I thought would be the perfect candidate for a Fitz Special, a 5½-inch Late Model New Service in .45 Colt. Although it had considerable pitting on the right side of the barrel and part of the cylinder, it was mechanically perfect. There was one major problem — it shot much too well to touch. Any .45 Colt capable of placing five

Top: Concealable power indeed! This "chopped" custom factory New Service was made for a peace officer in the 1930s. He had a pair! Bottom: *No. This is not some Python prototype. It's a Colt Model 1917, fully customized by King Gun Sight Company. Photos: Timothy Mullin*

Moon clips — whether full, half or quarter — made it possible to use the .45 ACP in Colt's big double-action revolvers.

double-action shots into less than 1½ inches at 50 feet is not to be messed with!

When a second Late Model New Service surfaced chambered in .44 Special, I sent it off to one of the premier gunsmiths in the country, Andy Horvath. Horvath has built more than a half-dozen single-action sixguns for me, and he turned this New Service .44 in to a Fitz Special. (That's why my "Fitz" is a .44 instead of a .45.)

In his 1930 book, *Shooting*, Fitz says of his Special:

"No claim is made to beauty in these arms but they will deliver the goods. I believe I am the pioneer butcher of revolvers for quick draw. Thirty years ago I tried out my first two-inch barrel and this was followed by the cut-away triggerguard, cut-off hammer spur, rounded butt, cut-off ejector rod, straightened trigger, etc."

I have been asked many times if cutting away the trigger guard is a safe procedure and if there is any danger in carrying a revolver cut in this manner. I've carried one for many years and to date am still walking without a limp. But I suggest many hours of practice with the Fitz Special

with the gun empty, drawing and dry snapping before actually firing it.

Fitz preferred the .45 Colt as it was the most powerful cartridge available at the time. However, it is interesting to see his choice of handgun hunting cartridges. He places the .45 Colt at the top of the list and says the smokeless powder load at 770 fps and a 250-grain bullet is sufficient for almost any purpose a hunting arm would be used for.

The Colt New Service .45 has a varied military history. We have mentioned how quickly the .38 Long Colt was found wanting after the Spanish-American War of 1898 and our troops found themselves facing an insurrection in the Philippines. The New Service was relatively new at this time, so they fell back on the SAA .45.

In between the resurrection of the SAA in 1899 and the adoption of the Government Model 1911, the New Service saw use. Two New Service Models were submitted to the army trials of 1906, resulting in the US Army Model 1909 which was chambered for the .45 Model 1909 cartridge, nothing more than a .45 Colt with a larger rim to aid extraction. A second model, the USMC Model 1909 differs only slightly in having a somewhat rounded butt. In 1911 1,000 US Navy Model 1909 New Services were purchased by our navy. The British also looked seriously at the New Service, not only purchasing them for use by the British forces but also the Canadians. (These were chambered in .455 Eley.)

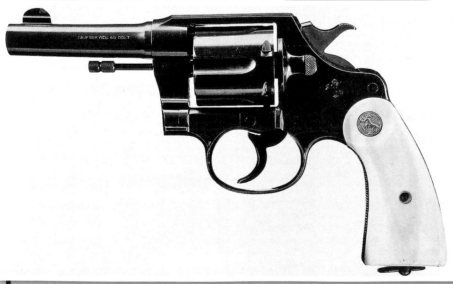

Top: The New Service platform was a natural for emblellishment, as these engraved, ivory-stocked specimens demonstrate. Above: Even a dyed-in-the-wool S&W fan like Ed McGivern was not immune to the appeal of the Colt New Service. This custom 4-inch, ivory-stocked .45 Colt specimen was his. *Photos: Timothy Mullin*

THE GREAT WAR AND AFTER

Even though we waited until 1917 for the U.S. Expeditionary Force to travel to Europe under General Pershing, there still weren't enough 1911s to go around. So the government turned to both S&W and Colt for a solution. That solution was to chamber both revolvers, the Smith & Wesson 2nd Model Hand Ejector and the Colt New Service to what was now the standard service cartridge — the .45 ACP. An engineer at Smith & Wesson came up with the half-moon clips which would hold three of the rimless .45 ACP cartridges not only making loading very fast, but extraction positive.

Approximately 152,000 Model 1917s were sent to Europe to arm our troops. These New Service Models all had 5½-inch barrels and, as mentioned, the military improved them by adding a collar to where the barrel meets the frame. These .45 ACP sixguns had smooth walnut grips, a lanyard ring in the butt and were marked on the underside of the barrel "United States Property."

Although many 1917s found their way into civilian hands after the Great War, the U.S. Army managed to keep close to 100,000 in its inventory, and those were pressed into service in World War II, mainly for duty with the Military Police at home and overseas.

Skeeter Skelton was a fan of the Colt 1917 and one of his first articles appearing in the long-gone magazine called *Gunsport* was entitled "The Poor Man's Magnum" in which he espoused the virtues of a heavily loaded .45 Auto Rim in the Colt Model 1917. Several

I've wanted to have a Fitz Special ever since I was the kid learning to shoot big-bore sixguns of the 1950's. There was very little hope of ever having an original, which would be very rare and very expensive, and definitely a collector's item.

Colt's groundbreaking Model 1878 double-action .45 compared to the Colt SAA.

years later he wrote another article titled "I Gave You The Colt, Now Give Me Back The Stud," which was about another Model 1917 .45 ACP he had totally customized. In both cases, Skeeter went with the 5½-inch barrel.

Another fan of the Colt New Service was the father of modern concealment leather, Chic Gaylord, although he opted for the .45 Colt chambering. In Chic's 1960 book *The Handgunner's Guide*, he paid high praise to the Colt New Service .45, calling it the best service revolver available. He carried it in a specially boned, tight-fitting, high-riding holster of his own design. In this same book Gaylord shows Detective Ganio's Monster Special, a short-barrel, round-butted .45 Colt New Service which was used with a 280-grain bullet over 10.0 grains of Unique.

Ed McGivern, normally known for speed-shooting S&Ws, had a special 4-inch Colt New Service .45 with ivory stocks and a slightly rounded butt. Texas Ranger Clint Peoples made up his own Fitz Special .45 ACP, with a highly abbreviated, round-butted grip frame with stag stocks.

The last 1940 Colt catalog touted the Colt New Service and the Colt SAA as two of the finest sixguns ever offered. They were, of course, correct. However, both models were dropped from production to make way for wartime needs, and the New Service was never to be seen again.

For further study of the Colt New Service, in addition to FitzGerald's book (which has been reprinted several times), I recommend *Colt's New Service Revolver* by Timothy J. Mullin (2009). For the Colt 1878, try *Colt's Double-Action Revolver Model of 1878* by the late Colt authority, Don Wilkerson (1998). All three of these books are must-haves for the student of .45 sixguns. ◎

John's old New Service .455 — converted to .45 Colt — is a real shooter.

Fit for a cover: These are the actual Great Westerns which appeared on the first cover of *GUNS Magazine* in January 1955.

THE GREAT WESTERN FRONTIER MODEL

CHAPTER 8

It is 1954. You are a young publisher about to launch a magazine strictly about guns. Outdoor magazines have been in existence for nearly a century, but your plans are different. No fishing. No camping. No outdoor recreation. Just *guns*. When the first issue hits the newsstands, the cover will be critical. So, what gun do you choose?

Remember, the .44 Magnum has not yet arrived. The only Rugers available are in .22 rimfire. Target shooters have not yet really discovered the .45 Auto. Fast Draw is just getting started. IPSC, IHMSA, handgun hunting and Cowboy Action Shooting are virtually eons away.

BACK TO THE FUTURE

Well, back to that first cover. *GUNS Magazine* Publisher George von Rosen reached back into history and featured a matched pair of Peacemakers. Many thought they were Colts. But they were, in reality, a matched pair of Great Western .45s.

In 1954 William Wilson began Great Western, offering what was basically the first all American-made replica of the Colt Single Action Army. Not made in Italy or Germany, these sixguns were made in North Hollywood, California.

When I saw that first January 1955 issue while

browsing a local newsstand, I had to buy it. That premier issue featured the Great Westerns on the cover, but the feature article on them, "Great Western, A Six-Shooter For TV Cowboys," would not appear until the May issue.

Not only did that premier issue of *GUNS* introduce the shooting world to the Great Western sixgun, it also featured such articles as "Shootin' Irons of the Old West," "Hickok–Hell's Own Marshall," "Guns For Hunting," "Fire On Full Automatic" and "Restoring An Old Muzzle Loader." Over the years the legends of shooting would appear in *GUNS* — Elmer Keith, Skeeter Skelton, Col. Charles Askins, George Nonte, Kent Bellah, Bill Jordan and others.

Perhaps the magaine's arrival had something to do with all the great sixguns also arriving in 1955. From Colt came the .357 Python, soon to be followed by Colt's resurrected SAA, the S&W .44 Magnum and Ruger's .357 Blackhawk.

THE FRONTIER SIX-SHOOTER

But let's get back to Great Western. Production of the Frontier Six-Shooter had begun in 1954. The Great Western looked so much like a Colt that the company actually used real Colts in the early advertising — in fact, some of the Great Western parts *came* from Colt. The Great Westerns pictured on that first cover of *GUNS* were chambered in .45 Colt with 4¾-inch barrels. The guns, which have no caliber markings on the barrels, have Colt-style hammers with the firing pin on the hammer. Since they are very early production sixguns, their serial numbers are GW183 and GW184. The ejector rod housings and frames were not case-colored but had the same plum-purple color found on the loading gates of many early Ruger single actions.

At first glance, Great Western Single Actions look identical to Colt SAAs. The early advertising used a Colt, disguised by fitting the plastic stag grips found on most Great Westerns. However, subtle differences can be seen in the hammer profile and shape of the trigger guard. Great Westerns show up on many TV westerns and

are easy to spot when the hammer is cocked. Colts have the firing pin on the hammer, while most Great Westerns have a frame-mounted firing pin like a Ruger. But unlike the Rugers, the Great Westerns have sort of an upside-down L-shaped hammer.

EARLY REVIEWS

In *Sixguns by Keith*, Elmer commented that the test Great Western Single Action he'd received was *" ... very poorly timed, fitted, and showed a total lack of final inspection. The hand was a trifle short, the bolt spring did not have enough bend to lock the bolt with any certainty, the mainspring was twice as strong as necessary and the trigger pull about three times as heavy as needed."*

Later in his book, however, Elmer was able to say:

"We are happy to report that Great Western has really gotten on the ball and is now cooking on all four burners. They overhauled their design and inspection departments, put in some gunsmiths who knew the score and are now turning out first-class single action copies. We have one in 4¾" .44 Special and it is a very fine single action in every way, perfectly timed, sighted, and very accurate. It has performed perfectly with factory loads and our heavy handloads and is very accurate at extreme ranges, the real test of any sixgun."

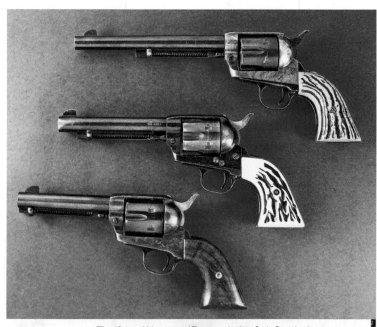

The Great Western .45, as with the Colt Single Action, came with three standard barrel lengths of 7½, 5½ and 4¾ inches.

John's rebuilt Great Western .45 rests on the cover of *Great Western Arms Company*, the welcome and much-needed definitive resource work on the history of the company as well as the single actions produced.

Henry M. Stebbins in 1961's *Pistols, A Modern Encyclopedia* had good things to say about the Great Western:

"Unlike the Colt Single Action, the Great Western hasn't stood still. Improvements have brought an efficient, modernized single action revolver. The stiff cocking of early Great Westerns is eliminated in current models. The mainspring is still flat, as we'd expect in this fairly close copy of the Colt; but cocking is now softer then with the first Great Western models. For durability, the hand, cylinder-bolt and trigger have been made of shock-resistant beryllium copper ... The Great Western Arms Company is ambitious and progressive. It's perfectly possible that they will build a single action that's of better quality than present or past Colts, as well as of more durable modern design. Some would even say, without qualification, that they now make the best."

More than 35 years ago I bought a 7½-inch Great Western .45 Colt barrel for $5 at a local gun show. All these years it has been sitting in my parts box. A few years ago at the same show I spotted a 7½-inch Great Western on a table at a very reasonable price. I told the fellow I'd take it, but I wanted him the pull the cylinder so I could check the bore. After working my way around the show, I came back

to examine the barrel to find out he'd sold the gun. Now, the only other person at the gun show who I thought could possibly be remotely interested in the gun was Brian Pearce, who writes for *Handloader* magazine. I found him, asked him about it and he pulled back his jacket to show me the Great Western in his belt.

Now it was his turn to try to get the cylinder out and he spent most of the rest of the weekend at that chore — he had to completely dismantle the gun and drive the pin out from the back. Turned out it was a movie gun and was basically welded together by years and years of black-powder shooting and no cleaning! After he got it apart, I bought it from him and turned it over to Tom at Buckhorn to make something out of it, after first giving him my old barrel and a new Colt .45 cylinder.

Meanwhile I acquired a set of imitation stag stocks for $15. That's more than I would have normally paid, but I'm glad I did. What I got were solid "jigged bone" plastic stags as used in the movies during the 1930s. They were fitted to my "new" Great Western and, for very little money, I now have a perfectly timed, accurate Great Western.

PROWLING THE USED BINS

It wasn't too long ago one could find excellent Great Westerns for around $125. In fact I got a chrome-plated one with a 4¾-inch barrel in .45 Colt. Before I had fired more than a few rounds through it, the forcing cone split. Now it wears a 4¾-inch nickel-plated Colt barrel.

Many of the parts of the Great Western Single Action are interchangeable with the Colt SAA except for the hammer, trigger and bolt screws. (The threads on the screws were changed to help prevent them from loosening under recoil.) Two years after the Great Western was introduced, Colt brought back the SAA, and despite the improvements in the Great Western guns, their fate was sealed. The company went out of business in 1964.

ABOUT THOSE COVER GUNS

Fast forward to January 2005. When I discovered that first issue of *GUNS*, I never dreamed what I would see 50

Both of these 4¾-inch .45 Single Actions have nickel-plated Colt barrels, however, the bottom one is a chrome-plated Great Western. It is identifiable by its frame mounted firing pin, L-shaped hammer and trigger guard configuration.

years later. There on the front cover of the magazine's 50th Anniversary issue was the blurb "Taffin Shoots the Great Western .45s from GUNS No. 1."

Those sixguns were shipped to me for the express purpose of shooting them to celebrate the 50th Anniversary of the magazine. All the time they had been in the hands of the family of the original publisher. But before I could shoot them, they needed some work.

The Great Westerns on the 1955 cover were not *quite* as bad as the one initially described by Elmer Keith, but close! I got permission to have them brought to perfection by long-time single-action gunsmith/trick shooter/shooting instructor, Jim Martin. As a young man, Jim Martin purchased Great Western kits, assembled them and sold them, using the money to buy more kits. You can bet his guns had much better actions than the originals.

If Jim Martin had been the head gunsmith for Great Western way back when, perhaps they would still be in business. These two early sixguns are now tuned and slicked the way a single action should be. As the hammer is cocked, the parts all work together instead of fighting each other. Jim

went several extra miles to get these sixguns finished and back to me in plenty of time to meet my deadline. Jim is not only a master 'smith, he is also a walking reference book of information. Thanks also go to Jim Cornwall of Kingman, Arizona, for turning the welded hammer around so quickly.

Fifty years after I first saw those Great Westerns, I actually got to shoot them and shoot they do! Using Black Hills .45 Colt 250 RNFP loads at 775 fps resulted in six-shot 50-foot groups of 1⅛ and 1⅜ inches. Seeing as how they are short-barreled single actions with a tiny V-notch rear and slim blade front, I would settle for that anytime. No reloads were tried much as I would have liked to since it is my long-standing rule never to shoot any of my reloads in someone else's personal guns.

Incidentally, Hy Hunter was an early distributor of Great Westerns, in fact the backstrap of both cover guns are inscribed "George von Rosen from Hy Hunter." Hunter would later import German made J.P. Sauer & Sohn Hawes versions. Audie Murphy also received a pair of .45 Great Westerns, and William Wilson, founder of Great Western, presented John Wayne with a pair of engraved Great Westerns. These were the two .45s the dying J.B. Books (portrayed by Wayne in *The Shootist*) carried. George Montgomery also used a pair of Great Western .45s in his TV series *Cimarron City*. Great Westerns arrived about the same time as the TV westerns, and they were much cheaper than Colt SAAs, so they show up on-screen often. Clint Walker (*Cheyenne*) carried a Great Western .45 in an Arvo Ojala Hollywood Fast Draw rig. Others packin' Great Westerns included Fast Draw expert Dee Woolem of Knotts Berry Farm. In the early episodes of *Gunsmoke*, James Arness used a Great Western .45 with a 7½-inch barrel, identified when cocked by the distinctively shaped hammer.

Great Westerns were made in the three standard barrel lengths of 4¾, 5½ and 7½ inches plus a 12½-inch Buntline Special. The standard model was a 5½-inch .45 Colt that sold for $99.50 in 1960 at a time when the resurrected Colt SAA .45 had a price tag of $125. Great Western also offered both pearl and ivory grips, engraving, nickel-plating and even adjustable target sights. As Fast Draw became more popular, Great Western offered a Fast Draw Model .45 Colt with a specially tuned action and a brass backstrap and trigger guard. They even had an ejectorless, short-barreled Sheriff Model. The Deputy Model was a 4-inch barrel version with a full-length barrel rib, adjustable sights, deluxe blue finish and walnut stocks instead of the standard imita-

tion stags. As far as I know, it was never offered in .45 Colt, just in .22 rimfire, .38 Special, .357 Magnum and .44 Special. And as mentioned, the company also offered Kit Guns for do-it-yourself gunsmiths at a price of about $20 less.

Great Western made several mistakes. First, it believed Colt would never again produce the SAA. When Colt did come back with the 2nd Generation run of SAAs in 1956, Great Western's days were numbered. Secondly, as too often happens with new businesses, it did not have the best-qualified people producing its product. Those early sixguns should have had the touch of a master single-action gunsmith before they ever left the factory. By the time they fixed the problem, the company then had to overcome those negative first impressions.

OPPORTUNITIES LOST

Great Western had a chance to really improve the single action. Instead of using a nearly indestructible coil spring operated action as did Ruger, the company chose to simply duplicate the old Colt SAA. Ruger capitalized one year later by bringing out the .357 Blackhawk, which not only had the coil spring action, but also a flat-topped frame with an adjustable rear sight. While Ruger had looked to the future, Great Western stayed stuck in the past. However, this should not obscure the very real enhancements Great Western brought to the single-action revolver. In fact, company literature of the day listed 14 reasons for selecting their single actions:

"(1) Great Westerns are made of 4130 Chrome Molybdenum steel, the same as used for stress parts in aircraft and guided missiles. (2) Barrels are made of medium carbon steel of the finest quality overseen by the man formerly in charge of manufacturing Weatherby barrels. (3) Cylinders are made of SAE 4140 Chrome Molybdenum steel heat treated to a tensile strength of 185,000 pounds per square inch. We have run .45 overloads at 100,000 pounds per square inch. (4) Both the bolt and trigger have been improved over the original and are guaranteed for 20 years, and a frame-mounted

The Great Western .45 came in three standard barrel lengths as well as a Buntline Special.

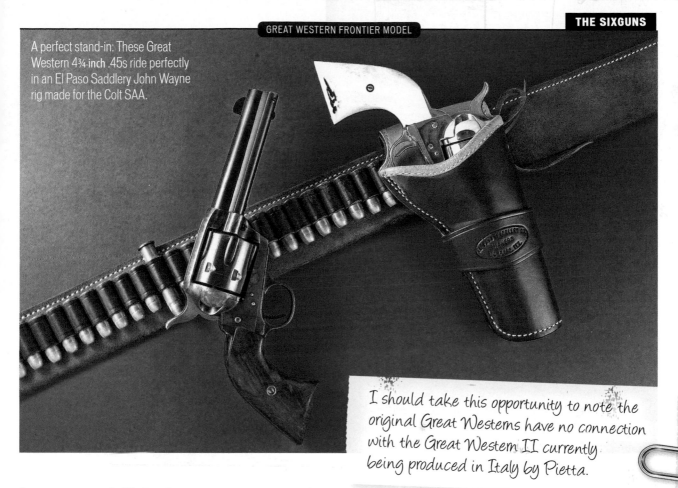

A perfect stand-in: These Great Western 4¾-inch .45s ride perfectly in an El Paso Saddlery John Wayne rig made for the Colt SAA.

I should take this opportunity to note the original Great Westerns have no connection with the Great Western II currently being produced in Italy by Pietta.

firing pin is used. (5) Stocks are imitation stags and are warp-resistant. (6) Late-model actions are carefully fitted and assembled with the smoothest and softest actions ever incorporated into a single action revolver. (7) Mainsprings have been designed for easier cocking. (8) The sear and bolt spring, which often failed in original guns, have been specially heat-treated and guaranteed for 50,000 movements. (9) There are no aluminum cast parts. (10) We offer a large variety of finishes including mirror blue, case hardened frame, chrome, nickel, gold, silver, or combinations thereof. (11) Great Westerns are the only single-actions offered in a variety of barrel lengths. (12) Great Westerns are the only single-actions offered in all popular calibers. (13) Front sights are purposely tall to allow for individual sighting in, and adjustable sights are also available. (14) The hammer is made of SAE 6150 Chrome Vanadium steel, giving greater strength and wear resistance than any other."

Of course, much of this is advertising hype; however, I have had experience with probably two dozen Great Westerns and have never had a spring fail or a part break, except for the above-mentioned forcing cone problem.

And Great Western really did test its guns for strength.

Starting with a pre-war SAA .45 as a base line, 27 grains of #2400 was loaded behind a 250-grain bullet, which ruptured the cylinder. Then the same load was tried in a Great Western with the result being not only the cylinder rupturing but the top strap buckled as well. But here is where it gets interesting. The company then took a Great Western after replacing the standard steel cylinder with a .45 Colt cylinder of SAE 4140 chrome molybdenum steel. This time 30 grains of #2400 was used with no negative results; no apparent changes. The gun still operated smoothly. I know I would not hold any Great Western in my hand and shoot such a load. My heavy hunting load with a 250-grain bullet in the larger Ruger .45 Colt Blackhawk uses 21.5 grains (which gives me over 1,400 fps).

One has to wonder if Great Western would have lasted longer had it improved the original SAA design with coil springs and a flat-top frame with adjustable sights. The 20-year guarantee on the bolt and trigger didn't mean much when the company only lasted 10 years. But the past is past. Meanwhile, I'll continue to shoot my Great Western .45s and treat them the same as other traditional single actions from Colt, Cimarron and USFA. ◎

THE SIXGUNS

A pair of 7½-inch 2nd Generation Colt SAA .45s. If you don't know by now, the 7½-inch barrel length is John's favorite configuration of the Peacemaker platform.

933
FPS
RCBS 45-250FN
10.0 HS-6

954
FPS

THE POST-WAR COLT SINGLE ACTION ARMY

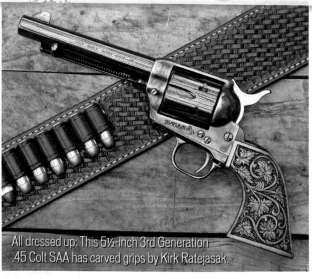

All dressed up: This 5½-inch 3rd Generation .45 Colt SAA has carved grips by Kirk Ratejasak.

CHAPTER 9

As we saw in the chapter on the pre-war Colt SAAs, production had ceased in 1940. By then most shooters looked upon the old Colt as being unable to measure up to the current crop of handguns. Even most of the Texas Rangers, who had been carrying SAA .45s for decades, had switched to 1911 Government Models or heavy-framed, double-action S&Ws.

Even Ranger Frank Hamer, who was called out of retirement in the early 1930s to head up the task force to capture Bonnie and Clyde, was carrying a 1911 in .38 Super as his

A 12-inch Colt Buntline Special .45 (top) over a 10-inch Cimarron import repro. Although very easy to shoot, the Buntline configuration is a hassle to pack.

backup gun. (Of course, his main sidearm was still "Old Lucky," his tried-and-true Colt SAA .45.)

Several factors had conspired against the Colt SAA. First, sales had plummeted over the years as the public had discovered the .357 Magnum double action and, of course, the 1911. Old Colt machinery, some of it dating back to the 1870s was wearing out, and we would soon be in the midst of World War II and its demands for wartime production. There was no longer any room for the SAA in Hartford.

THE NEXT RUN

However, history takes strange twists and turns. The postwar TV boom and the western TV heroes it popularized, plus the 1953 introduction of Bill Ruger's .22 Single Six, helped set the stage for the resurrection of the original Colt Model P.

In 1955 the 2nd Generation Colt SAAs began. And the first chambering was, of course, .45 Colt. It was to last until 1975, and included 12-inch-barreled Buntline Specials and 3-inch-barreled ejectorless Sheriff's Models.

Still basically the same gun as the 1873 Peacemaker, the "new" Colt was made of stronger steels. As far as quality, the 2nd Generation guns — at least at the beginning — were as good or better than anything from the first run.

Sometime in the winter of 1956/1957, I purchased the first of the new 2nd Generation Colts to arrive in my area. It just "happened" to be a 7½-inch .45. In the TV age of Matt

Dillon and the soon-to-arrive Paladin, what else could it be? Both James Arness and Richard Boone carried their 7½ inch SAAs in a fast-draw rig crafted by Arvo Ojala. In November 1958, I had my first date with the girl who would go on to become my wife, Diamond Dot. Where did we go? To pick up my own black basket-weave Ojala rig. Now, all these years later, I still have Dot and that holster!

The Colt .45 SAA was used extensively in Fast Draw, and I soon learned it was necessary to smooth it up, not only for faster operation but also to keep it working. A proper tuning by a qualified gunsmith helps the parts work together instead of against each other and practically removes any chance of spring breakage. Even to this day the Colt SAA uses flat springs; they are no problem *if* it the gun goes under the hands of a 'smith who totally understands how the old design works.

The 2nd Generation guns are virtually identical to the originals except for some very minor changes such as serial numbers, barrel markings and lack of inspector's marks. Instead of carrying on from the 1st Generation serial number range, Colt chose to use an "SA" suffix on the new guns and begin the serial numbers with 1002SA. (They would go to just over 73000SA when production ended in 1975.) Stocks (or grips if you prefer) were checkered hard rubber until around 50000SA, when a plastic-type material was used. Around 1970 the plastic stocks were made with the eagle

Three generations of 4¾-inch Colt SAAs (from bottom left clockwise): Bisley Model, ivory-stocked 1st Generation, stag-stocked 2nd Generation and 3rd Generation with snakewood stocks.

design below the screw hole. Approximately 36,000 2nd Generation .45 Colt Single Actions were produced, with 5½-inch barrel lengths being the most predominant, followed by the 7½-inch versions and then the 4¾-inch length.

In 1957 Colt resurrected the Buntline Special. In the chapter covering the original SAAs — the 1st Generation sixguns produced from 1873 to 1940 — I covered the original Buntline Specials, as well as the three standardized

This very dressy pair of stag-stocked, nickel-plated Colt SAAs looks right at home with an El Paso Saddlery two-gun rig.

barrel lengths of 4¾, 5½ and 7½ inches. However, shooters could have any length they wanted on special order. If you recall, Ned Buntline presented five "Buntline Specials" to five lawmen in Dodge City in the late 1870s. Researchers have uncovered 22 of these with 19 chambered in .45 Colt fitted with a wire stock and a long-range rear sight.

In somewhat modern times, most of us know of the Buntline Special from the old TV series *The Life and Legend of Wyatt Earp* starring Hugh O'Brian in the title role. O'Brian carried a Buntline Special, first in a homemade holster and later in a custom Arvo Ojala Hollywood rig. Such actors as Henry Fonda, Burt Lancaster, James Garner, Randolph Scott, Joel McRae, Jimmy Stewart, Harris Yulin, Kevin Costner and Kurt Russell all played Wyatt Earp.

In all of these movies I can only recall seeing the Buntline Special in the hands of Kurt Russell in *Tombstone* and in the hands of Harris Yulin in the otherwise forgettable *Doc.* Yulin's was a 12 inch, whereas Russell used a 10 inch in a crossdraw holster. The one he used, which is currently available as a replica from Cimarron Firearms, has a shield on the right-hand stock signifying this long barreled .45 was presented to Wyatt Earp by the grateful citizens of Dodge.

My 2nd Generation .45 Buntline Special is an excellent

shooting sixgun – certainly much easier to shoot than any of the other three standard barrel lengths. It is, however, *not* the most practical packin' sixgun. I simply cannot imagine carrying one on an everyday basis as Wyatt Earp claimed he did. There's a reason the military cut so many of the original Cavalry Models from 7½ to 5½ inches in barrel length, and also why the 4¾-inch version became known as the Civilian Model. The 2nd Generation Buntline Special was quite popular with slightly over 4,000 being produced – about 10 percent of the total .45 Colt SAA production in the 20-year 2nd Generation run.

A RE-RESURRECTION OF SORTS

By 1975 history began to repeat itself and the 2nd Generation machinery was worn out to the extent the SAA was removed from production again. This time, however, it would not take 15 years to come back. Within a couple of years, Colt began the 3rd Generation run, beginning at serial number 80,000SA. To lower costs, which had skyrocketed on Colt SAAs (to say the least!), the ratchet on the back of the cylinder and the hand were changed, the full-length cylinder pin bushing was dropped in favor of a collar in the front of the cylinder only, and for some very strange reason, the threads were changed on the barrels. Of the two minor changes, the reconfigured hand was changed for easier assembly, and the cylinder no longer had a full-length bushing, but a button bushing at the front end to reduce production costs. To these two tweaks, add the change from the original "black-powder" screw in the front of the frame to hold the cylinder pin to a spring-loaded catch, a change that occurred before the turn of the century.

So, in total, we've had only three basic changes in the Colt SAA design in over 120 years. This doesn't count a changed hammer profile, the change in the type of lettering on the barrel, and a different location for the serial numbers. These were minor variations having nothing to do with the operation of the sixgun itself. (One change that should be noted is the cylinder pin bushing, which has now gone back to the original configuration, with the collar button replaced by a full-length bushing.)

The 3rd Generation Colt Single Action lasted into the late 1980s, when the market was flooded with all types of variations as to finish, barrel lengths and often second-class examples before the production was to cease again for the third time. After being killed off three times, one would think the Colt SAA would finally be dead and buried. Not so. It came back again!

With the latest resurrection, the Colt SAA has followed a somewhat strange path, being sometimes offered as a production gun and other times as a custom shop offering. The bad news is quality has also been spotty, but the great news is the latest Colt SAA sixguns being produced are of excellent quality, with close attention paid to fit and finish. Colt has added new machinery and is trying to do things as they should be done. They want to produce the finest single-action sixgun possible. I'd say they have succeeded.

All the new Colts I have seen are excellently finished with a beautiful deep blue on everything but the mainframe which contains the breathtaking case-hardened colors Colt has long been known for. Grips are the standard checkered rubber/plastic black eagles. Metal-to-metal fit is excellent, with no overhanging edges, such as where the trigger guard meets the bottom of the mainframe. Grips are also fitted exceptionally well, with no sharp edges hanging over. The "ears" of the top of the backstrap and the curve of the back of the hammer are also fitted very well. This has not always been true in the past. I was especially impressed with the

This 2nd Generation SAA is a true classic and always will be.

More custom touches: A pair of 4¾-inch 2nd Generation Colt SAA's with pearl (left) and stag (right) stocks.

lockup of the cylinder. The bolt is fitted to the notches in the cylinder, the cylinder is fitted to the base pin, and the base pin is fitted to the frame so well there is very little side-to-side or front-to-back movement of the cylinder.

The actual timing of all sixguns is near-perfect. An old test to check for timing is to place thumb pressure on the cylinder, producing resistance as the hammer is cocked. If the timing is off, the cylinder will not lock completely into battery. Every new Colt I have examined has passed the test. These guns are put together right!

RELOADS FOR A WARHORSE

My first .45 Colt Single Action of nearly 60 years ago taught me a lot about reloading. In those early days, it

was very difficult to find components, and the only bullets I could find were made for the .45 ACP, hard cast weighing about 230 grains. My powder of choice then was #5066. I did not have a powder scale then and this was definitely a mistake. Instead I set my powder measure using the printed table provided. On the first shot the 7½-inch barrel of that .45 did a complete 90-degree arc and pointed skyward. (These loads were definitely hotter than needed.) However, like the dumb teenager I was, I thought the best thing to do was to shoot them all up quickly and get rid of them. Dumb! But somehow the good Lord watches out for fools, drunks and dumb teenagers. Both I and the sixgun survived.

After this experience I purchased a good beam balance

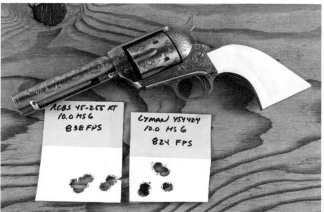

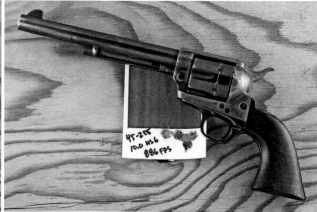

Jim Riggs engraved, ivory-stocked 2nd Generation 4¾-inch SAA (left) and less-dressy 2nd Generation 7½ inch (right). Both proved their mettle on paper.

to weigh my charges. Then I went into my second reloading era, when I thought everything needed to be loaded to the hilt. At the time Elmer Keith's recommended load for the .45 Colt was his 260-grain bullet over 18.5 grains of #2400. I bought a single-cavity mold, melted lead over my mother's kitchen stove and proceeded to follow Keith's lead. I also discovered the maximum load in the manuals of the time using 10.0 grains of Unique behind the Keith bullet. So everything I loaded was either 18.5 grains of #2400 or 10.0 grains of Unique. Those days are behind me and I only load these charges rarely. In fact, I've backed off more to 8.0 to 8.5 grains of Unique for my everyday working loads. Most 2nd and 3rd Generation .45 Colt SAAs will have cylinder throats measuring around .454 to 455 inch, so I routinely size cast bullets to .454 inch for my Colts.

THE SAA TODAY

I have been assailed by some of my fellow writers for advancing the Colt Single Action Army as a self-defense handgun. I will not draw back from that, but I do *not* advocate it as the best defensive handgun for everyone. I do maintain it is still a viable choice in the hands of someone who can handle it, as I have done for over 50 years. I would not feel overmatched if I found myself armed with a .45 Colt SAA against someone with the latest Wondernine.

I have seen the best handgunners in the world shoot both semiautos and double-action sixguns. I have also seen Peacemaker experts like Bob Munden handle a Colt SAA with blinding speed.

I have been shooting the Colt .45 SAA for nearly 60 years. Let us all hope and pray 60 years from now, we will still enjoy the freedom that only firearms ownership can bring, and that sixgunners will still be enjoying the Colt Single Action Army.

If you're not affected by the graceful lines of the Colt SAA, you've crossed over the line from enjoying handguns as works of art to the drab world of viewing them as working tools, such as computers or claw hammers. If this is the case, it's time to slow down and enjoy the finer things once again. ◎

TEST-FIRE: COLT SINGLE ACTION ARMY 2ND GENERATION 7½-INCH .45

LOAD	VELOCITY	5 SHOTS, 20 YARDS
Lyman #454309WC/8.0 gr. Unique	982 fps	1⅜"
Lyman #454424KT/8.0 gr. Unique	889 fps	1¼"
Lyman #454424KT/9.0 gr. Unique	955 fps	1½"
Lyman #454424KT/20.0 gr. #4227	1,055 fps	1⅜"
Oregon Trail 255SWC/20/0 gr. #4227	1,037 fps	1"
Oregon Trail 250RNFP/6.0 gr. N-100	844 fps	1¼"
RCBS #45-270SAA/8.0 gr. Unique	924 fps	1⅜"
RCBS #45-270SAA/8.5 gr. Unique	958 fps	1¾"
RCBS #45-270SAA/18.5 gr. #4227	950 fps	1¾"

JOHN'S SELECT LOADS FOR THE .45 COLT SAA

BULLET: RCBS #45-250FN Sized .454 Inch **LOAD:** 10.0 gr. HS6

LOAD	VELOCITY	5 SHOTS, 20 YARDS
7½" 2nd Generation	984 fps	1⅛"
7½" 3rd Generation	933 fps	7/8"
7½" 3rd Generation	954 fps	3/4"
4¾" 3rd Generation	815 fps	1¼"
5½" 3rd Generation	815 fps	1⅝"

BULLET: RCBS #45-255KT Sized .454 Inch **LOAD:** 10.0 gr. HS6

7½" 2nd Generation	886 fps	1⅛"
7½" 3rd Generation	906 fps	1¼"
4¾" 2nd Generation	838 fps	1⅛"
5½" 3rd Generation	772 fps	1⅜"

BULLET: Lyman #454424KT Sized .454 Inch **LOAD:** 20.0 gr. #4227

7½" 2nd Generation	1045 fps	1¼"
7½" 3rd Generation	1069 fps	1¼"
7½" 3rd Generation	1013 fps	1⅛"
4¾" 2nd Generation	949 fps	1¼"
4¾" 2nd Generation	984 fps	1¼"
4¾" 3rd Generation	907 fps	1⅜"

BULLET: Oregon Trail 255-gr. SWC Sized .454 Inch **LOAD:** 18.5 gr. 5744

7½" 2nd Generation	913 fps	1"
7½" 3rd Generation	906 fps	1¼"
7½" 3rd Generation	901 fps	1¼"
7½" 2nd Generation	924 fps	1⅛"

BULLET: Lyman #454424KT Sized .454" **LOAD:** 10.0 gr. HS6

4¾" 2nd Generation	824 fps	1⅛"
4¾" 3rd Generation	766 fps	1⅜"
5½" 3rd Generation	749 fps	1⅜"

THE SIXGUNS

One of the things John really likes about the new production Colt Frontier is the excellent Elliason rear sight (below, inset).

THE COLT NEW FRONTIER

CHAPTER 10

The original Colt Single Action Army was a study in perfection when it arrived in 1873. It balanced perfectly, pointed naturally and was chambered for a powerful cartridge — the .45 Colt with a 255-grain bullet at around 900 fps. It's been replicated by many manufacturers and its influence can even be seen in today's Ruger and Freedom Arms lineup.

As good as it was back in the frontier times, Colt set about to improve it. By the late 1890s the West had pretty well been tamed. Shooters were using sixguns for something besides fighting and self-defense — namely target shooting.

So Colt did two things to try to make the SAA better suited for punching paper. First, the frame of the SAA was flat-topped and fitted with very crude adjustable sights. Second, it was then turned into the Bisley Model in 1896, with a wide hammer and trigger and a reconfigured grip frame better suited for target shooting. Neither one of these Flat-Top Target Models lasted very long. In fact,

shooters asked that the Bisley be made into a regular SAA by keeping the grip frame and wide hammer and trigger, but going back to the standard "hog-wallow trough" rear sight found on all SAAs. The target-type improvements just didn't go over very well.

THE NEW FRONTIER

It would be nearly 70 years before Colt tried to improve the SAA again, but this time they did it perfectly. In 1960 John F. Kennedy was elected president and a new era arrived

COLT NEW FRONTIER

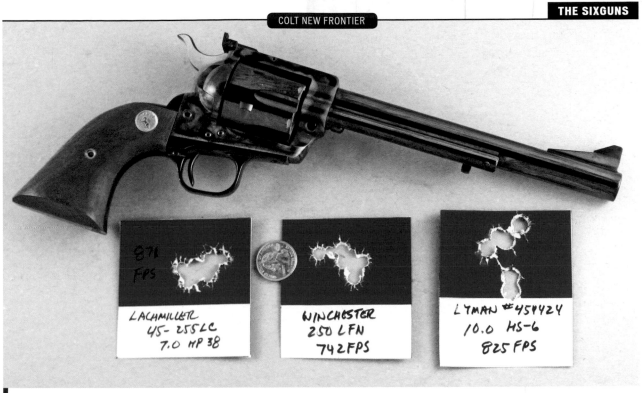

This 7½-inch barreled Colt New Frontier was quite fond of two of John's handloads as well as a Winchester factory load.

called the "New Frontier." To help celebrate this new era of looking toward the future, Colt decided to issue an upgraded SAA, and in late 1961, the New Frontier Model was introduced in honor of it. To further honor the young president, Colt went to work on a special engraved presentation model to present to JFK; however, the dark day of November 22, 1963, occurred before the project was finished.

The mainframe of the New Frontier was given a heavy flat-top frame and fitted with an adjustable rear sight matched up with a ramp front. The frame was beautifully case-colored (as only Colt could do it). The rest of the gun was in Colt Royal Blue. I thought it was about the most beautiful sixgun I had ever seen. However, I was in college and working to support my young family at the time. There would be no New Frontier for me, but I could dream.

UPSCALE SIX-SHOOTER

In 1962 a standard Colt SAA cost $125. The New Frontier, however, was at an unreachable $140. This was at a time when Ruger Blackhawks were going for less than $100, and the superb Super Blackhawk in .44 Magnum was selling for $116. But had I been able to look into the future, I would somehow have borrowed the money and bought the New Frontier. Today it would be worth no less than 15 times

the original price. I've since learned a lesson. Namely, Colt single actions do *not* go down on value.

The Colt SAA may be the choice of traditionalists, but the New Frontier maintains the beautiful looks, feel and balance of the SAA with the added advantage of adjustable sights. It is a rare fix-sighted sixgun that shoots perfectly to point of aim. Even if it does, it may only be with one particular load. If such a sixgun shoots low, the front sight can be filed down. Too high and the front sight must be made taller — not such an easy fix. If the windage is off, the barrel must be turned using a special vise. But the New Frontier requires nothing

The flat-top influence: An ivory-stocked New Frontier (right) compared to "New Frontierized" Ruger Blackhawk (left).

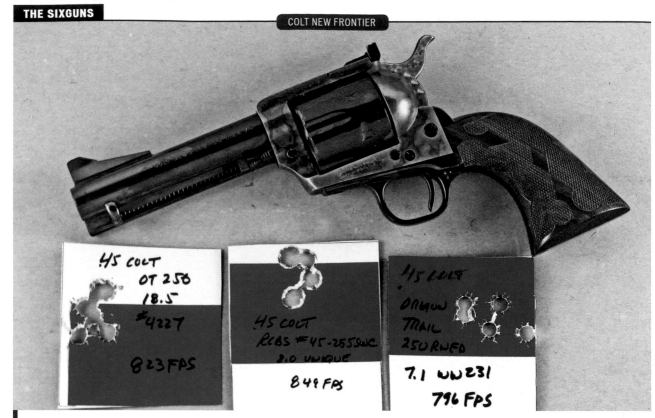

.45 COLT
OT 250
18.5
#4227

823 FPS

.45 COLT
RCBS #45-255SWC
8.0 UNIQUE

849 FPS

.45 COLT
OREGON
TRAIL
250 RNFD

7.1 WW231
796 FPS

Obviously, John tailored these three handloads to bring out the best in an ebony-stocked 2nd Generation New Frontier.

more than a proper-fitting screwdriver to change point of impact. This advantage turns it into a viable hunting handgun.

DIFFERENT NUMBERS, DIFFERENT RUNS

The first run of Colt New Frontiers, known as 2nd Generation sixguns, began at serial number 3000NF and finished in 1974 at serial number 7888NF. This first run of magnificent "modern" Colt Flat-Top Target sixguns saw the .45 Colt offered in the three standard barrel lengths of 4¾, 5½ and 7½ inches plus just under 75 of the 12-inch Buntline Special New Frontiers.

For many years, in fact several decades, I used my 2nd Generation 7½-inch New Frontier and was bothered by the fact it actually shot slower than my 4¾- and 5½-inch .45 Colts. The problem was excessive barrel/cylinder gap. Finally when Hamilton Bowen needed to borrow a New Frontier .45 to do some measuring I sent him my sluggish .45 and asked him to set the barrel back and tighten the barrel/cylinder gap while he had it. When it came back what a difference it displayed! Muzzle velocities were now up where they should have been and the extra added bonus was the fact groups also tightened up. It simply shot more accurately with a tight barrel/cylinder gap. My normal loads picked up 75-100 fps over what I had been getting with the barrel as it came from the factory.

Most sixgunners, at least those who hold the Colt SAA in high regard, pick the 4¾-inch barrel length as the easiest to pack and the fastest from leather. The same feeling carries over to the New Frontier. About 30 years ago, I decided to build up my first Perfect Packin' Pistol, Colt .45 style.

TEST-FIRE:
COLT 2ND GENERATION
NEW FRONTIER 7½-INCH .45

LOAD	VELOCITY	5 SHOTS, 25 YARDS
Lyman #454309WC/8.0 gr. Unique	982 fps	1⅜"
Lyman #454424KT/8.0 gr. Unique	889 fps	1¼"
Lyman #454424KT/9.0 gr. Unique	955 fps	1½"
Lyman #454424KT/20.0 gr. #4227	1,055 fps	1⅜"
Oregon Trail 255SWC/20.0 gr. #4227	1,037 fps	1"
Oregon Trail 250RNFP/6.0 gr. N-100	844 fps	1¼"
RCBS #45-270SAA/8.0 gr. Unique	924 fps	1⅜"
RCBS #45-270SAA/8.5 gr. Unique	958 fps	1¾"
RCBS #45-270SAA/18.5 gr. #4227	950 fps	1¾"

COLT NEW FRONTIER

THE SIXGUNS

For sheer "packing perfection," it's mighty tough to top a 4¾-inch barrel.

Colt had already ended the 2nd Generation run of .45 New Frontiers, and the 4¾-inch barrel length was virtually impossible to find. However, what I did find was a 2nd Generation 4¾-inch New Frontier barrel in .45 Colt for a very reasonable price. Now it was time to look for a .357 Magnum New Frontier.

Luckily, when Diamond Dot and I were on our way over to see my mother, we stopped at a little gun shop where we found one at a very reasonable price.

So the .45 barrel and the .357 New Frontier went off to John Linebaugh to be made into a tight-chambered .45 New Frontier. John cut the .357 Magnum cylinder to a minimum-dimensioned .45 Colt and gave it a tight barrel/cylinder gap. At the time, most .45 cylinders had chamber throats larger than necessary and were cut so that brass expanded more than needed when fired. When I got the gun back, I fitted it with creamy ivory stocks with Colt medallions and then loaded it with the Lyman/Keith #454424 bullet hard cast and sized to .452

inch. My reward for all the time and expense? A one-hole group at 25 yards.

Today, 30 years later, that little sixgun still shoots very well. But I treat myself and my sixguns somewhat kinder now and rarely use extra heavy loads.

Some years later I came up with another 2nd Generation 4¾-inch New Frontier .45 barrel and began to look for another .357. Once I acquired one, barrel and gun were sent off to gunsmith Tom Sargis with the same instructions I'd given to

This new-production .45 Colt New Frontier is well set off with custom stocks and El Paso Saddlery leather.

SIXGUNS AND THEIR CARTRIDGES

COLT 2ND GENERATION NEW FRONTIER 4¾-INCH .45

LOAD	VELOCITY	5 SHOTS, 20 YARDS
Lachmiller #45255LC/8.0 gr. Unique	928 fps	1 5/8"
Lyman #454424KT/8.0 gr. Unique	868 fps	1 3/4"
Lyman #454424KT/7.0 gr. HP38	792 fps	1 1/4"
Oregon Trail 255SWC/8.0 gr. Unique	961 fps	1"
Oregon Trail 250RNFP/7.1 gr. WW231	853 fps	5/8"
Oregon Trail 250RNFP/6.2 gr. N-100	823 fps	1 3/8"
Oregon Trail 250RNFP/18.5 gr. #4227	908 fps	1 3/8"

John Linebaugh. Currently the Linebaugh New Frontier wears Colt ivories while the Sargis sixgun is fitted with one-piece fleur-de-lis ebony stocks by Paul Persinger.

In 1978 the .45 New Frontier went back into production joining the 3rd Generation run of SAAs. Like the SAA, the ratchet on the back of the cylinder and the hand were changed, the full-length cylinder pin bushing was dropped in favor of a collar in the front of the cylinder only, and for some strange reason, the threads were changed on the 3rd Generation barrels. From 1873 until 1975, the barrels were 20 threads per inch, but all 3rd Generation Colts were — and are — 24 tpi. The upside to this is 24 tpi is also what Ruger frames and barrels are, so I bought all of the New Frontier barrels a local gun shop had when they went out of

business. I've used them to build several custom sixguns on three-screw Ruger single actions.

The most bothersome change to me was the new profile of the 3rd Generation hammers — both on the SAA and the New Frontier. The early ones appeared to have a ground-off spur with an unappealing, flattened-off profile. Thankfully, all hammers are now properly contoured. Serial numbers for the 3rd Generation New Frontiers began at 01001NF (using five digits instead of four). Although production ended in 1982, a few were assembled from parts for the next two years.

Shortly after this, my friend and fellow gunwriter, Wiley Clapp, and I queried the Colt representative at a press conference about the possible return of the New Frontier. He told us we were probably never going to see it again. I'm certainly glad he was wrong!

ANOTHER RESURRECTION

The year 2011 marked the 175th anniversary of Colt SAAs, going all the way back to the percussion Paterson of 1836. All New Frontiers produced in 2011 have a special Anniversary Marking on the barrel consisting of "1836 — 175th Anniversary — 2011" and serial numbers begin at 20000NF. All three standard barrel lengths, 4¾, 5½ and 7½ inches are offered in .45 Colt. The first production run consisted of the 7½-inch barrel and the 4¾ inch followed shortly thereafter. I have not heard of any 5½-inch .45s being produced as of this writing.

Because the 7½-inch gun was first off the line, it was the first one I tested. Nice as the earlier ones are, they pale in comparison to this current New Frontier. It's simply the most beautifully finished factory Colt single action I have ever seen. You can practically see your ancestors in the blued parts! It is also exceptionally well fitted with no sharp edges. Grip frame to mainframe fit is as it should be. If you run your finger over the seams you feel a nice, smooth transition. Lockup is tight, the trigger pull — while not perfect — is certainly more than adequate. Panels are nicely fitted to the grip frame, and although they're very plain, they fit my hand perfectly. I'll take proper

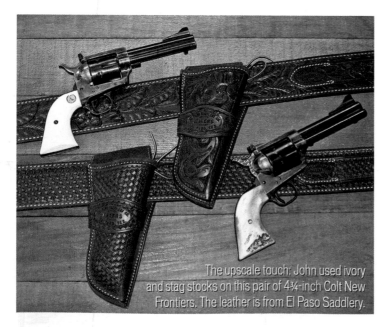

The upscale touch: John used ivory and stag stocks on this pair of 4¾-inch Colt New Frontiers. The leather is from El Paso Saddlery.

COLT NEW FRONTIER

A new production .45 Colt New Frontier — particularly in 7½-inch trim — makes a viable hunting handgun when loaded with hollowpoint cast bullets.

fitting and shape over fanciness anytime; although, of course, I've already fitted custom grips of deluxe walnut to mine.

CHAMBERS AND BULLETS

As a bullet caster I have a great advantage, namely being able to tailor bullet diameters to fit each particular sixgun. There is a lot of variation found in the chamber throats of .45 Colt sixguns. Older Ruger Blackhawks will often be found with exceptionally tight throats — some as small as .449 inch — while older Smith & Wessons have some as large as as .457 inch. Currently, both companies are staying right at .451-.452 inch. Applying a pin gauge to the New Frontier gave me a uniform reading of .455 inch for all six chambers. I keep a generous supply of reloads on hand with both .452- and .454-inch bullets, so for the most part I chose the latter. However, I was pleasantly surprised to find the smaller bullets also shot well, as did factory ammunition.

One of the great attributes of Colt SAAs and New Frontiers is how user-friendly they are. Loads in the 800-1,000 fps range are exceptionally pleasant to shoot, with felt recoil at a minimum. When you pull the trigger the hammer begins its long arc to strike the primer, and as the gun fires, you experience a gentle nudge instead of heavy recoil. Much of that is attributable to the SAA grip frame. Naturally, things change a little - but not much - when you go to heavier hunting handloads. Using 250- to 260-grain cast Keith bullets at 1,100 fps results in more felt recoil, but certainly nothing punishing. This ancient cartridge may be more than 140 years old, but it is still viable for hunting in the New Frontier.

All Colt single actions, including the New Frontiers, have the traditional action with no transfer bar. This means they *must* be carried with only five rounds and the hammer down on an empty chamber. The earlier 3rd Generation New Frontiers did away with the full-length cylinder bushing, going instead to a button in the front end. Two improvements have been made to this latest run — the full-length bushing is back, and more importantly, the rear sight has been changed. The original adjustable rear was certainly adequate, but Colt has now gone to the excellent Elliason rear sight. Adjustments are more precise, and the back of the sight is totally flat and serrated to block glare. I wouldn't mind equipping all my New Frontiers with Elliasons.

It was awhile in coming, but Colt is definitely doing it right. For a time, especially in the late 1980s and early 1990s, quality slipped somewhat. But that's all in the past and the company is doing everything possible to turn out both sixguns worthy of the Colt name. The latest examples of the SAA and New Frontier are as close to perfection as I have ever seen in any Colt single actions. ◎

COLT 3RD GENERATION NEW FRONTIER 7½-INCH .45 COLT

LOAD	VELOCITY	5 SHOTS, 20 YARDS
Lachmiller #45-255/7.0 gr. HP38	859 fps	1½"
Lyman #454424 KT/10.0 gr. HS-6	825 fps	1¼
Lyman #454424 KT/20.0 gr. #4227	997 fps	1⅜"
Lyman #454309WC/8.0 gr. Unique	946 fps	1¾"
RCBS #45-255KT/10.0 gr. HS-6	841 fps	1¼"
RCBS #45-250 FN/10.0 gr. HS-6	884 fps	1¾
RCBS #45-270/8.0 gr. Unique	905 fps	1½"
Oregon Trail 255 SWC /7.0 gr. HP-38	859 fps	1½
Oregon Trail 255 SWC/8.0 gr. Unique	888 fps	1⅝"
Oregon Trail 250 RNFP/8.0 gr. Unique	917 fps	1¼
Oregon Trail 250 RNFP/6.0 gr. Red Dot	818 fps	1⅛"
Oregon Trail 250 RNFP/6.0 gr. N-100	766 fps	1¼
Oregon Trail 255 SWC/7.0 gr. HP-38	825 fps	1½"

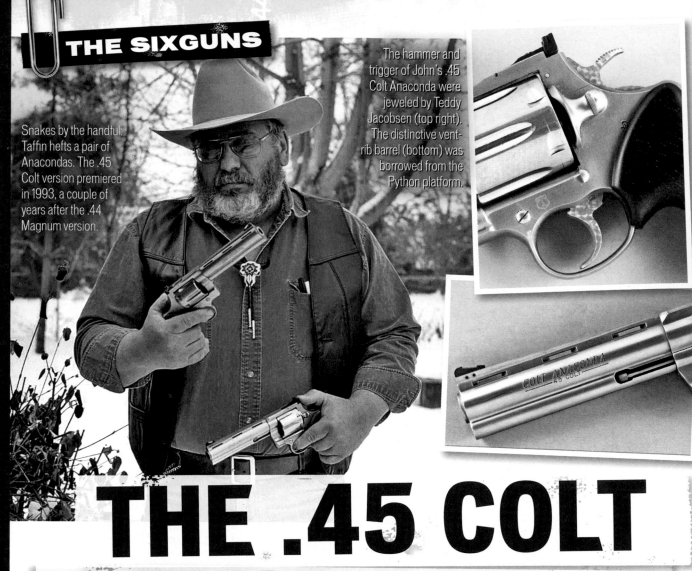

Snakes by the handful: Taffin hefts a pair of Anacondas. The .45 Colt version premiered in 1993, a couple of years after the .44 Magnum version.

The hammer and trigger of John's .45 Colt Anaconda were jeweled by Teddy Jacobsen (top right). The distinctive vent-rib barrel (bottom) was borrowed from the Python platform.

THE .45 COLT ANACONDA

CHAPTER 11

When Colt stopped production of both the Single Action Army and the New Service in 1940, it left the great .45 Colt cartridge something of an orphan. But although the guns were gone, the cartridge retained countless ardent admirers. The .357 Magnum and the .45 ACP may have been more up to date at the time, but that was no consolation to those who fancied the .45 Colt.

The true believers were easy to pick out of any crowd. Mention ".45 Colt" and their eyes would suddenly take on a faraway look. It wouldn't do any good to try to talk to them for a few minutes, as they had gone back into history, smelling powder smoke while slowly running all the great .45 Colt revolvers of the past through their minds.

A LENGTHY EVOLUTION

In the distant future, of course, these same sixgunners could expand their thoughts to the exceptionally rare Smith & Wesson Model 1950 Target .45 Colt and the sixgun which helped modernize it — the .45 Colt Ruger Blackhawk.

A lot of things happened in the mid-1950s as far as six-guns were concerned. S&W brought out its .44 Magnum, while Colt — after a 15-year layoff — resurrected the .45 Colt SAA. Surely, many hoped, Colt would bring back the New Service, but it was not to be.

In the time prior to World War II, Colt's premier service revolver was the .38 Special Official Police. Fitted with target sights and a heavy barrel, it became the Officer's Model

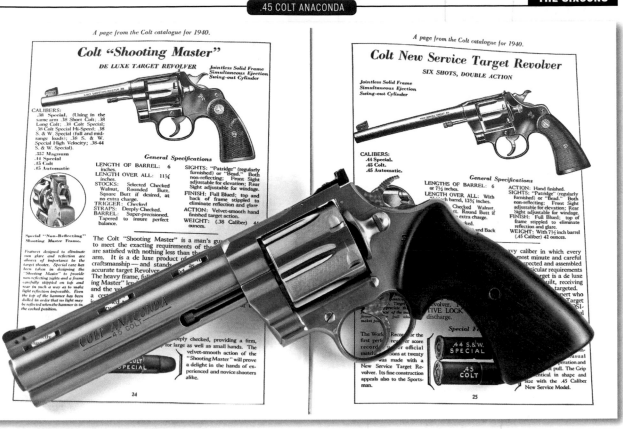

The .45 Colt Anaconda is a worthy successor to the Colt New Service.

Match. Then in 1954, Colt decided to chamber the .357 Magnum, using the Official Police platform, and the first Colt .357 Magnum arrived, complete with a heavy barrel and adjustable sights. Within a short time this sixgun was upgraded with a heavy underlug barrel with a ventilated rib, a smoothed and tuned action and the magnificent Colt Royal Blue finish, and the .357 Magnum Python arrived. This was immediately recognized as the Cadillac of Colt revolvers — surely a successor to the .45 Colt New Service could not be far behind.

But it took a spell. Thirty-five years after S&W's .44 Magnum arrived, Colt finally brought out its first big-bore double-action revolver since before World War II. It wasn't the Colt New Service. It wasn't the Colt Python on a larger frame. It was a new design, the Anaconda. Yes, it did look somewhat like the Python with its heavy underlugged/vent rib barrel, but it had a different action than the Python.

Those first .44 Magnum Anacondas looked great, felt great and shot terribly. The problem was the barrels. This was soon corrected, and we wound up with an excellent shooting gun. Could we hope it would soon be chambered in .45 Colt? Would Colt get back on the true path?

While I enjoyed my .44 Magnum Anaconda, I held on

to it with an eye to the past while thinking about the future. I went back to that last 1940 Colt catalog and lusted over the wonderful New Services offered then. There was the .45 Colt Shooting Master with a 6-inch barrel and Patridge front sight mated with a windage adjustable rear, tuned and smoothed hand-finished action and checkered walnut stocks. Turning to the next page my eyes fell on the .45 Colt New Service Target with a 7½-inch barrel. These — along with the regular New Service — still beckoned. Would they ever be resurrected?

The copywriter of that catalog may have been a bit florid, but he was pretty accurate when he said:

"The New Service Revolver was designed for those requiring a specially sturdy firearm of sufficiently large caliber for the most serious service without excessive weight. It withstands the rigors of heat, cold, rain, or snow as well as excessive use, as many as 250,000 rounds having been fired from a New Service Revolver without noticeable impairment of accuracy."

He continued in the same vein:

"It is the Model chosen by men who frequently find themselves far from gunsmiths and whose lives may depend upon the ability of their firearms, for it is capable

SIXGUNS AND THEIR CARTRIDGES

Above: The .45 Colt Anaconda is capable of handling very stout loads — making it a versatile choice for handgun hunting. Left: The evolution of the Colt .45 Double Action includes the Model of 1878, the New Service and the Anaconda.

of stopping any animal on the American Continent ... The New Service is essentially a holster Revolver for the man in the open–Mounted, Motorcycle and State Police; the Hunter, Explorer and Pioneer."

Surely this part of history could not be lost forever — and it wasn't. Shortly after the arrival of the .44 Magnum Anaconda, Colt did the right thing and chambered it in .45 Colt. It took more than half a century, but in 1993 Colt was once again producing a big-bore sixgun chambered for the original big-bore cartridge.

KINGS OF THE SNAKE FAMILY

The .45 Colt Anaconda was announced with either 4-, 6-, and 8-inch barrels. My original test gun was the 6-inch version. This sixgun is all stainless steel weighing in at 51 ounces and is slightly larger and several ounces heavier than S&W's Model 29 .44 Magnum. The Anaconda is definitely able to handle .45 Colt loads heavier than standard, making it an excellent hunting handgun.

If you look at it carefully, it appears to be a cross between a King Cobra and a Python — two other members of the

Colt "snake family." Although the barrel looks like it came off a Python, it's larger in diameter. The finish on my .45 Colt Anaconda is excellent, being better than that found on most stainless steel handguns of its time, which was 20 years ago. In fact, the finish on mine is better than that found on the original .44 Magnum version I acquired in 1991.

The entire gun is nicely polished except for the flattened-off top of the frame and barrel, which is highly appreciated, non-reflective gray. So are the hammer and trigger, which would look better if they were either polished or case-colored.

The sights are strictly from the King Cobra — an adjustable rear with a white outline and a ramp front with a pale red insert (harder for me to see in the sunlight than the bright red insert used on S&W sixguns of the time). My needs would be better served with plain black sights. However, the front sight does fill the rear outline correctly and is fastened to the base with two pins that have never loosened.

AFTERMARKET ENHANCEMENTS

When I got my .45 Anaconda, the double-action trigger pull was not bad at 11 pounds but needed the touch of a custom gunsmith. So I sent it off to Teddy Jacobsen for some work. Teddy is an ex-cop and understands the needs of law enforcement officers as well as civilian shooters. He gave the gun a thorough cleaning and complete action job, lubing all the internal parts with Tetra G. He also installed

Wolff hammer and trigger return springs, all of which brought the DA pull down to a smooth 9 pounds. And the improved single-action pull went to a crisp 3¼ pounds.

To dress up the gun, Teddy polished the cylinder flutes and polished and jeweled both the hammer and trigger. The factory grips furnished were finger-grooved rubber and were too small for my fat fingers. They were also mismatched and did not go together properly. This was no matter, as I replaced them. At the time, my friend Deacon Deason of BearHug was still with us and came up with a prototype pair of walnut grips made as close as possible to the Skeeter Skelton style found on many of my Smith & Wessons.

The original BearHug stocks were just plain-Jane walnut for fit testing. After I reported back to Dean that they were perfect for my hands, he fitted the Anaconda with an extra-special pair of Macassar rosewood grips (guaranteed to set a sixgunner's heart beating a little faster). The combination of the grips and Teddy's tuning and polishing made the big .45 something special — a sixgun radiating pride of ownership. (Deacon passed away in 1994 while I was on safari in Africa, and I think of him every time I shoot the gun).

For the original test-firing the .45 Colt Anaconda I fitted it with a 3x scope to better test the accuracy, however my plan was to keep this as an iron-sighted hunting handgun, which is what I have done for the past 20 years — often carrying it in an El Paso Saddlery Tom Threepersons holster.

The Anaconda .45 has proven to be accurate with both standard loads and heavy loads, using jacketed and hard-cast bullets. Some favorite loads include Keith's original #454424 with 18.5 grains of #2400, for over 1,125 fps and five shots in less than an inch at 25 yards.

The RCBS equivalent, #45-255KT, shoots just as well and only a few feet slower with 22.0 grains of #4227. My favored heavy bullet load is the Hornady 300-grain XTP-JHP over 21.5 grains of Winchester's 296 for 1,100 fps. This one has a very slight edge in accuracy over the other two cast bullet loads. There is nothing to be found in the desert, sagebrush, foothills or mountains of Idaho which can't be handled with the .45 Colt Anaconda and an appropriate load.

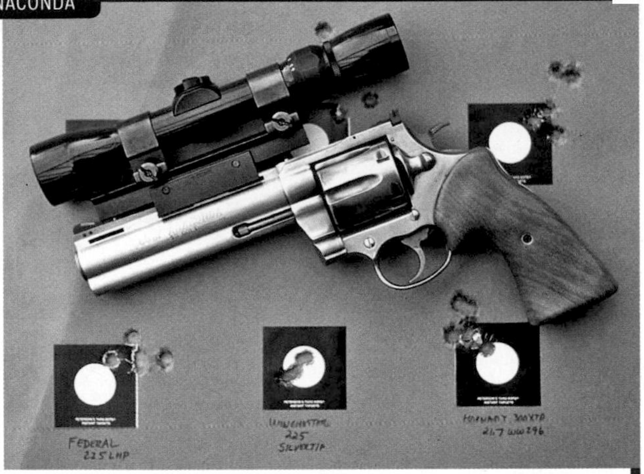

Traditionalist that he his, John prefers to pack his .45 Colt Anaconda without optics, although he did employ a 3x handgun scope to check out its 25-yard accuracy potential.

EPILOGUE

The Colt New Service lasted just over 40 years and disappeared on the eve of World War II. The Anaconda in .45 Colt arrived in 1993 and was gone before the turn of the century. The good news is Colt is now once again producing beautifully crafted single-action sixguns and semiautomatic pistols. The "bad" news is they are two years behind. This backlog makes it tough to imagine them resurrecting any other classic revolver. But dare we hope for the return of a Colt big-bore, double-action revolver? ◎

.45 COLT ANACONDA 6-INCH (3x SCOPE)

LOAD	VELOCITY	5 SHOTS, 25 YARDS
CCI Blazer 255-gr. Lead	727 fps	1"
Federal 225-gr. Lead HP	808 fps	3/4
Winchester 225-gr. Silvertip	839 fps	5/8"
LBT 300LFN/18.5 gr. #2400	1,120 fps	1"
Lyman #454424KT/9.5 gr. Unique	1,008 fps	7/8"
Lyman #454424KT/20.0 gr. #4227	1,044 fps	1 [illegible]
Lyman #454424KT/22.0 gr. #4227	1,127 fps	1¼"
Lyman #454424KT/18.5 gr. #2400	1,135 fps	7/8
Lyman #452490GC/10.0 gr. Unique	1,097 fps	1¼"
Lyman #457191/18.5 gr. #2400	1,140 fps	1 [illegible]
NEI #310.451KT/21.5 gr. WW296	1,103 fps	1⅛"
RCBS #45-255KT/22.0 gr. #4227	1,110 fps	7/8
RCBS #45-300SWC/21.5 gr. H110	1,123 fps	1⅜"
Hornady 300XTP-JHP/21.7 gr. WW296	1,095 fps	3/4
Oregon Trail 255SWC/9.0 gr. Unique	962 fps	3/4"
Oregon Trail 300RNFP/21.5 gr. H110	1,193 fps	1⅞"

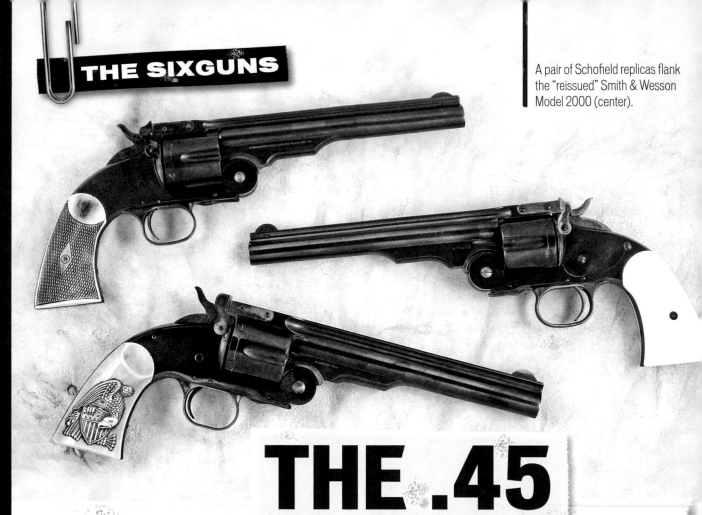

A pair of Schofield replicas flank the "reissued" Smith & Wesson Model 2000 (center).

THE .45
SMITH & WESSON
SCHOFIELD

Replica Schofields have been offered in barrel lengths of 3, 5 and 7 inches.

CHAPTER 12

As a teenager growing up in the 1950s, I had an older neighbor who also loved single actions. I was drawn to them like a moth to the flame. First, of course, was a Colt SAA. Then there was a Colt 1860 .44 1860 cap-and-ball.

His third sixgun, however, was a .44 Russian Smith & Wesson. Up to that time, I had always thought S&W made double-action sixguns only. After all, what movie cowboy hero ever carried a Smith? The .44 Russian S&W lacked the marvelous balance of its Colt counterpart, but even as untrained as I was, I could recognize it as a truly marvelous piece of engineering.

That Smith & Wesson was so intriguing I went to the

John does a bit of rangework with his Navy Arms Schofield. Combat-target results were impressive (left), even when he tried a bit of "single-action rapid fire."

It would be four years after the first big-bore Smith & Wesson before the Colt SAA would be offered. Even with Smith & Wesson's head start, there is a most important reason why the Colt "Won the West" (and just about every B-movie hero carried one). The S&W .44s were mostly sold overseas. Of 60,000-plus 3rd Model Russian .44s produced from 1874 to 1878, only 13,500 went to the domestic market. The rest went to Russia, Japan and Turkey.

THE RUNNER-UP

Although the U.S. Army adopted the .45 Colt SAA over the more sophisticated Smith & Wesson .44 American, the Colt was slower to unload than the auto-ejecting S&W.

While the Smith & Wesson had a great advantage in ease of unloading and reloading, it also required two hands to operate the latch on the top of the barrel. Col. George Schofield of the 10th Cavalry set about to improve things. Schofield changed the latch from the back of the barrel assembly to the mainframe, allowing it to be pushed in with the thumb of the shooting hand rather than opened with the off hand. This provided for one-handed operation, even from horseback.

In 1873 a test was set up placing the (now designated) Schofield Model against the Colt SAA. While mounted on a moving horse, the horseman had to empty the sixgun, remove six cartridges from his belt pouch and reload. It took

library to try to find some information on it. However, it was not until the Roy Jinks and Robert Neal's definitive *Smith & Wesson: 1857-1945* appeared in 1966, followed by 1977's *History of Smith & Wesson* did I really learn much about the history of the company's single-action revolvers.

As we have seen after the Civil War, Colt continued to manufacture the 1851 .36 Navy and 1860 .44 Army as the principal fightin' sixguns for both the civilian and military markets. Smith & Wesson had the Rollin White patent for bored-through cylinders and did make some small-caliber cartridge handguns during the war. In 1869 Smith & Wesson went big bore with the .44 American, a top-break, six-shot single action. The American went through numerous changes culminating in the .44 Russian New Model No. 3 — the gun I found so fascinating in my neighbor's collection.

26 seconds to unload the Colt, and it was then reloaded in 60 seconds. The improved S&W Schofield took two seconds to unload, and it was then reloaded in 26 seconds. One minute is an awfully long time to reload, especially when you're being shot at! The Schofield took only one-third as much time to unload and reload as the Colt. The army was convinced and, although they did not drop the Colt SAA, they *did* order Schofields.

While the Colt could handle the shorter .45 S&W ammunition, the S&W would not chamber the longer .45 Colt. This potential logistical problem was ultimately solved by dropping the Schofields. They became government surplus in 1880, and many of the 7-inch Schofields had their barrels cut back to 5 inches, making them quite popular with Wells Fargo agents. It has also been postulated the Schofield was dropped because Smith & Wesson had other guns to build for other markets and no longer wanted the Schofield contract.

A TOP-BREAK TEMPLATE

Although it is unlike any other .45 single-action or double-action sixgun available with neither ejector rod nor swingout cylinder, the Schofield operates much like the first handgun many of us dinosaurs ever shot, a break-open Harrington & Richardson .22.

Today, of course, all Schofield models are collector's items. If I had an original I would probably shoot it very sparingly and with black powder only, as I do with my S&W

American, Model No. 3 Russian, New Model No. 3 and double-action Frontier.

Although I don't have an original Schofield, I have the next best thing — a replica. About the time I began shooting sixguns seriously, Val Forgett of Navy Arms started importing .44-caliber replica cap-and-ball revolvers. Over the next four decades, replicas of Colt and Remington cartridge single actions came forth in varying levels of quality. Then in the early 1990s, the first replica Schofield was offered by Navy Arms.

THE FIRST SCHOFIELD REPLICA

The Model 1875 is quite faithful to the original. There are a few changes. The cylinder on the Uberti/Navy Arms Schofield is longer than the original and, since there was neither ammunition nor brass available when the project was conceived, instead of being chambered for the original .45 S&W (or .45 Schofield), it was chambered in .45 Colt. The first ones had 7-inch barrels and were soon followed by a 5-inch Wells Fargo Model.

My first Schofield replica was a blued 7 inch with smooth walnut stocks. The left panel bears the stamp mark of "1877," but there are 19th-century martial inspection initials on both sides per the original. The Navy Schofield is nicely finished with a case-colored trigger guard, hammer and latching system. The rest of the gun is a deep blue. Two screws hold the female part of the locking latch above the cylinder. When the rear screw is backed out, the latch can be lifted upwards allowing the cylinder to be removed.

Uberti has steadily increased its quality over the years, and the finish and fit of the Schofield Model leaves nothing to be desired. The replica even has the same problem as the original — it's so tightly fitted that black-powder loads foul things up very quickly. Sights are as they were on the original — a half-moon German silver front and a very wide rear "V" (with a small "U" at the base of the "V"). My replica shoots right to point of aim with my now-standard .45 Colt load of 255-grain bullets at 800-900 fps.

The two top contenders: Smith & Wesson's Model 2000 .45 S&W Schofield and Colt's Single-Action Army .45 Colt.

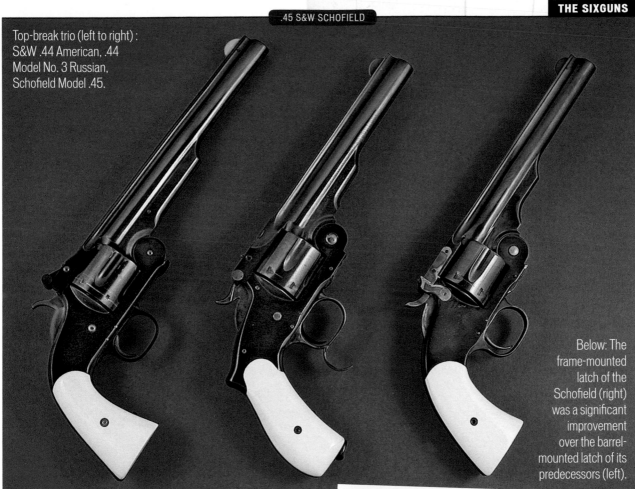

Top-break trio (left to right): S&W .44 American, .44 Model No. 3 Russian, Schofield Model .45.

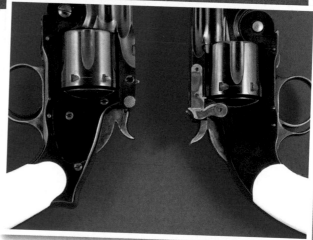

Below: The frame-mounted latch of the Schofield (right) was a significant improvement over the barrel-mounted latch of its predecessors (left).

TOP-BREAK OPERATION

We have a large range of .45 Colt sixguns available today in varying strengths, and the Schofield is for sensible standard-pressure loads only. It locks up tightly and is at the same level — perhaps a bit less — as a Colt SAA. To operate the Schofield, put the hammer on half-cock, push the barrel catch with your thumb and swing the barrel down with your off hand. This will cause the automatic ejector to kick out the fired cases. Reload the cylinder and bring the barrel up until it latches tightly. If you only want to remove one or two fired cases, open the barrel just enough to start the ejector upward so you can remove and replace them — then close the action.

Loads in the 650-750 fps range are exceptionally pleasant to shoot in the Schofield. One of my favorite hand-loads consists of the 230-grain hard cast .45 ACP bullet over 7.5 grains of either Unique or Universal for about 625 fps. This load is quite accurate – I've gotten 25-yard groups at well under 1½ inches for five shots.

The Lyman/Keith #454424 — which weighs in at 260 grains from my alloy — and seated over 8.0 grains of either Unique or Universal, clocks out at over 800 fps from my Navy Schofield and shoots into 2 inches at 25 yards.

I also like to shoot the more traditional Lachmiller #45-255LC, which duplicates the original 255-grain conical bullet of the .45 Colt load from the 1870s. I like to cast this bullet fairly soft, lube it with a black-powder lube such as SPG, and place it over 30.0 grains of FFFg black powder for right around 800 fps. It is quite accurate, however, it only takes less than a cylinderful for black-powder fouling to cause cylinder

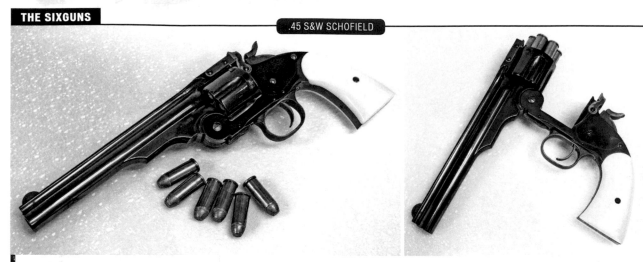

The S&W Model 2000 is chambered for the original .45 S&W, also known as .45 Schofield (left). Empties are easily and simultaneously ejected (right) via the top-break operation — a considerable tactical advantage over the gate-loading/unloading system of the Colt SAA.

binding. (I assume this was the same problem experienced in the 1870s.) To keep the Schofield shooting, I use a spray bottle of Windex to spritz around the front and back of the cylinder after every few shots. Not a traditional frontier-style technique, but it does keep things working!

By the time the first replica Schofield arrived in the 1990s I had already spent nearly four decades shooting Colt SAAs. After curling my hand around the Colt grip frame for so long, the Schofield grip frame took some getting used to. I find the Schofield quite pleasant to shoot, but it would certainly take quite a bit of practice on my part to be able to handle it as fast and easily as a Colt. With the original 7-inch barrel, the Schofield balances well and has excellent pointability. The wide rear sight and narrow front blade combination are quick to pick up and act much like a peep sight on a levergun. As with all traditional single action sixguns, the best safety on the Schofield is found between your ears. It comes with the

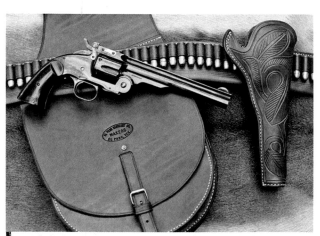

It is easy to step back into history with a .45 Schofield and traditional leather from El Paso Saddlery.

necessary hammer block safety to allow its importation, but it still should be carried with only five rounds and the hammer resting on an empty chamber at all times. The half cock is not a safety – engaging it will allow the cylinder to rotate, possibly bringing a live round under the hammer.

FROM REPLICA TO REISSUE

Val Forgett had worked diligently to bring forth the first Model 1875 Schofield replica. Then in 2000, for the first time since 1875, shooters could have a brand new, *real* Smith & Wesson Schofield! To celebrate the 125th Anniversary of its classic, the company offered the Schofield 2000 — built on modern machinery from the S&W Performance Center while still adhering to the original design, including a cylinder that only accepts the .45 Schofield cartridge.

Since S&W engineers didn't have the original drawings to work from anymore, they had to work from an original Schofield, borrowed from S&W historian/collector, Roy Jinks. At the time, the company had this to say about the reintroduction:

"American firearms historians have come to recognize what Colonel Schofield had instinctively understood the first time he held the Smith & Wesson Model 3 Schofield in his hand–it was the best revolver ever invented for the Horse Soldier. Now, 125 years later, Smith & Wesson reintroduces the Schofield. The Schofield Model of 2000 is a modern, top-break, single action from the Smith & Wesson Performance Center. It features the design concepts of the original Model 3 Schofield and incorporates the technical and engineering

advantages the intervening 125 years have made possible. With its seven-inch barrel, bright blue finish, and walnut grips, the Schofield Model of 2000 is a modern classic."

The deeply blued finish of the Schofield Model 2000 is nicely set off with a case-colored trigger guard, hammer and latching system. Just as with the original and subsequent replicas, two screws hold the female part of the locking latch above the cylinder and when the rear screw is backed out, the latch can be lifted upwards allowing the cylinder to be removed. The overall fit and finish is excellent as one would expect from the Performance Center.

The original Schofield was only produced from 1875 to 1877 with less than 9,000 guns being manufactured. The Model 2000 was produced much slower and for a shorter period of time. It was virtually hand built one at a time, with a retail price somewhere in the range of $1,200-$1,300. The original Schofield sold to civilians for $17.50. Smith & Wesson had no problem selling all the Model 2000 Schofield produced; however, it was not cost-effective for them as they could produce other guns faster and sell them for more money, so the bean counters won out.

A sixgun as nice as the Smith & Wesson Model 2000 deserved custom grips and custom leather. Eagle Grips offers the best imitation ivory I have seen with its UltraIvory. Although it costs only about one-third as much as the real thing, you have to look *very* closely to tell the difference. The craftsmen at Eagle expertly fitted a pair of UltraIvories to the Model 2000 and followed my wishes to decrease the thickness by about one-third of the factory grips. They not only look great, but they also feel exceptionally good.

I had the sixgun and the grips. All that was left to complete the picture was grand leather, and nothing looks better with a blued sixgun with ivory grips than black leather. To complete the project, I called Rudy Lozano at Black Hills Leather for a double holster setup to carry two S&W single actions. I chose The Oklahoma rig — a Mexican loop-style holster with two loops, with the holsters and matching belt fully lined, border-stamped and then dyed black. It looks like a traditional gun-fighters rig from the 1870s.

A few years back if I wanted to experiment, I had to make .45 Schofield brass by trimming .45 Colt cases. Now Starline offers excellent .45 Schofield brass, and Black Hills has both 180- and 230-grain factory loads. This is very mild, pleasant-shooting ammo with the 230-grain load clocking 650 fps from a 7-inch barrel. For the re-loader, Lyman's Cowboy Dies for the .45 Colt are also set up to load .45 Schofield. A different shellholder is required as the Schofield rim is slightly larger in diameter than the Colt.

SCHOFIELD OR COLT SAA?

Gunfighters on both sides of the law carried Schofields, and we definitely know that Schofield Number 366 belonged to Jesse James. He may have been carrying it when he was shot by Bob Ford. Jesse apparently carried both a Colt Peacemaker and a Schofield. (I wonder if he used .45 S&W ammunition in both?) I have often contemplated what I would have done had I lived in the 1870s and had to make a choice between an S&W Schofield or a Colt. Perhaps I'd have done as Jesse James did and have 'em both! ◎

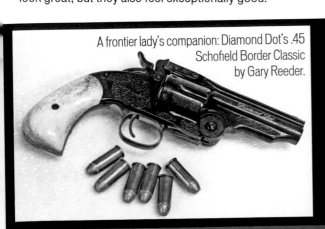

A frontier lady's companion: Diamond Dot's .45 Schofield Border Classic by Gary Reeder.

DIAMOND DOT'S
SPECIAL SCHOFIELD

Several years ago Diamond Dot's boss wanted do something special for her. Looking at Gary Reeder's website, he found just the thing – a custom Schofield known as the Border Classic. To build it, Reeder cut the barrel back to 3 inches, added fitted mastodon ivory stocks, some engraving and a special deep blue job. So for her birthday that year, Diamond Dot received a very special Uberti/Navy Arms/Gary Reeder Border Classic .45 Colt.

THE SIXGUNS

John has been a devotee of the Model 1917 since his teenage years. Back then, the price was right on this classic.

THE S&W .45 HAND EJECTORS

CHAPTER 13

In 1881, Smith & Wesson brought out its first double-action revolver, the .44 Double Action First Model, also known as the New Model Navy No. 3 — basically its top-break New Model No. 3 with a DA trigger added. The main chambering was .44 Russian; however, some were manufactured chambered in both .38 WCF (.38-40) and .44 WCF (.44-40). Although the cylinder was certainly long enough for the .45 Colt, I don't know of any DA S&W top-breaks so chambered.

By the 1890s both Colt and S&W were working on a more modern DA revolver with a swing-out cylinder. Colt arrived first with the New Service, but in 1899, S&W's .38 Military & Police arrived. It would be late 1907 before the company came out with a big-bore swing-out.

Any serious sixgun student knows the first modern big-bore S&W DA was the magnificent 1st Model, New Century .44 Military Model of 1908, or as it is lovingly called by shooters and collectors, the Triple-Lock. This new revolver was also chambered for the new .44 Special, becoming the first of the big-bore Hand Ejectors. The name comes from the fact the top-breaks all featured automatic simultaneous cartridge ejection, while the newer swing-outs required you to push the front of the ejector rod to kick out the cartridges. The Triple-Lock received its name from the fact the cylinder locked at the back, at the end of the ejector

One of John's more potent .45 Colt handloads delivered fine accuracy in this Model 25-5.

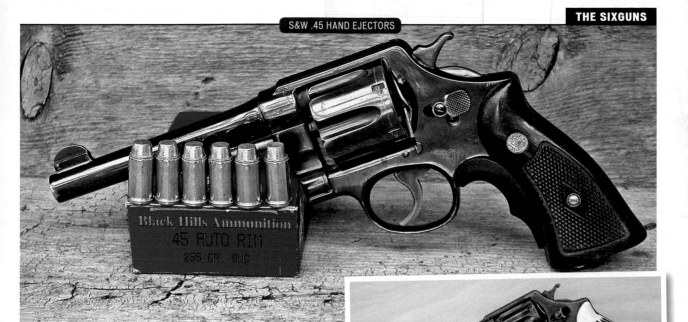

The .45 Auto Rim option: Model 1917 (top). The 2nd Model Hand Ejector (bottom) was converted from .455 Eley.

rod, and with a precisely machined third lock at the front of the cylinder.

The 1st Model Hand Ejector is mostly found in .44 Special; however, a few where in .45 Colt and many more were destined for the British market and were .455 Mark II chambered. The Triple-Lock was relatively short-lived, being produced from 1908-1915, at which time the enclosed ejector rod and third lock were dropped, resulting in the 2nd Model HE. This model was also mainly produced in .44 Special for the civilian market, with about 700 each offered in .45 Colt and .455. However, almost 75,000 were produced as military models in .455 for the British and Canadian governments, and by 1917 it was the U.S. military's turn for .45 Smith & Wessons.

The answer was the Smith & Wesson 2nd Model HE and the Colt New Service, both of which were standardized with 5½-inch barrels and chambered in .45 ACP. To make this rimless cartridge work in the cylinders, an S&W engineer came up with the half-moon clip to hold three cartridges, which not only provided proper headspace but also provided for extraction. (Half-moons have evolved into full moons, allowing six cartridges to be loaded and ejected at once.)

The 1917 S&W in military dress was produced from September 1917 to January 1919, with almost 164,000 being produced. The frame is stamped "US Army Model 1917" and the left side of the barrel is marked "S&W D.A. 45." There is also a U.S. Ordnance flaming bomb marked on the left side of the frame. The 1917 Smith was modernized further

at approximately serial number 185,000 with the addition of a hammer-block safety, which remains on S&W sixguns today. Military models were finished in standard blue with smooth walnut grips; commercial versions have a deeper blue and checkered diamond grips with S&W medallions.

The rugged 1917 S&W was made even better by the arrival of .45 Auto Rim ammunition from Remington in the early 1920s. Many outdoorsmen and law officers were soon carrying a 1917 loaded with .45 Auto Rim. Even by the time I started shooting in the mid-1950s, there were still plenty of reasonably priced 1917s.

THE MODEL 1950

In 1946 Smith & Wesson had reintroduced the 1917, which then became the Model 1950 in 1951. It is virtually indistinguishable from the 1917 except for a few minor changes, plus a change from the old long action to the short one. At least 200 of these 1950 Models were chambered in .45 Colt, the rest being .45 Auto Rim.

SIXGUNS AND THEIR CARTRIDGES

S&W's Thunder Ranch Model 22-4 embodies Clint Smith's concept of a "fighting sixgun." John agrees wholeheartedly, despite that newfangled frame-mounted firing pin!

Even today, the 1917/1950 S&W — basically now nearly 100 years old — is still a viable self-defense gun when loaded with either .45 Auto Rim cartridges or a full-moon clip holding six .45 ACPs. Back things up with a couple of loaded full-moon clips in your pocket, and you're on pretty sound footing.

When the Triple-Lock was dropped in 1915, the enclosed ejector-rod housing also disappeared. The ejectorless rod housing of the 2nd Model HE would remain right up to the eve of World War II. However, even as the 2nd Model HE arrived in 1915, there were those who clamored for a return to the Triple-Lock or at least to the enclosed ejector-rod housing. This finally resulted in the arrival of the 3rd Model HE or Model 1926. All of these were in .44 Special as far as is known and were produced from 1926 to 1941. Production was interrupted during WWII, and started up once again from 1946 to 1949. The 3rd Model was a popular heavy-duty sixgun, especially among southwestern lawmen and outdoorsmen. Earlier in its production life it was used as the

platform for both the .38/44 Heavy Duty and Outdoorsman of 1930, as well as the .357 Magnum of 1935.

A 4TH MODEL

As we recovered from the wartime production of the 1940s and entered the 1950s, S&W brought forth the 4th Model HE — the Model 1950 Target in .45 ACP/.45 Auto Rim. Around 2,700 were made before it disappeared from the company catalog. A very few were offered in .45 Colt. Over the years I'd been able to come up with several 1950 Targets chambered in .44 Special. Although it was dropped in the mid-1960s, a special run of 800 5-inch, old-style tapered barrel .45 Colt Model 26-1s (the new designation) were made for the 50th anniversary of the Georgia State Patrol in 1987. Not being a bullseye shooter, I would've been very happy to have one of these later Model 26-1s; however, I had never even seen one in all my years of attending local gun shows. I had yet to find either a pre-26 1950 Target or Model 26 .45 ACP Target Model — and finding one in .45 Colt was virtually impossible.

PROJECT GUN

Several years ago, my friend Paco Kelly gave me a 1950 Target .45 Colt barrel, and a project immediately began to form in my mind. I next acquired a Highway Patrolman .357 Magnum Model 28-2 in excellent condition and sent it — along with the .45 barrel — to John Gallagher. What I wanted was the type of sixgun chosen by the Georgia State Patrol. Gallagher rechambered the cylinder to .45 Colt, cut the barrel to 5 inches, remounted the front ramp and fitted a post front sight, tuned the action, set the single-action trigger pull at just under 3 pounds and refinished the barrel to match the matte blue of the Highway Patrolman. I finally had my 1950 Target chambered in .45 Colt.

The 1950 Target barrels do not have the best reputation for shooting cast bullets, so I was prepared, if necessary, for this to be a dedicated jacketed-bullet .45. I worried needlessly. It shoots jacketed, hard-cast, and surprise of surprises, it even likes Speer's soft-swaged 250-grain lead semiwadcutters, which really shouldn't shoot well in the shallow-rifled 1950 Target barrel. In fact, I almost did not try the box of .45 Colt ammunition I had loaded with the soft Speers and 7.8 grains of Unique. (I normally use 8.0 grains, but the powder measure was throwing the slightly lighter charge so I stayed with it.) The results were nothing short of incredible. Six shots at 20 yards give me one ragged hole at an easy-shooting 770 fps. Actually, every load I tried shot very well in the Gallagher S&W.

It turned out the custom Gallagher was only the beginning. That summer I walked into Boise Gun Co. and found not one, but *two* 1950 Targets — one in .44 Special, the other in .45 ACP. I wound up swapping a Merwin-Hulbert for both.

Shortly after that I found myself in the hospital with a 10 percent chance of survival. (I did survive, for which I feel very blessed.) While I was recuperating, Matt from Buckhorn came over with *another* pair of 1950 Targets in excellent shape — again one in .44 Special and the other in .45 ACP. I had the asking price and got them.

CLARK, MICULEK, JORDAN

It has been my good fortune over the past 45-plus years to meet some of the finest gentlemen in our industry. One such fellow figure was Jimmy Clark.

In 1990 I aided Chairman Hal Swiggett in presenting the Outstanding *American Handgunner* Awards Foundation bronze to Jimmy Clark in his home area of Shreveport, Louisiana. There were 10 nominees that year, and I was the only one to accompany Hal and Bill Jordan to Shreveport.

This particular Shreveport September was absolutely stifling in its heat and humidity. The banquet was held on Friday and I was set to fly back out on Monday. Jimmy Clark saved me from a terrible fate by taking me home for the weekend, saving me a boring several days stuck in a hotel. It stands out as one of the most memorable times in my life. I met all of Jimmy's family including his wife, son Jim Jr., daughter Kay, as well as the gunsmiths in his shop. On Saturday morning I met a young sixgunner named Jerry Miculek who was just starting to make a name for himself. Bill Jordan also showed up around the same time. I shot with Jerry early in the morning (he beat me, of course), with both of us using his 8⅜-inch Smith & Wesson .357 Magnum. We quit shooting at 9 a.m. when the temperature and humidity both hovered at 100 degrees. In spite of the heat, I had a wonderful time with all of them. Jerry, of course, not only went on to become the fastest double-action shooter the world has ever known, but he also married Jimmy's daughter, Kay.

JIMMY CLARK'S CONTRIBUTION

Jimmy was born in Texas in 1923 and served in the Pacific as a Marine during WWII. He was called back in during Korea and spent most of his time working on pistols for the military. He was one of the early pioneers of accurizing the .45 ACP and also one of the first to chamber the 1911 for the .38 Special. He was also an early pioneer in

Packing a Model 25 .45 Colt with a 6½-inch barrel calls for a serious shoulder rig, like this classic from Al Goerg.

SIXGUNS AND THEIR CARTRIDGES

John was able to wring some rally good groups out of the Smiths on the range.

the use of long barrel/long slide 1911s. All the time he was pistolsmithing he was also competing, being the fifth man to break 2600 in the NRA course in 1950 and 10 years later was the fourth man to achieve 2650 out of a possible 2700.

In 1949 Jimmy did a short-action job on a 1917 Smith & Wesson .45 ACP revolver. He had found he could shoot the revolver better than the 1911s available at the time. Unfortunately, as he was reloading, a double charge of powder snuck in and took the gun apart. In 1951 Jimmy bought two Smith & Wesson 1950 Target .45 ACP revolvers, tuned the actions and found he had a revolver which would shoot jacketed bullets pretty well, but as he says:

"They were a disaster with our handload using the Hensley & Gibbs #130 cast bullet and 3.5 grains of Bullseye. I returned both revolvers to the factory explaining the problem. After several months, I received them back with very small groups the boys at the factory claimed to be fired at 50 yards. I again tried various loads with the same terrible results. The guns were retired and never fired again."

In 1954 Jimmy was complaining to someone at an S&W exhibit booth, not knowing he was talking to then-President Carl Hellstrom about those 1950 Target revolvers. The discussion became quite heated and Hellstrom did not — at first — appreciate what Jimmy had to say. But the more Hellstrom thought about it the more he realized Jimmy knew what he was talking about. The following year, 1955, Jimmy won the Mid-Winter Matches and was awarded a brand-new 1955 Target. Jimmy found it shot every bit as good as his 1911 autos.

Jimmy later told me:

"I often take my old Model 1955 out of the safe and fire hardball ammo at long ranges. It is an excellent plinker at 100 yards or so at anything that floats along the banks of the Red River. Needless to say, it is one of my most prized possessions."

The 1955 Target that Jimmy Clark "inspired" S&W to offer was basically an upgrade of the original 1950 Target .45. The barrel was changed to a heavyweight bull-barrel style, and target trigger, target hammer and target stocks were added. I also believe the company changed the rifling to better accept cast bullets.

I've had considerable experience using cast bullets in three 1950 Targets, a 1955 Target and the later Model 25. They all shoot cast bullets exceptionally well, however I normally go heavier than the old 200-grain H&G #130. I also size them according to the chamber's throats on each individual gun (these are .454 inch or larger). Jimmy probably stayed with the 200-grain bullet because of lighter recoil. If he had followed my path, the 1950 Target might have shot well for him, but then we would never have seen the 1955 Target. Sometimes, things work out just the way they're *supposed* to.

It is easy to see how the blending of the 1955 Target .45 ACP with the 1950 Target .44 Special resulted in the original .44 Magnum in 1956. Elmer Keith may have inspired the cartridge, but it looks like Jimmy had a hand in bringing about the gun.

By mid-1960 Smith & Wesson took an ax to its catalog and dropped the 1950 Target Model, the 1955 Target Model and the .38/44 Outdoorsman. All of these had become numbers instead of models in the late 1950s, with the 1950 Target and 1955 Target chambered in .45 being renamed the Model 26 and 25. But eventually a special run of 10,000 Model 1955s would be offered as S&W's 125th Anniversary Model in 1977, chambered not in .45 ACP but .45 Colt.

But one problem existed with the .45 Colt models in that S&W used the relatively short .45 ACP cylinder of the Model 1955, which precluded the use of .45 Colt bullets set in their proper crimping grooves. Bullets that worked fine in Colt SAAs did not work in these DA sixguns. In order for the cylinder to function, bullets often had to be crimped over the shoulder rather than in the crimping groove. The company corrected this with the Model 25-5 .45 Colt. A dead ringer for the Model 29

S&W 1955 TARGET 6½-INCH .45 AUTO RIM

LOAD	VELOCITY	5 SHOTS, 25 YARDS
Lyman #452423 Keith/8.0 gr. Blue Dot	709 fps	1"
Lyman #452423 Keith/5.5 gr. Unique	832 fps	1"
Lyman #452490GC Thompson/6.0 gr. Universal	955 fps	1¼"
Oregon Trail 255-gr. SWC/5.5 gr. Unique	870 fps	1"
Oregon Trail 255-gr. SWC/6.0 gr. Unique	920 fps	1⅛"
Oregon Trail 255-gr. SWC/7.0 gr. Unique	931 fps	3/4"

.44 Magnum, S&W's first standard production model in .45 Colt first saw the light of day in 1979.

The Model 25-2 ran side by side with the 25-5 for a one-two marketing punch in both .45 ACP chambering and also in .45 Colt. The former carries a short cylinder designed for the .45 ACP cartridge, while the latter fills out the cylinder window.

It would be hard to find a sixgun better suited to defensive use than a Model 1955 Target .45 ACP, once properly customized, personalized and tuned. All that is really needed is to cut the barrel to 4 inches and replace the target trigger and hammer with the less-cumbersome and slicker handling standard hammer and trigger. Throw in an action job, maybe replace the Baughman front ramp sight with a flat-post Patridge front and a *serious* sixgun

Big-frame big bores: Smith & Wesson 1950 Target Models.

TEST-FIRE:

EVERYDAY WORKING LOADS FOR S&W .45 SIXGUNS

4-INCH MODEL 25-5 .45 COLT

LOAD	VELOCITY
Lyman #454424 Keith/9.0 gr. Power Point	816 fps
Lyman #454424 Keith/9.0 gr. Unique	883 fps
Lyman #454424 Keith/20.0 gr. #4227	932 fps
RCBS #45-270 SAA/18.5 gr. #4227	861 fps

4-INCH MODEL 25-2 AUTO RIM

LOAD	VELOCITY
Lyman #452423 Keith/7.5 gr. Unique	1,045 fps
Lyman #454424 Keith/7.0 gr. Unique	894 fps
Lyman #4544424 Keith/14.0 gr. #2400	848 fps
Oregon Trail 255-gr. SWC/7.0 gr. Unique	847 fps
Black Hills 255-gr. SWC	766 fps
Buffalo Bore 255-gr. Hard Cast	858 fps

emerges. Just about every ammo manufacturer offers excellent defensive loads for the .45 ACP that are relatively mild in a large (N) frame, allowing quick recovery between shots.

Chambered in .45 ACP, the Model 1955 allows the use of .45 ACP cartridges with or without the use of either half-moon or full-moon clips. The use of these clips especially of the full-moon style rivals the speed of reloading a 1911. If you choose .45 Auto Rim ammunition, a half- or full-moon clip isn't needed.

John has a traditionalist's love of the .45 Colt — particularly when it's chambered in a sweet-shooting sixgun like S&W's Model 25 Classic.

The 4-inch Model 25-5 in .45 Colt is also an easy packin', easy shootin' defensive sixgun. There are a number of excellent factory loads offered in .45 Colt — namely Speer's 200-grain "Flying Ashtray" JHP, Winchester's 225-grain Silvertip HP and Federal's 225-grain lead semiwadcutter. There are also heavier options from Buffalo Bore and Cor-Bon. While not as fast as .45 ACP rounds in a full-moon clip, a .45 Colt DA S&W can be quickly recharged with a speedloader.

Before the run of Model 25-5s ended, they were available in 4-, 6- and 8⅜-inch barrel lengths. The latter is one of my favorite sixguns for accurate sixgunnin' and just plain fun. Loaded with 260-grain Keith-style semiwadcutters at 1,100 fps, it makes a practical close-range deer and black bear handgun.

A few years back I ran an exhaustive test looking for what I call "pleasure loads" — superbly accurate loads for the .44 Special, .41 Magnum, .44 Magnum, .45 AutoRim and .45 Colt using Smith & Wesson sixguns. Surprise of surprises, the .45 Colt Model 25-5 proved to be the most accurate overall.

The key to accuracy is to tailor cast bullets to the cylinder chamber throats. I have seen cylinders from different manufacturers made for the .45 Colt anywhere from .449 to .458 inch. Usually, the proper size bullet will shoot accurately. The .45 Colt has proven to be superbly accurate in my 4-inch Model 25-5 when I use a 255-grain bullet over 9.0 grains of Unique (for 900 fps) and groups in 1 inch or less at 20-25 yards. For defensive use, Winchester's Silvertip HP at 800 fps would be effective and relatively easy-shooting.

SPECIAL RERUNS

Although the original classic .45 Hand Ejectors are long gone, S&W resurrects some of them from time to time. Three fairly recent examples have been the .45 HEG (Hand Ejector Gold), the .45 Thunder Ranch Special and the .45 Classic. The former and latter are both chambered in .45 Colt, while the Thunder Ranch Special is .45 ACP/.45 Auto Rim.

All of the original HE models were offered in basic blue, often S&W's beautiful Bright Blue — and some fixed-sight models can be found with nickel plating. They are the most

6.0 POWER PISTOL

.45 AUTO RIM BLACK HILLS 255

.45 AUTO RIM OT 255

John's Model 1955 Target sports stocks by Herrett's. He generally can't resist dispensing with factory grip panels whenever possible.

beautiful DA revolvers ever offered. However, 70 years after the introduction of the Triple-Lock, the road marked "Sixgun Perfection" took a major detour.

First, stainless-steel began to appear with the .44 Magnum Model 629. Then came heavily under-lugged barrels. Finally came round-butt grip frames on all S&W sixguns, and the old ways were gone! I realize I am biased when it comes to what a revolver should look like, and I definitely believe in standard barrels, square butts and blued finishes. I will not argue with you if you prefer the new ways, but I won't change my mind about the new ones.

Yes, I realize that today we are privileged to have what are probably the best-built sixguns ever offered, certainly the strongest and most accurate, it is simply that they do not stir the depths of my soul like the sixguns of old. And at my age, my soul and spirit need a great deal of stirring!

However, my spirit soared with the advent of the .45 HEG from the Performance Center nearly a dozen years ago, which, under the S&W numbering system, is Model 25-10. In an age of endless heavy-barreled, round-butted, stainless-steel revolvers, suddenly we had something almost completely different. It was very close to Sixgun Perfection. Let's highlight what they did perfectly. The barrel is marked ".45 Colt Ctg." You might have expected it to be .44 Special, but thanks to the popularity of Cowboy Action

Shooting, the .45 Colt at the time was probably the most popular big-bore sixgun cartridge. (Cowboy Action shooters look mostly to smaller cartridges now.) The finish is reminiscent of the old S&W Bright Blue, the barrel is the slim profile found on pre-war revolvers, with the front ramp integral with the barrel. The sights are an adjustable rear with a gold bead post front, the standard trigger is smooth, while the hammer has a unique teardrop shape. All in all, it was a most-pleasing sixgun.

I had a few quibbles with it — the barrel length is 6 inches instead of the standard 6½ inches of pre-war days. The grip frame is round-butt instead of the original square one, and for some odd reason, there is a third locking feature at the front of the cylinder, but the second lock-up at the end of the ejector rod housing is gone. Due to modern manufacturing techniques, the old style hammer-mounted firing-pin has been replaced by a frame-mounted pin; and instead of the precisely machined third locking feature of the 1st Model HE, it has a ball detent at the front of the yoke that locks into the back of the ejector rod enclosure.

I can live with the 6-inch barrel as I even have a vintage Berns-Martin breakfront holster found in New Mexico years ago and it fits a large frame 6-inch Smith & Wesson. The lack of a third locking feature does not bother me at all nor does the frame mounted firing pin, and the round-butt grip

One of John's custom projects involved rechambering this S&W Highway Patrolman Model 28 to .45 Auto Rim and replacing the original .357 barrel with one from a 1950 Target barrel in .45 Auto Rim at the beginning of the project.

frame has been taken care of, so you might say I was 99.9 percent pleased with the .45 Colt HEG.

Although some .45 Colt chambered sixguns are certainly capable of handling heavy-duty .45 Colt loads in excess of 30,000 psi, I have no intent — nor do I see any reason — to push this new-old sixgun. This is a standard sixgun, weighing 38 ounces with the Skeeter Skelton stocks from BluMagnum installed, for standard loads. The single-action trigger pull measures just slightly over 4 pounds, which is easy for me to live with. My everyday working load for this sixgun is the RCBS #45-270 SWC over 18.5 grains of H4227 for 900 fps and groups just slightly over one-inch. For a jacketed bullet load, I can be happy with the Hornady 250, Sierra 240 or Speer 260 jacketed hollowpoint over 9.4 grains of Unique for the same 900 fps muzzle velocity and equally good groups. Even at 900 fps, the big flat-nosed .45s speak with great authority.

Beginning around 1990 and right up to today, the revolver has mainly been pushed to second place when it comes to fighting handguns, while the semiautomatic has become firmly entrenched in first place. However, this does not mean the age-old sixgun is no longer viable.

A FIXED-SIGHT FIGHTING SIXGUN

Several years ago Clint Smith prevailed on S&W to produce a fighting sixgun, and that is exactly what they did with the Model 21-4 chambered in .44 Special and the 22-4, its counterpart in .45 ACP/.45 Auto Rim. These are fixed-sighted, enclosed ejector rod, 4-inch barreled, heavy-

duty sixguns reminiscent of the old .38/44 Heavy Duty of the 1930s. The fixed sights consist of a square notch rear sight at the top of the frame matched up with a half-moon, pinned-in front. The great advantage of fixed sights is the fact they are virtually impossible to get out of whack. Adjustable rear sights are great advantage for sighting in for individual shooters and/ or different loads; however, they are certainly not as strong as fixed sights. Having said that, I will also say I have never broken an adjustable rear sight. The older fixed-sight Smith & Wessons had the front sight as an integral part of the barrel rather than being pinned, and the former is certainly stronger while the latter allows easy installation of a taller front sight.

The .45 Model 22-4 shot low for me, and it was just a matter of picking the most used load and filing the front sight accordingly to bring the point of impact even with the point of aim. I like to use 255-grain SWC cast bullets in .45 Auto Rim brass over 6.0 to 7.0 grains of Universal or Unique for 850-950 feet per second. I also like the Black Hills 230-grain JHP .45 ACP rounds loaded in full-moon clips. This is not just a fighting handgun, as it also makes an imminently practical everyday packing/outdoor sixgun. The only way it could be any better for this duty is if it was in stainless steel.

Smith & Wesson's .45 Classic never really existed in the past as an actual sixgun but is actually a hybrid of sorts. It has the longer cylinder of the later .45 Colt Model 25-5 matched up with the slim barrel profile of the .45 Auto Rim/.45 ACP in the 1950 Target/Model 26. Wherever it came from it is definitely welcomed. As we have said (repeatedly) back when the original classic N-frame sixguns were being made they had 6½-inch barrels. This was true from the original Triple-Lock through the next three .44 Hand Ejectors, as well as the .38/44 Outdoorsman, the .357 Magnum and the original .44 Magnum. For some unknown reason when the .41 Magnum was introduced, the barrel was 6 inches, and then in 1979 this was standardized. Then came the heavy underlugged barrels on nearly every S&W

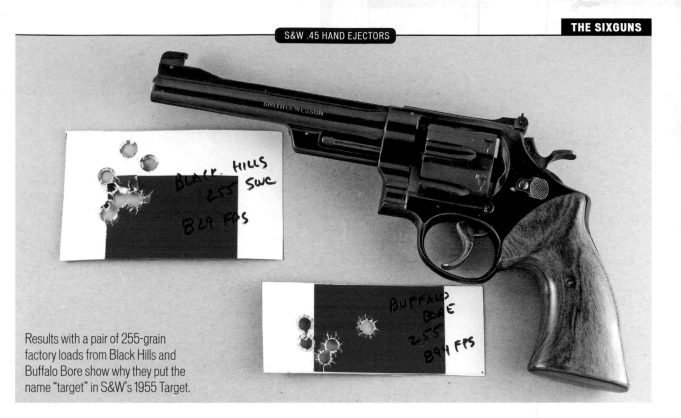

Results with a pair of 255-grain factory loads from Black Hills and Buffalo Bore show why they put the name "target" in S&W's 1955 Target.

sixgun. The non-heavy underlugged 6½-inch length came back with the .44 Magnum 50th Anniversary Model in 2006, and to whoever decided to put it and the square butt back on all the Classic Models I say a hearty Thank You!

Smith & Wesson really did it right with this .45 Colt Model 25 Classic, as all six chamber throats are a uniform .452 inch. The chamber throats are not all they got right on this modern Classic. The cylinder locks up tightly, the barrel/cylinder gap is set at .004 inch, and the trigger is smooth and creep free, although a little heavy at six pounds for the single-action pull. The finish is a bright blue reminiscent of the legendary finish from the 1950s. The upper sideplate screw is back, both the trigger and hammer are the target type, and the latter is an improved profile over the target hammers of 50 years ago.

Sights are a fully adjustable square notch rear sight matched up with a Patridge front sight and both are blue as all iron sights should be. The front sight is pinned in, allowing it to be changed if a different height or type is required, and removal of the rear sight assembly reveals the top strap is drilled and tapped for scope mounting. Stocks are a slim profile, hand-pleasing, target-style of nicely grained walnut with the old-style diamond around the screw holes and enough checkering for a good grasp. One very

small but pleasant detail is the attractiveness of the Smith & Wesson medallions set in each great grip panel; they have a very nice antique brass look to them. If there is anything wrong with the looks of this big-bore sixgun I can't find it! Remember, we don't get in a snit over the lock which is a 21st-century reality; anyone who does misses out on some grand sixguns.

Not only are most modern sixguns stronger and held to tighter tolerances than their counterparts from 50+ years ago, but they also usually shoot even better. And this Model 25 Classic does shoot at both ends of the spectrum. The factory Remington 255-grain LSWC at 877 fps and my handloads of the Lyman/Thompson #452490GC over 14.0 grains of Blue Dot at 1,011 fps put five shots into ⅞ inch at 20 yards. With proper tolerances, it is a rare .45 Colt from any maker that will not shoot. ◎

One of S&W's best "classic reissues" is the Hand Ejector Gold in .45 Colt.

THE SIXGUNS

Here are three variations on S&W's .45 ACP/.45 Auto Rim theme (top to bottom). A 4-inch stainless Model 625-4 Springfield Armory Commemorative, a 5-inch full-lugged stainless Model 625-2, and a 4-inch blued Model 25-2.

THE SMITH & WESSON MODEL 625

CHAPTER 14

I n 1988 Smith & Wesson did something quite radical to its lineup of .45 sixguns. Let's take a quick look at how they got there:

After World War II, the design of S&W revolvers was modernized to the present short action, replacing the older — some would say smoother — long action. In 1950 the old 1917 .45 received a ribbed 6½-inch barrel, a micrometer rear sight, a post front and began winning matches as the 1950 Target Model .45. Within a very few years, the 1950 Target received a heavy bull barrel and became the 1955 Target Model, to become known as the Model 25 in 1957.

The 1950 and 1955 .45s were gone from the lineup by the mid-1960s, but the .45 ACP/.45 Auto Rim revolver was a concept that would not die. In 1988 it came back to life as the Model 1988, thanks to S&W's Bill Jensen. Since the

A Hogue-stocked Model 625-2 in .45 ACP/.45 Auto Rim proved its mettle with two of John's handloads and a Black Hills factory offering.

arrival of the Model 1988, we have also seen the arrival of Jerry Miculek, who has done amazing things with this fast-shooting S&W .45.

The 1988 .45 ACP (or Model 625-2) was intended to provide revolver shooters in both IPSC and Pin Shooting

Although John is a fan of the classic slender barrel configuration, he does appreciate the "shootability" of 5-inch, heavy-barreled .45s featuring full-length underlugs.

with the best possible tool for the job. There are many things right about this revolver. The caliber is ideal for all types of action shooting and defensive purposes. No other big-bore cartridge is available in so many different loadings nor so widely accepted and respected.

There's no folderol on this sixgun. Both hammer and trigger are standard-style, not the cumbersome wide "target" type, and the trigger is smooth to allow your finger to slide over the face of it in fast double-action shooting. The sights are plain black, no white-outline rear, no red insert in the front ramp to cause the gun to shoot to different points of aim according to the available light.

But here's where things get radical. For the first time, an N-frame revolver was available with a 5-inch heavy L-frame-style barrel with a full underlug, plus a rounded K-frame-style butt. Both of these factors combine to provide even less felt recoil than is normally experienced with mild-shooting .45 ACP (or .45 Auto Rim) loads.

The heavy barrel and mild recoil, the proven fight-stopping capabilities of the .45 ACP, the round butt (friendly to the small-handed), and satin stainless finish all add up to a first-class fighting handgun.

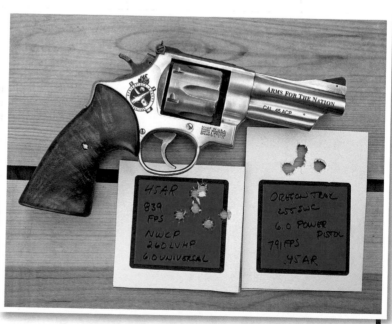

Obviously, these targets shot with the S&W's .45 ACP/.45 Auto Rim Springfield Armory Commemorative Model 625-4 show the gun's propensity for heavier bullets. The stocks are by BluMagnum.

"Spare and a Pair." The two Mountain Guns on the left are in .45 Colt. The one on the right is in .45 AR.

Add in the advantages of moon clip loading, and it's easy to see how popular this sixgun was destined to become. S&W originally announced that only 5,000 would be made and quickly realized that wouldn't be enough. The company has continued to make the Model 625 in several different barrel lengths.

There are things you can do to make it an even slicker defensive sixgun. The rear sight is easily rounded to prevent it from snagging on clothing. The barrel just begs to be cut to 3 or 4 inches for the fastest possible draw out of a high-riding hip holster, and S&W took this step quite quickly. Throw in an action job for a smooth DA trigger pull and you've to a near-perfect fighting sixgun.

A GRIP ON THINGS

With the arrival of the Model 625, S&W went with Pachmayr round-butt, finger-groove grips. This was a vast improvement over the standard factory wood stocks of the time. Many shooters like finger-groove grips, but for anything chambered for mild-recoiling standard cartridges, I do not believe that finger-groove grips belong on anything designed for fast work. When my hand hits the grip, I want whatever position I get to

be *right*. This is not possible with finger grooves.

A better choice would have been the Pachmayr round-butt K-frame standard grips. I had them on a Model 29, but trying to install them on the Model 625 proved they were slightly too small. So I called my friend, the late Deacon Deason of BearHug Grips. He sent me a smooth walnut pair with an open backstrap, filled in behind the trigger guard and front strap. At my request, they were not cut for a speed-loader but simply thinned down on the left side to allow the fast use of full-moon clips. As time went on, I stole the walnut BearHugs for use on a harder-kicking sixgun and went with (would you believe?) Hogue finger-groove grips. Why? They fit my fingers well for *deliberate* shooting.

OTHER CHANGES

The overall configuration of the Model 625 had a couple of advantages over previous models. Its heavier barrel reduces felt recoil — the gun simply seems to "hang" better on target and, though I prefer the old square-butt style, I must admit that the round butt allows for a greater range of custom grips. The stainless finish also gives you less to worry about in terms of rust.

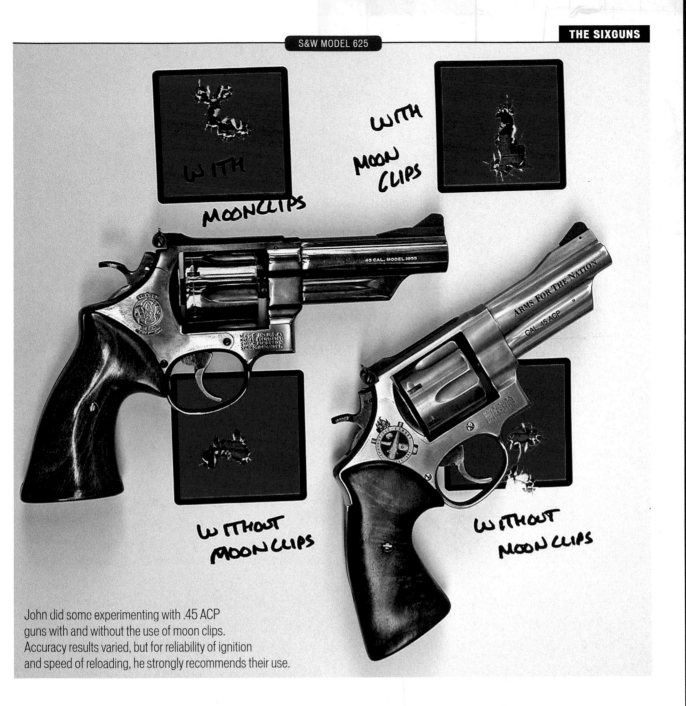

John did some experimenting with .45 ACP
guns with and without the use of moon clips.
Accuracy results varied, but for reliability of ignition
and speed of reloading, he strongly recommends their use.

Since my original Model 625-2 was obviously an excellent candidate for a duty/defensive sixgun, I called El Paso Saddlery for a belt holster. "Are you familiar with the new 625-2?" I asked the late Bob NcNellis, El Paso's genial owner.

"*Familiar* with it? I'm shooting one in IPSC," he replied. "Do you know where I can get another?" Within a few minutes I had ordered a basket weave Tortilla — El Paso's answer to the pancake — as my packin' rig for the gun.

The Tortilla rides high and tight to the body, providing both comfort and security for the relatively heavy Model 625. A quick move of the hand and a snap of the thumb-break security strap, and I soon found the big sixgun comes into action *fast*.

THE MOON CLIP QUESTION

We often hear .45 Auto Rim revolvers can be used with .45 ACP ammunition without moon clips. When .45 ACP ammunition is used, we're told, the mouth of the case theoretically butts up against the shoulder in the cylinder. Maybe yes, maybe no. Depends on the individual sixgun. When I tried it with my original Model 625-2, I experienced one or two misfires in each cylinderful when I used Blazer aluminum-cased ammunition. I can only assume the rounds either slid forward over the shelf in the chamber as the firing pin hit the primer, or that the cases were a mite short for the chamber, allowing them to move forward.

With other brands of ammunition, accuracy without the

255 KT
20.0 H4227
893 FPS

45
Colt

.45 COLT
275 KT

18.5 H4227
873 FPS

RCBS 45-270
8.5 UNIQUE
812 FPS

Targets shot with the .45 Colt
Mountain Gun Model 625-6 justified
John's hope for S&W to finally offer it.

clips was good, but not outstanding (except for Federal Match ammo). But when I used full-moon clips, every group shrank in size, some to one-half the size of groups *without* the clips.

This sold me on the use of moon clips. As a bonus with the use of clips, it is impossible for one fired case to slip under the extractor star as often happens with rimmed cartridges. A full-moon clip of .45 ACPs loads — and unloads — fast and positively. For defensive use it would be foolish and/or dangerous not to use the clips with ACP ammo.

Once I was satisfied with the performance of my Model 625-2 using .45 ACP loads and clips, I then switched to my real goal, mainly using .45 Auto Rim loads. So I worked up some of my favorite .45 ACP handloads using Auto-Rim brass. Any handgun that is going to be shot a lot — and this one was destined to be — must be capable of handling cast bullets, unless you have an unlimited supply of jacketed bullets or an unlimited supply of cash to buy them! For me, at

least, and a whole lot of other "dinosaur" sixgunners, the cast bullet is still king when it comes to doing a lot of shooting.

I assembled some of my favorite cast bullet/load combinations, and then I ran into my first problem. Over the years I have learned (usually the hard way) not to load a whole batch of ammunition without trying out loads to see if the handgun they're intended for will actually accept them. Nothing can be taken for granted when assembling ammunition, even though you'd expect loads that have been used for years in the Model 25-2 Smith & Wesson would also work in the Mosel 625-2. Not so! Plans were made on paper to load Keith bullets crimped in the crimping groove and using .45 Auto Rim brass. These had worked well in the past, and my plans called for using the Lyman #452423, a 240-grain semiwadcutter, and the Lyman #454424, a 260-grain SWC. I ran both through the lubri-sizer and, as I got ready to load them, a little voice urged "Better try 'em first!" I loaded the first round with the #454424 and the loaded round — which dropped into my Model 25-2 and seemed to rattle around a bit — would not chamber in the 625-2. Switching to the #452423, which was specifically designed for the .45 Auto Rim, gave me the same result.

My last hope for a heavy SWC bullet was the Lyman-Thompson #452490GC. The first round was loaded with the gas-checked 250-grain SWC and, finally, success! This excellent bullet has a front band small enough to allow it to fit (albeit quite snugly) the chambers of my Model 625-2, and it has since proven to be a good choice for the gun with 7.0 grains of Herco for a muzzle velocity of 929 fps. This combination can put six shots into a ¾-inch group at 25 yards — great shooting for a big-bore sixgun with cast bullets. Both 8.0 grains of Herco (1,000 fps) and 13.0 grains of #2400 (1,017 fps) shot into 1¼ inches.

The Keith-style .45 Colt 260-grain #454424 could be used by crimping over the front band in Auto Rim brass and 7.0 grains of Unique gave it a satisfying 900-plus fps (with six shots going into 1⅜ inches). You may note all of these loads eclipse the long-standard 255-grain .45 Colt factory loading by 50-150 fps. What does this mean? The Model 625 is also a viable close-range deer and black bear sixgun.

My results with Speer's 250-grain swaged SWC were also very satisfying. This bullet is very soft and doesn't work with every load/powder/ gun combination. But when I loaded it over 6.0 grains of Unique and crimped in the crimping groove, for slightly over 750 fps, it proved an accurate, mild-shooting, easily assembled defense and small game load. But you should stay under 800 fps with this one to avoid excessive leading.

My long-time favorite cast bullets for use in the .45 ACP have been Lyman's #452460, Hensley & Gibb's #68 and RCBS's #45-201KT. All three of these SWCs weigh in right at the 200-grain mark and usually are excellent performers in semiautos. They did the same in my revolver. In fact in my original testing, Lyman's #452460 and 6.0 grains of WW231 delivered a six-shot group of ½ inch center-to-center. That's astounding for a big-bore sixgun, especially when you consider how far the bullet has to jump from the cylinder to the forcing cone and rifling.

Accuracy with cast bullets was so far above my Model 25-2, at the time I called S&W to ask Tom Campbell whether or not the barrel specifications had been changed. He told me the barrel was cut the same as those supplied on the Model 25-2, but there was a reason for the accuracy improvement. The chamber throats of the Model 625-2 were held to .453 inch. What this means is the cast bullet does not have to swell up in the cylinder and then be swaged down again when it hits the rifling. The result? Much better cast-bullet accuracy.

ANOTHER CHAMBERING

In 1988 the Model 625-2 was one of the best ideas to come out of S&W in many a moon. The only possible thing for anyone to complain about was the fact it was in .45 Auto Rim/.45 ACP instead of .45 Colt. But someone at the factory wisely decided to head off the grumbling. One year later the Model 625-5 arrived — a dead-ringer for the Model 625-2

Bright idea: Here is a very rare 4-inch nickel-plated Model 26/1950 Target.
Photo: Timothy Mullin

with one major difference — a .45 Colt chambering. Everything good about the Model 625-2 applies in spades to the newer Model 625-5. Now I have them both.

Way back in the 1970s, S&W chambered its 1955 Target in .45 Colt as the Model 25-5, but it proved to be a "buyer beware" situation as several had oversized chambers – some ran as large as .456 inch or even more. But with the coming of the Model 625, the company got serious about quality .45 Colt sixguns. Every Model 625 in .45 Colt I've examined since adheres to tight tolerances with properly sized chamber throats.

However, S&W didn't stop there. As 1990 arrived, it looked back to the past, all the way back to the 1950 Target Model. The company even went back farther to the Model 1926 Target Model, and even still farther to the Triple-Lock Target Model. All three of these are exceptionally rare with 4-inch barrels in their original incarnation. As far as collectors know, only one Model 1926 exists in Target configuration with a 4-inch barrel and the majority of all three models

are chambered in .44 Special. A very, very few 1950 Target Model .45 ACP/.45 Auto Rim with 4-inch barrels were ever manufactured, and even less put together in .45 Colt. However, Smith & Wesson looked to these classics when it came time to make the next step.

First, they made a special run of sixguns possibly even better suited to defensive use than the Model 25-2 .45 ACP or Model 25-5 .45 Colt.

These Model 625-4 stainless steel sixguns were marked as Springfield Armory Commemoratives and are chambered in .45 ACP/.45 Auto Rim. The 4-inch barrels on these are the pre-1955 slim style found on all S&Ws prior to the bull barrels brought forth on the 1955 Target and .357 Combat Magnum in 1956. This makes them a little lighter for packin' and places the point of balance back in your hand rather than ahead of the cylinder.

THE MOUNTAIN GUN

Then it was time for S&W to *really* reach out to old-school sixgunners. First, one of those 4-inch slim barrels was put on a Model 629 chambered in .44 Magnum, and the idea of the Mountain Gun was born. Added to the lightweight barrel profile and stainless steel construction was a round-butt grip frame. The concept was an instant success. But it was no time to stop there. The next Mountain Gun was the same basic 4-inch sixgun – this time chambered in .45 Colt. Now if you think about this, the Mountain Gun concept went against everything else that seemed trendy at the time – namely building bigger, heavier revolvers to help counteract felt recoil. Everyone knows big thumper calibers need extra weight for dampening recoil, but the Mountain Gun concept does just the opposite as it accentuates recoil with its lighter weight.

But the point of a Mountain Gun is to

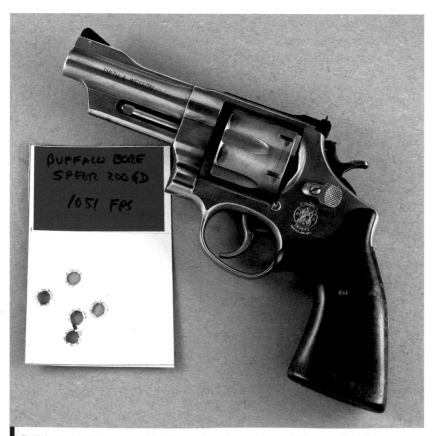

Buffalo Bore's 200-grain .45 ACP loads featuring the Speer 200-grain Gold Dot Hollow Point delivered excellent results in this Model 625-4.

offer an easy-to-pack, short-barreled revolver – one destined to be shot very little with heavy loads. Mountain Guns became exceptionally popular and remain so. The .45 Colt version is officially known as the Model 625-6. Although it is all stainless steel, it does have a case-hardened blue steel trigger and hammer. The trigger has the smooth face favored by serious double-action shooters. The single-action pull, incidentally, is just slightly over 4 pounds. The front sight is a blue steel Baughman on a stainless ramp base that is part of the rib machined into the barrel proper. The rear is fully adjustable with a black blade.

When you remove the rear sight assembly by loosening the two screws – one of which serves as the elevation screw – you'll find three holes drilled and tapped in the top strap. This signifies the Mountain Gun is scope-ready. I doubt if very many – if any – sixgunners would carry a 4-inch .45 Colt revolver with an optical sight. However, the option is there, and it is a welcome feature for really testing load accuracy.

Another Mountain Gun improvement is found in the cylinder release latch. The sharply checkered oval of the past was replaced by a less severely checkered and easier-operating teardrop design. As with most S&W sixguns of today, the .45 Colt Mountain Gun came round-butted with rubber finger-grooved grips.

But I sent my hand pattern off to Herrett's Stocks to aid them in carving a set of smooth walnut "Detective" stocks I thought would go well with the Mountain Gun. I was right. They fill in behind the trigger guard, but thanks to their open-back feature, are not overly bulky. They also extend far below the bottom of the butt to accept my three chubby gripping fingers perfectly.

I am a firm believer in the "pair and a spare" philosophy first brought forth by Kent Bellah in the 1950s. So once I had a chance to come up with a second .45 Colt Mountain Gun, I grabbed it. I now have two in .45 Colt and the third in .45 ACP/.45 Auto Rim. I only carry them one at a time and for this I use the Hank Sloan holster crafted by Mike Barranti. Sloan, an FBI man, designed it with a tension-adjustable screw and Elmer Keith added the hammer cover to protect the lining of your jacket. It's an excellent rig for a 4-inch N-frame. ◎

TEST-FIRE:

.45 AUTO RIM S&W 625-2 (5 INCH)

LOAD	VELOCITY	5 SHOTS, 20 YARDS
Black Hills 255-gr. SWC	803 fps	1¼"
Buffalo Bore 255-gr. +P	1,057 fps	1⅝"
Sierra 240-gr. JHC/6.0 gr. Universal	737 fps	1⅜"
Sierra 240-gr. JHC/7.0 gr. Unique	964 fps	1⅝"
Speer 200-gr. JHP/7.0 gr. Unique	897 fps	1½"
Lyman #454424 Keith/6.0 gr. Unique*	864 fps	2"
Lyman #454424 Keith/7.0 gr. Unique*	907 fps	1⅜"
Lyman #454424/6.5 gr. Herco*	927 fps	2"
Lyman #452490GC/7.0 gr. Herco	929 fps	3/4"
Lyman #452490GC/8.0 gr. Herco	1,000 fps	1¼"
Lyman #452490GC/13.0 gr. #2400	1,026 fps	1¼"

*Crimped over front shoulder

S&W .45 AUTO RIM MOUNTAIN GUN (4 INCH)

Black Hills 255-gr. SWC	791 fps	1½"
Buffalo Bore 255-gr. +P	1,026 fps	1⅝"
Buffalo Bore Speer 200-gr. GDHP +P	1,232 fps	1½"
Sierra 240-gr. JHC/6.0 gr. Universal	714 fps	1¾"
Sierra 240-gr. JHC/7.0 gr. Unique	972 fps	1¾"
Speer 200-gr. JHP/7.0 gr. Unique	900 fps	1⅜"
Lyman #452490GC/13.0 gr. #2400	1,012 fps	1⅝"
Lyman #454424/5.5 gr. Unique	766 fps	2"
Oregon Trail 255-gr. SWC/6.0 gr. Unique	887 fps	1¾"
Oregon Trail 255-gr. SWC/7.0 gr. Unique	921 fps	1¾"

S&W .45 COLT MODEL 625 (5 INCH)

Oregon Trail 255-gr. SWC/9.0 gr. Unique	923 fps	1½"
Oregon Trail 255-gr. SWC/20.0 gr. #4227	906 fps	1¼"
Hornady 250-gr. XTP-JHP/20.0 gr. #4227	906 fps	1½"
Speer 260-gr. JHP/20.0 gr. #4227	899 fps	1¼"

S&W .45 COLT MOUNTAIN GUN (4 INCH)

Oregon Trail 255-gr. SWC/9.0 gr. Unique	927 fps	1½"
Oregon Trail 255-gr. SWC/20.0 gr. #4227	898 fps	1¾"
Hornady 250-gr. XTP-JHP/20.0 gr. #4227	868 fps	1¾"
Speer 260-gr. JHP/20.0 gr. #4227	859 fps	1⅜"
Lyman #454424 Keith/9.0 gr. Power Pistol	777 fps	1¾"
Lyman #454424 Keith/9.0 gr. Unique	870 fps	1⅜"
Lyman #454424 Keith/20.0 gr. #4227	893 fps	1"
RCBS #45-270SAA/18.5 gr. #4227	872 fps	1⅛"

THE BOOK OF THE .45

SIXGUNS AND THEIR CARTRIDGES

Smith & Wesson's 21st-century X-frames — the .460 and .500 S&W Magnums.

THE SMITH & WESSON MODEL 460XVR

John topped his SSK single shot with a Leupold variable to get the most of the .460's long-range potential.

CHAPTER 15

With the coming of the .357 Magnum, most shooters believed we had reached the pinnacle of pistol power, but that was 1935. Later, of course, Dick Casull started the experiments which led to his .454, Smith & Wesson brought out the .44 Magnum, and John Linebaugh came forth with his .500 and then .475 Linebaugh chamberings.

All arguments as to which of these was the most powerful revolver ceased in 2003 with S&W's introduction of the X-frame Model 500 chambered in the new .500 S&W Magnum. It could launch a 440-grain bullet from its 8⅜-

S&W MODEL 460XVR

The .460 works well with the normal heavy-duty sixgun powders. A variety of hard cast bullet weights (inset) are available for it from Cast Performance Bullet Company and Oregon Trail.

inch barrel at nearly 1,700 fps.

However, using the same basic X-frame as on the Model 500, S&W then introduced the Model 460 Extreme Velocity Revolver chambered in .460 S&W Magnum. It was time to drop back and put a little more enjoyment in shooting while still maintaining extreme power. And compared to the .500's heaviest factory load, the .460 is pure pleasure. Even with its full-house factory load of a 395-grain bullet at close to 1,600 fps, I can truthfully say, from the massive X-frame, it's not too bad.

The combination of four plus pounds weight, interchangeable muzzle compensator and finger-groove rubber grips all work together to keep felt recoil at a tolerable level. I have since replaced the rubber grips with walnut Jordan Troopers from Herrett's (to me they feel and look better). When I tested the .500 in 2003, I swore it would be my last time doing the extensive shooting necessary to develop loads for sixguns at that power level — my wrists and hands just wouldn't take it anymore. But the fact I put over 1,000 rounds through the .460 in my initial testing demonstrates just how much more user-friendly this latest S&W Magnum really is.

BUILT FOR SPEED

Just as it did in 1935 with the .357 Magnum, S&W claimed the high-velocity record for a revolver again in 2005 — the .460 factory round from Cor-Bon, using the 200-grain Barnes XPB bullet, is rated at 2,300 fps. When you consider there are many rifles out there in the same velocity neighborhood with lighter bullets, it's impressive to see just what S&W accomplished. To me, the .460 is a whole lot more practical than the .500. At least those who purchase the 460XVR will probably spend a lot more time shooting this "smaller" 21st century powerhouse.

The Model 460XVR itself weighs 73 ounces when equipped with an 8⅜-inch barrel. According to S&W, the barrel features gain-twist rifling, made possible by a proprietary Electro Chemical Rifling (ECR) method which produces superb accuracy. Gain twist simply means the rifling twist becomes faster toward the muzzle.

S&W MODEL 460XVR

Groups shot at 100 yards with the SSK .460 Encore.

Does it really produce better accuracy? I don't know, but it certainly shoots very well in my hands. Finish is an all satin-stainless steel, capacity of the cylinder is five shots, and the single action trigger pull on mine weighs out at 3¾ pounds — plenty light for a gun this size. The rear sight is fully adjustable and can be removed to reveal holes already drilled and tapped to accommodate a scope mount base. The front sight features interchangeable blades and is provided with a gold bead and an optional Hi-Viz green dot. Even before shooting I installed the green dot and found it very easy to see. Unlike red ramp front sights, which disappear or wash out in bright sunlight for me, the green dot just seems to glow with more intensity.

There is always a lot of hype around any new product, and I really questioned one statement made by S&W in its advertising:

"If you zero its sights at 200 yards, you will bag your buck with a center hold. Zero to 250 yards with no hold over! Just center it and fire. A 460XVR will do the rest."

I know S&W is trying to emphasize the extremely flat trajectory of a 200-grain bullet at 2,300 fps. However,

shooting deer at 250 yards with a revolver is something I will never recommend. I have some extremely accurate revolvers mounted with scope sights, and my self-imposed maximum distance for shooting game is around 125 yards. In fact, there was so much controversy stirred up by this 250-yard claim, S&W quickly backed off from it. That type of shot is for scope-sighted, single-shot pistols chambered in rifle-style cartridges, and even then it requires knowledge of the actual distance, a solid rest and an animal willing to stand still and present a broadside shot. Yes, I know about Elmer Keith and his 600-yard shot on a mule deer using a 6½-inch Smith & Wesson .44 Magnum with iron sights. This needs to be put into proper perspective. First, there are very few Elmer Keiths (if any) around. Secondly, Keith himself admitted it was a desperate attempt to stop a deer — which had been wounded by a rifle shooter — attempting to make it over the top of a ridge and get away to die a lingering death.

OTHER GUN/LOAD OPTIONS

Even before S&W was able to provide test guns, SSK Industries was chambering the Encore in the .460 S&W

S&W MODEL 460XVR

THE SIXGUNS

Two factors help mitigate felt recoil besides the .460 X-frame's weight — the rubber grips (right) and the interchangeable compensator below the distinctive green fiber-optic front sight (left).

Magnum. So in addition to the XVR, I also have had real shooting experience with a 10-inch SSK Custom Encore for testing loads. J.D. Jones of SSK provided the Encore barrel topped with a Leupold variable. With this combination I got 100-yard groups right at 1 inch with factory Cor-Bon loads. This combo I *would* use at 250 yards, if conditions were right.

Although S&W introduced the Model 460 XVR at the 2005 SHOT Show, it decided to do more testing before releasing the guns. Endurance tests of 5,000, 10,000 and 15,000 rounds were performed, as engineers paid special attention to any flexing of the frame with proof loads. As you'd expect, the 460XVR — just like the Model 500 — is manufactured with specials steels and special heat-treating. I had absolutely no malfunctions with the 460XVR except two instances of primers flowing around the firing pin with

the Cor-Bon 200-grain load. This was toward the end of the testing process and the cylinder was pretty dirty, as I had not cleaned the gun nor even run a brush through the barrel. This neglect is not normal, however; and the overall performance testified to the quality of the Model 460XVR. The last five rounds fired grouped into 1¼ inches at 25 yards. The majority of the loads I used were with hard-cast bullets, and the gun seemed to show no propensity for leading. This also speaks highly of the quality of the gas-checked bullets from Cast Performance Bullet Co. and Oregon Trail Bullet Co. that I used. Of course, I also used jacketed bullets from Barnes, Belt Mountain, Hornady and Sierra.

THE COR-BON CONNECTION

When S&W developed the .357 Magnum, it did so in conjunction with Winchester. Twenty years later the .44 Magnum came about with the cooperation of Remington. It's interesting to see both the .500 Magnum and the .460 Magnum ammunition not being developed by one of the older companies, but rather Cor-Bon, a relative newcomer on the scene, but usually an outfit on the cutting edge of ammunition development, especially for handgun hunter and law-enforcement use. Several types of factory

Cor-Bon offers .460 factory loads ranging from a 200-grain spitzer to a 395-grain hard cast. The .460 uses a longer case than the .500 S&W Magnum (right).

SIXGUNS AND THEIR CARTRIDGES

Recoil of the .460 is less than the .500 S&W Magnum, but it's still enough to give John's arms a noticeable "lift."

TEST-FIRE:
S&W MODEL 460XVR (8⅜ INCH)
FACTORY .460 LOADS

LOAD	VELOCITY	4 SHOTS, 25-YARDS	4 SHOTS, 50 YARDS
Cor-Bon 200-gr. XPB	2,324 fps	1⅜"	2¼"
Cor-Bon 250-gr. XPB	1,853 fps	5/8"	2½"
Cor-Bon 325-gr. A-frame	1,634 fps	1⅝"	1¾"
Cor-Bon 395-gr. HC	1,561 fps	2⅛"	4¼"

FACTORY .454 CASULL LOADS

LOAD	VELOCITY	4 SHOTS, 25 YARDS
Buffalo Bore 325-gr. LBT	1,586 fps	1⅜"
Buffalo Bore 360-gr. LBT	1,405 fps	1⅞"
Cor-Bon 300-gr. JSP	1,533 fps	2¼"
Cor-Bon 335-gr. HCFP	1,556 fps	1⅞"
Win. 250-gr. Partition Gold	1,793 fps	2"

FACTORY .45 COLT LOADS

LOAD	VELOCITY	4 SHOTS, 25 YARDS
Buffalo Bore 260-gr. JHP	1,410 fps	1½"
Buffalo Bore 325-gr. LBT	1,359 fps	2¼"

SSK .460 ENCORE (10 INCH)

LOAD	VELOCITY	3 SHOTS, 100 YARDS
Cor-Bon 200 gr. XPB	2,589 fps	7/8"
Cor-Bon 250-gr. XPB	2,091 fps	1⅜"
Cor-Bon 325-gr. BC A-frame	1,987 fps	1⅜"
Cor-Bon 395-gr. HC	1,787 fps	Poor
Barnes 200-gr. JHP/40.0 gr. L'il Gun	2,228 fps	1¾"
Hornady 300-gr. XTP-JHP/36.0 gr. AA#9	1,986 fps	1½"*
Sierra 300-gr. JFP/40.0 gr. L'il Gun	2,102 fps	2"*

*Starline Brass; CCI #200 Large Rifle Primers

loads available for the .460 S&W Magnum comes in Cor-Bon's distinctive black, white and blue boxes.

I have had experience with four factory offerings for the .460 S&W Magnum from Cor-Bon. First we have the muzzle velocity champion ammunition giving the Model 460XVR the undisputed title as not only the "Highest Velocity Revolver in the World" but also holder of a second title of "The Most Powerful .45 Caliber Revolver in the World." Both stem from the use of Cor-Bon's sizzling 200-grain Barnes' XPB load (MV: 2,300 fps; ME: 2,350 ft/lbs). As we go up the line using heavier bullets, of course, the muzzle velocity changes dramatically as does the muzzle energy.

The 250-grain XPB spitzer is rated at 1,900 fps (ME: 2,004 ft/lbs); the 325-grain Bonded Core A-frame, 1,650 fps (1,965 ft/lbs); and the 395-grain Hard Cast, 1,550 fps (2,108 ft/lbs).

I fired all four from both an 8⅜-inch Model 460XVR and a 10-inch SSK Encore. The S&W was equipped with the standard factory sights, while the Encore was equipped with a Leupold 2.5-8x LER scope on a SSK T'SOB mount.

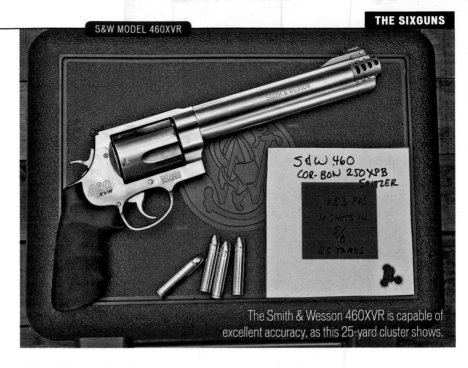

S&W MODEL 460XVR

The Smith & Wesson 460XVR is capable of excellent accuracy, as this 25-yard cluster shows.

These are the muzzle velocities I got from the S&W: the 200-grain XPB at 2,324 fps; 250-grain XPB at 1,853 fps; the 325-grain A-frame at 1,634 fps; and the 395-grain Hard Cast at 1,561 fps. You will notice Cor-Bon does *not* pad its velocity ratings.

When I switched to the 10-inch, the muzzle velocities were significantly higher (as expected). In the same order, this is how things added up: 2,589 fps, 2,091 fps, 1,987 fps and 1,787 fps.

From an accuracy standpoint, the results for the Encore delivered 100-yard, rifle-type groups with the 200-grain XPB, 250-grain XPB and the 325-grain A-frame. However, the 395-grain Hard Cast would not stay on paper.

When I switched back to the S&W, all four loads shot well for me at 25 yards and opened up a bit at 50 (the 395-grain HC load was slightly over four inches). In all fairness, it is very difficult to come up with a barrel twist that can handle such a wide range of bullet weights. You can have optimum results with 200- or 400-grain bullets, but I suspect it would be very hard to have one barrel provide extreme accuracy for both.

YES, IT'S A .45

This is a book on .45s and, although advertised as a .460, this latest magnum from S&W is actually a .45, taking the same diameter bullets as the .45 Colt and .454 Casull. That is, in a properly chambered cylinder, it will handle bullets in the .451- to .452-inch diameter range. The Model 460XVR also accepts the .45 Colt and .454 Casull as "lighter" loads, although it is difficult to regard some of the heavy-duty .45 Colt and .454 Casull factory loads as *light*. But I found both would be good enough to serve as an "understudy" for the .460.

However, the same precaution should be taken into consideration as when using .38 Specials in a .357 Magnum, or .44 Specials in a .44 Magnum, or .45 Colts in a .454 Casull. Extensive use of the shorter cases in the longer cylinders can result in a ring developing in the chamber right above the case mouth. If the cylinder is not routinely (and thoroughly) scrubbed after using the shorter cases, it may be difficult to chamber the longer rounds. Keep those chambers clean and there should be no problem.

Life is full of trade-offs and the Model 460XVR is a perfect example. Its weight of 4½ pounds (plus the compensator and rubber grips) make it relatively easy to shoot but difficult to pack. However, any "shoulder holster" designed to ride across the stomach should do much to aid ease of carry.

Regardless of its bulk, I like the Model 460XVR if for no other reason than it is not a .500 S&W Magnum! ◉

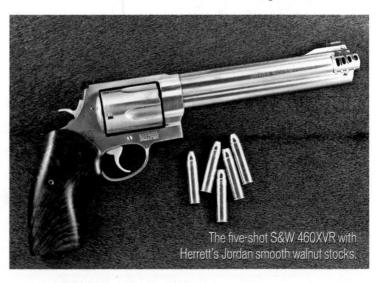

The five-shot S&W 460XVR with Herrett's Jordan smooth walnut stocks.

The original Old Model .45 Colt Blackhawk was made in two standard barrel lengths — 7½ and 4⅝ inches .

RUGER .45 BLACKHAWK & BISLEY

CHAPTER 16

In 1955 Bill Ruger modernized the centerfire single action with the introduction of the Blackhawk. Using the virtually unbreakable coil-spring action of his Single-Six .22, Ruger enlarged the frame to the size of the Colt SAA and chambered it for the .357 Magnum. He also flat-topped the frame and incorporated a fully adjustable micro rear sight matched up with a ramp front. Barrel length of the original Ruger .357 was an easy packin' 4⅝ inches, and the grip frame was identical to that of the Colt. With it, Ruger had given sixgunners the perfect outdoorsman's revolver.

Writing in 1955, Elmer Keith said:

"We would have preferred a slightly larger frame and a cylinder a bit larger in diameter, especially for the .45 Colt cartridge, but this .357 Ruger is one honey of a gun and amply heavy for the .357 and .44 Special and will give the standard chamber wall thickness if Bill ever chambers it for the .45 Colt."

Perhaps the .44 Special *would* have followed on the heels of the .357, but in late 1955, the .44 Magnum arrived. Ruger tried to chamber the Blackhawk for the new .44, but when a prototype blew during proof-testing, he wisely increased the size of the frame and the diameter of the cylinder.

Keith may not have had his .45 Colt, but the basic plat-

This Ruger stainless steel New Model Blackhawk in .45 Colt has been thoroughly "Bisley-ized."

form for building one was there with the beefed-up frame.

Both the .357 and .44 Magnum Blackhawks are now known to collectors as "Flat-Tops." They would be in production until 1963, when what are now known as the "Old Models" emerged. Since Ruger had introduced the .44 Magnum Super Blackhawk in 1959, the Flat-Top .44 Magnum was dropped with the advent of the Old Models. These three-screw variants had two "improvements." The same protective ears found on both sides of the rear sight of the Super Blackhawk were now incorporated into all Ruger single actions, and the grip frame was changed from the XR3 "Colt-style" to the XR3-RED size, allowing more room between the back of the trigger guard and the front strap. To me, this change was ill-conceived and, whenever possible, I've fitted the original XR3 to my working Old Model Blackhawks.

The .44 Magnum Flat-Top was now gone, however the .357 Magnum was joined by the .41 Magnum in 1965, a .30 Carbine version in 1968 and, finally, the .45 Colt in 1970. At the time I was attending graduate school in Missoula, Montana, and trying to find any way to keep my sanity while being away from my family. I wandered into the local gun shop, and there it was — a .45 Colt Blackhawk with a 7½-inch barrel. I didn't even notice the extra .45 ACP cylinder as I made arrangements for it to be shipped to my FFL dealer back in Idaho. Turned out the Old Model would only remain

in production for three years more, and a few were even made with the Super Blackhawk brass grip frame.

A POWER PLATFORM

Just as Keith had suggested, Ruger wisely went with the .44 Flat-Top/Super Blackhawk platform. This opened whole new vistas for the ancient .45 Colt. For the first time since 1873, we now had a sixgun capable of using the large capacity of the old black-powder case. With the coming of smokeless powder in the 1890s, its large volume could not be utilized with higher pressures of smokeless considering the available sixguns at the time. The larger .45 Blackhawk allowed us to shoot 250-grain cast bullets at .44 Magnum velocities. And, even more importantly for the handgun hunter, we could now safely drive 300-grain bullets at 1,200 fps.

At the time, however, we had no extra-heavy .45 Colt sixgun bullets. So many of us resized 300-grain .45-70 bullets down to .452 inch. Cast bullets worked pretty well, but jacketed ones had to be thoroughly lubed with oil before sizing. My friend Jim Taylor and I both settled on a charge of 18.5 grains of #2400, which clocked out at 1,100 to 1,200 fps, depending on barrel length. With the coming of specially designed 300-grain bullets for the .45 Colt — plus the advent of both Hodgdon's H110 and Winchester's 296 powder — heavy loads became much easier to put together.

The Bisley Model grip frame on a pair of Rugers (top and bottom) compared to the the grip frame configuration of Keith's No. 5 (center).

test. I carefully molded bullets of the proper alloy for use with black powder, sized and lubed them with a lubricant specifically designed for black powder, and loaded them into balloonhead .44 Russian brass. The first 25 shots, without cleaning in between, cut one ragged hole at 25 yards. So, was the accuracy reputation of the .44 Russian true? Or was it the sixgun? Perhaps it was both.

The Bisley, in various calibers, lasted until 1912. However, in the mid-1920s, a young cowpoke by the name of Elmer Keith was starting to become known in the gun writing circles. A fellow by the name of Harold Croft of Pennsylvania took the train all way across country to meet with Keith, who was then ranching outside Durkee, Oregon. Croft did not believe what Keith had been writing about long-range shooting with a sixgun, so he brought a suitcase full of .45 Colt sixguns to actually see what Keith could do.

Croft's ideas had been turned into reality by Sedgley and Houchins, two well-known gunsmiths of the time. He took four Featherweight .45 Colts which had been flat-topped and fitted with adjustable sights to Durkee. Keith liked what he saw and — along with the ideas of Harold Croft and gunsmiths Neal Houchins, R.F. Sedgley and J.D. O'Meara, working together — a standard Colt SAA was welded up to make a heavy flat-top. The grip frame was made by mating a standard Colt SAA trigger guard and a Bisley backstrap. The latter had

These .45 Colt Flat-Top New Models were commissioned by Lipsey's — one of Ruger's top distributors. The leather is by El Paso Saddlery.

John feels the Bisley Blackhawk grip configuration is the best choice for handling some of his livelier handloads.

I do not believe any properly designed revolver cartridge is any more inherently accurate than any other.

to be shortened and reshaped somewhat to come up with what Keith perceived as the perfect grip frame. The chambering was .44 Special, and Keith called it his No. 5. Keith had switched to the .44 Special a few years earlier when he blew up at least one — maybe more — .45 Colt SAAs. He was probably using a black-powder gun matched up with all the powder he could grind up to the consistency of flour and packed in the cartridge case under a 300-grain .45-70 bullet. Had the cylinder been a little stronger — and had Keith had more modern powder to work with — his No. 5 may well have been chambered in .45 Colt.

Keith tried to convince Colt to produce this modernized Bisley, but his pleas fell on deaf ears. Colt has never seen fit to resurrect the Bisley. However, what Colt would not do, Bill Ruger later would. Keith's ideas — adjustable sights on a flat-topped frame — was realized in the Super Blackhawk. But did his legendary No. 5 influence Ruger's eventual Bisley? In R.L. Wilson's *Ruger & His Guns,* we find this quote from then-president, Steve Sanetti:

"Many shooters like the grip frame shape and the curved 'Bisley' style hammer/trigger configuration of the Ruger. Many believe that we simply copied Elmer Keith's No. 5 grip design, but I can tell you that these designs are strictly from Larry Larson and Bill Ruger, with a nod to the original Colt Bisley. Nobody copied Keith's design."

They may not have copied Keith's design, but they surely took a peek at it! Keith's No. 5 grip frame was made to fit his rather small hands; Ruger's is longer to accommodate average and larger-sized hands. But the basic idea of mating an SAA trigger guard with a Bisley backstrap is still there.

I feel that it is, without a doubt, the most comfortable single-action grip frame for shooting heavy loads. There are trade-offs however. The Bisley grip frame is the most comfortable for me, but the bottom of the curved trigger catches the bottom of my trigger finger which for many years now has built up scar tissue and is also larger than the corresponding finger on my left hand.

The Ruger Bisley arrived in 1985. Two sizes were originally produced, Super Blackhawk and Single-Six. The larger version arrived only with a blued finish, a 7½-inch barrel and a choice of four chamberings: .357 Magnum, .41 Magnum, .44 Magnum and .45 Colt. The Single-Six version was offered in .22 Long Rifle and .32 H&R Magnum, with both fixed and adjustable sighted versions having 6½-inch barrels.

Ruger Bisleys come and go in the Ruger catalog. Currently only two standard centerfire models are offered, 7½-

The Ruger Old Model .45 Blackhawk on the left has been customized to look like the Colt New Frontier on the right. The leather is from El Paso Saddlery.

inch blued versions in both .44 Magnum and .45 Colt. There have also been special runs for major distributors — most often these are 5½-inch stainless steel versions.

In 1992 Ruger took its basic stainless steel Super Blackhawk and fitted it with a heavy-ribbed barrel cut with scallops to accept Ruger scope rings. Dubbed the Hunter Model, it was also fitted with a longer ejector tube and ejector rod for more positive removal of fired cartridges. This is without a doubt one of the best bargains ever offered to the handgun hunter. I am not a fan of the Super Blackhawk grip frame — the square-backed trigger guard catches the built-up scar tissue on my middle finger. Ruger must have been thinking of me when they introduced the Bisley Hunter Model — the same basic sixgun fitted with a Bisley grip frame, hammer and trigger. It's the best bargain out there for handgun hunters — especially so for those who prefer a scoped handgun.

TAMING THE BIG STUFF

Just prior to the arrival of the Bisley, John Linebaugh of Cody, Wyoming, began building custom heavy-duty,

five-shot single actions. He began with the .45 Colt and then designed two cartridges — the .500 and .475 Linebaughs. These latter two were originally made by using trimmed down .348 Winchester and .45-70 brass. They fired heavy cast bullets of 380 to 440 grains at magnum velocities. John maintains without the Bisley grip frame, most sixgunners could not handle these cartridges. My original .357 Bisley was sent off to John and converted to .500 Linebaugh.

My other three Bisleys were basically kept stock — except for the addition of fancy walnut stocks by Charles Able. I recently sent all three of them to Ben Forkin of Forkin Custom Classics to be given the works. Barrel lengths were cut to 5½ inches, new front sights were fitted mated up with Bowen rear sights, the actions were totally tuned and tightened, and they were all then reblued except for the mainframes, loading gates and hammers (which were all case-colored by Doug Turnbull). These are about as beautiful as a Bisley gets. Normally I prefer the 7½-inch barrel on most single actions, especially for hunting, but on the Bisley I prefer the balance of a 5½-inch barrel.

This New Model .45 Colt Blackhawk customized by Milt Morrison was presented to Taffin in 1995 by The Shootists.

MORE CUSTOM RUGER .45'S

Several years ago I had Jim Stroh build a 5½-inch five-shot heavy-duty .45 Colt on a Super Blackhawk. It features an interchangeable front sight system, unfluted full-sized .45 Colt cylinder, and a matte blue finish. It didn't take me long to find I couldn't handle it with the Super Blackhawk grip frame, so it was sent back to Stroh who used Bisley parts to turn it into a Bisley Model. Now I can shoot it with pleasure.

When the Bisley Vaquero arrived, I bought two of them, one blue and one stainless, so I could take all the Bisley parts and fit them to a pair of 4⅝-inch .45 Colt Blackhawks, one blue and one stainless. Either is a great candidate for the coveted title of "Perfect Packin' Pistol."

A DOWNSIZED COLT .45

As we've seen, by 1972 it seemed the smaller "first edition" Blackhawk was gone forever, but to celebrate the 50th Anniversary of the Colt SAA-sized original, Ruger brought out a flat-top New Model to match the original in 2005. As an added bonus, they brought back the original XR3 grip frame configuration (in steel instead of the original alloy). Ruger even resurrected the original micro rear sight.

This was, of course, a one-shot, one-year deal. That could've been the end of it, except for the farsightedness of one of our top firearms distributors, Lipsey's. When that original .357 Blackhawk arrived back in 1955, Elmer Keith wanted

SELECTED LOADS
FOR RUGER .45 COLT SINGLE ACTIONS

GUN	BARREL LENGTH	LOAD	VELOCITY	5 SHOTS, 20 YARDS
BULLET: OREGON TRAIL 255-GRAIN SWC				
OM Blackhawk	7 ½"	20.0 gr. 4227	996 fps	1 ½"
OM Blackhawk	7 ½"	8.5 gr. Unique	989 fps	1 ⅛"
NM Blackhawk	7 ½"	18.5 gr. #2400	1,214 fps	1 ¼"
Bisley Blackhawk	5 ½"	9.0 gr. Unique	922 fps	1 ⅝"
OM Blackhawk	4 ⅝"	20.0 gr. 4227	967 fps	1 ⅝"
OM Blackhawk	4 ⅝"	8.5 gr. Unique	951 fps	1"
BULLET: LYMAN KEITH #454424				
OM Blackhawk	7 ½"	10.0 gr. Unique	1,115 fps	1 ½"
NM Blackhawk	7 ½"	10.0 gr. Unique	1,034 fps	1 ⅛"
Bisley Blackhawk	5 ½"	20.0 gr. 4227	967 fps	1 ½"
OM Blackhawk	4 ⅝"	9.0 gr. Unique	976 fps	1 ⅝"
OM Blackhawk	4 ⅝"	10.0 gr. Unique	1,073 fps	1 ⅜"

HEAVY HUNTING LOADS
FOR RUGER .45 COLT SINGLE ACTIONS

BULLET	LOAD	4 ⅝"	7 ½"
Lyman #454424 Keith	20.0 gr. #2400	1,168 fps	1,241 fps
NEI #451.310 Keith*	21.0 gr. WW296	1,124 fps	1,196 fp
Lyman #454628GC**	18.5 gr. #2400	1,190 fps	1,273 fps
Lyman #454424GC**	21.0 gr. WW296	1,102 fps	1,174 fps

* 310-gr. SWC   **305-gr. FNGC

TEST-FIRE: LIPSEY'S RUGER FLAT-TOP NEW MODEL (5½ INCH)

.45 COLT

BULLET/LOAD	VELOCITY	5 SHOTS, 20 YARDS
Black Hills 250-gr. RNFP	750 fps	1⅜"
Federal 225-gr. LSWCHP	817 fps	1¾"
Speer 250-gr. GDHP	839 fps	1½"
Winchester 225-gr. Silvertip	782 fps	1⅛"
Lachmiller 45-255-gr. LC/8.5 Unique	939 fps	1¾"
RCBS #45-255-gr. KT/8.0 gr. Unique	922 fps	1⅛"
Hornady 255-gr. L/7.1 gr. WW231	748 fps	7/8"
Oregon Trail 250-gr. RNFP/8.0 gr. Unique	833 fps	1¾"
Oregon Trail 250-gr. RNFP/7.1 gr. WW231	769 fps	1⅜"
Oregon Trail 250-gr. RNFP/18.5 gr. #4227	841 fps	7/8"
Oregon Trail 250-gr. RNFP/6.2 gr. N-100	818 fps	1⅛"
Oregon Trail 255-gr. SWC/6.2 gr. WW452AA	796 fps	1¾"
Speer 250-gr. LSWC/7.8 gr. Unique	759 fps	1"

.45 ACP

BULLET/LOAD	VELOCITY	5 SHOTS, 20 YARDS
Black Hills 185-gr. JHP	1,001 fps	1"
Black Hills 230-gr. JHP	825 fps	3/4
Black Hills 230-gr. JHP +P	939 fps	1⅛"
Black Hills 230-gr. FMJ	817 fps	1⅜"
Black Hills 230-gr. RNL	892 fps	1⅝"
Federal 185-gr. JHP	945 fps	1¼"
Federal 230-gr. FMJ	788 fps	1¼"
Federal 230-gr. H-S HP	928 fps	1⅜"
Remington 185-gr. JHP	1,071 fps	1"
Speer 200 FMJ	864 fps	1"
Speer 230 FMJ	847 fps	1¾"
Winchester 185 Super Match	800 fps	1"
Winchester 230 FMJ	845 fps	3/4"
Winchester 230 BEB	905 fps	1"
Oregon Trail 200SWC/5.0 gr. Bullseye	863 fps	1"
Oregon Trail 200 SWC/7.0 gr. Unique	1,070 fps	1"
H&G #68/7.2 gr. Unique	1,094 fps	1"
Lyman #452460/7.0 gr. Unique	895 fps	1"

future models in .44 Special and .45 Colt. Neither one ever materialized, mainly due to the arrival of the .44 Magnum one year later. To safely hold the new .44 Magnum, both frame and cylinder were, of necessity, increased in size.

In 2005 I talked to Ruger's then-president about using the New Model .357 Magnum Flat-Top as the basis for a .44 Special version. He didn't say yes, but then again, he didn't say no and, thanks to Lipsey's placing an order for 2,000 units, the .44 Special became a reality (a year later it became a standard catalog item). Lipsey's then took the next logical step and ordered the New Model .357 Magnum Flat-Top in a .45 Colt version — in both blue and stainless steel — with 4⅝- and 5½-inch barrel length options. They didn't stop there, but went ever further and made the .45 Flat-Top Convertibles with an extra .45 ACP cylinder along with each sixgun.

Let me repeat the fact that the New Model .45 Colt Flat-Top Ruger Blackhawks are basically the same size as the original .357 Magnum Blackhawk and the Colt SAA. After the original .45 Blackhawk arrived back in the early '70s, handloaders found they could go well above loads suitable for the Colt SAA, and most reloading manuals started featuring a special section for the .45 Ruger Blackhawk. Some of the loads so listed are in the 25,000-32,000 psi range and *must never* be used in the new Flat-Top .45. For me that means 250- to 260-grain bullets should be kept under 1,100 fps. Save the heavier loads for larger frames.

Over the years .45 Colt sixguns have been plagued with chamber throats in the cylinders which have not adhered to any sort of standard specifications. I have found .45 Colt cylinder throats as tight as .449 inch and as large as .457 inch with the ideal being somewhere around .451-.452 inch. Tight cylinders are a relatively easy fix, requiring only a throat reamer and the skill to use it. Of course, overly large cylinder throats can be overcome by using larger diameter bullets, or in extreme cases, the cylinders can be replaced. Sending a .452-inch bullet down a .457-inch chamber throat doesn't do much for accuracy. But both of the cylinders on these Ruger .45 Convertibles have been cut correctly. With the blue version, the .45 Colt cylinder has uniform throats at .451 inch, while all of the .45 ACP holes measure .452 inch. With the

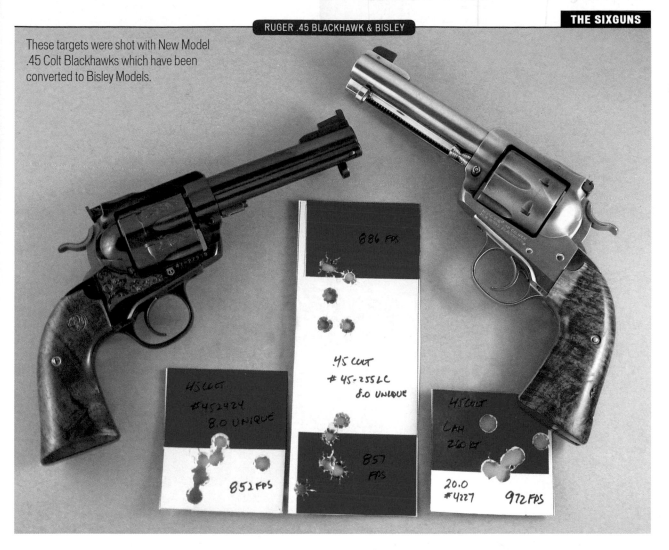

These targets were shot with New Model .45 Colt Blackhawks which have been converted to Bisley Models.

stainless, both the .45 Colt and .45 ACP cylinder throats are all a uniform .451 inch. This is a large part of the reason these sixguns shoot so well.

Both the blued and stainless steel versions are offered in 4⅝- and 5½-inch barrel lengths. Sights consist of a black micro rear with a nice square notch matched up with a black ramp front with a sloping blade. Too often, stainless sixguns have stainless steel front sights, which are tough to pick up in bright light. Normally, New Model Ruger single actions come with trigger pulls heavier than I prefer. Normally I remove one grip panel and slip one side of the trigger return spring off its post, resulting in a lighter pull. With these two guns, this resulted in trigger pulls of 2½ to 3 pounds. The steel grip frames are basically the same size and shape as the original alloy XR3s — very close in size and shape to the original Colt SAA, which is the best grip ever devised for standard loads in a single action.

The grip panels are faux ivory with black Ruger medallions. The panels on the blue version are such that the pinhole on the grip doesn't quite match up with the pins on the grip frame, resulting in an overlap on the backstrap and an underlap on the frontstrap. The stainless gun has grip panels with a correct fit. Both are so nice, I've fitted them with custom grips.

Whether I use standard (or slightly above) .45 Colt or .45 ACP loads, felt recoil is never close to punishing. I normally like to load standard .45 Colts with 250- to 260-grain cast bullets at around 900-1,000 fps. Elmer Keith's original bullet, Lyman's #454424 weighs around 260 grains from my alloy; however, some .45 Colt cylinders are just a smidgen short when this bullet is crimped in the crimping groove.

Several years ago Dave Scovill set about to basically redesign the Keith bullet by slightly shortening the nose and adding more weight in the body. The result is the RCBS #45-270SAA, which weighs around 280 grains from my wheelweight alloy. Loaded over 10.0 grains of Unique, it clocks just over 1,000 fps and groups into an inch, making it an excellent everyday workin' load. ◎

THE SIXGUNS

John set up this 7½-inch Redhawk .45 Colt as a dedicated hunting tool. The barrel-mounted scope is held with Ruger rings. The grips are by BearHug.

RUGER REDHAWK .45 & SUPER REDHAWK .454

Whether you want to shoot .45 Colt or .454 Casull, Cor-Bon offers a plethora of high-performance loads in either caliber.

CHAPTER 17

In 1992, I found myself in Bill Ruger's office to conduct an interview. I was ushered into his modest office — piled high with gun magazines of every description — which contained some notable firearms, as well as a prototype semiauto pistol on his desk. We were talking about things in general when we were interrupted with a phone call — one that he was told he had to take. Although I could only hear Bill's end of the conversation, I knew it was not good news. As I sat there, Bill received word of the seriousness of his son Tom's illness.

Sharing something as difficult as this with a man makes you feel close to him, and I've had a very special feeling for

Bill ever since then — in addition to the appreciation I've always had for his firearms genius.

During our conversation I asked Bill about bringing out a .45 Colt Redhawk. I have no way of knowing if it had any

For everyday packing, John prefers his .45 Redhawk in 4-inch, iron-sighted trim.

bearing on his decision, but we now have a Redhawk chambered in the grand, old cartridge. Over the years the Redhawk had been offered in .357 Magnum and .41 Magnum in addition to the standard .44 Magnum offering. The two former chamberings are now long gone, but the big .44 and the .45 Colt remain.

The .45 Colt version is probably the sturdiest double-action .45 ever offered. It has been available in 5½-inch as well as 7½-inch versions. Both can be had with — or without — the option consisting of two scallops on the barrel to accept Ruger scope rings.

BIG RED

The only fault most of us can find with the Redhawk is the fact that it is difficult to get a really good trigger on Big Red. It is strange to read the account of the engineers and designers of the Redhawk as they talk about the smooth double-action trigger pull and good single-action pull. Not quite. My two Redhawks came with single-action trigger pulls that measure 6¾ and 6¼ pounds.

The Redhawk gains its strength in many ways. The threaded area of the frame is very thick, double what you find in many other sixguns, and the massive cylinder is locked at the rear and front of the cylinder itself rather than at the end of the ejector rod. The barrel carries a heavy rib and the top strap is brute-strong. My .45 Colt Redhawk is the scope-ready 7½-inch version, complete with Ruger rings for mounting a 2x Burris LER pistol scope. I've since added a 5½-inch easy packin' version. The 5½-inch is equipped with an easy-to-see baby blue Ruger front sight. And to help soften the recoil of stout loads, I put on a set of Uncle Mike's finger-groove grips to replace the factory wood stocks. For the scoped gun, I used BearHugs. Both sets of aftermarket grips were appreciated when I started launching 265-grain bullets at 1,465 fps, 335-grain bullets at 1,275 fps and 360-grain bullets at 1,180 fps.

With the scoped .45 Redhawk, accuracy is exceptional, despite the heavy trigger pull. Of all the loads initially tested — five factory heavy-duty hunting loads and 23 handloads using both cast and jacketed bullets with weights from 250 grains up to 335 grains — the average group size for five shots at 25 yards was just over an inch. Astounding!

The factory hunting loads I tried included two from Buffalo Bore and two from Cor-Bon. Buffalo Bore's 300-grain Speer clocked out at 1,367 fps over the skyscreens of my

RUGER REDHAWK .45 COLT (7½ INCH)

TEST-FIRE

LOAD	VELOCITY	5 SHOTS, 25 YARDS
Buffalo Bore 300-gr. Speer	1,367 fps	3/4"
Buffalo Bore 325-gr. LBT	1,392 fps	3/4"
Cor-Bon 265-gr. BC +P	1,347 fps	1"
Cor-Bon 300-gr. BC +P	1,271 fps	1 3/8"
Hornady 250-gr. XTP/20.0 gr. #2400	1,137 fps	7/8"
Hornady 300-gr.XTP/21.2 gr. H110	1,064 fps	1"
Lyman/Casull 300-gr. GC/21.5 gr. WW296	1,240 fps	7/8"
LBT 260-gr. KT/10.0 gr. Unique	1,059	3/4"
LBT 260-gr. KT/21.0 gr. #2400	1,294 fps	1 3/8"
CPBC 265-gr. LBT/26.0 gr. WW296	1,464 fps	1"
CPBC 325-gr. LBT/21.0 gr. WW296	1,234 fps	1"
CPBC 335-gr. LBT/21.0 gr. WW296	1,275 fps	1 1/8"
CPBC 360-gr. LBT/19.5 gr. WW296	1,180 fps	1 1/4"
Lyman/Keith #454424/18.5 gr. #2400	1,093 fps	1 1/4"
Lyman/Thomp. #452490GC/23.0 4227	1,165 fps	1 1/8"
Lyman/Thomp. #452490GC/20.0 gr. #2400	1,306 fps	7/8"
NEI 310-gr. KT/21.2 gr. H110	1,127 fps	1 1/8"
NEI 325-gr. KT/21.2 gr. H110	1,208 fps	1 1/4"
Sierra 240-gr. JHP/24.0 gr. H4227	1,058 fps	7/8"
Sierra 240-gr. JHP/25.0 gr. WW296	1,250 fps	1 3/8"
Sierra 240-gr. JHP/26.0 gr. WW296	1,301 fps	7/8"
Hornady 250-gr. JHP/24.0 gr.H4227	1,087 fps	1 1/2"
Hornady 250-gr. /26.0 gr.WW296	1,292 fps	1/2"
Hornady 250-gr. XTP/26.0 gr. H110	1,364 fps	1 3/8"
Speer 260-gr. JHP/24.0 gr. H4227	1,124 fps	3/4"

Oehler Model 35P and delivered five shots in ¾ inch at 25 yards. The Buffalo Bore 325-grain LBT exhibited the same accuracy with a muzzle velocity of 1,392 fps. These loads are *not* for the faint of heart and are suitable only for modern, heavy-framed .45 Colt sixguns. The Cor-Bon load I tried included its 265-grain Bonded Core +P at 1,347 fps and a 300-grain Bonded Core +P at 1,271 fps. Both were right at an inch at 25 yards.

Those four heavyweights, however, are for big-boned, heavily muscled critters. For whitetails I like Hornady's 250-

grain XTP over 20 grains of Alliant #2400. In the 7½-inch Redhawk, this one clocks 1,137 fps with near pinpoint accuracy (⅞ inch). Cast Performance Bullet Co. offers hard-cast LBTs for use in the Redhawk. I assemble them with Winchester's 296 and CCI #350 Magnum primers. The 265-grain bullet over 26.0 grains yields 1,464 fps and groups at an inch. For the 325-grain LBT, I use 21.0 grains for 1,234 fps (also an inch). The 335 grainer with the same charge comes in at 1,275 fps (1⅛ inches), while the super-heavy 360 grainer over 19.5 grains groups into 1¼ inches with a muzzle velocity of 1,180 fps. All of these loads will penetrate from here to Sunday.

REDHAWK IMPROVEMENTS

The Redhawk has been a most popular hunting handgun in its original .44 Magnum chambering. So much so that it was joined — rather than supplanted — by the Super Redhawk as Ruger had planned. But there is a large segment of the sixgun shooting population that holds to the idea that anything the .44 can do, the .45 can do better.

The 7½-inch .45 Colt Redhawk is a good choice for hunting big game. The original Redhawks were — and are — bull strong. They handle heavy loads easily and beg for more, but the shooter is another matter. With the relatively small factory wood stocks, I find felt recoil with heavy bullet loads to be punishing, so both my long-barreled Redhawks wear custom grips.

Ruger has made two changes from the original Redhawk. The factory 4-inch barreled model wears totally new grips. Instead of the smallish, smooth wooden stocks found on the older guns, these carry finger-grooved, pebble-grain rubber grips from Hogue.

The original Redhawk also featured fully adjustable sights — with an interchangeable front sight system. On the 4-inch gun they have since decided to go with a fixed front ramp-style blade and a red insert. I usually "black out" the red and wish they'd have stayed with the interchangeable system on the "packin" Redhawk.

For an every day carrying load for the 4-inch .45 Colt Ruger Redhawk, I normally go with the 260-grain Lyman/

Meet an exceptionally serious snubbie — the .454 Alaskan. In this truncated stomper, the .45 Colt capability is a welcome one from a 2¾-inch barrel (inset).

Keith #454424 over 9.0 grains of Unique for around 950 fps and superb accuracy. For a heavier load, Sierra's 300-grain JSP over 22.0 grains of #4227 clocks 1,100 fps. I consider this one too heavy for smaller-framed .45s.

A BIGGER BIRD

Once S&W stood the sixgunning world on its ear with the .44 Magnum, many thought it would be impossible for any sixgun to surpass it in power. They were proven wrong when, in 1983, the .454 Casull arrived in the Freedom Arms sixgun. In 1987, however, Ruger's Redhawk was made even larger and stronger with the Super Redhawk. It, too, was chambered for the big, bad .454 Casull.

The Super Redhawk is not even a bigger Redhawk or an improved Redhawk. It's simply a stronger — though different — sixgun. So, why was it introduced? The answer is, trouble had arisen with the Redhawk about the time the company had decided to change the Redhawk so it had the grip and trigger mechanism of the GP-100. Before this could be done, though, a few Redhawks started blowing the barrel shanks at the threaded portion. To combat this, the frame was extended to enclose about 2½ inches of the barrel which, in turn, made room for both of the scope rings to be on the frame rather than on the barrel. Now we know why the Super Redhawk is such a strange looking sixgun!

Then about the time Ruger decided to change the Redhawk to this configuration, it was discovered the problem with the Redhawk was not a design flaw or weakness but, of all things, was being caused by the lubricant being applied to the threads of the Redhawk barrel before it was screwed into the frame. So what to do now? Do you drop the very popular Redhawk because of a problem that did not exist? Do you forget the new design and stay with the Redhawk? Or do you bring out the Super Redhawk while still keeping the Redhawk? Sixgunners everywhere are happy Ruger chose the latter option.

SIXGUNS AND THEIR CARTRIDGES

How did Ruger view the new Super Redhawk? Its literature read:

"The ultimate development in a heavy frame double action revolver of unusual appeal for today's outdoorsmen, hunters, and silhouetters shooters. It has all the mechanical features and patented improvements of Ruger's newest double action the GP-100 with a number of important additional features. Unique new Ruger Cushioned Grip panels are anatomically designed to fit the hands of a majority of shooters. The extended frame is designed to accommodate the Ruger Integral Scope Mounting System which positions the scope rearward for superior balance and performance. Interchangeable front sight system. Offered in stainless steel in a variety of barrel lengths."

This is, of course, typical hype surrounding any new gun. However, if you cut through it, you'll find Ruger was correct about the "anatomically designed" grips. They ain't pretty but

they work! First chambered in .44 Magnum, the stainless-steel-only Super Redhawk has proven itself to be everything it was claimed to be. It handles the heaviest .44 Magnum loads with ease and is also easy on the shooter. Its four-pound weight (more if a scope is added) combined with the cushioned grip panels make a real comfort difference.

Next Ruger took a giant step forward and chambered its Super Redhawk for the .454 Casull. For those not knowing just what the .454 Casull is about we can easily compare it to a .44 Magnum that uses a 240-grain bullet at 1,400 fps; the .454 Casull is .45 caliber and its 260-grain bullet has a muzzle velocity of 1,800 fps. To obtain this performance one has to raise the 35,000-40,000 pressure range of the .44 Magnum up to 60,000 or more. That is very significant additional strain placed on a sixgun frame and cylinder.

Rumors of a .454 Ruger started circulating late in 1997. I was told all about it at the 1998 SHOT Show by someone who told me they had the straight skinny on the project and it would be a single-action Bisley Model with a five-shot cylinder plus an auxiliary cylinder for .45 Colt. A single-action Bisley, a five-shooter with an extra cylinder. Sounded good to me. What did we get? A double-action Super Redhawk, a six-shooter, with one cylinder. So much for those in the know!

John found the Super Redhawk to combine brute .454 power with remarkable precision. And it proved remarkably easy to shoot.

The Super Redhawk even though it is chambered in .454 Casull, and even though both Freedom Arms and Taurus use five-shot cylinders, is a true sixgun with six cartridge holes in the unfluted cylinder. No one should even consider having a .44 Super Redhawk rechambered to .454. When I asked Ruger what changes were made to accommodate the newer, higher-pressure cartridge, I was informed of two major changes. The steel used in the KSRH-7454 (Model number assigned to the Super Redhawk .454) is of a higher grade than that used for the .44 Magnum model, and the heat treating is different. Neither of these can be duplicated by any gunsmith that would convert the .44 to .454 and Ruger, of course, will not convert any existing guns to .454.

The .454 Super Redhawk looks like a .44 Super Redhawk, yet it doesn't somehow. The same lines are there. The same strange profile of the mainframe is maintained. But the overall effect is quite different due to the color — it's called the Target Grey finish. Instead of wood-colored inserts, the Super Redhawk has black laminated grip panels for an almost-futuristic effect. Being very traditional when it comes to sixguns, I like blued steel matched with ivory or some form of fancy stocks of staghorn or exotic woods. But after I installed a nickel-finish 4x Burris using Ruger stainless rings, I found I ended up with a businesslike — but attractive — big-bore handgun.

There are a few other differences. The barrel twist on the .44 Magnum Super Redhawk is 1:20, while that found on the .454 version is a slower 1:24 (to handle the faster and heavier bullets). Due to the slightly larger holes found in the cylinder and barrel of the .454 Super Redhawk, it is a few ounces lighter than the .44 Magnum Redhawk.

OTHER DIFFERENCES

The Super Redhawk's cylinder is marked for the use of .454 *and* .45 Colt ammunition. Freedom Arms has always cautioned against this in its guns for one simple reason. If you fire a lot of .45 Colt loads, a ring will build up in the cylinder just ahead of the case mouth. If you don't scrub it out, it makes the insertion of the .454 cartridges difficult in tight chambers and could also cause pressures to rise dramati-

The Alaskan is very imposing from the front end (above). And the wall thickness of the cylinder (below) is equally impressive.

cally if those rings prevent the .454 crimp from opening as it should when the gun is fired. So if you use .45 Colt ammo in your Super Redhawk, remember to scrub!

Because the Super Redhawk sprang from the GP-100, several other improvements are apparent. The standard Redhawk has never been known for a great trigger. By using the basic GP-100 design, the Super Redhawk employs separate springs for the trigger and hammer, resulting in a much smoother out-of-the-box pull. The Redhawk has one of the best grip frames ever found on a double-action sixgun, but the Super Redhawk's is even better — it's basically a stud allowing for a lot of latitude in terms of custom grips. However, the factory grip on the Super Redhawk is very comfortable with heavy loads (most double-action grip designs are not), and the grip design is much more comfortable during long strings of fire than the Redhawk grip.

Scope rings on the Super Redhawk mount solidly on

SIXGUNS AND THEIR CARTRIDGES

the frame via one large screw, each combined with semi-circular recesses on each side. For added strength, a lug on the bottom of each ring mates with a recess on top of the frame. This allows each ring to be anchored side to side as well as front to back. Once the scope is zeroed, it can be removed and reinstalled with no (or very little) change in point of impact. With nothing more than a quarter to loosen or tighten the base screws, you can have almost-instant access to either scope or iron sights. Standard sights include a red-insert front which is removable by depressing a plunger at the front of the sight base, thus allowing the use of replacement colored nylon front sights which are available as an option. The rear sight is fully adjustable and features a white outline.

The .454 is a serious cartridge and one that must be approached seriously. When I first approached the new .454 Super Redhawk, I was expecting to be spend some grueling moments at the bench. But I shouldn't have worried. It's relatively easy-shooting. Even so, I did not start with top-end loads but worked my way up. First came heavy loaded .45 Colt rounds with 300-grain bullets at 1,100 fps, then 340-grain bullets at 1,250, and then — and only then — did I progress to every .454 factory load at my disposal, with, of course, a few of my .454 handloads.

All my shooting was done with the Burris 4x scope

mounted in Ruger rings. The added weight served to help make things easier. *Any* .454 kicks, but I kept it to a minimum with Uncle Mike's shooting gloves. In all of my shooting, absolutely no malfunctions of any kind occurred, and all fired cases ejected easily from the Super Redhawk's cylinder.

Starting with the .45 Colt loads, my normal powder charge for bullets 300 grains and heavier is 21.5 grains of WW296 or H110. (When I set the powder measure, it weighed out at 21.2 grains, which was fine with me.) My favorite bullets for this application are BRP's 300-grain gas check, LBT's 325-grain WFN, two of NEI's standard Keith designs (300- and 324-grain SWC) and, finally, SSK's really big .45 bullet — a 340-grain FN. Groups for five shots at 25 yards run right at 1 inch for these loads, with muzzle velocities from 1,100 to 1,250 fps. Practically speaking, these are the only loads I'll really need, as they will take care of deer, black bear and wild boar easily.

Next up the .45 Colt ladder are factory loads from Buffalo Bore and Cor-Bon. Buffalo Bore's 300-grain Speer and 325-grain LBT's both shot at around 1,330 fps grouped in 1⅛ inches and ⅝ inch, respectively. Cor-Bon choices also include a 265-grain Bonded Core, a 300-grain BC and a 300-grain JSP. All of these are around 1,275 fps and grouped at 1 inch or less. The upshot of the .45 Colt stuff? Nothing wrong with the way the .454 Super Redhawk shot it – factory or home brewed.

Then I got to the more serious .454 loads from Winchester and Cor-Bon for the really tough stuff. Winchester offers a 260- and 300-grain JFP which are dead ringers performance-wise for the loads formerly offered by Freedom Arms. In the Super Redhawk they clock out at 1,745 and 1,544 fps, respectively, and group at 1 inch or less. My favorite from Winchester for most hunting applications is the 260-grain Partition Gold that clocks out over my Oehler Model 35P at a smoking-hot 1,803 fps. When the Super Redhawk was still relatively new, I handed one to my friend Ray Walters and asked him to shoot it and tell me what he thought the load was. It was loaded

The Target Grey-finished Super Redhawk has been offered in .480 Ruger (top) as well as .454 Casull. The .454 version, of course, will also handle the stoutest .45 Colt loads you can stand.

with six rounds of the Partition Gold. After firing a cylinderful, Walters guessed it was a 240-grain load at 1,400 fps. He was *quite* surprised to find he was so far off the mark. It really does shoot easy!

Cor-Bon covers all the bases .454-wise. From thc Super Redhawk's 7½-inch barrel, its offerings are very impressive and include a 265-grain Bonded Core (1,641 fps), a 285-grain BC (1,505 fps), a 300-grain BC (1,515 fps), a 320-grain Penetrator (1,508 fps), a 335-grain Hard Cast (1,508 fps) and a 360-grain Penetrator (1,441 fps). These are all designed for serious hunting applications against big animals. In short, the .454 Super Redhawk can be called upon to hunt anything that walks. *Anything.*

A SUPER SNUBBIE

Ruger's "biggest little" sixgun is the Alaskan. This latest Super Redhawk chambered in .454 is designed to be an easy-to-pack survival sixgun — especially in any areas where the big bears roam. To come up with the Alaskan, the barrel of the Super Redhawk is cut off flush with the extended frame. There are no scope cut-out recesses, and a ramp-style front sight is installed on the frame. For grips, the Alaskan has Hogue's rubber finger-grooved Tamer Monogrip (a very welcome addition when firing heavy .45 Colt or .454 loads). Instead of the Target Grey finish of the standard model, we have what appears to be regular matte stainless steel.

The Alaskan may have been designed primarily for use in bear country; however, for anyone who spends time in the outdoors and feels a lot more comfortable with a portable and powerful sixgun at hand, the Alaskan handles the full range of .45 Colt and .454 Casull loads. Standard-level .45 Colt loads are extremely pleasant to shoot in this relatively heavy 42-ounce sixgun. With heavy .45 Colt loads, 300-grain bullets at 1,200 fps or more, the Hogue Tamer Monogrip with its slightly pebbled surface, finger grooves and cushioned back strap begins to be appreciated. Any sixgun loses muzzle velocity with a short barrel, but the Alaskan exhibits a lot less loss than expected. Cor-Bon's .454 loads stay potent with the 260-grain bullet at 1,535 fps and the 300-grain bullet at 1,345 fps. That's still a lot of power.

RUGER SUPER REDHAWK .454 (7½ INCH

.45 COLT LOADS

LOAD	VELOCITY	5 SHOTS, 25 YARDS
Buffalo Bore Heavy .45 Colt 325-gr. LBT-LFN	1,332 fps	5/8"
Buffalo Bore Heavy .45 Colt 300-gr. Speer PSP	1,335 fps	1¼"
Cor-Bon Magnum .45 Colt +P 265-gr. BC	1,277 fps	1"
Cor-Bon Magnum .45 Colt +P 300-gr. BC	1,256 fps	7/8"
Cor-Bon Magnum .45 Colt +P 300-gr. JSP	1,289 fps	1"
Lyman/Casull 300-gr.FNGC/21.2 gr. H110	1,122	1"
LBT 325-gr.WFN/21.2 gr. H110	1,120 fps	1¼"
NEI 310-gr. Keith / 21.2 gr. H110	1,116 fps	1"
NEI 325-gr. Keith / 21.2 gr. H110	1,231 fps	3/4"
SSK 340-gr. FN / 21.2 gr. H110	1,249 fps	1⅜"

.454 CASULL LOADS

LOAD	VELOCITY	5 SHOTS, 25 YARDS
Cor-Bon 265-gr. BC	1,641 fps	1¼"
Cor-Bon 285-gr. BC	1,505 fps	1"
Cor-Bon 300-gr. BC	1,553 fps	1¾"
Cor-Bon 300-gr. JSP	1,515 fps	1⅛"
Cor-Bon 320-gr. Penetrator	1,508 fps	7/8
Cor-Bon 335-gr. HC	1,508 fps	1⅝"
Cor-Bon 360-gr. Penetrator	1,441 fps	1¼"
Winchester 260-gr. JFP	1,745 fps	1"
Winchester 300-gr. JFP	1,544 fps	7/8"
Winchester 250-gr. JHP	1,259 fps (Med. Vel.)	2"
Winchester 260-gr. Part. Gold	1,803 fps	1¼"

Muzzle blast, as expected, is heavier than anything most of us will ever encounter on any sixgun. Thanks to the grips, the Alaskan remains controllable. Anyone armed with one would have a very good chance of surviving a big bear attack. Ruger's advertising says of the Alaskan: "Ruger proudly introduces the perfect revolver for a trek into dangerous game country."

This may well be more than advertising hype, but for my personal use, I prefer the 4-inch barreled .45 Colt with heavy loads over the 2¾-inch barrel of the .454 Alaskan. ◎

THE SIXGUNS

The stainless steel New Vaquero (center) is flanked by a pair of beefier stainless steel original Vaqueros.

RUGER .45 VAQUEROS

CHAPTER 18

My first centerfire Ruger was a .357 Magnum Blackhawk. While it did not have the beautiful flowing lines of the Colt Single Action Army, it was close. And, as I was soon to find out, it was superior in some respects.

Colt flat springs broke, namely hand and bolt springs. Ruger coil springs did not. I was later to find the springs on properly tuned Colt SAAs rarely broke, but I didn't know it at the time and was using stock, untuned Colts for fast draw. It didn't take me long to realize that the ideal solution would be a Colt SAA with Ruger lockwork. That, of course, never happened, but something else did.

BACK TO THE FUTURE

In the early 1990s Bill Ruger showed me what was to be the next Ruger single-action .45 Colt. Cowboy Action Shooting had arrived, and thousands of shooters looked for traditional sixguns for competition. They wanted guns with the old hog wallow groove cut in the top strap instead of fancy adjustable sights. All Ruger centerfire single actions since 1955 had been equipped with modern adjustable sights. So, with no traditional Rugers being available, Cowboy Action competitors went with Colt SAAs or imported replicas thereof. Finally, somebody at Ruger smelled the Cowboy Action coffee and decided to come forth with a traditional single action.

What Bill had shown me that day was the prototype Vaquero. At the time the company was trying to improve its case-coloring before bringing it out. Ruger apparently decided this was not going to happen and released what it had.

When the Vaquero premiered in 1993, it exceeded all

John found the New Vaquero in .45 Colt to be exceptionally accurate.

OT 255 SWC
8.5 UNIQUE
968 FPS

sales expectations. Cowboy Action shooters, outdoorsmen, single-action fanciers, hunters, plinkers, *everyone* had to have one. First chambered in .45 Colt, the Vaquero came in the three standard barrel lengths — Gunfighter (4⅝ inches), Artillery (5½ inches) and Cavalry (7½ inches). In the depressed handgun market at the time, the Vaquero was a tremendous success. The vast majority of the sixguns on the firing line were soon Rugers.

To put together the Vaquero, Ruger started with the basic New Model Blackhawk, removed the adjustable sights, reshaped the top strap and gave it the traditional groove, then replaced the ramp front sight with a simple blade. The Vaquero quickly became a byword for anyone wanting a virtually indestructible .45 sixgun for heavy-duty use.

Although Ruger would go on to offer the Vaquero in other chamberings, the very first one was a 7½-inch blued .45 Colt with a case-colored (not case-hardened) frame. It soon followed with a stainless steel version of the same.

Until the arrival of the Vaquero, all centerfire Ruger single actions were easy to sight in simply by using a screwdriver. Dealing with fixed-sight sixguns isn't quite as easy. There was no problem windage-wise, at least for me, as my Vaqueros were dead on in that respect. It was simply a matter of filing the "too tall" front sight to the proper height. My first 7½-inch Vaquero originally shot 3 inches low with 300-grain bullets and 8 inches low with 260-grain bullets.

In the past, when I had filed on the Italian-made replicas, this was fairly easy. However, my first file strokes on a Ruger front blade told me I was now dealing with a much tougher steel.

The 7½-inch stainless steel New Vaquero .45 Colt should be used with "Colt-level" loads only.

TWEAKING AND MODIFYING

Once the stainless steel version arrived, it became very popular with those who roamed the wilds, especially in the the 4⅝-inch configuration. (I've always wondered why Ruger didn't just use the traditional 4¾-inch Colt SAA configuration.)

My original Vaquero with a 7½-inch barrel was soon radically changed. By that time I had also acquired a pair of 7½-inch stainless ones and outfitted them with stag grips, but I decided to do something else with my original .45. The barrel was shortened to 3½ inches, and one of Qualite's Pistol & Revolver bird's-head grip frames was installed to turn that Cavalry Model into an easy-packing concealment sixgun.

I kept using the 7½-inch stainless steel pair in Cowboy Action matches, especially with black-powder loads, but I also used them for testing .45 Colt loads — both standard and heavy — with bullet weights ranging from 250 to 325 grains. Before writing *Action Shooting Cowboy Style*, I thoroughly tested over 50 sixguns chambered in .45 Colt. My two 7½-inch stainless Vaqueros (one of which came from Ruger, the other from a pawnshop), turned out to be the No. 1 and No. 2 sixguns in terms of overall accuracy during my testing.

As the Vaqueros became more readily available, I came up with a pair of perfect packin' pistols. They were blued 4⅝-inch .45s, and I had them fitted with carved ivory-style stocks by Precision Pro Grips. I also sent them off to Jim Stroh to have the triggers set back to look — and feel — more like those on a Colt SAA.

Dave Lauck of D&L Sports also worked on another of my Vaqueros — a 5½-inch stainless model. He cut the barrel even with the ejector rod housing, fitted the gun with stag stocks and removed the sharp edges at the front and back of the grip frame just enough to give it a "round butted" look. The end result turned out to be one of the easiest sixguns to pack of all the ones I own.

BIRTH OF THE BISLEY VAQUERO

The original Ruger Bisley grip configuration was inspired, of course, by the legendary Colt Bisley. I immediately embraced it as an excellent solution for mitigating felt recoil from big-bore sixguns. I wasn't the only one. John Linebaugh also started using the Bisley rather than the Blackhawk or Super Blackhawk for his five-shot conversions to .475 and .500 Linebaugh. And, for the first time, the recoil of these cartridges became manageable.

The next step for Ruger was to mate the Vaquero with a Bisley platform to produce the Bisley Vaquero (for years, custom gunsmiths had been fitting Bisley grip frames to Ruger Vaqueros). Ruger surprised everyone by unveiling the first factory Bisley Vaquero at the 1997 SHOT Show. It made such an impression that it was voted Handgun of the Year by Shooting Industry's Academy of Excellence.

The first Bisley Vaqueros out of the factory were blued .45 Colts, and stainless ones soon followed. Stainless Bisley Vaqueros were heartily welcomed by many shooters,

This New Vaquero in stainless with a 5½-inch barrel is a Perfect Packin' Pistol candidate.

especially those who pack their sixguns outdoors in all types of weather. For this, the Bisley Vaquero was perfect. Belt it on, load it with heavy-duty .45 Colt ammunition and forget about it until it is actually needed. It will do the job.

THE QUESTION OF FRAMES

When Colt introduced the Bisley concept in 1896, it made the mainframe higher in the back than the standard SAA. The grip frames do not interchange. Ruger did the same thing to a lesser degree. The Bisley grip frame is slightly higher than the Super Blackhawk, and although the Bisley grip frame does fit the Blackhawk, Super Blackhawk and Vaquero mainframes, it requires removing metal along the top of the backstrap to blend the grip frame to the mainframes of those models. It was obvious that Ruger did not redesign the Bisley grip frame to fit the Vaquero.

Nevertheless, the .45 Colt Bisley Vaquero is one good lookin' sixgun. Shooters who use theirs with full-house loads definitely appreciate the easy handling and diminished felt recoil the Bisley variation affords.

Bill Oglesby totally tuned and tightened a stainless steel 4⅝-inch .45 Colt specimen of mine, finished the frame and ejector rod in matte stainess and left the rest of the gun in bright polished stainless. He then refitted and refinished the factory Bisley stocks. What an improvement! With no adjustable sights to ever get out of whack, this is definitely a hard-duty, weather-resistant sixgun, capable of handling heavy .45 Colt loads with ease.

One of my .45 Colt Bisley Vaqueros groups into 1 inch with 9.0 grains of Unique and Bull-X's 255-grain bullet with

The Bisley Vaquero (right) compared to a custom "Bisley-fied" New Model Blackhawk (left).

Dave Lauck of D&L Sports shortened the barrels, fitted stag stocks, and slightly rounded the butts of these Vaqueros — one in .45 Colt, the other in .44-40 — making them both easier to pack.

a muzzle velocity of 1,025 fps. The Lyman/Casull 300-grain FP gas check and RCBS's #45-300-grain FN gas check are top performers when both are loaded over 21.2 grains of H110. The Lyman clocks out at 1,083 fps, while the RCBS design — with more bullet in the case — goes 1,144 fps. These are very potent loads in a .45 Colt sixgun. Both group very close to 1 inch.

THE NEW VAQUERO

More than 750,000 Vaqueros were produced before production was stopped in favor of the New Vaquero. How significant is that number? In just over a decade Ruger produced more than twice as many Vaqueros as the entire 1st Generation run of Colt SAAs produced from 1873 to 1940. I'm not sure why the original Vaquero was stopped in favor of the New Vaquero, especially since the Redhawk and Super Redhawk have run side-by-side for two decades. I do know this has caused all kinds of confusion, with some calling the original Vaquero the "Old Model" Vaquero. There is no such thing. There *is* the large-framed original and the standard-framed New Vaquero. When I

chastised custom sixgunsmith Gary Reeder for using the term "Old Model," he said he had no choice as it was necessary to avoid confusion. I can handle that. At any rate, both have transfer bars and are safe to carry fully loaded with six rounds.

Comparing the New Vaquero, standard Vaquero and traditional Colt SAA reveals the New Vaquero is much closer in size to the Colt than it is to the standard Vaquero and will fit most holsters designed for the Colt as well. The cylinder diameter of the New Vaquero is 1.675 inches compared to 1.654 inches for the Colt and 1.730 inches for the standard Vaquero. This is important because it means loads for the New Vaquero .45 should be much closer to Colt levels than to Vaquero/Blackhawk levels. I see no reason to exceed 1,000-1,100 fps with a 260-grain bullet in the New Vaquero. This load shoots comfortably, is very accurate and, short of *really* big game, will handle any sixgun chore most of us will ever encounter.

Cylinder length of the New Vaquero is 1.611 inches, slightly less than the Colt SAA's 1.622 inches and quite a bit less than the Vaquero's 1.704 inches. This means .45 Colt loads using 300- to 350-grain bullets won't normally fit in the New Vaquero's cylinder without protruding from the front of the chamber and preventing the cylinder from rotating. (This is actually a good thing, as these heavy loads do not belong in the downsized New Vaquero.)

In addition to its smaller size, several other improvements were made in the New Vaquero. The ejector rod head is larger, allowing more comfort and positive action when ejecting spent shells, plus the cylinder now lines up correctly with the ejector rod. With the New Vaquero, an audible click tells you the chamber is in line with the rod.

With the first Ruger sixgun, the Single-Six .22 of 1953, the grip frame was virtually identical in size and shape to the 1st Generation Colt SAA. This XR3 frame was carried over to the .357 Blackhawk of 1955 and the .44 Magnum version one year later. In 1963 the grip frame was changed to the XR3-RED, allowing more room between the back of the trigger guard and the front of the grip strap. This is the grip frame found on the original Vaquero, but the New Vaquero has the original XR3 size and shape, and older XR3 grips will fit. Almost. For whatever reason, the location of the grip pin is off just enough to require filling the old hole in the grip and drilling a new one.

one tough sixgun capable of handling heavy .45 Colt loads, but I like the New Vaquero even more. One caveat: Many reloading manuals have separate .45 Colt sections dealing specifically with heavy loads for Ruger sixguns. These are *not* to be used with the New Vaquero. My favorite "heavy" load for the New Vaquero is the 260-grain Keith bullet over 9.0 grains of Unique or Universal for 1,050 fps.

The original Vaquero will handle any loads I normally put in a .45 Colt Blackhawk. I don't use these heavy loads as much anymore, so my old Vaqueros have been pretty much supplanted by the New Vaquero. Whether with a 4⅝-, 5½- or 7½-inch barrel, my stainless New Vaqueros are regularly fed 260-grain, hard-cast Keith bullets over 8.0-8.5 grains of Unique or Universal for right around 850-950 fps, depending upon barrel length.

The New Vaquero is just about a perfect fixed-sighted single action for outdoor use. But just to prove once again how gun designers like to go to the edge of perfection and then step back, we have that weird New Vaquero hammer. Apparently, it was thought lengthening the hammer spur would make it easier to cock. Actually, just the opposite is true, and it is flat-out ugly. My New Vaquero hammers have either been shortened or replaced with Super Blackhawk or Montado hammers. They look better and are much easier to operate. ◎

A FINAL WORD

The New Vaquero grip frame is also slightly narrower than the older style and — combined with the slimmer checkered rubber grips, which are also slimmer than the original Vaquero's wood ones — makes it feel awfully good in my hand. In fact, these are the best-feeling Ruger factory sixgun stocks I've ever encountered. Instead of the medallions found in Ruger stocks since 1953, the New Vaquero grips have the Ruger eagle molded in the grip itself.

I like the original Vaquero. It is

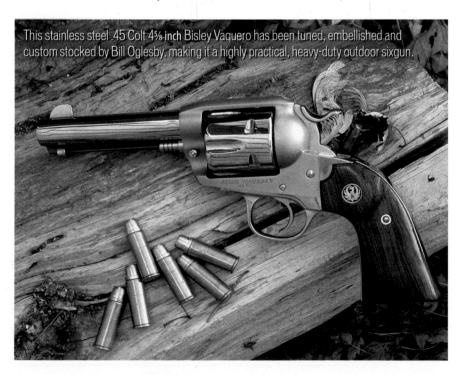

This stainless steel .45 Colt 4⅝-inch Bisley Vaquero has been tuned, embellished and custom stocked by Bill Oglesby, making it a highly practical, heavy-duty outdoor sixgun.

THE SIXGUNS

Three versions of the stainless steel Old Army: 7½-inch (adjustable and fixed-sighted) and 5½-inch (fixed-sighted). John feels the stainless Old Army versions with either sight setup are the best percussion sixguns ever offered.

RUGER OLD ARMY .45

CHAPTER 19

My experiences with percussion sixguns began with originals in the mid-1950s. I had both a Colt 1860 Army and a double-action Deane & Adams. Unfortunately, as with too many other handguns and long guns in my later teenage years, I traded them away. (I'd love to have that 1860 Army back. It was in excellent shape!)

With the addition of an R&D .45 Colt cylinder, the Old Army does double duty.

Most of the original percussion revolvers from the 1840s to the 1860s were considered to be .44 caliber. Colts such as the 1847 Walker, 1st, 2nd and 3rd Model Dragoons, 1860 Army — along with Remington cap-and-ball sixguns — were so classed, despite the fact they normally take a roundball with a diameter of .451 to .454 inch.

Since then just about every percussion pistol ever made

has been replicated. Some have been very good; some not so good. Some were obviously put together for a quick sale with no regard for whether or not such a pistol ever existed. Other makers took great pains to be authentic.

However, if you want the best possible cap-and-ball sixgun — and you're not a stickler for authenticity — the choice comes down to Ruger's Old Army. It has always

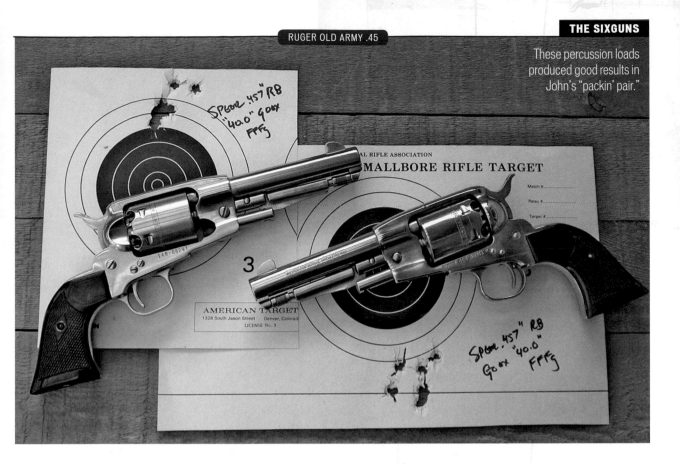

These percussion loads produced good results in John's "packin' pair."

been considered to be .45 caliber and takes a .457-inch roundball or conical bullet.

Forty plus years ago when Bill Ruger decided to offer a percussion revolver, he insisted it would be the best ever manufactured. He wanted a top strap like the one on the 1858 Remington, and he wanted it to be as strong as his Super Blackhawk.

MODERNIZING A CLASSIC

The result was the Old Army with adjustable sights, a 7½-inch barrel and your choice of blue or stainless steel. My friend and I purchased the first pair to arrive in Idaho. The stainless version was definitely welcomed as it made cleanup so easy. In fact, some new owners even talked of putting their Old Army in the dishwasher, after removing the

An adjustable-sighted stainless steel Old Army fitted with Super Blackhawk grip frame (top) compared to a fixed-sighted stainless model with an R&D .45 Colt cylinder secured in place with a Belt Mountain base pin (bottom).

RUGER OLD ARMY .45

OLD ARMY
SPEER .457" RB
"40.0" 2
PYRODEX
P

OLD ARMY
SPEER .457 RB
"40.0" TRIPLE-7
FFFg
2

4

These typical percussion loads fired in the
Old Army yielded pretty consistent results.

grip panels, of course. I never thought of doing such a thing and, in fact, have never had a dishwasher anyway!

Ruger's Old Army is a completely modernized version of the cap-and-ball sixgun. The chambers are tapered to provide a very tight seal and help prevent a double discharge, but it is still a good idea to use a wad or top off each chamber with either a black powder lube or Crisco. This not only prevents a second chamber from igniting but also, perhaps even more importantly, helps to keep the bore clean. Because the Old Army takes a larger diameter bullet than the standard .451 or .454 inch size of Colts or Remingtons (be they original or replica), the Ruger is capable of excellent accuracy. In my 7½-inch Old Army, a 225-grain conical bullet over 35 grains (by volume) of Pyrodex P results in a muzzle velocity of 870 fps and will put six shots in an inch at 25 yards. Energywise, this is the equivalent of .45 ACP hardball. Using 40 grains of Pyrodex P or Triple-7 FFFg resulted in velocities well over 1,000 fps and excellent accuracy with a .457-inch roundball – and that moves us past .45 ACP

hardball and into +P territory. This is, of course, all with an adjustable-sighted sixgun and black powder.

One of the problems with both original and replica percussion guns – especially the Walker and some of the Dragoons — was the propensity for the loading lever to unlatch and fall down when the sixgun was fired. With the Old Army, the loading lever is positively locked into place and will not drop down upon firing. The loading lever, rammer and cylinder base pin are an interrelated assembly which are removed from the gun by simply turning a large screw in the front of the frame by means of a coin or screwdriver. The loading lever of the Old Army exerts the best leverage in seating the ball over the powder of any percussion revolver ever produced.

The Old Army was built on Ruger's Old Model action. Until production ceased it remained the only Ruger single action with a traditional half-cock setting and no transfer bar safety. But it can be carried safely with six rounds, as there are safety recesses in between each chamber for

> *If you want the best possible cap-and-ball sixgun — and you're not a stickler for authenticity — the choice comes down to Ruger's Old Army.*

resting the hammer in. These recesses should *always* be used unless the hammer is resting upon an empty chamber.

The Old Army's stainless-steel nipples are set deeply into the cylinder to help prevent fragments of fired caps from falling in the mechanism or behind the cylinder and causing a jam. This type of problem has never occurred with any Old Army I have used. It is also the only percussion revolver that can be dry-fired without damage, as the hammer nose is designed to clear the nipples by .005 inch.

I have been shooting one of the original stainless-steel Old Army models for over four decades, using it often in the past in black-powder matches. Although I've replaced several sets of nipples, it is still as good as new. For my use it has been fitted with a Super Blackhawk grip frame and ivory micarta grips. Mine is also one of about 500 that came through with the "Black Powder Only" inscription upside-down on the cylinder.

A SHORTER SOLUTION

The original Old Army from the early 1970s was offered in both blue and stainless with adjustable sights. The last version offered before they were dropped from production (I have no idea why) was an easy-packin' 5½-inch barreled version featuring fixed sights. It, too, could be had in blued or stainless.

Most cartridge shooters seem to prefer shorter barrels, and until the 5½-inch Old Army came along, cap-and-ball traditionalists had been restricted to the longer barrels on factory guns, or they had to have them custom-cut to shorter lengths.

The Old Army makes an attractive short-barreled sixgun. Before production ceased I acquired a pair of 5½-inch stainless-steel models which came with Ruger's faux ivory grips with a black eagle medallion. These were removed and replaced by Eagle Grips Gunfighter Grips in checkered black buffalo horn. The dark color contrasts

Taffin prefers three propellants for use in the Old Army — Goex FFFg, Hodgdon Pyrodex and Triple 7.

beautifully with the stainless steel. When shooting black powder, especially if each chamber is topped off with Crisco or a similar lubricant, things tend to get a little messy and greasy. This is part of the fun, although with smooth grips things can get slippery as well as a little messy. Even though there's not much recoil with an Old Army (relatively speaking) there *is* enough to make the checkered grips pay off.

To carry my pair of 5½-inch Old Armys, I called on Bob Mernickle for a special custom rig. I wanted the trimmest and lightest setup possible, dark brown to match the buffalo horn grips. Mernickle did it right. The belt is tapered on both ends to receive the buckle and sizing holes without the need of sewn-on billets. Holsters are the Slim Jim-style, made to hang straight so they can be worn butts to the rear or to the front. Bob finished off the belt with a gunfighter stitch that he also carried over into both holsters. Since these are cap-and-ball sixguns, no cartridge loops were called for.

Both perform well with Speer's .457-inch roundball, Thompson's lubed wad and CCI's #11 percussion cap. The three powders I normally use in 35.0- and 40.0-grain charges (by volume) are Goex FFFg black powder, Hodgdon's Triple-7 FFFg and Pyrodex P. With 35.0 grains of Triple-7 FFFg, velocity is 925 fps with six shots in 1⅜ inches at 20 yards. Moving up to 40.0 grains of Triple-7 FFFg yields 1,130 fps and a group of 1¾ inches. These velocities are right at — or even exceed — what I've gotten with the 7½-inch barreled Old Army.

THE CARTRIDGE OPTION

Thanks to Taylor's & Co. and R&D, the Old Army can easily be changed into a cartridge-firing sixgun. Taylor's offers R&D conversion cylinders chambered in .45 Colt. These are available in both blue and nickel finishes (which matches the stainless Old Army very nicely). In order to use the conversion cylinders, remove the original cylinder and use the same base pin serving as part of the Old Army loading lever with the new cylinder. An even better solution is to use the Belt Mountain replacement base pin. For use with cartridge cylinders, this base pin, which is easily removable, does away with the original loading lever assembly making it much easier to remove the cylinder for loading cartridges. Currently, Belt Mountain offers a spring-loaded

Belt Mountain offers a special base pin with a spring-loaded catch for convenience if you want to use cartridge cylinders in your Old Army.

John carries his 5½-inch Old Army Ruger .45s in this Slim Jim rig by Bob Mernickle.

latch to secure the base pin, making it unnecessary to use the screw through the side of the frame.

The R&D cylinder comes with a back plate with six firing pins, safety notches between chambers and a locating pin in the back of the cylinder which mates up with a corresponding hole in the conversion ring/back plate. To load, remove the back plate, place cartridges in the cylinder, replace the back plate *carefully*, place the cylinder back in the frame and replace the base pin. To unload, remove the cylinder, take off the back plate and remove the cartridges. If they do not fall out by gravity, use a rod or wooden dowel to tap them out from the front of the cylinder.

The workmanship on the R&D cylinders is excellent. I ordered two and both were near-perfect fits in my Old Army frames as well as in two older 7½-inch models. With most .45 Colt loads — and the R&D cylinders in place — both revolvers shoot just slightly below point of aim at 20 yards, but they group very well. Having cartridge cylinders fitted to percussion revolvers allows a great deal of versatility without adding extra sixguns.

When we entered the cartridge era in the early 1870s, many sixgunners had their revolvers converted to cartridges by adding a new cylinder. But the smart ones held onto their old cylinders just in case they found themselves without ammunition. They could still survive by loading their own in the original cylinders. Thanks to the Old Army and Taylor's R&D .45 Colt cylinder, this sensible measure can still be used today.

With the R&D .45 Colt cylinder in place in the Ruger 5½-inch Old Army, a 235-grain bullet lubed with SPG and seated over 35.0 grains of Swiss FFFg yields 920 fps and six shots in 1½ inches at 20 yards. With the Oregon Trail 250-grain RNFP over 6.0 grains of Red Dot, velocity is 863 fps with the same accuracy.

Some sixgunners do use the Old Army for hunting and this should be done within reason. If a standard .45 Colt load or a .45 ACP +P load would be appropriate for the game, then the Old Army is also appropriate. I would certainly choose conical bullets and full-house black-powder or Pyrodex charges when using the percussion cylinder. ◉

THE SIXGUNS

John relaxes after a shooting session with the .45 Colt Rodeo (left). USFA offered this model in all three traditional barrel lengths (right), but the 7½-inch specimen he's holding is quite rare.

USFA .45 SINGLE ACTIONS

CHAPTER 20

t was sometime around 1990. Sitting there in front of me was the one of the most beautifully finished single-action sixguns I had ever seen. The bluing was so deep you could almost see your great-grandfather in it. The case-coloring looked as if it belonged in an art museum. No, it wasn't an original Colt SAA. It was in an exhibition booth for United States Patent Firearms Manufacturing Company (USPFA), and it was in the business of selling Colt replicas. But there was a difference. Its sixguns were not only fitted and finished in this country, the work was done in the old Colt Armory.

At the time USPFA was relatively new. It had taken over the old manufacturing facility of Colt Patent Firearms. In keeping with this, USPFA's catalog was a beautiful

A finely finished (inset) and ivory-stocked USFA Single Action compared to the plain-Jane Rodeo.

Fire Arms (USFA). Making the switch to a totally American-made sixgun was neither quick nor easy, but when it was accomplished, the company catalog changed dramatically. What remained was just about the finest traditional factory-built SAA replica I had ever seen.

stroll through history with both color and black-and-white photos, and period-style 19th century advertising for the cap-n-ball Colts, various pocket pistols and, of course, "Single Action, Central Fire, Army, Six Shot, .38, .44, and .45 Inch Calibre, Revolving Pistols."

Replicas basically began with Great Western in Los Angeles in 1954, and they lasted less than 10 years. Italian replicas started coming in sometime around the late 1950s, and it was a long time before the quality and authenticity of current replicas came about, thanks mainly to the efforts of the late Val Forgett of Navy Arms and Mike Harvey of Cimarron Firearms. But USFA replicas — just as with the Great Western sixguns — are totally a domestic effort.

GOING ALL-AMERICAN

USPFA's Custom Shop offered non-standard barrel lengths, engraved sixguns, plus grips of gutta percha, stag, pearl and ivory. All their sixguns — cartridge and percussion — were beautifully assembled in this country using Italian parts. It was just the first step in USPFA's Doug Donnelly's dream of providing an all-American-made single action. During the process, the name was changed to United States

USFA NO. 1 AND NO. 2

For my first experience with the counterpart American-made USFA sixgun, I ordered a .45 Colt with a 4¾-inch barrel. After many years of testing virtually every sixgun offered, I am not easily impressed. As I unpacked the USFA

The USFA .45 Colt Rodeo II came in a satin nickel finish.

gun, I immediately realized *this* one had been done right. Most factory single actions (one major exception being those from Freedom Arms) need some work to either tune them or fit them enough to really satisfy someone who has been shooting them as long as I have. Not this time!

The mainframe and hammer were beautifully case-colored in what is described as Armory Bone Case, while the rest of the gun was finished in a deep Dome Blue. Grips furnished as standard were checkered hard rubber with a

All in the finish: It may have been less expensive than the standard Single Action, but USFA's .45 Colt Cowboy shoots just as well.

MEISTER 250 RNFP
18.5 #4227

794 FPS

"US" molded in. Normally, I prefer to fit sixguns with custom grips made of ivory, stag or exotic wood. However, in the case of the USFA single action, the grips were so perfectly fitted and felt so good I was very hesitant to change them. Tempted as I was to keep them, I fought the feeling and this .45 now wears ivories.

One of the things I always look at critically is the radiusing of the lower part of the back of the hammer and the two "ears" formed by the back strap where it screws into the mainframe on both sides of the hammer. A well-made single action will exhibit a smooth mating of the contours of all three. This USFA sixgun — and all subsequent ones I've acquired — are very nearly perfect in this respect. The same careful fitting can also be found where the top of the face of the hammer meets the top strap. The fit of the trigger guard to the bottom of the mainframe is so perfectly done you can run your finger over it and not feel where one part begins and the other ends. The same is true where the back strap meets the frame.

The front of the ejector rod housing as well as the cylinder are both beveled for easier holstering. The next two things are what are most often lacking — or in need of correction — in other single actions are the chamber mouth diameters and trigger pulls. This first USFA .45 Colt sixgun passed with 100 percent with all

John shoots one of his favorite styles of sixguns, USFA's beautifully finished Flat-Top Target.

six chambers measuring a uniform .452 inch. The trigger pull is three pounds, while the cylinder locks up tightly, both in the hammer-down and cocked position.

Standard USFA Single Actions are available with a V-notch or square-notch rear sight. Mine was ordered with the square notch — which is perfectly filled in with just a smidgeon strip of daylight on both sides of the square-profile front sight. You also have a choice of a cross pin or screw-in "black powder" cylinder pin latch. I went with the more modern spring-loaded version.

One of the inherent problems found in fixed-sight guns is getting them to shoot to point of aim. This can be affected by the load used, how you see the sights and how you grip the gun. But I had really struck pay dirt with this sixgun. Not only is it dead-on for windage, it also shoots most of my .45 Colt loads right on the money in terms of elevation.

I can't remember ever experiencing a traditional single action in nearly five decades where everything was right in a single package. The only possible way I can see to improve a USFA sixgun is by spending some time polishing the interior parts with a stone.

Since acquiring this first USFA .45, I have added a second, set up and finished exactly as the first. However, this one has a 7½-inch barrel and is fitted with an auxiliary .45 ACP cylinder for versatility. Its longer sight radius makes it easier for me to shoot, but I have kept the original factory grips. Someday that will change, but I'm not in any rush right now.

LOADS LOADED, SHOTS FIRED

For the .45 Colt, one of my favorite bullets is RCBS's #45-270 SWC, a Keith-style number that weighs out at 281 grains, cast 20:1 of lead and tin. With 8.0 grains of Unique it only travels around 800 fps from a 4¾-inch barrel. However, at that weight it's plenty for most applications. Another longtime favorite of mine has been the Lyman Keith bullet #454424 over 20.0 grains of #4227. In this short-barreled USFA sixgun, this load clocks out at 965 fps and places five shots in 1 inch at 20 yards. I've found this load to give good results in a lot of sixguns — even ones initially reluctant to shoot well.

With the 7½-inch gun, this same bullet over 9.0 grains of Unique clocks out at 985 fps and puts five shots in ⅞ inch at

SIXGUNS AND THEIR CARTRIDGES

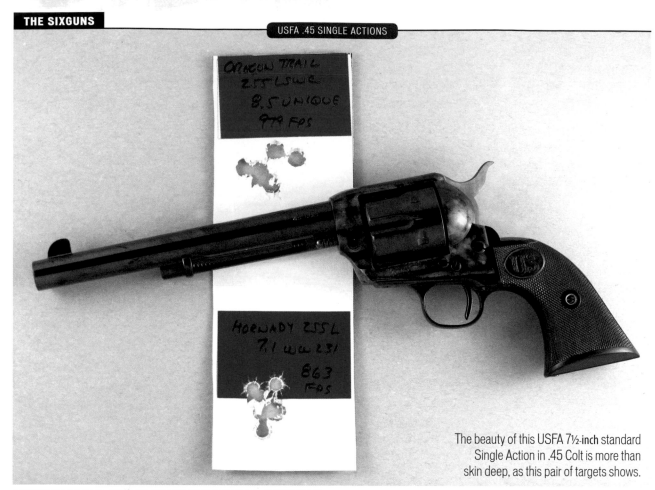

ORECON TRAIL
255 LSWC
8.5 UNIQUE
979 FPS

HORNADY 255L
7.1 WW 231
863 FPS

The beauty of this USFA 7½-inch standard
Single Action in .45 Colt is more than
skin deep, as this pair of targets shows.

This 4¾-inch USFA .45 Colt Single
Action is perfectly set off by an Austin
floral-carved holster by El Paso Saddlery.

the same distance. With the .45 ACP cylinder in place, Black Hills' 230-grain RNL and 230-grain JHP +P, as well as Winchester's 230-grain FMJ, all shoot one-inch groups at 918 fps, 974 fps and 866 fps, respectively. I'm always amazed how well .45 ACP loads shoot from these long .45 Colt cylinders!

The basic .45 USFA Single Action has a 4¾-, 5½- or 7½-inch barrel and is finished in Old Armory Bone Case and Dome Blue. Custom touches include a case-colored hammer, full blue or nickel finish. You can also opt for walnut, pearl or ivory stocks, and special engraving all the way up to full-coverage scroll.

OTHER MODELS

Three special models have also been offered, the Rodeo, Rodeo II and the Cowboy. (The latter is *not* to be confused with the Colt Cowboy of about 15 years ago.) All three standard versions have been offered in 4¾- and 5½-inch lengths in .45 Colt, and very rarely with the 7½-inch barrel length. USFA has also offered an "antique" version — the Gunslinger, a sixgun made to look as if it had been in service for many decades, with a much-used and distressed-looking finish.

After accomplishing the switch to an all-American sixgun with a finish as good or better than anything offered over the past 135 years, USFA decided to offer a much less expensive version, the Rodeo. Internally, it was identical to its standard Single Action except a different finish was used to cut costs.

This approach was not without precedent. In 1935 Smith & Wesson began offering the beautifully finished

Factory .45 ACPs shoot well through
the auxiliary cylinder of the USFA .45 Colt.

.357 Magnum, but in 1954, by using a matte blue finish on the same basic revolver, the S&W Highway Patrolman could be offered for a much lower price (about 35 percent less).

The next version was the Rodeo II. This is the same basic sixgun as the Rodeo, but instead of the Rodeo's matte blue finish, the Rodeo II is satin nickel. The grips are also different. Instead of checkered black rubber, they're a brown-colored version called "Burlwood" to somewhat duplicate the older gutta percha grips of the 19th century (which often took on a brown hue). The Rodeo II also features screws finished in carbona (fire blue). They make a very pleasing contrast to the nickel finish.

Grips furnished as standard on both the standard single action and the Rodeo are checkered hard rubber with a "US" molded into the top part of the grip. These stocks, or grips if you prefer, are so perfectly fitted to the frame they feel like they've been custom fitted — the Cowboy is also the same basic sixgun as the standard Single Action, made with the same materials to the same tolerances. The only difference is the exterior finish, which is polished blue throughout instead

of the standard blue/case-color combination. The Cowboy was cataloged in all three standard barrel lengths in .45 Colt.

My 4¾-inch .45 Colt Cowboy is a beautifully shooting .45 Colt with Black Hills 250-grain RNFPs grouping in ¾ inch for five shots at 20 yards. CCI's Blazer 200-grain JHP delivered five shots into one ragged ⅜-inch hole at the same distance.

My best handload has proved to be Speer's 250-grain GDHP over 9.0 grains of Unique for a one-inch group and a velocity of 932 fps. My everyday working load — a 260-grain Keith bullet over 8.0 grains of Unique — clocks 887 fps and groups in 1¼ inches. (I can surely live with that.) But for those who don't reload, Buffalo Bore offers a 255-grain Keith bullet load at just over 1,000 fps in the short-barreled Cowboy. This is an excellent load for roaming desert, sagebrush, foothills or mountains while packing a .45 Colt.

All USFA single-action sixguns are traditional, meaning they have no transfer bar and are only safely carried when loaded with five shots and the hammer down on an empty chamber. In addition to the models mentioned, they have also offered replicas of the Colt Bisley Model, the Flat-Top Target

SIXGUNS AND THEIR CARTRIDGES

Short and sweet: John shoots his nickel-plated 2½-inch barreled Sheriff's Model. Like all traditional USFA sixguns, it should only be carried with five rounds in the cylinder and the hammer down on an empty chamber.

(complete with late 19th century-style target sights) and the short-barreled, ejector rod housing-less Sheriff's Model. One of the "problems" inherent in the traditional single action was the slowness in loading and unloading compared to the auto-ejecting top-breaks and swing-out double actions. USFA's Sheriff's Model is even slower, as its super-short barrel precludes an ejector rod housing/ejector rod. You have to use your fingernail or a piece of rod to poke out the empties.

SHORT AND SLICK

I've always been intrigued by the Sheriff's Model. I even owned a real Colt one once. It was chambered in .41 Long Colt and I paid $35 for it. I wish I still had it, but it went in one of my teenage trades. It didn't have much finish left, but it functioned fine and would be worth a whole lot more than $35 today! In the early 1960s, Colt resurrected the .45

Sheriff's Model in a special run available through Centennial Arms. They were beautiful little sixguns.

By the time the Third Generation Colt SAAs appeared, I had one more chance when a special run of dual-cylindered .44-40/.44 Special Sheriff's Models were offered sometime in the 1980s. I just couldn't get excited about them this time. Duke Venturino has one and it is one of his favorites — when loaded with shotshells — for keeping the rattle-snake population down around his diggings. I haven't seen a rattlesnake around here for at least 20 years, so I couldn't use that as a reason.

Later, however, I found I still wanted a Sheriff's Model, so I got one of USFA's — a nickel-plated .45 Colt with a 2½-inch barrel. As with all original Sheriff's Models, the USFA version has the "black powder" frame, wherein the base pin is held in place by a screw through the front of the frame.

The Sheriff's Model rates as "Perfectly Pleasurable Packin' Pistol." Although it wouldn't make it on the list of the Ten Most Desirable defensive firearms, I'd feel well armed with it stuck in the back pocket of my jeans. Former Texas Ranger Frank Hamer, the man who ended the deadly career of Bonnie and Clyde, said if he ever needed more than the five rounds in his .45, he was guilty of sloppy "peace officering." So I guess if Hamer could do it with five, so can I.

The USFA Sheriff's Model had a higher retail price than the standard USFA single action, plus there was a significant extra charge for the nickel-plated finish. My practical side said "Don't buy it." But I rarely ever listen to that spoilsport anymore.

With standard .45 Colt loads, felt recoil stays at the pleasurable level. Every time I pull the trigger, a big hole shows up in the paper or a soda pop can does a little dance. And since the only use I can possibly see for golf balls are as targets, if I hit one just right with a 255-grain bullet, they'll go 25 yards or more.

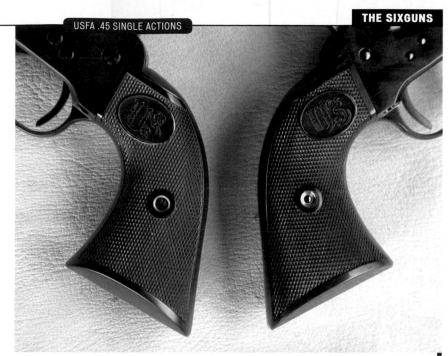

USFA .45 SINGLE ACTIONS

USFA offered their checkered rubber grips in both black (left) and Burlwood (right), designed to replicate the color of 19th century gutta percha stocks.

MORE MODELS

In the late 1950s I was newly married, working the night shift in the factory, and spending my days at Boyle's Gun Shop. One day a fellow came in with three guns he wanted to sell for a total of $65, and John Boyle bought all three. Two were nondescript and long forgotten. The third gun, however, was a 7½-inch Colt Flat-Top Target. USFA eventually came out with an excellent replica, complete with the same adjustable sights as found on the original.

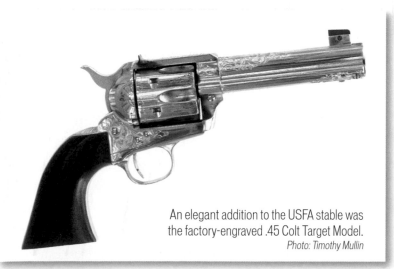

An elegant addition to the USFA stable was the factory-engraved .45 Colt Target Model.
Photo: Timothy Mullin

Another interesting variation from USFA was the Omnipotent. This single action had a Colt 1877 Lightning-style grip frame giving it quite a different feel. These were at least cataloged in all barrel lengths, but I don't believe very many ever left the factory. There was also a true rendition of the Colt Buntline Special complete with a ladder-style rear sight which could be raised up from its mortise in the top strap. There were also Bisley Models and Bisley Target Models and even Sheriff's Model Bisleys.

POSTSCRIPT

As I've discussed the USFA sixguns, I've had a hard time traveling back and forth between the present and the past for the simple reason as this is written, it appears USFA is about to close its doors. From what I have heard, which seems to be from very reliable sources, the CNC machinery has been sold and sixguns are only being assembled with parts on hand. I never like to be mistaken; however I hope I am in this case. USFA has produced some excellent .45 sixguns, and I am very pleased with mine. They will all definitely be passed on to the grandsons. ◎

A perfect presentation: The Freedom Arms Anniversary Model with all the trimmings.

FREEDOM ARMS .454 CASULL MODEL 83

CHAPTER 21

Four years after Wayne Baker and Dick Casull began Freedom Arms in March 1979, the first factory-built five-shot .454 Casull left the factory. The .454 Casull single-action revolver was now reality; however, it would be several years before it was widely accepted by the general shooting public.

In 1985 Baker sent me a 10-inch Premier Grade .454, and I set it up with silhouette sights. I used it for the long-range game, switched to standard sights or a scope for hunting, and fired thousands of heavy test loads through it. I subsequently bought the gun, and it remains as tight as the day it left the factory.

From the very beginning, the Freedom Arms .454 — now known as the Model 83 — has been built to exacting tolerances. Cylinders are line bored, that is locked into the

frame and then a pilot hole drilled to begin to form each chamber, which should be locked into precise alignment with the barrel in any sixgun for top accuracy. Freedom Arms revolvers are hand-fitted from the very beginning of mating one particular cylinder to one particular barrel and frame. Freedom Arms does not build a gun to a specific price point. They build the best revolver possible, *then* set the price. That price is high, but it is a rare buyer who would say it isn't worth it.

IN THE BEGINNING

During the 1950s, many used Colt SAAs were available for $50 (a week's pay for me in 1956!). The economics of the situation combined with his passion for the old Colt led Dick Casull to begin experimenting with it, as Elmer Keith

John flattened this African warthog with the Field Grade .454.

did two decades earlier when he used the Colt SAA for his custom .44 Specials.

Casull played with the .44 Special for awhile, but when Winchester brought out solid head .45 Colt cases to replace the old folded-head, or "balloon-style" brass, the .45 Colt became the main thrust of his experimenting. The .45 Colt SAA's thin cylinder walls meant little or no margin of safety when using heavier than standard factory loads. The old folded head cases, which started the persistent idea that .45 Colt brass is weak, had given way to stronger brass. But the guns themselves were still relatively weak.

Casull bulged a number of cylinders working with the .45 Colt. When he started using frame-mounted firing pins to handle the higher pressures he was getting, cylinders and top straps blew, and ignition problems developed.

A five-shot cylinder would be necessary to realize the full potential of the .45 Colt cartridge. So Casull made them up using 4140 steel. They had to be as large as possible and still be able to fit the cylinder window of the Colt frame. The geometry of the Colt had to be changed, of course, to have the action work as a five-shooter instead of six. Initial loads

utilizing a 250-grain cast bullet attained muzzle velocities of 1,300 fps — close to the performance of the .44 Magnum which would arrive a few years later. But Casull, who was still in his early 20s at the time, wanted more.

He figured a way to heat-treat Colt SAA frames to 40 Rockwell without warpage. Around 1954, using specially built P.O. Ackley .45-caliber 1:24 twist barrels, the five-shot Colts were now capable of 1,550 fps with 250-grain bullets. The results were gratifying, but Casull wasn't satisfied. He wanted power, of course, but he wanted it with an adequate

John hasn't gotten all the way to his idea of the "Perfect Packin' Pistol," but the 4¾-inch Freedom Arms .454 is a big step toward the goal.

FREEDOM ARMS .454 CASULL MODEL 83

John set up two of his Freedom Arms .454s for hunting. The 10-inch Premier Grade sports a 4x scope, the 7½-inch Field Grade a 2x.

safety margin. By now, he was reaming .45 Colt primer pockets to accept rifle primers, and ignition problems were overcome with duplex and triplex loads. (This was before the availability of H110 and WW296, which make duplex and triplex loads unnecessary.)

It became obvious the Colt SAA had been taken as far as possible. The answer would have to be a new frame. So, starting from scratch, Casull built frames from 4140 steel and five-shot cylinders from 4150. Parts were engineered as needed, and the .454 Casull — by then labeled the .454 Magnum — became a reality. During the 1960s a number of .454s were built, and also Ruger Super Blackhawks were converted to five-shot .454 Magnums.

Plans for a factory in Freedom, Wyoming, came together in 1979. In 1983 the first factory-produced .454 was sold, it was called the Premier Grade, mainly chambered in .454, a small number in .45 Colt and .44 Magnum. In 1987, I was privileged to see the then-unannounced "new" Freedom Arms .454. I immediately felt it would outsell the original. To bring the price down, especially for those who wanted a .454 hunting revolver, they had created a "Field Grade," as opposed to the highly polished, presentation-grade Premier. The Field Grade carried a bead-blasted finish, which eliminated many hours of careful polishing. Instead of the special, meticulously fitted Premier Grade laminated

This may well be the ultimate "Sheriff's Model." The Deputy U.S. Marshal .454 may lack an ejector rod, but it doesn't lack for raw power!

With the use of auxiliary cylinders, John's 4¾-inch .454 handles (top photo from left): .454 Casull, .45 Colt, .45 ACP, .45 Winchester Mag.

grip, the Field Grade was furnished with bolt-on Pachmayrs for another cut in production costs. Finally, a special base adapter was fitted to the frame to accept Ruger rear sights. Total savings in the retail price came to about 30 percent, which put the Field Grade in the same price range as the Colt Python and Gold Cup. Internally, nothing was changed. Not a thing. Field Grade cylinders are still line-bored. Barrel/cylinder gaps for both grades are under .002 inch. The standard barrel lengths for Model 83s with adjustable sights are 4¾, 4, 6, 7½ or 10 inches — all are scope-ready. Fixed-sight versions are also available in some barrel lengths. (To me, fixed 4¾-inch would be the ideal perfect packin' pistol for emergencies involving big, mean critters.)

The Model 83 — in either grade — is a traditional five-shot single action. When carried fully loaded with five rounds, it utilizes a hammer safety that engages when the hammer is placed in the safety notch. I prefer to carry my Freedom Arms revolvers with only four rounds and the hammer down on an empty chamber.

As mentioned previously I received my first test gun, a 10-inch .454 from Freedom Arms, in 1986. My first *American Handgunner* article on the .454 resulted in my being hired as a staff writer doing both features and the column *Siluetas* for each issue. With the decline in long-range silhouette competition, however, *Siluetas* ended and *The Sixgunner* began.

Over the past several decades I have tested and written about the Freedom Arms Model 83s and Model 97s. I have worked with them in .454, .44 Magnum, .45 Colt, .32 H&R

Magnum, .32-20 and .22 Long Rifle. All are excellent examples of what a single-action sixgun can be. I certainly cannot take the pounding of hundreds of full-house loads through the .454 as I was able to do in the 1980s, but that first .454 will always have first-place in my sixgunnin' heart. Take a look at the sidebar to see a "real time" excerpt from my first article on the .454. A lot has happened since I wrote it. That first article had the most comprehensive reloading data ever published on the .454, and it remains so today. The .454 no longer is the "The Most Powerful Revolver Cartridge." Freedom Arms has added the .475 Linebaugh and .500 Wyoming Express chamberings to its Model 83, and Smith & Wesson has the X-frame revolvers firing the .500 and .460 S&W Magnums. The .454 may no longer be the biggest and most powerful cartridge, but it remains one of the best of the big-bore revolver cartridges available in a truly portable sixgun.

After shooting the 10-inch .454 extensively and developing hundreds of handloads — and using it for silhouette shooting and hunting — I wanted more .454 sixguns. Next came the direct opposite, a packin' pistol with a 4¾-inch barrel. It may not be the best target pistol, nor the best hunting pistol, not even the best silhouette pistol. Those three niches are all too specialized. My quest has been for a handgun that rides easily on the hip, can be counted on to deliver the goods quickly and efficiently, and is small enough to rest under a pillow or bedroll at night.

Every sixgunner has specific ideas about packin' pistols.

Shootin' and packin': John lights one off in his original .454 back in 1986 (right). He quickly learned that a short sling made packing the 10-inch .454 a whole lot easier.

I've never found the absolute perfect one, but I've certainly enjoyed the search. My 4¾-inch adjustable-sighted .454 received two custom touches — a factory action job before it left Wyoming and the fitting of ivory micarta grips. This was before the Field Grade .454 was available, and had it been around, I might have taken a serious look at a Field Grade fixed-sight model and filed the front sight down to match perfectly with one load. But had I done so I would never have had access to the full range of power level — a 240-grain bullet at 1,800 fps, a 260 at 1,750 and a 300 at 1,600! All of these were unheard of before the arrival of the .454.

I must admit to using more .45 Colt loads than .454 loads, as I did not always need upper-level .454s. If I lived in grizzly or brown bear country, I would, but I don't. One of my favorite .45 Colt loads is the Lyman/Casull 300-grain hard-cast, gas-checked Casull bullet over 21.5 grains of WW296. This is only a 1,100 fps load, but it is very accurate out to long range. I have used it to a full 800 yards shooting at two-foot square targets, and actually managed to hit them once in awhile by watching the bullets strike up dust and walking them in.

AUXILIARY CYLINDERS

Later, Freedom Arms made the .454 packin' pistol even more versatile by offering an auxiliary cylinder in .45 ACP. I

sent my 4¾-inch .454 back to the factory to have it fitted not only with a .45 ACP cylinder, but a .45 Colt cylinder as well. Why a .45 ACP cylinder? Simple. I have hundreds, probably thousands of rounds of various .45 ACP loads around. When used in the Casull, they make for pleasant shooting, and I do not have to chase brass all over Idaho. Nor do I have to mess with full- or half-moon clips. With a single-action revolver, both rimmed and rimless brass all extract the same way. Shoot 'em. Drop 'em in the Dillon Case Vibrator. Load 'em on the Dillon 550. Repeat. The .45 ACP cylinder also allows experimenting with the grand, old round that would never be possible in any other handgun. Retro-fitted auxiliary cylinders lock up tightly and are fitted just as precisely as the original .454 cylinder. The back of each cylinder is marked with the caliber, while the original .454 cylinder is serial numbered to the gun so each cylinder is easily identified.

I was well pleased with the new versatility of my 4¾-inch Model 83. I could carry it with the .454 cylinder fitted with either full-house loads or milder — though still heavy — .45 Colt loads. Installing the .45 Colt cylinder precludes the use of some loads I like, as the wide front bands on the bullets will not enter the tight cylinder, although they work fine in the .454 cylinder. But if you use .45 Colt loads in the .454 cylinder, keep the cylinder brushed out so a ring does not form.

SELECT LOADS FOR THE FREEDOM ARMS .454 CASULL

LOAD	MV: 4¾"	MV: 7½"	MV: 10"
BULLET: FREEDOM ARMS/LYMAN 260-GR. GAS CHECK. #454628			
PRIMER: REMINGTON #7½ BENCH REST RIFLE • TEMPERATURE: 60-80 DEGREES			
22.0 gr. #2400	1,268 fps	1,371 fps	1,420 fps
24.0 gr. #2400	1,414 fps	1,516 fps	1,563 fps
26.0 gr. #2400	1,465 fps	1,590 fps	1,623 fps
28.0 gr. #2400	1,555 fps	1,663 fps	1,706 fps
30.0 gr. #2400	1,668 fps	1,803 fps	1,849 fps
32.0 gr. #2400	1,754 fps	1,876 fps	1,924 fps
34.0 gr. WW296	1,628 fps	1,750 fps	1,795 fps
37.0 gr. WW296	1,779 fps	1,903 fps	1,972 fps
33.0 gr. H110	1,606 fps	1,727 fps	1,780 fps
35.0 gr. H110	1,712 fps	1,841 fps	1,888 fps
37.0 gr. H110	1,543 fps	1,650 fps	1,710 fps
BULLET: NEI/SSK INDUSTRIES 270-GR. GC #270.451			
22.0 gr. #2400	1,264 fps	1,352 fps	1,380 fps
28.0 gr. #2400	1,504 fps	1,626 fps	1,659 fps
30.0 gr. #2400	1,628 fps	1,760 fps	1,796 fps
32.0 gr. #2400	1,741fps	1,862 fps	1,910 fps
35.0 gr. H110	1,668 fps	1,783 fps	1,820 fps
36.0 gr. H110	1,699 fps	1,817 fps	1,864 fps
38.0 gr. H110	1,822 fps	1,959 fps	1,989 fps
BULLET: NEI 300-GR. #310.451 KEITH-STYLE*			
23.0 gr. WW296	1,256 fps	1,357 fps	1,378 fps
25.0 gr. WW296	1,378 fps	1,489 fps	1,512 fps
27.0 gr. WW296	1,465 fps	1,567 fps	1,607 fps
29.0 gr. WW296	1,538 fps	1,663 fps	1,688 fps
21.0 gr. H110	1,034 fps	1,135 fps	1,270 fps
24.0 gr. H110	1,256 fps	1,342 fps	1,363 fps
26.0 gr. H110	1,381 fps	1,477 fps	1,500 fps
28.0 gr. H110	1,498 fps	1,602 fps	1,643 fps
29.0 gr. H110	1,509 fps	1,632 fps	1,674 fps
21.0 gr. #4227	1,159 fps	1,258 fps	1,284 fps
24.0 gr. #4227	1,318 fps	1,438 fps	1,452 fps
18.0 gr. #2400	1,120 fps	1,229 fps	1,277 fps
20.0 gr. #2400	1,276 fps	1,394 fps	1,417 fps
22.0 gr. #2400	1,383 fps	1,509 fps	1,533 fps
18.0 gr. AA#9	1,165 fps	1,259 fps	1,302 fps
20.0 gr. AA#9	1,264 fps	1,362 fps	1,419 fps
22.0 gr. AA#9	1,315 fps	1,449 fps	1,500 fps
24.0 gr. AA #1680	1,000 fps	1,160 fps	1,180 fps
26.0 gr. AA#1680	1,122 fps	1,238 fps	1,292 fps
BULLET: NEI 325-GR. #325.451 KEITH-STYLE*			
20.0 gr. H110	1,049 fps	1,159 fps	1,185 fps
23.0 gr. H110	1,282 fps	1,371 fps	1,392 fps
25.0 gr. H110	1,352 fps	1,454 fps	1,480 fps
28.0 gr. H110	1,495 fps	1,599 fps	1,640 fps
18.0 gr. #2400	1,207 fps	1,288 fps	1,323 fps
21.0 gr. #2400	1,369 fps	1,466 fps	1,482 fps

*All NEI Keith-style bullets are crimped over the front band.

LOAD	MV: 4¾"	MV: 7½"	MV: 10"
BULLET: NEI/SSK 340-GR. #345.451			
22.0 gr. H110	1,037 fps	1,220 fps	1,233 fps
26.0 gr. H110	1,332 fps	1,493 fps	1,497 fps
28.0 gr. H110	1,435 fps	1,585 fps	1,610 fps
30.0 gr. H110	1,513 fps	1,672 fps	1,706 fps
32.0 gr. H110	1,605 fps	1,773 fps	1,800 fps
19.0 gr. #2400	1,130 fps	1,288 fps	1,291 fps
21.0 gr. #2400	1,212 fps	1,352 fps	1,368 fps
24.0 gr. #2400	1,402 fps	1,516 fps	1,563 fps
20.0 gr. #4227	995 fps	1,094 fps	1,116 fps
22.0 gr. #4227	1,095 fps	1,236 fps	1,257 fps
24.0 gr. #2400	1,225 fps	1,340 fps	1,373 fps
BULLET: HORNADY 250-GR. XTP-JHP			
30.0 gr. WW296	1,282 fps	1,386 fps	1,422 fps
32.0 gr. WW296	1,437 fps	1,537 fps	1,560 fps
34.0 gr. WW296	1,565 fps	1,691 fps	1,735 fps
16.0 gr. HS6	1,080 fps	1,241 fps	1,279 fps
18.0 gr. HS6	1,242 fps	1,321 fps	1,382 fps
20.0 gr. HS6	1,374 fps	1,457 fps	1,477 fps
17.0 gr. HS7	1,065 fps	1,172 fps	1,224 fps
19.0 gr. HS7	1,210 fps	1,316 fps	1,348 fps
21.0 gr. HS7	1,315 fps	1,436 fps	1,462 fps
22.0 gr. #4227	1,030 fps	1,133 fps	1,136 fps
25.0 gr. #4227	1,105 fps	1,240 fps	1,248 fps
BULLET: FREEDOM ARMS 240-GR. JHP			
36.0 gr. H110	1,637 fps	1,795 fps	1,865 fps
38.0 gr. H110	1,770 fps	1,950 fps	1,955 fps
29.0 gr. #4227	1,384 fps	1,437 fps	1,452 fps
31.0 gr. #4227	1,450 fps	1,572 fps	1,577 fps
32.0 gr. #4227	1,511 fps	1,600 fps	1,637 fps
BULLET: FREEDOM ARMS 260-GR. JHP			
30.0 gr. H110	1,362 fps	1,472 fps	1,510 fps
32.0 gr. H110	1,427 fps	1,526 fps	1,557 fps
34.0 gr. H110	1,503 fps	1,656 fps	1,675 fps
36.0 gr. H110	1,596 fps	1,810 fps	1,814 fps
30.0 gr. #4227	1,390 fps	1,488 fps	1,508 fps
32.0 gr. #4227	1,485 fps	1,622 fps	1,631 fps
33.0 gr. #4227	1,540 fps	1,662 fps	1,683 fps
BULLET: FREEDOM ARMS 300-GR. JSP			
28.0 gr. H110	1,351 fps	1,412 fps	1,478 fps
30.0 gr. H110	1,450 fps	1,529 fps	1,570 fps
33.0 gr. H110	1,628 fps	1,717 fps	1,743 fps
27.0 gr. #4227	1,218 fps	1,344 fps	1,397 fps
29.0 gr. #4227	1,348 fps	1,473 fps	1,491 fps

SIXGUNS AND THEIR CARTRIDGES

Full-dress Freedom Arms: In celebration of its 25th Anniversary in 2008, the factory offered this Aniversary Model .454.

Replacing the .454 cylinder with the .45 Colt cylinder lets me use factory .45 Colt loads (and equivalent handloads) in the Casull, as well as some of my heavier loads made up for the Ruger .45 Blackhawk. The full-house .45 Colt/.454-style loads are loaded only with bullets that will enter the .454 Casull cylinder and not others such as the Colt SAA.

For a pleasant day of plinking or close-range varminting, in goes the .45 ACP cylinder. Since the best factory defensive loads are not made for the .454 or .45 Colt, but for the ACP, that would be the best choice if the gun was intended as a house or camp defender. Even with all this versatility, something in the back of my head kept nagging me to take one more step. What in the world could it be? Well, of course, I needed a .45 WinMag cylinder. Off it went back to Freedom Arms and the Triple Threat became a 4-Way Threat.

I soon added a third .454, a 7½-inch which went with me to Africa. My Field Grade .454 is a 7½-inch version with a few

options. Since I find the Pachmayr grips a trifle large for my hand, and also prefer the traditional look of a standard single action grip, I went the route of ordering black micarta grips fitted to the Field Grade. They look extremely attractive when mated with the subdued bead blasted finish of the stainless steel .454. Since all Freedom Arms Single Actions come with a heavier than desirable trigger pull, I also ordered an action job with the trigger set at 2½ to 3 pounds, the same weight range specified on all my Freedom Arms single actions. Finally, I prefer the standard Freedom Arms sights instead of the Ruger rear that is standard on the Field Grade. The Premier Grade rear sight has also been changed positively and now carries the deeper notch I prefer for precise shooting. With the options I ordered, I feel this 7½-inch Field Grade .454 Casull is about as close to perfection as you can get in an all-around single-action revolver. For tough outdoor service in a 52-ounce portable package, this is it.

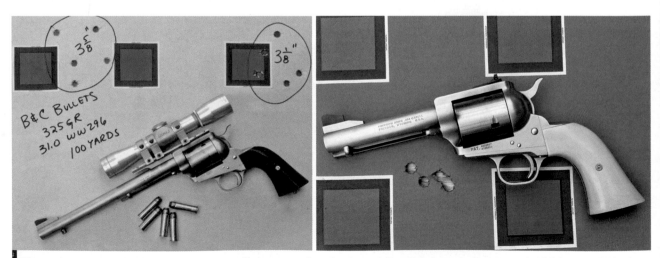

Power plus precision: At 20 yards, John got excellent accuracy from his 4¾-inch Freedom Arms single action using full-house .454 loads (right). The scoped, long barrel version (left) was equally impressive at 100 yards.

BULLETS, BULLETS, BULLETS

With the velocities possible in the .454, many jacketed bullets may be found wanting. The original Freedom Arms bullets had a jacket of .032 inch. Any bullet used for the highest performance should also be as heavily jacketed. For lighter jacketed bullet loads in the .454, I turn to Sierra's 240-grain JHC, Hornady's 250-grain JHP or Speer's 260-grain JHP. These .45 Colt bullets have lighter jackets than the original Freedom Arms .454 bullets and will work best at velocities around 1,600 fps or less. The same thing applies when it comes to cast bullets. The .454 is a natural for cast bullets if they are chosen — and loaded — wisely. Some 240- to 260-grain cast bullets will not perform as well at the higher speeds as they lose accuracy when pushed too fast. Different guns react differently, so experimentation may be necessary. My best results have been with gas-check bullets in the 300-grain range.

One 255-grain cast bullet designed for the .45 Colt also works well in the .454 — Lyman's #454424 designed by Elmer Keith back in the 1920s. For a heavy load with this one, I like 25.0 grains of #2400 for 1,600 fps. For a mild load, I go with 16.0 grains of HS6 for 1,300 fps and no unburned powder granules to work their way into the tight-fitting parts of the Freedom Arms revolver. My most accurate loads with the .454 are all assembled with bullets in the 300-grain weight range and up. There are a number of excellent heavyweight designs by NEI, Lyman and SSK. NEI's contributions are both "Keith-style" bullets. Because of their nose length, they require crimping over the front band when used in the .454.

The NEI bullets are #310.451 and #325.454. The first three numbers give the approximate weight and the last three indicate the caliber. For the 310-grain bullet, I prefer 18.0 grains of #2400 (1,230 fps), 21.0 grains of #2400 (1,450 fps) and 25.0 grains of H110 (1,500 fps). These are not full-house loads but are plenty for most shooters and most chores. For the slightly heavier 325-grain Keith bullet, I like 21.0 grains of H110 for a pleasant-shooting 1,225 fps or

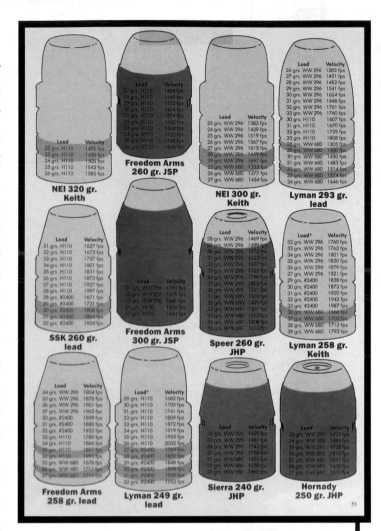

John's maiden voyage: This exhaustive chart of loads appeared in the July/August 1987 issue of *American Handgunner.*

26.0 grains for a bull-busting 1,500 fps. Both of these bullets shed their velocity very slowly and, when started at 1,500 fps, will still be traveling nearly 1,200 fps at 200 yards. That is a *lot* of downrange energy.

The heaviest practical bullet for the .454 is also one of the most accurate. This is the J.D. Jones-designed SSK #345.451, which drops a 340-grain bullet with my hard-casting mixture. Start at 22.0 grains of H110 for 1,200 fps and go all the way up to 32.0 grains of H110 for right at 1,800 fps (all the recoil I wanted 25 years ago and don't even want to contemplate now). Lyman's heavyweight .454 bullet is #454629. It's a 300-grain flatpoint, gas-check design by Dick Casull himself. This one has been specifically designed to withstand the high velocities possible with the .454 Casull. My starting load for it is 26.0 grains of WW296 for 1,400 fps, and I stop at 32.0 grains of WW296 for 1,700 fps.

POWER PLAY!

EXCERPTS FROM THE PAST

AMERICAN HANDGUNNER JULY/AUGUST 1987

Special Handgun Hunting Issue

JULY/AUGUST 1987 — $2.50 IN CANADA $3.50

AMERICAN HANDGUNNER

CENTIMETER
is a new 10mm combat cartridge ideal for self-defense and competition

THE TRUTH about handgun hunting from expert J. D. Jones

THE SAGA of handgun hunting, a gripping essay by Massad Ayoob

THE CUSTOM .44 for handgun hunting from Bill Wilson

THE .454 CASULL hotter than the .30-06?

You Can Win an Andy Cannon fighting revolver designed by Massad Ayoob in our **CUSTOM GUN GIVEAWAY**

"Here, John, try this one. Each time Dick Casull spoke those words he handed me another of his special loads for his .454. I spent three delightful days at Freedom, Wyoming, much of the time spent visiting with, talking to, and above all, learning from Dick, the firearms genius behind the .454 Casull. We were spending the afternoon running some of his special-purpose loads through his 12" octagon barreled .454 Freedom Arms single action. He had claimed 2,350 fps for this gun with his 260-grain cast bullet over a very stiff charge of Winchester 296 ignited by Remington Bench Rest Rifle Primers.

"Now I had no reason to doubt his claims, but I had been experimenting with the .454 for almost a year prior to my journey to Freedom and the best I could do from my 10" was slightly over 2,000 fps, and this resulted in stuck cases. That was before I learned a few secrets from Dick about special-purpose loads. If Dick did manage to come through with his claims, a 260-grain bullet at 2,350 fps the muzzle energy would be 3,188 ft-lbs! Now that is 14 percent more than the energy produced by a 150-grain bullet from a .30/06!

This from a straight-wall pistol cartridge fired from a 12-inch revolver barrel!

"I nestled the .454 down on the sand bags, got a good grip on the stock, and squeezed the trigger. Recoil was fierce, and as the gun came down out of recoil I checked the velocity reading on my Oehler Model 33 Chronograph: 2,344 fps! The next four rounds showed virtually the same reading, and all cases ejected with a tap on the extractor rod. No wonder this load shot through 3/8" steel, as Dick had demonstrated the day before and which I was fortunate to capture on videotape.

"After trying this load, I did not think there would be anything else left to try. How wrong I was. Now it was time for Dick's big load, a 400-grain cast bullet at 1,600 fps. Compare this with the factory .45/70 with a 405-grain bullet at 1,300 fps from a 32" rifle barrel. The recoil of this load proved to be not quite as bad as the 260-grain/2,350 fps number, but it was right up there. The chronograph again substantiated Dick's claim: 1,606 fps.

"Pressures for the .454 Casull factory loads and reloads run to 60,000 CUP and more. The gun is built to take it, and indeed, has tremendous safety built into it. Primer pockets will blow and cases may split if pressures are too high, but the revolver will take it. Because of the pressures involved — higher even than many rifles — only rifle primers should be used in reloading for the .454 Casull. Dick himself recommends Remington Benchrest Rifle Primers. The original brass for the .454 was nothing more than .45 Colt brass lengthened from 1.285" to 1.385". The case was lengthened simply to prevent its entering .45 Colt chambers. Some .45 Colt chambers on the sloppy side will chamber the .454, but anyone trying something like this is literally playing with dynamite. No .45 Colt will even come close to handling the .454 and will probably blow with the first round and could have disastrous results. Don't even think of trying it!

"The new batch of brass has been beefed up in the web area and has a small primer pocket for the use of small rifle primers. Older brass is head stamped; ".454 Casull NAA" while the newer batch of brass is marked with: "F-A 454 Casull." The newer brass, even though heavier, will give slightly less muzzle velocity than the older brass because of the change from large to small rifle primers. My original lot of 500 rounds of brass has been loaded heavily 10 times or more and I have lost two cases, one with the neck split and the other with a vertical split down the side. It is amazing what the brass will take when used in the tight chambers of the Casull revolver ...

"The .454 Casull is first and foremost a hunting handgun. Larry Kelly used it with 300-grain JFP's–loaded by Freedom Arms to 1,700 fps — on his recent African safari. Kelly used the .454 on hippo, croco-

dile, Cape buffalo and lion. Only one bullet was recovered, that used on the Cape buffalo. Kelly said: 'The .454 Casull left nothing to be desired — accurate, dependable, and capable of taking any animal on earth.' High praise from the premier handgun hunter. The .454 has also been used with success in America on elk, moose and Alaskan brown bear, plus many deer and black bear ...

"The .454 Casull has made its reputation as 'The Worlds Most Powerful Revolver.' This it is, and it is not likely to be challenged by any production gun. It is also an extremely accurate revolver. My 10", even when equipped with iron sights, seems to have built-in radar. It is one of those all-too-rare revolvers which just seems to shoot everything well. The reason for this is the close tolerances held by Freedom Arms and also the barrel twist of 1:24, which not only stabilizes 250-grain bullets but is perfect for the 300-340-grain ones ...

"The 4¾" .454 requires more concentration and I have not been able to shoot it as well as a longer barrel .454. However, using 400-grain bullets at 1,400 fps from the short barrel, I have put five shots in 7/8" at 25 yards. Even the 4¾" Casull shoots extremely well at long range. A 300-grain bullet with a muzzle velocity of 1,400 fps is still traveling 1,150 fps at 225 yards. This is a lot of downrange energy. I will not insult any reader's intelligence by saying that the .454 is pleasant to shoot. Exciting, yes. Exhilarating, definitely. Fun? Absolutely. The grip design is a good one and helps lessen felt recoil. But there is no way to have as much muzzle energy as the .454 is capable of without paying for it. If, however, you can handle a heavily loaded .44 Magnum you can also handle a .454. The .454 Casull from Freedom Arms is the most expensive American-made production revolver available. It is also the strongest, probably the best built, and capable of outstanding accuracy ..." ◎

Two Model 97s in .45 Colt persuasion:
the easy-carrying 5½ inch with adjustable sights
and the shockingly compact 3½-inch Round Butt.

FREEDOM ARMS MODEL 97

CHAPTER 22

Fourteen years after the introduction of the five-shot Model 83 .454 Casull revolver, Freedom Arms introduced its "90 percent gun," the smaller Model 97. The first such single actions offered — in what came to be known as the Mid-Frame — were true sixguns, with six-shot cylinders in .357 Magnum. They could be had with either fixed or adjustable sights and with 5½- or 7½-inch barrels. As soon as the .357 Magnum arrived, dedicated sixgunners began to speculate about a larger caliber. We did not have to wait long for a five-shot .45 Colt — the most compact single action chambered for *the* classic big-bore sixgun cartridge ever factory-produced.

The .45 Colt Model 97 is one ounce lighter than a 5½-inch Colt SAA at 38 ounces, two ounces lighter than the same barrel length in the Colt New Frontier. It also has the same natural feel and pointability as the Colt, but there all similarity ceases. The grip shape of the M97 is longer and straighter than the Colt SAA (a case could be made to the effect it's actually an improvement).

With its light weight, the Model 97 does exhibit some recoil with 255-grain bullets at 1,000 fps-plus, and although not totally unpleasant, it is does take its toll when hundreds of rounds are fired in a day. It's nothing like the same amount of full-house .454s from the larger Model 83, but it will leave some soreness in your shooting

John took advantage of a 4x LER scope to shoot this group at 25 yards with Winchester .45 Colt 225-grain Silvertips.

hand. Most shooters will definitely find loads in the 850-fps range are a whole lot more pleasant, especially during lengthy range sessions.

The Model 97 is a thoroughly modern sixgun made of stainless steel, hand-fitted parts and extremely close tolerances. It also features a transfer bar safety. The five-shot Model 97 .45 Colt is safe to carry fully loaded with a round under the chamber, but old habits of mine are hard to break. As an aside, every single action — including Freedom Arms models — should always have the hammer fully cocked and then carefully lowered. If the hammer is lowered from the half-cock notch, it is easy to lock up the action and put the sixgun out of commission temporarily.

The Mid-Frame Model 97 adheres to the same high quality and attention to detail as its full-size Model 83. Model 97 .45 Colt barrels are exactly the same stock as used on the Model 83. Each gun is made of stainless steel; cylinders and barrels are line-bored.

STACKING UP TO THE COMPETITION

Size-wise here is how the Freedom Arms Model 97 .45 Colt compares with three other .45 sixguns — a 3rd Generation Colt New Frontier, an Old Model Ruger .45 Blackhawk and the Freedom Arms Model 83 .454 Casull. Using the Hornady Digital Caliper, I come up with the following measurements:

	M97	M83	RUGER	COLT NF
CYLINDER LENGTH	1.627"	1.780"	1.748"	1.610"
CYLINDER DIAMETER	1.575"	1.751"	1.723"	1.649"
CHAMBER THROATS	.4515"	.4515"	.451"	.456"
CYLINDER WALL THICKNESS	.058"	.123"	.085"	.063"
THICKNESS BETWEEN CHAMBERS	.0905"	.129"	.0585"	.048"

A check with the calculator shows that the cylinder wall thickness of the .45 Colt Mid-Frame Model 97 is about 50 percent that of the Model 83 .454, 70 percent of the Old

John shoots his favorite barrel length — the 7½-inch Model 97 (top) and the same model (left) in 5½-inch trim.

my 300-grain loads will fit the Model 97's cylinder. When bullets are seated properly they protrude through the front face of the cylinder preventing cylinder rotation. However, Buffalo Bore offers a special loading for the Model 97 using a 300-grain Hornady XTP-JHP at 1,200 fps that will work. Recoil, of course, is *heavy*, but the power is there if you need it.

GOOD-TIME PACKIN'

Because my favorite sixgun is a .44 or .45 with a 7½-inch barrel, I could have opted for a Model 97 with that barrel length. I *was* tempted, but I didn't. My wife is the main fisherman in the family, and I wanted her to be able to easily pack this sixgun for several days in comfort. This is a sixgun for enjoyable times — plinking with the kids, hiking, close-range varminting and, if the chance presents itself, a deer at (very) close range. An awful lot of coyotes, deer and black bear have been taken with the standard .45 Colt load, including the original black-powder cartridges. The Freedom Arms Model 97 is right at home for these types of situations with a 255-grain bullet at 800 to 1,000 fps.

For easy packin' qualities, I settled on the 5½-inch barrel, and to complete the picture I ordered adjustable sights and black micarta grips. As with all Freedom Arms revolvers, the Model 97 is all-stainless steel (no lawyer-driven warning

Model Ruger and 92 percent of the Colt SAA. The Model 97 is slightly smaller than a Colt SAA and quite a bit smaller where it counts than the Ruger and Freedom Arms .454. For most uses, it remains a standard-size sixgun for standard loads. The .45 Colt Model 97 with its five-shot cylinder allows more metal between chambers, almost 90 percent more than a Colt SAA. Unlike the Colt with its near paper-thin walls, the Model 97 has the cylinder bolt slots between the chambers rather than underneath them.

The Model 97 in .45 Colt is probably as strong as the Ruger .45 Blackhawk. But I have no intention of using heavy .45 Colt loads tailored for the Ruger or Freedom Arms Model 83 very often. My max loads for the .45 Blackhawk are 300-grain hard-cast bullets at 1,100-1,200 fps. For the Model 97 I mostly stay with 255-grain bullets at around 1,000 fps or less. I am not concerned about strength, but more about practicality and recoil. None of

labels!). The Model 97 is even more versatile with one other addition — a .45 ACP cylinder allowing for an additional range of target and defensive loads. With its interchangeable front sight system on the adjustable-sight models, the height of the front blade can be easily changed when you go from, say, .45 ACP 185-grain JHPs to 260-grain hard-cast .45 Colt loads.

The Freedom Arms Model 97 (far right) compared to (from top left, down) the Colt New Frontier, Freedom Arms Model 83 and Ruger Blackhawk.

I do not prefer a light trigger pull on any sixgun or rifle, and — from the factory — the trigger on my Model 97 scales out at 3½ pounds. This is just about perfect for a single-action workin' sixgun. The action is smooth, the cylinder locks up tightly, with almost no perceptible movement fore, aft or side to side. The barrel/cylinder gap is almost imperceptible.

Double-action sixguns in .45 ACP need full or half-moon clips for reliable ignition and the best possible accuracy. A single-action sixgun like the Model 97 doesn't. Instead, the ledge at the front edge of the cylinder catches the mouth of the rimless .45 ACP case and provides the headspace. All ACP rounds I tested in the Model 97's auxiliary cylinder func-

tioned perfectly, except for some misfires with Cor-Bon's 165-grain Plus-P JHPs. A call to Cor-Bon confirmed that the 165s did have a kiss of a crimp which was causing the problem.

My Model 97 has been fired extensively with both .45 Colt and .45 ACP loads. Excellent groups were common with both cylinders, using both iron sights and a Leupold LER 4x scope mounted with an SSK base and rings. The rear sight assembly removes easily by loosening two screws, then lifting it out of its recess in the top of the frame to reveal three drilled and tapped holes to accept the SSK mount. I am a slow typist to be sure; however, it takes less time to do all of this than for me to type out the directions! Both the rear sight assembly and scope mounts of the Model 97 fit in — not on — the top of the frame.

CYLINDER CONSIDERATIONS

Favorite loads for the Model 97 .45 Colt style definitely include Hodgdon's #4227 and 250- to 260-grain bullets. With RCBS's 45-250FN, a deadringer for the original .45 Colt bullet of the 1870s,

The .45 Colt Model 97 Round Butt 3½-inch deserves John's title of Perfect Packin' Pistol. Bullet weights are, of course, constrained by the relatively short cylinder length.

or Oregon Trail's 255-grain SWC and 20.0 grains of #4227, muzzle velocity is 1,000 fps, and group size is right at an inch

OREGON TRAIL
255 SWC
7.0 HP 38
736 FPS

The .45 Colt Model 97 Round Butt is easy packin' and quite accurate.

at 25 yards. With the 4x Leupold in place, smaller groups at the same distance were commonplace.

Close attention must be paid to overall cartridge length due to the relatively short cylinder. It is necessary to crimp

Buffalo Bore offers
Heavy Duty 300-grain JSP
.45 Colt loads specially tailored
for the short cylinder of the Model 97.

some bullets over the front shoulder to keep them from protruding out the front of the cylinder. The abovementioned Oregon Trail load is especially pleasing, as this powder has never failed me in the .45 Colt. When all else fails, reach for #4227. If the gun doesn't shoot with 18.5 to 20 grains of #4227 and a 255-grain bullet, it will probably never work with anything.

We have such a vast array of .45 ACP ammunition available today it makes a lot of sense to have an extra ACP cylinder for any .45 Colt, especially one which has adjustable sights. With the .45 ACP cylinder and loads fired both with the adjustable sights and Leupold 4x scope in play, they show this .45/.45ACP sixgun to be no slouch in the little brother department. With Winchester's 185-grain FMC Match, four shots cut one ragged little hole at 25 yards measuring 3/8 inch. Pretty impressive from a single-action revolver *without* moon clips.

PACKABLE PERFECTION

The 5½-inch Freedom Arms .45 Colt Model 97 is definitely a top candidate for the title of Perfect Packin' Pistol. All of us on the quest for the elusive ideal have different ideas of just what it should be. It changes with our lifestyle, where we live, where we wander, our age, our attitude and on and on and on. The PPP can be chambered in anything from the wonderful little .22 Long Rifle up to one of the really big bores, such as the .475 and .500 Linebaughs. But as I have gotten older, I especially look to lighter sixguns as a PPP candidate, and this Model 97 is right up there now on my list. It has also been joined by another excellent candidate.

About 10 years ago at the SHOT Show, Freedom Arms unveiled another Model 97 variant. The first round-butted, short-barreled Model 97 was a 3½-inch barreled, fixed-sight .45 Colt weighing exactly two pounds. That is about as easy to pack as anything you can find. To come up with it, Freedom Arms rounds only the heel of the butt, leaving the toe intact. I tried it this way for a while and decided it would work much better for me if that toe was also slightly rounded out. I had my gunsmith at Buckhorn do about a quarter-inch round-butting to stop my little finger from getting bitten by the square toe — a great improvement.

For my use in the 3½-inch Model 97 Round-Butt, I've pretty much settled on 250- to 260-grain bullets in the 900-1,000 fps range. The same loads will average 150-200 fps more in 7½-inch sixguns, so they are a handful (for me) in this relatively lightweight little .45. When the situation calls for something heavy duty, I go with a hard-cast WFNGC (Wide Flat-Nose Gas-Check) bullet over 18.5 grains of #2400. Because the cylinder length requires deeper seating of this bullet, muzzle velocity

is just under 1,000 fps, and the load provides all the recoil I want on a steady basis. However, when traveling, it is a comforting insurance policy. It turns the Round-Butt Model 97 into a "Pocket Perfect Packin' Pistol." ◎

TEST-FIRE: MODEL 97 5½-INCH .45 COLT

LOAD	MV	IRON SIGHTS	4X SCOPE
Blazer 200-gr. JHP	892 fps	1"	1⅛"
Black Hills 255-gr. SWC	897 fps	1½"	1¾
Winchester 225-gr. Silvertip HP	854 fps	1⅞"	7/8"
Or.Trail 250-gr. RNFP/8.0 gr. Unique	906 fps	1¼"	1¼
Or. Trail 250-gr. RNFP/20.0 gr. #4227	979 fps	1⅞"	1¼"
Or. Trail 250-gr. RNFP/6.0 gr. N100	912 fps	1⅞"	3/4
Or. Trail 250-gr. RNFP/6.0 gr. Red Dot	887 fps	1⅜"	7/8"
Or. Trail 250-gr. RNFP/6.0 TiteGroup	851 fps	3/4"	7/8
Or. Trail 255-gr./20.0 gr. #4227	1,000 fps	1⅛"	1"
RCBS #45-250-gr.FN/8.0 gr. Unique	974 fps	2⅛"	1¼
RCBS #45-250-gr.FN/20.0 gr. #4227	1,030 fps	1"	1"
RCBS #45-250-gr.FN/7.0 gr. WW231	939 fps	1¾"	3/4
RCBS #45-255-gr.KT/18.5 gr. #4227	929 fps	1⅜"	1⅛"
RCBS #45-255-gr.KT/6.0 gr. Red Dot	850 fps	1¾"	3/4"
RCBS #45-255-gr.KT/6.0 gr. TiteGroup	889 fps	1¾"	5/8"

TEST-FIRE: MODEL 97 5½-INCH .45 ACP

LOAD	MV	IRON SIGHTS	4X SCOPE
Black Hills 200-gr. JHP	982 fps	1¾"	1⅜"
Blazer 200-gr. JHP	858 fps	1⅞"	1¼"
Blazer 230-gr. FMJ	994 fps	1⅞"	1⅜"
Federal 230-gr. FMJ Match	876 fps	1¾"	1¼"
Hornady 200-gr. XTP-JHP	924 fps	1½"	1"
Remington 185-gr. JHP	1,063 fps	1⅜"	1¼
Speer 230-gr. Gold Dot JHP	898 fps	1¼"	1¼"
Speer Lawman 200-gr. JHP	1,029 fps	2½"	1¼
Winchester 230-gr. FMJ	717 fps	2½"	1¼"

All groups are four shots at 25 yards. Leupold 4X Long Eye Relief Scope used for shooting scoped groups.

John's Improved No. 5 in .45 Colt has been stocked with sheep horn by Roy Fishpaw. Above it is the South Texas Army in .44 Magnum.

TEXAS LONGHORN ARMS
IMPROVED NO. 5

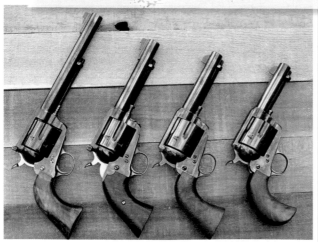

Bill Grover offered four models of his "right-handed" single actions with (from left) the West Texas Flat-Top Target, Improved No. 5, South Texas Army and Border Special.

CHAPTER 23

On July 4, 1925, a young cowboy decided to celebrate by firing his Colt .45 SAA. He was using black-powder loads, but the bullets were oversized — and he had ground the black powder to finer granules. When the charge ignited, the top half of the cylinder and the top strap parted company from the old Colt. This not only caused him to switch from the .45 to the .44 Special, but it also started a writing career which would span six decades.

From the late 1920s until 1955, Elmer Keith continually promoted the .44 Special as the ideal sixgun cartridge using

At left is a No. 5 grip frame by Gordon Marts on a Bisley Model Colt compared to the grip frame of the Texas Longhorn Arms Improved No. 5.

his personally designed #429421 Keith bullet weighing in at 250 grains with a muzzle velocity of 1,200 fps using Hercules #2400. Over the years, Keith featured his sixguns in his articles, and as a teenager I purchased a copy of *Sixguns by Keith* and spent hours studying the pictures of his many custom sixguns. After I met Keith for the first time, he supplied me with a list of all his old sixgun articles from the *American Rifleman,* and I was able to add those to my file.

Keith was, as he called himself, a "gun crank" and wasn't satisfied with stock factory sixguns, so he enlisted the help of some top gunsmiths and engravers. Most of his .44 Specials and .44 Magnums as well as his rifles and trophy animals are part of the Keith Collection displayed at the Boise, Idaho, Cabela's Elmer Keith Museum. It is worth the trip just to see Keith's No. 5, as he called it, as well as approximately 60 other firearms, both sixguns and rifles.

Even though Keith switched to the .44 Special in the late 1920s, he did not totally give up on the old .45 Colt. Hanging on my wall are several photos of Keith drawing an ivory-stocked .45 Colt SAA with a 4¾-inch barrel, adjustable rear sight, barrel band front sight and wide hammer. When I was privileged as a Member of the Elmer Keith Museum Foundation Board to examine Keith's personal sixguns, I found an old black-powder .45 Colt SAA along with four SAA .44 Specials. The .44s included a 7½ inch with a King short action job, a one-of-a kind 7½-inch Flat-Top Target, a custom 5½-inch Flap-Top Target with a Keith-designed folding three-leaf rear sight and the No. 5 SAA. The No. 5 was an extensively customized 5½-inch Flat-Top Target Model with a special grip made by combining a Bisley backstrap and Colt SAA trigger guard. The seeds of the No. 5 were planted by another gun crank, one Harold

The No. 5 grip frame represents a blend of the Colt Single Action Army and Bisley Model grip frame.

Croft of Philadelphia. In the late 1920s, Croft packed a suitcase full of sixguns and took the train all the way across the country to Elmer Keith's small ranch in Durkee, Oregon. Today that trip would take a few hours of actual flight time; in those pre-Depression days it took several days.

Croft made his long trek because he was curious. Keith had been writing about long-range shooting at several hundred yards with a sixgun, and Croft wanted to see it for himself. In his book Keith says:

"He brought a suitcase full of good sixguns, mostly .44 Special or .45 Colt caliber and asked me to demonstrate some of the long-range shooting I had been writing about. Seven hundred yards across a dry, dusty field I had a target four feet square. By laying on my back with my saddle used for a head and shoulder rest, and shooting with both hands held between my drawn up knees, I proceeded to lob slugs on that target. I hit it with every gun he brought along before the gun was empty except a two-inch barreled .45 single action slip gun with a Newman

hammer. It required 11 shots to find the target with that short-barreled gun ... With the good .44 Special and .45 Colt guns with barrels of four to 7½" it was no trouble to find the target in a shot or two, and with some I hit the four-foot target with three out of five shots."

At the time Croft was having lightweight pocket pistols built on Colt SAA and Bisley platforms, while Keith was more interested in full-sized single actions for long-range shooting and everyday packing. Croft's ideas had been turned into reality by Sedgley and Houchins, two well-known gunsmiths of the time. Sedgley did the frame work and Houchins did the sights, stocks and action work.

Croft took Keith four Featherweight .45 Colts, two on SAA frames, two on Bisley models. To produce the Featherweights, the recoil shield was hollowed out, the ejector rod was removed, the frame was narrowed down in front of the trigger guard, and the loading gate hollowed out. The frames were also flat-topped and fitted with adjustable sights. All of the Croft Featherweights weighed

Sentimental favorite: John lines up a shot with his .45 Colt Texas Longhorn Arms Improved No. 5.

between 30 and 32 ounces and were written up by Keith in a 1928 issue of *American Rifleman*.

Keith liked what he saw and, along with the ideas of Harold Croft and gunsmiths Neal Houchins, R.F. Sedgley and J.D. O'Meara, working together, the top strap of a standard Colt SAA was welded up to make a heavy Flat-Top Target design. These improvements followed:

1) *The old flat mainspring was replaced by a U-type spring.*

2) *A Bisley wide hammer was welded on to a standard one.*

3) *High Patridge-type adjustable front and rear sights were installed.*

4) *The base pin latch was changed from the traditional spring-loaded cross latch to a Keith-designed solid vertical lever to prevent the base pin from moving forward under recoil. It rotates 90 degrees for pin removal.*

5) *The grip frame was the mating of a standard SAA trigger guard with a Bisley backstrap reconfigured to Keith's specifications.*

Keith called his new sixgun the No. 5, as it had been patterned after Croft's numbers M1 to M4. The M1 to M4 were originally in .45 Colt, while Keith's No. 5 was a .44 Special. Two of the Croft sixguns have surfaced lately, and I had a chance to both handle and shoot a part of real sixgun history. Both have two dates on them, and I am assuming one date is for the original completion to .45 Colt and the other represents the changeover to .44 Special after

Croft had visited Keith who convinced him the .44 Special was better suited for heavy loads.

At least once a month I made the short pilgrimage to the Elmer Keith Museum where I never tired from looking at Keith's .44 Special and .44 Magnum sixguns — they inspired and rejuvenated me. But there is only one original No. 5, and when I was given the privilege of placing Keith's sixguns in the museum, it was given a prominent spot in the center of the display.

John's Improved No. 5 .45 Colt sits, appropriately enough, in the last No. 120 Keith holster to come out of the old George Lawrence Company.

One of Bill Grover's last sixguns was this stainless steel .45 Colt South Texas Army.

BILL GROVER WAS "RIGHT"

I first "met" Bill Grover in the pages of *GUNS* magazine more than 30 years ago, and then followed this up by meeting him in person at a 1987 gathering of The Shootists. That early article was on how Bill rebuilt a pair of 4¾-inch Colt SAAs for noted speed shooter Thell Reed. Shortly after the article appeared, Bill went from gunsmith to gunmaker as he opened the doors of Texas Longhorn Arms.

Bill was born in Kentucky in 1944. This explained his southern drawl. (He spoke in loving terms of "mah pistols.") Bill always said Sam Colt was left-handed and built his single actions — beginning with the Paterson — that way. All Colt percussion revolvers are most easily capped by switching the sixgun to the left hand and then doing the capping with the right. Colt died before the advent of the cartridge revolver, but all cartridge single actions from Colt are naturally handled by switching the gun to your left hand, which then operates the cylinder as your right hand ejects the spent cartridges and reloads the cylinder.

For Bill, this proved Colt was a lefty, for if the guns had been built for a right-handed shooter, the loading gate and ejector rod would have been on the left side so the sixgun would never leave the hand. It certainly makes sense to me, as I always switch any Colt, Freedom Arms or Ruger sixgun to my left hand for loading and unloading. To cor-

rect this, Grover formed Texas Longhorn Arms to produce "right-handed" sixguns. On all of Grover's single actions, the loading gate and ejector rod are found on the left side, and the cylinder rotates counterclockwise.

The "natural" way to load or unload a TLA single-action sixgun is to keep it in the right hand as the left hand opens the loading gate, and ejects the cartridges as the right hand rotates the cylinder. The problem with all of this is the fact that the "left-handed" way seems natural after being in use for nearly 150 years before the arrival of TLA, so I've had to force myself to learn to operate its sixguns correctly.

The company originally offered three right-handed sixguns, chambered mostly in .44 Magnum, .44 Special and .45 Colt on the same basic platform. Each was completely fabricated of 4140 steel with coil springs and a frame-mounted firing pin. Bill maintained that a properly timed TLA sixgun would *stay* properly timed if it were handled correctly. This means no line around the cylinder from the drag of the locking bolt.

TLA guns have several eye-pleasing features. All trigger guards are rounded. The triggers themselves are also rounded, contoured like a shotgun trigger and set far back in the trigger guard. The three frame screws do not protrude all the way through the frame, leaving the left side of the sixgun clean for engraving. Also all screw slots line

These targets were shot by John with his Improved No. 5 in .45 Colt. The cylinder pin locking lever (inset) on this series was patterned after the original and was designed to prevent the pin from moving forward when heavy loads are used.

up together, a feature requiring careful fitting. One of the TLA sixguns was the West Texas Flat-Top Target, a 7½-inch single action with adjustable sights and a grip frame closer to that of the 1860 Army than the Colt SAA; it is ³⁄₁₆ inch longer than the traditional single action grip frame. I find it most comfortable. Bill Grover let me borrow his personal West Texas Flat-Top Target with a 7½-inch barrel and chambered in .44 Special, and after much cajoling on my part, Grover agreed to sell me this Flat-Top Target. When I finally caught Grover at the right time, he not only agreed to sell me the Flat-Top but also offered, if I would send it back, to fit it with two more cylinders, one in .44 Magnum and the other in .44-40. I agreed to meet Bill in Texas for a hunting trip and try to take three animals, one with each cylinder, .44-40, .44 Special and .44 Magnum. Both of us were successful, and I took three critters, one with each caliber.

When the TLA West Texas Flat-Top Target came back to me with all three cylinders, Grover also included one of his Texas High Rider holster systems. The High Rider works with any single-action sixgun and is especially handy with 7½-inch barrel lengths. It is worn high, either strong-side or

cross-draw and consists of a holster proper and a belt slide. The holster fits inside the belt slide and locks into place with the bottom end of a loop on the front of the holster that snaps to the belt slide. To remove the holster, simply unsnap and raise the holster out of the belt slide. (This same rig is now offered by Ted Blocker Holsters.)

That Flat-Top Target went back to Texas one more time for a fourth cylinder chambered in .44 Russian and was scheduled to make another trip to be fitted with a .44 Colt cylinder. Now some may ask, why bother since a .44 Magnum cylinder will also handle the .44 Special, .44 Russian and .44 Colt? For those who understand, no explanation is necessary. For those who don't, no explanation is possible. Over the years this .44 Flat-Top has taken a lot of game, and I always think of Bill when I use it.

Grover's second right-handed single action was the South Texas Army with fixed sights, a barrel length of 4¾ inches, and usually offered in .44 Special or .45 Colt. Unlike the TLA West Texas Flat-Top Target, my South Texas Army has only one .44 Special cylinder. The South Texas Army has Colt SAA-style fixed sights and a grip frame much closer to the 1860 Army than the 1873 SAA. The former grip has a slightly different angle — being a little straighter than what's on the SAA — and allows room for your little finger, which no longer has to either dangle in space or be wrapped under the butt.

TLA grip frames are exceptionally comfortable when shooting heavy loads. Both the Flat-Top and South Texas Army are fitted with beautifully shaped and fitted one-piece stocks of fancy walnut and mesquite, respectively. This sixgun also needed a companion .45 Colt version which, unfortunately, did not materialize.

The late, great Bill Grover shows off a specially engraved and ivory-stocked Improved No. 5.

The Texas Border Special was fitted with a round-butt grip long before they became popular on Ruger Vaqueros and custom sixguns. Bill did this to make it easier to conceal and to reduce felt recoil with heavy loads. This traditionally styled defensive sixgun packs very easily in a hip holster or even behind the belt, and the specially designed wide hammer makes cocking fast and easy.

In 1987 Bill Grover set out not to copy the Keith No. 5, but to improve on it while keeping the original flavor. The grip straps, grip contour, base pin and lever latch are all identical to Elmer's original No. 5. I have handled both sixguns at the same time and, when it comes to the grip frame, the original No. 5 and The Improved No. 5 feel and look the same. Grover's original plans were to build 1,200 Improved No. 5s in .44 Magnum with 5½-inch barrels. After testing the original, I ordered serial number K44, which I now have, and also eventually purchased an identical model in .45 Colt. Bill's plan to produce 1,200 .44 Magnums never came to pass, nor did his dream of 1,000 each of the West Texas Flat Top Target and South Texas Army.

My first Improved No. 5 was in .44 Magnum, but I naturally wanted a companion .45 Colt, and this time it actually did work out. When I was chairman of the Outstanding American Handgun Hunter Awards Foundation, Bill Grover donated a No. 5 in .45 Colt as raffle prize. I was not eligible to be in the drawing, but the fellow who won it felt he did not have much use for the gun, so he sold it. *Guess* who bought it?

A VERY SPECIAL NUMBER

Now I had a .45 Colt Improved No. 5 and one of the first things I did was send it off to Roy Fishpaw for some suitable grips. Roy suggested I go with sheep horn, which I did. Grips made from sheep horn are mostly straw colored with an almost translucent effect, and often have black streaks when the horn comes from Rocky Mountain Bighorn and red streaks if the "donor" is an Alaskan Dall.

The Improved No. 5 has a larger cylinder and frame than a Colt SAA, being more on par with the Ruger .45 Colt Blackhawk, thus it handles heavier loads easily. Some favorites of mine for this TLA .45 are the Lyman/Keith

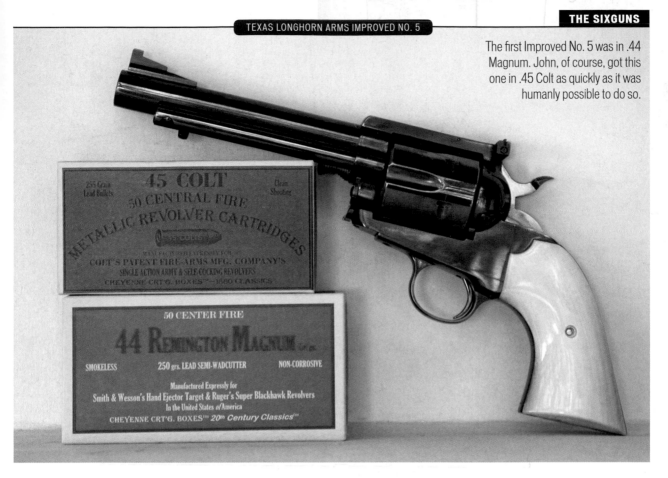

The first Improved No. 5 was in .44 Magnum. John, of course, got this one in .45 Colt as quickly as it was humanly possible to do so.

#454424 over 20.0 grains of #2400 for over 1,300 fps, and the NEI Keith-style 310- and 325-grain bullets over 21.2 grains of H110 for 1,100-1,200 fps. For an everyday working load I go with the Lyman/Keith bullet over 9.0 grains of Unique for right at 1,000 fps.

In addition to his TLA models, Grover also built a few other custom guns. Two of these for me were both .44 Specials using Ruger Old Model frames. One is a 7½-inch with custom fancy walnut grips by Charles Able. The other a 4¾-inch packin' pistol with a Colt SAA grip frame fitted with one-piece ivory stocks by BluMagnum. The long-barreled sixgun is serial number JT1. The packin' .44 Special is one of seven. The first for Skeeter Skelton was SS1. Mine is SS4. Others belong to Bart Skelton, Bob Baer, Jim Wilson and Terry Murbach. Bill made SS7 for himself.

Sadly, there will be no more. As you might understand, both of these sixguns are very special to me.

WHAT COULD HAVE BEEN

Dreams help us to maintain hope in this life. Bill and I shared two of them. The first, and largest, would see both of us hunting Africa extensively using TLA sixguns. This was to happen as soon as Texas Longhorn Arms became prosperous. The second dream was to see me designing what I considered the perfect single-action sixgun and Bill making it. Neither dream ever came true. Texas Longhorn Arms closed its doors in the late 1990s. Relatively few TLA sixguns were actually produced. When used ones are now found for sale, they are quite pricey. Grover and I were planning a No. 5 using a Colt New Frontier as the basic platform. I had the sixgun as well as a Bisley backstrap and was negotiating for a Bisley hammer. Alas, it was not to be.

Bill was a master gunmaker but a lousy businessman. He never expected such a demand for his Improved No. 5s and was unable to keep up with production. That hurt his business tremendously, along with his penchant for trusting the wrong people. Ultimately, the inevitable happened. With the closing of TLA, Bill was greatly affected physically. So much so he never really let any of us know just how sick he really was. Diabetes, kidney failure and the amputation of both legs in September 2004 was more than his body could handle. He went home in October of the same year.

So long, Bill, keep the campfire burning until I get there. ◉

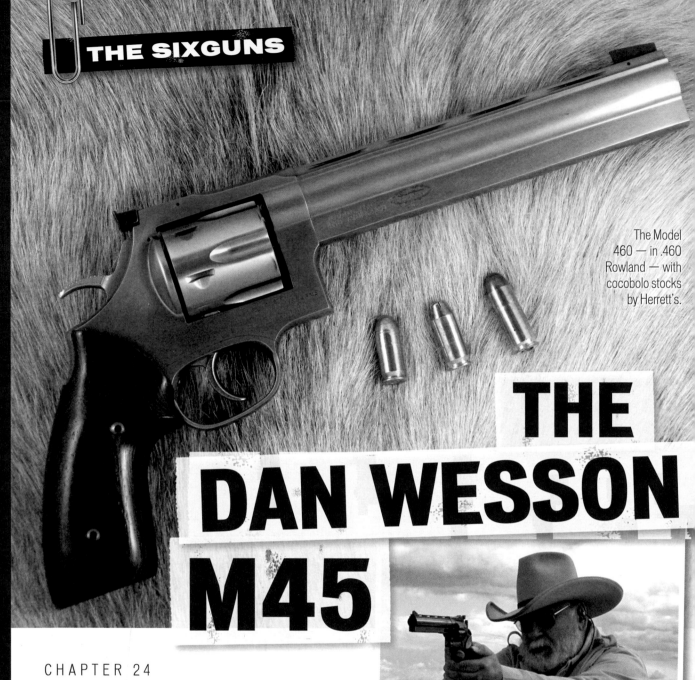

The Model 460 — in .460 Rowland — with cocobolo stocks by Herrett's.

THE DAN WESSON M45

CHAPTER 24

My first true silhouette sixgun was the Dan Wesson .357 Magnum with a heavy 10-inch barrel. It was incredibly accurate and was followed by other Dan Wesson silhouette models in .44 Magnum, .357 SuperMag and the ill-fated .375 SuperMag. (The .445 SuperMag came along a mite too late for me to use in my silhouette days.)

However, Dan Wesson's popularity with the silhouette shooters was a good news/bad news proposition. As long as there were plenty of silhouette shooters, DW had a waiting market, but once that sport began to decline, the company was caught in a squeeze. When I visited the folks at DW in the early 1990s, it was obvious the company was struggling. It was not too long after the doors were closed

John waited awhile to get his own Dan Wesson in .45 Colt. Here he is, making up for lost shooting time!

and the Dan Wesson was no more. Many sixgunners were saddened by the demise of a truly innovative revolver.

A DIFFERENT APPROACH

Dan Wesson's original plan was to offer a basic revolver with interchangeable cylinders and barrels. This was refined

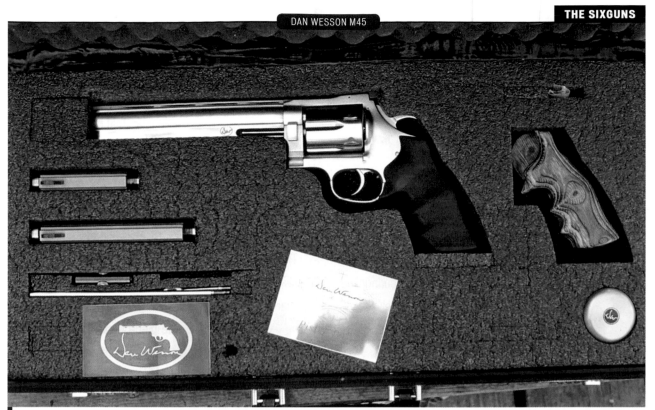

The Model 460 came in this specially padded case complete with extra barrels and extra Hogue finger-grooved wooden stocks.

somewhat when the revolver emerged in the 1970s as a sixgun featuring interchangeable barrels only. Normally, revolver barrels must be removed with the use of a vise and an action wrench. But the DW — thanks to a barrel/shroud combination with a locking nut at the front of the barrel — made it possible for anyone to change barrels by using the special wrench supplied with every sixgun.

The interchangeable barrel feature had an added bonus. DW sixguns were exceptionally accurate because the barrel locked at the front of the shroud and the barrel/cylinder gap was set tightly by the user when the barrel was installed. DW was also the first to offer interchangeable front sight blades. A sixgunner could choose from a black post, ramp, red, white or yellow inserts for the front sights. The advantage for silhouette shooters was the fact the front sights were offered in several widths and heights.

Yes, DW revolvers were accurate. but they had several problems. The front of the cylinder face and the back of the barrel were not always parallel to each other, making it difficult to set the cylinder gap. Chambers were often rough, and actions were almost always so. All of these problems, combined with the decline in silhouette shooting, eventually killed the DW sixgun.

REVOLVER RESURRECTION

However, the DW revolver did come back, produced not in Massachusetts, but in New York. Using mostly new machinery, Bob Cerva, the new owner of the company, turned out some beautiful sixguns. The first example I had from the new facility was an 8-inch heavy-barreled, stainless-steel .44 Magnum. It had a smooth action, smooth cylinder chambers and a barrel/cylinder gap that featured parallel lines. In fact, the cylinder chambers did not even have to be polished, as they came from the chambering operation with a smooth finish. The result? No more cases sticking in the cylinder.

Dan Wesson Firearms not only produced sixguns in .357 Magnum and .44 Magnum chamberings, but also the .445 and .414 SuperMags. Only a very few .414s were originally produced before the factory shut its Massachusetts facility. But from the new regime in New York, I not only received a .414 but also a .360 and a .460 (which we will look at shortly). It was not long before the new Dan Wesson Firearms was sold to CZ-USA. In the process the company found it could make 1911s quicker and sell them easier than it could revolvers.

The original DW factory did not ignore .45 Colt shooters. (Campfires and bacon frying just do not seem complete without packin' a .45 Colt.) But despite the numbers of

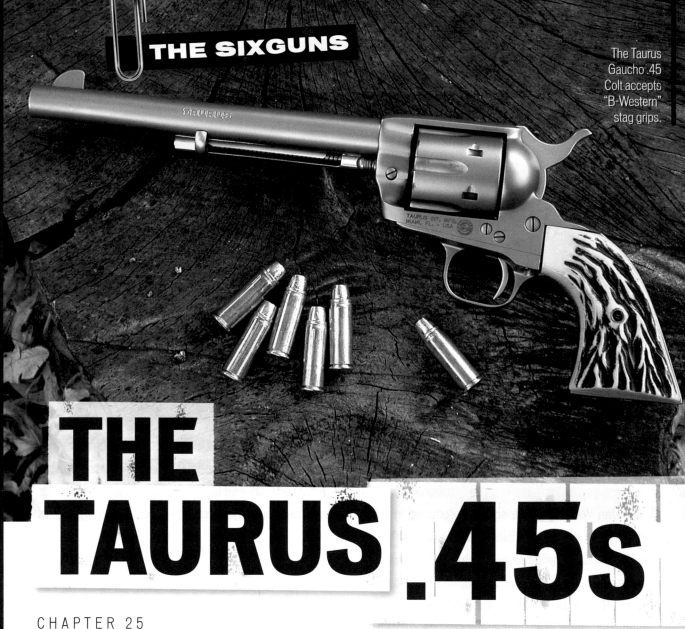

THE SIXGUNS

The Taurus Gaucho .45 Colt accepts "B-Western" stag grips.

THE TAURUS .45s

CHAPTER 25

Taurus revolvers have been around for a long time. Although they've been providing exceptional value for the money, there was always something missing for me in the area of aesthetics. This changed in the late 1990s, so I'm assuming someone came on board who understood what a sixgun should look like. Up to then, they had been offering the Model 44 — a good-shooting .44 Magnum which, unfortunately, fell a little short in the looks department, especially with the end of the barrel profile and the design of the stocks. It just didn't have that "real sixgun" look.

A RAGING SUCCESS

At the 1997 SHOT Show, Taurus unveiled a new big-bore revolver, the Raging Bull. Someone obviously spent a good deal of time at the drawing board, and the prototype displayed did not look like it would handle .454 Casull-type pressures. In fact, that particular gun did not look like it even had a forcing cone. As far as I know, no one ever had the opportunity, or perhaps the desire, to test it. But this changed over the course of the year, and when Taurus unveiled the production model a year later, all who saw and handled it were quite impressed.

Although first announced in a five-shot .454 Casull version, as well as six-shot versions in .44 Magnum and .45 Colt, I personally have never seen one in .45 Colt and cannot say if any were ever actually produced. I have had considerable experience shooting both a blue and a stainless .44 Magnum as well as three of the .454s — an 8-inch blue model as well as two 6-inch stainless versions (one satin-finished, the other high gloss). In shooting all five of these guns, the only problem I've encountered has been trying to ignite .454s with rifle primers when shooting double action.

John feels in terms of aesthetics, the Taurus Raging Bull .454 represents the company's "breakthrough" offering. Those red-backed rubber grips go a long way toward reducing felt recoil.

John shoots his .45 Colt Gaucho. He got it in his favorite barrel length — 7½ inches.

A general look at the Raging Bull is the first order of business. As mentioned earlier I have always been somewhat biased against foreign-manufactured sixguns. Not because they aren't necessarily functional or durable, simply because they were not pleasing to my eye — they seemed about as exciting as a claw hammer or a nail gun. That changed with the advent of the Raging Bull. To me, it is the best-looking DA sixgun to come along since the original Smith & Wesson .44 Magnum of 1956.

Just about everything has been done right both as to form and function. The trigger, which is the same width as the trigger guard, is smooth with no checkering or serrations to irritate your trigger finger during long strings of fire. At the same time, the hammer spur has the right amount of checkering to allow for positive single-action cocking. This user-friendly checkering is also on both cylinder release latches for a non-slip surface. Yes, I said *both*. It takes two thumbs to open the cylinder — there is a conventionally situated latch on the left side of the frame behind the recoil shield, plus a second locking latch on the crane in front of the cylinder. This provides secure lockup, but both latches must be pressed simultaneously to unlock the cylinder. There is no locking latch at the end of the ejector rod. The cylinders of the Raging Bulls are basically cut and formed from cube-shaped pieces of steel with a diameter of 1.770 inches and a length of 1.760 inches.

The heavy barrels are of the full underlug variety with a recess for the ejector rod. Integral to each barrel is a heavy rib with three ventilated slots on the 6½-inch versions and with one more added for 8⅜-inch barrel lengths. Barrel, underlug and ventilated rib are all machined from one solid piece of steel, as is the ramp for the front sight. This heavy barrel measures 1.650 inches from top to bottom.

The front sight itself is a pinned-in black blade. It matches up with a fully adjustable rear sight (also black)

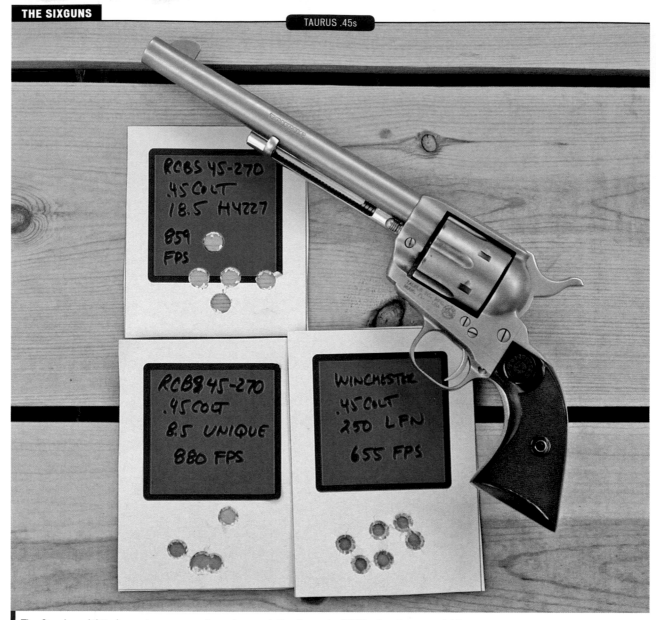

RCBS 45-270
.45 COLT
18.5 H4227
859 FPS

RCBS 45-270
.45 COLT
8.5 UNIQUE
880 FPS

WINCHESTER
.45 COLT
250 LFN
655 FPS

The Gaucho exhibited amazing accuracy for a sixgun retailing for under $500 when it was available.

featuring a slanted rear blade to help prevent glare. This is the best type of sights for my eyes at this stage of my life. Since the front sight blade is pinned, it can easily be changed out for a taller, shorter, wider or narrower blade if you want. On each side of the barrel below the front sight there are four ports to help control muzzle flip when shooting full-house loads. There is no rifling in the ported section, so in reality a 6½-inch sixgun is really slightly over 5 inches in true barrel length, while the 8⅜-inch versions are rifled for approximately 7 inches. This does not seem to have any adverse effect on muzzle velocity as .454 Raging Bulls are relatively "fast-shooting" revolvers.

There are two things to remember concerning ported sixguns. First, they are noisy and hearing protection is an absolute must, especially for anyone who may be standing off to the side or close by. Perhaps even more important is the fact when using cast bullets, material can be thrown through the ports that can be dangerous to bystanders. Ported guns should *never* be fired with anyone standing where they could get hit with any trash coming out of the ports

Stocks on all Raging Bulls are highly functional, pebble-grained black rubber with a cushioned red insert along the backstrap area. Using red instead of black for the cushion was a good move as it identifies every Raging Bull at a glance and adds a distinctive touch to normally drab black rubber grips.

The Raging Bull .454 is a heavy sixgun, weighing 55

The Raging Bull is also available in high-gloss stainless, which mimics nickel plating, yet is considerably more rugged.

ounces in the 6½-inch barrel length. If I have any complaint at all about the Raging Bulls it is in regard to the trigger pull. Using the RCBS Premium Trigger Pull Scale, the single-action pull on mine weighed 4¾ pounds, so I had Tom at Buckhorn Gun bring it down to a more usable three pounds.

I will not say any of the .454 sixguns from Taurus are "pleasant-shooting" when using full-house loads. You simply cannot escape recoil, but Taurus has made these sixguns as pleasant shooting as possible with the heavyweight construction, ported barrels and cushioned rubber stocks, which are smaller at the bottom to provide a secure grip during recoil.

Taurus' .454 Raging Bull has been in the field now for nearly 20 years. Unlike Ruger's .454 Super Redhawk, which has a six-shot cylinder, the Raging Bull has a heavy five-shot cylinder with .155 inch of steel between chambers and outside walls of .110 inch in width.

SELECT LOADS

One of my favorite .454 Casull loads is assembled with the Lyman/Casull 300-grain #454629GC over 31.5 grains of H110 or WW296 in Starline brass ignited with Remington 7½ Small Rifle primers. From a 6½-inch Taurus Raging Bull this load clocks out at 1,530 fps and places four shots in 1⅜ inches at 25 yards. Here are some factory .454 load results in the same gun.

SOUTH AMERICAN SINGLE ACTION

By the early 1990s, Cowboy Action shooting was booming, so it was only natural for many companies to start supplying traditional single-action sixguns for the sport. Ruger introduced the Vaquero (the Mexican version of a cowboy), following up with the slightly smaller New Vaquero.

TEST-FIRE: TAURUS RAGING BULL .454 CASULL (6½ INCH)

LOAD	VELOCITY	4 SHOTS, 25 YARDS
Buffalo Bore 325-gr. LBT	1,570 fps	2½"
Buffalo Bore 300-gr. JFN	1,618 fps	1¾
Buffalo Bore 360-gr. LBT	1,432 fps	2½"
Cor-Bon 265-gr. Bonded Core	1,549 fps	1⅞
Cor-Bon 285-gr. Bonded Core	1,473 fps	1⅞"
Cor-Bon 300-gr. Bonded Core	1,579 fps	2¼
Cor-Bon 300-gr. JSP	1,486 fps	1⅝"
Cor-Bon 320-gr. Penetrator	1,482 fps	1½
Cor-Bon 335-gr. Hard Cast	1,463 fps	1⅞"
Cor-Bon 360-gr. Penetrator	1,405 fps	2½
Winchester 260-gr. Partition Gold	1,744 fps	7/8"
Winchester 260-gr. JFP	1,720 fps	1¼
Winchester 300-gr. JFP	1,622 fps	1⅞"

SIXGUNS AND THEIR CARTRIDGES

Hamilton Bowen converted this .38/44 Heavy Duty Smith & Wesson to .45 Colt, Dan Love did the engraving and Paul Persinger carved the ivory stocks. Hamilton calls it "the nicest S&W to ever leave my shop."
Photo: Arlo Brown

Taffin's friend Paco Kelly commissioned this Ruger Bisley Vaquero .45 (right) from Gary Reeder. Gary's "Ultimate .45" is a dual-cylindered Ruger Blackhawk with custom front sight, custom grips and black chromex finish.

Peacemaker Specialists "Royal Flush" .45 with one-piece ivory stocks, silver plating and a proprietary Gunslinger Deluxe action job. The holster is by Thad Rybka.

Peacemaker Specialists "Last Frontier" is a completely reworked 2nd Generation .45 Colt New Frontier with color casehardened hammer, fire-blue screws and one-piece elephant ivory stocks.

Below: This Freedom Arms Model 97 is from Hamilton Bowen. The top strap has been modified to S&W M&P style, and it has been fitted with a new round barrel. Then Hamilton fitted a windage-adjustable dovetail sight and shortened the grip frame and converted it to Colt SAA-style. Ivory grips were then fitted by Paul Persinger and a lanyard ring installed. The rough-out holster is from Thad Rybka.

Packable powerhouse: Gary Reeder's .455 Alaskan Express features custom sights and a modified grip frame.

This 3rd Generation .45 Colt also got the 1880's package from Peacemaker Specialists, including remarked barrel, checkered hammer spur, beveled and fluted cylinder and Helfricht-style engraving.

d-style double action: This custom .45 Colt iple-Lock belonged to Bob Nichols, author of a seminal ork on speed shooting. *Photo: Timothy Mullin*

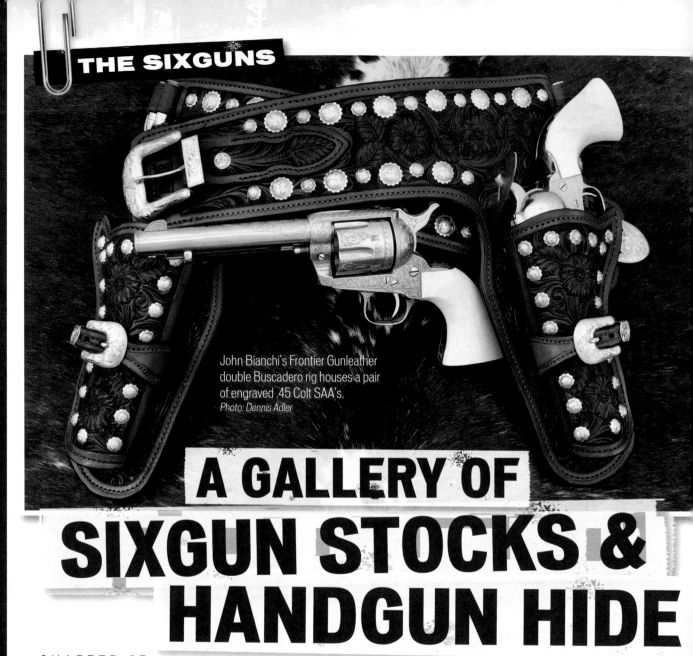

THE SIXGUNS

John Bianchi's Frontier Gunleather double Buscadero rig houses a pair of engraved .45 Colt SAA's.
Photo: Dennis Adler

A GALLERY OF
SIXGUN STOCKS &
HANDGUN HIDE

CHAPTER 27

Beauty combines with function when it comes to sixgun stocks and holsters. Single-actions rarely need stocks replaced for function but rather to satisfy the aesthetic whims of the owner. Ivory, ram's horn, mother-of-pearl, staghorn and exotic woods really improve the looks and bolster pride of ownership of your prized single-action Ruger, Colt or Freedom Arms sixgun. With double-action revolvers, it's a different story as most DA factory stocks leave a lot to be desired when it comes to function. However, by choosing the right ones, you can improve both function *and* form.

As far as holsters go, every good sixgun deserves

This style rig from El Paso Saddlery was favored by John Wesley Hardin (left). A Tom Threepersons-style (right) as offered by Walt Ostin.

John Wayne popularized this style holster in many of his movies. It is offered by El Paso Saddlery as "The Duke."

good leather. As with most other things such as tires, brakes and parachutes, cheap leather can be way too "expensive" in the long run. So with all this in mind, let's stop the words and start the pictures. ◉

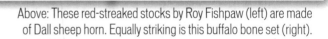

Above: These red-streaked stocks by Roy Fishpaw (left) are made of Dall sheep horn. Equally striking is this buffalo bone set (right).

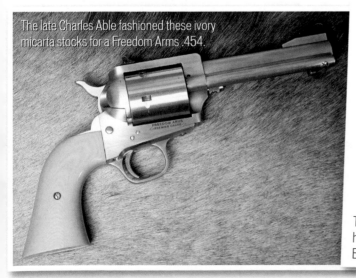

The late Charles Able fashioned these ivory micarta stocks for a Freedom Arms .454.

Tom Threeperson-style holsters by (left to right): El Paso Saddlery, George Lawrence and Walt Ostin.

Originally designed by Walter Roper, these stocks (left) are available from Keith Brown. A .45 Colt S&W (center) got its stocks from BluMagnum. A Dan Wesson (right) became more "shootable" with Herrett's Jordan Trooper stocks.

Andy Anderson designed this Gunfighter-style holster in the 1960s.

There's always wood! Fancy walnut stocks by Scott Kolar would grace any single-action sixgun.

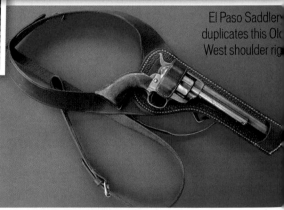

El Paso Saddlery duplicates this Old West shoulder rig.

Speed and comfort: A fast-draw rig by Thad Rybka is also excellent for everyday carry.

These .45 Auto Rim S&Ws wear factory and staghorn Magna grips.

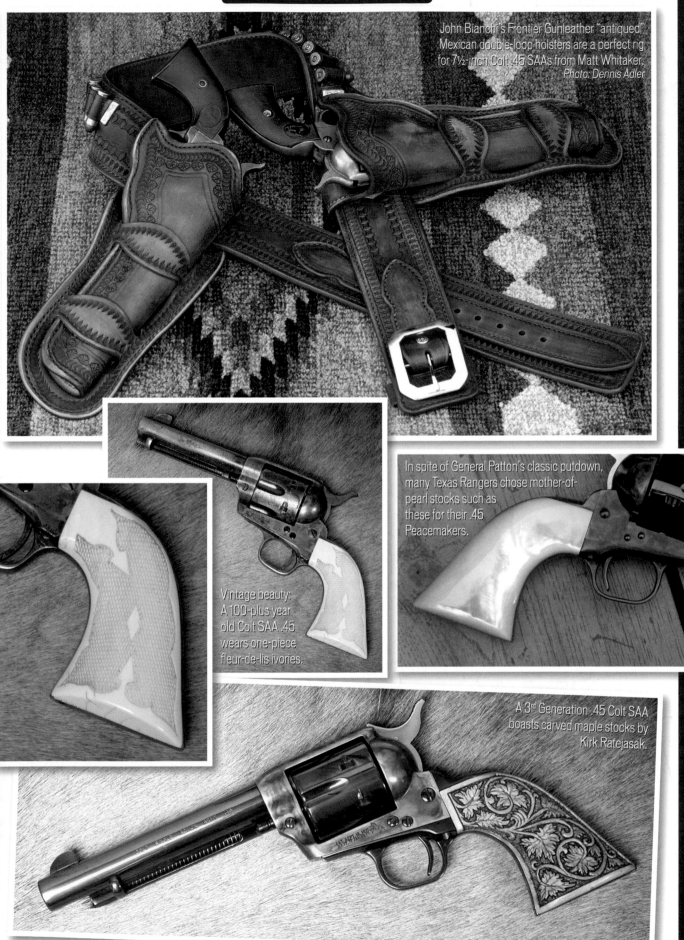

John Bianchi's Frontier Gunleather "antiqued" Mexican double-loop holsters are a perfect rig for 7½-inch Colt .45 SAAs from Matt Whitaker. *Photo: Dennis Adler*

In spite of General Patton's classic putdown, many Texas Rangers chose mother-of-pearl stocks such as these for their .45 Peacemakers.

Vintage beauty: A 100-plus year old Colt SAA .45 wears one-piece fleur-de-lis ivories.

A 3rd Generation .45 Colt SAA boasts carved maple stocks by Kirk Ratejasak.

Staghorn grips are a worthy accessory for this Colt New Frontier .45.

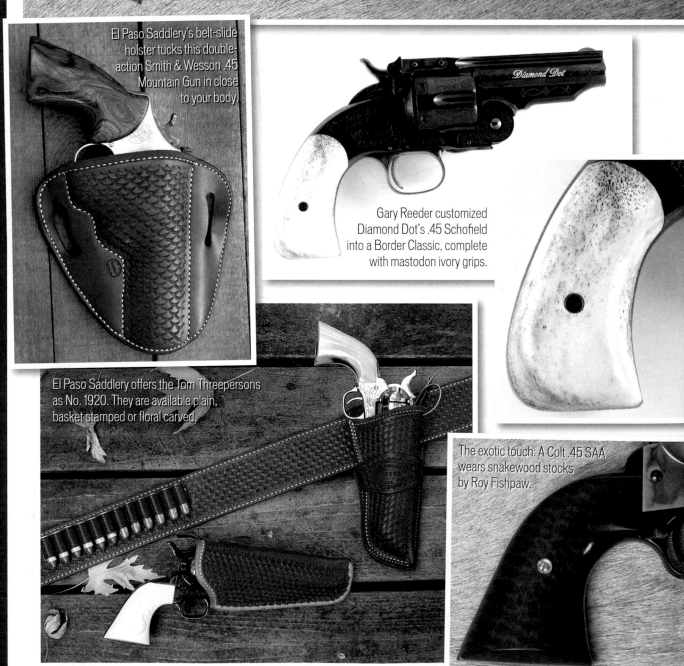

El Paso Saddlery's belt-slide holster tucks this double-action Smith & Wesson .45 Mountain Gun in close to your body.

Gary Reeder customized Diamond Dot's .45 Schofield into a Border Classic, complete with mastodon ivory grips.

El Paso Saddlery offers the Tom Threepersons as No. 1920. They are available plain, basket stamped or floral carved.

The exotic touch: A Colt .45 SAA wears snakewood stocks by Roy Fishpaw.

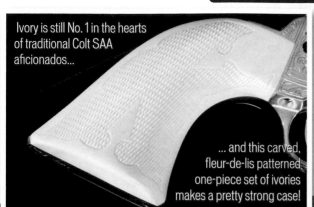

Ivory is still No. 1 in the hearts of traditional Colt SAA aficionados...

... and this carved, fleur-de-lis patterned one-piece set of ivories makes a pretty strong case!

This engraved 2nd Generation .45 Colt SAA is fitted with carved ivories by Eagle Grips.

A copy of the holster worn by Nick Adams in *The Rebel* TV series was crafted by Bob Arganbright. Bob also did this carved Hollywood Fast Draw holster (below).

A large DA S&W in .45 Colt carries easily in the Al Goerg shoulder holster, which is now available from Gary Reeder Custom Guns.

A real gunfighter rig is this short-barreled Colt SAA fitted with an 1860 Army grip frame and a special holster designed for speed. *Photo: Bob Arganbright*

THE SIXGUNS

Loading and unloading through the gate is a one-at-a-time propostition. Use the ejector rod while lining up the chambers to kick out the brass.

MANAGING THE SINGLE-ACTION SIXGUN

CHAPTER 28

I bought my first .45 single-action revolver — a brand-new production Colt SAA — in 1956. It was soon followed by a long line of Colts, Great Westerns and Ruger Blackhawks. Over more than half a century since that first Colt, I have learned from both personal experience as well as the writings of several experts on the handling and use of the single-action revolver. These men included Eugene Cunningham (author of *Triggernometry*), Walter Rogers (who modified the Colt SAA to suit himself), Elmer

Keith and Skeeter Skeleton (whose writings always stirred my sixgunnin' spirit). What follows are my Top 10 tips for operating the .45 sixgun.

1 LOADING

The proper way to carry a loaded traditional single-action six-shooter is with one empty chamber under the hammer.

Tuff Strips are an easy way to carry extra rounds for the single action and help speed up the loading process (left).

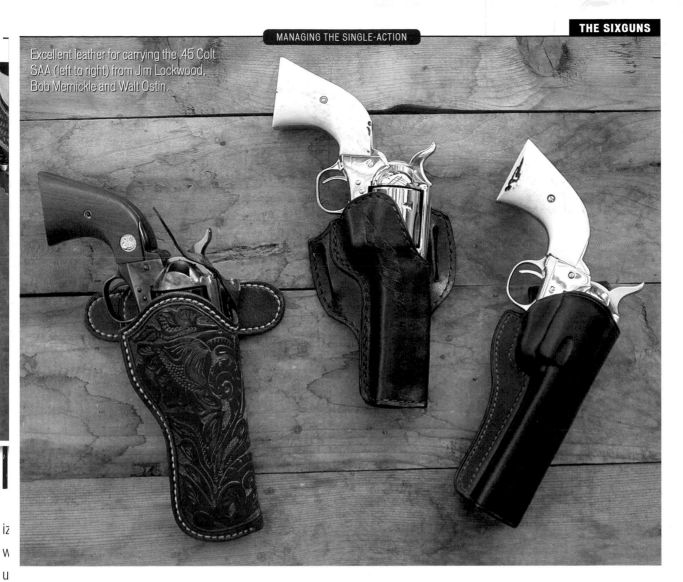

Excellent leather for carrying the .45 Colt SAA (left to right) from Jim Lockwood, Bob Mernickle and Walt Ostin.

Here's how to set things up correctly: Open the loading gate, pull the hammer back to the half cock notch, load one round, rotate the cylinder skipping the next chamber, and then load four more cartridges.

The next step is to safely rotate the cylinder so the empty chamber is under the hammer. If the "load one-skip one-load four" has been done correctly, you then simply pull the hammer back to the full cock notch and then *carefully* lower it while releasing the trigger. The hammer will now be resting on an empty chamber. Practice this with *dummy* cartridges until it is second nature. Please note the hammer is never let down from the half-cock notch, but is brought back to the full-cock notch before lowering. One of the best ways to lock up any traditional single action is to lower the hammer from the half-cock notch. The internal parts will not be in the right place, and this can really foul things up.

With the New Model Ruger — or any other single action with a transfer bar — fully loaded carry is, of course, com-pletely safe. When the hammer is down, the transfer bar is retracted and the hammer does not contact the firing pin. To load this style of sixgun, opening the loading gate releases the cylinder bolt, allowing free cylinder rotation. Cartridges are loaded through the loading gate and when the loading gate is closed, the cylinder may need to be rotated slightly to once again engage the cylinder bolt. There is no need to touch the hammer through the loading and unloading process.

2 UNLOADING

I also see all kinds of contortions gone through by those trying to unload the traditional single action. I open the loading gate and bring the hammer back to the half-cock notch. Then I shift the gun to my left hand, which cradles the tip of the hammer and the backstrap. With my right hand I work the ejector rod with the barrel pointed downrange and tilted slightly upwards. This drops all of the empties into my cradled left hand.

THE REPLICA SIXGUNS

Cimarron's .45 Colt Wyatt Earp Special (center) compared to a Colt (top) and Great Western Buntline (bottom).

THE .45 SIXGUNS OF CIMARRON

CHAPTER 30

When replica cartridge sixguns started to arrive in the United States, something was haywire. Those foreign-made Colt SAA copies from the 1960s, 1970s and well into the 1980s carried brass backstraps and trigger guards, and the case-colored frames looked like a poor spray-on finish. Much cheaper than original Colts, these sixguns filled the movie screens of the period, most often in "Spaghetti Westerns" made in Italy or Spain. They were not bad shooters generally speaking, but they made a traditional sixgunner shudder to say the least.

CIMARRON'S MODEL P

That has all changed and the major credit goes to Mike Harvey and Cimarron Arms. Harvey, an old western buff himself, purchased the defunct Allen Firearms and began the arduous process of convincing the Italians — mainly the Uberti factory — to upgrade its single actions to be true copies of the original 19th century Colt SAA. Brass back straps and trigger guards gave way to steel. Cimarrons from Uberti are now finished exceptionally well, with rich bluing and case colors far removed from the original finishes. Grip frames feel like Colts and one-piece style walnut grips are very well shaped and rounded in the right places, with no square blocky feel or high spots.

Handguns cannot be imported without a safety that will survive the drop test. Cimarron opts for a safety on the hammer that operates as a block when the hammer is drawn to the safety notch. This is a real safety, not the weak arrangement of the old Colt SAA. But even with it, I prefer the tried and true "empty chamber under the hammer" precaution.

CIMARRON .45 SIXGUN

Cimarron's "Original" is showcased on the Model P at left. The blued/case colored one on the right has been fitted with an 1860 grip frame.

The three traditional barrel lengths — 4¾, 5½ and 7½ inches — are offered. The .45 Colt chambering is standard and is certainly the No. 1 favorite with replicas. With blue and case-colored finish and one-piece walnut grips, the Cimarron Model P retails for well under an American-made single action from Colt or USFA.

All barrel lengths are available as a Black Powder Model with screw-in retainer for the cylinder pin and a Bullseye ejector rod head or the Pre-War Model with half-moon ejector rod head and spring loaded cross pin cylinder latch. Black Powder Models are not relegated to the exclusive use of black powder only. The designation denotes a look of authenticity, not a strength factor. Single Actions are available in a charcoal blue or fire blue finish. The latter is a true blue rather than a black finish and is very bright. It also is quite fragile and soon wears off a sixgun that is used extensively. For those who prefer, all models are also available in full-nickel finish, and for a real trip back into history, Cimarron offers an antiqued finish they call "Original" to recall well-worn Colts from the 1870s.

Several years ago Cimarron began offering the Model P in stainless steel. At the time I ordered two 7½-inch .45s and was well pleased with their performance enough that I not only purchased both of them, but I also had them fitted with custom ivory-style stocks from Buffalo Brothers. In talking with my friend Bob Baer in Texas a few months ago, he told me I had to get one of the new stainless steel Model Ps as they were the finest sixguns he had seen in a long time. I was already ahead of him.

The storekeepers and sheriffs among us have not been forgotten, and the .45 Colt is offered with a 3½-inch barrel complete with ejector rod and housing. These 'little' sixguns are found particularly attractive amongst the crowd of shootists that I prefer to ride the river with. Any models may be ordered with full Cattle Brand engraving or A, B or C engraving consisting of one-quarter, one-half, or full coverage, respectively.

Most Cimarrons will shoot low for most shooters with most loads, but the front sight can be filed to your particular point of aim. This is a vast improvement over that of just a few years back when all replicas were coming through with too little front sight, causing them to shoot high. It is very difficult to fix a high-shooting single action. On the other hand, one that shoots low can be easily adjusted with a little file work.

VARIATION ON A THEME

To come up with something just a little different, Harvey studied the single-action grip and changed it by fitting the old 1873 Colt-style single action with a grip frame that is a dead ringer for the 1877 Colt .38 Lightning or .41 Thunderer double actions. They are called the New Thunderer Model. Mine in .45 Colt proved an excellent shooter when I custom tailored loads with cast bullets sized to .454 inch instead of the standard but smaller .452 inch.

My production New Thunderer is extremely well finished with deep, dark bluing on all parts except hammer and frame which are case colored. Metal to wood fit is excellent, and the dark walnut grips are fine-lined checkered and look and feel very good. A nice touch is the use of charcoal blued screws for the grip frame and frame. These provide a subtle contrast to the dark blue of the rest of the gun. The New Thunderer grip frame starts out as a round butt but as it curves up a pronounced double-action style hump is encountered. It

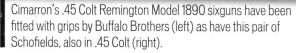

Cimarron's .45 Colt Remington Model 1890 sixguns have been fitted with grips by Buffalo Brothers (left) as have this pair of Schofields, also in .45 Colt (right).

looks strange at first, but it is highly functional in controlling standard .45 Colt loads in the short-barreled New Thunderer. Instead of the rolling-in-the-hand feeling afforded by the standard single-action grip, the Thunderer feels more like a double-action grip, and the sixgun does not twist or roll in the hand. However, my hand is so used to the traditional Colt Single Action grip frame my New Thunderer has been retrofitted with a standard grip frame. I just don't change very easily.

LONG-BARREL VARIANT

Cimarron has another unique offering in its Wyatt Earp Model. Originally, Colt provided any barrel length above standard on special order including some 16-inch guns with ladder-style adjustable rear sights. During the run of 2nd Generation Colts, a 12-inch Buntline was offered. However, what is most important concerning the Cimarron Model P "Buntline" being offered is the fact that it is a duplicate of

the Buntline Special used by Kurt Russell in his memorable turn as Wyatt Earp in 1993's *Tombstone*.

Watching the movie closely, it is apparent that the Buntline Special used has a 10-inch barrel, not the standard 12-inch length of the 2nd Generation sixguns. Also when Russell as Wyatt removes his special Colt from its presentation box, we see the medallion that is inlaid in the right hand stock. This is also carried out in Cimarron's version as the badge-shaped shield contains the inscription, "Wyatt Earp Peacemaker, From the Grateful People of Dodge City, Apr 8th 1878." Notice there is no mention of Ned Buntline.

The 12-inch sixguns are a little muzzle heavy; however, I find that feeling lacking with 2 inches less barrel. It just seems to hang on target better. The Wyatt Earp Peacemaker is also offered in the Original finish, but by the luck of the draw, the sixgun furnished to me for testing, and subsequently purchased, was the traditional blued/case-colored scheme. Screws are bright nitre blue finish, rather than the traditional blue-black. The action is smooth, the cylinder locks up tightly, trigger pull is a little creepy but not heavy (at least not since I installed a lighter mainspring). This sixgun not only shoots exactly where it is pointed, but it also delivers nice, tight groups.

Targets shot with the .45 Colt Cimarron Stainless Steel Model P show a high level of accuracy potential.

CARTRIDGE CONVERSIONS

The Richards Conversion, the improved Richard-Mason Conversion and the 1871-72 Open-Top all served as transition revolvers from the 1860 Army to the Colt Single Action Army. They are a very important part of sixgun history and original examples are quite valuable. Fortunately for those who wish to shoot such revolvers, all three have been available for quite some time, with most of them chambered in .44 Colt. This cartridge, in both its original and modern version, has a smaller rim than the .44 Russian as the cylinder of the converted 1860 Army is not large enough to accept the

CIMARRON .45 SIXGUN

Cimarron's Remington 1858 Cartridge Conversion is furnished with a .45 Colt cylinder.

larger rims on the Russian without them overlapping. Now, thanks to Cimarron, we have the newest version of the Richards Conversion, the Richards II, which not only has room for the larger diameter rims, but the frame and cylinder have also been made larger to accept the .45 Colt.

In comparing the Cimarron Richards II to Diamond Dot's original Richards Conversion, I find the latter has a cylinder diameter of 1.621 inches while the newer version measures 1.677 inches to handle the larger .45 Colt. The original Richards Conversion used a heeled bullet of the same diameter as the outside of the brass cartridge case. To be able to fire the original, and we do shoot it with black powder only, I load a hollowbase pure lead bullet into modern .44 Colt brass. Upon firing, the base of the bullet expands to contact the rifling. The Cimarron replica makes things much simpler. It is built to handle standard smokeless powder loads, and the barrels are dimensioned as any current .45 Colt, so it is not necessary to use soft lead bullets.

The .45 Colt Cimarron Richards II is an all-steel revolver instead of having the brass trigger guard of the original. Mainframe, hammer, breech plate and loading gate are all case-colored with the balance of the revolver being nicely polished blue-black. The

grip frame is the comfortable 1860 Army style, very well fitted with one-piece walnut stocks with good grain. For my eyes and hold, it shoots about 6 inches high with most loads. This can be corrected by the installation of a higher front sight. Probably an easier solution would be to deepen the rear sight notch on the hammer and take a little off the top of the hammer to effectively lower the rear sight. The Richards II loads the same as any traditional single action. Place the hammer on half-cock to allow the cylinder to rotate and load/unload through the gate. The ejector rod has a large head, making it very easy to operate.

THE REMINGTON NEW ARMY

The Remington .44 New Army percussion revolver was the first sixgun actually converted to metallic cartridges. Cimarron has not forgotten the Remington and also offers an

John fitted his Cimarron New Thunderer .45 with a standard Model P grip frame.

THE REPLICA SIXGUNS

The late, lamented Hartford Armory 1890 Remington .45 Colt.

HARTFORD REMINGTONS & STI TEXICANS

CHAPTER 31

My favorite subject through high school was history. My teachers made the subject come alive, and I wish they still were as well — so I could thank them for instilling a love of the subject — especially American history — in me. As I became a shooter, history became even more important to me as firearms have played such an important role in it.

Remington Model 1875s compared — an original (top) and the Hartford Armory version (below).

The most prolific period of single-action sixgun development was about 1870 to 1874. First came Smith & Wesson with the introduction of the Model 3 American, followed by the Colt SAA in 1873 and the Remington Model 1875 shortly thereafter.

Remington was already supplying single-shot Rolling Block rifles to the Egyptians and had a large contract to

deliver the Model 1875 sixgun chambered in .44 Remington to them as well.

When I first started getting serious about sixguns, it was very easy to find Colts but almost impossible to come across Remingtons. (If the reverse had been the case, I might have had a lifelong love affair with Remingtons instead of Colt's Model P). Everyone knows how comfort-

The .45 Colt Texican came with a casehardened frame and hammer. The aggressively checkered stocks were John's only real complaint.

able the Colt SAA grip frame is for shooting; however, at this stage of my life, I've discovered the fact the Remington grip frame to be even more comfortable. This discovery came about with the shooting of new sixguns from Hartford Armory, which very briefly produced replicas of the 1875 and 1890 Remingtons.

And as much as I love Colt SAA's, I have to admit the Remingtons were an inherently stronger design. Where Colt used three parts — mainframe, backstrap, and trigger guard bolted together Remington used a one-piece engineering marvel incorporating the mainframe and grip frame with no screws to loosen while shooting. Unlike the open-top design of Sam Colt's percussion revolvers, the early Remingtons had a solid top strap. The first Remington cartridge revolvers arrived in 1874. The first few hundred where chambered in .46 Remington; however, this was soon changed to .44 Remington with approximately 16,000 being manufactured by 1878 (most of which went to the Egyptian government). All had 7½-inch barrels and featured a pinched-post front sight and lanyard ring.

Somewhere between 2,000 and 4,000 Model 1875s were produced over

the next three years with a blade front sight, mostly without the lanyard ring and chambered in .44-40 and .45 Colt. Some minor changes were made in 1881, with between 4,000 and 5,000 being manufactured before the Model 1890 arrived. The last few (less than 1,000) Model 1875s were chambered in .44-40 with 5¾-inch barrels. In 1883, approximately 1,000 nickel-plated Model 1875s were purchased by the U.S. government to arm the Indian police. E. Remington & Sons suffered a bankruptcy in 1888, the company name was changed to Remington Arms, and a few "Model 1888" single actions were produced before the arrival of the Model 1890.

These Model 1890s were produced in .44-40 with less

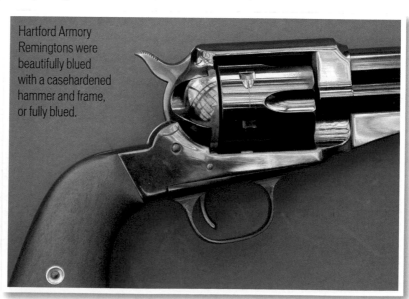

Hartford Armory Remingtons were beautifully blued with a casehardened hammer and frame, or fully blued.

The Hartford Model 1890 .45 Colt handles heavy-duty, 300-grain loads with ease.

sured a uniform .451. Just as with the original Remingtons, both the Hartford Model 1875 and 1890 were provided with pinched-post front sights, which I found quite easy to see. With the strength and accuracy afforded by these new Hartford Armory sixguns, they should have been very popular with handgun hunters.

HARTFORD ARMORY MODEL 1890 (7½ INCH) .45 COLT

LOAD	VELOCITY	5 SHOTS, 25 YARDS
CPBC 265-gr. WFNGC/18.5 gr. #2400	1,167 fps	1¾"
Lyman #454490GC/20.0 gr. #2400	1,280 fps	1¾"
Boar Slammer 325-gr. GC/19.5 gr. H110	1,142 fps	1¼"
Fusilier 300-gr./18.5 gr. #4227	1,053 fps	1½"
Fusilier 300-gr./9.0 gr. Unique	1,021 fps	1½"
Park Cor-Bon 335-gr. Hard Cast	1,065 fps	1⅛"
Lyman 325-gr./18.5 gr. #4227	1,076 fps	1⅜"
Oregon Trail 300-gr./18.5 gr. #4227	1,015 fps	1¼"
Oregon Trail 300-gr./9.0 gr. Unique	1,007 fps	1¼"
SSK 340-gr. FN/21.2 gr. H110	1,229 fps	1½"
Hornady 250-gr. XTP-JHP/20.0 gr. #2400	1,203 fps	1⅞"
Hornady 300-gr. XTP-JHP/21.2 gr. H110	1,027 fps	1¾"

DOUBLE THREAT

Is it possible to have a fixed sighted sixgun performing both Cowboy Action *and* hunting chores? When testing the Model 1890 at 25 yards with several different bullet weights and muzzle velocities, I found a difference of 9½ inches in vertical placement on the target. A Cowboy Action revolver does not require perfect shot placement, but a hunting handgun does. Hartford Armory solved this by offering a screw-in front sight available in different heights with a special wrench for removal and installation. As it is, the Model 1890 shot close enough to point of aim in my hands to allow it to be used for hunting with 300-grain bullets.

It is not easy to teach such an old dog like me new tricks; however, this new-old design from Hartford Armory went way to the top of the list of favorite single-action sixguns. This was an absolutely great sixgun. You may have noticed I have been writing about it in the past tense. I have no idea what happened, but very few of these were actually made before Hartford Armory stopped production. These were absolutely high-quality sixguns with a commensurate high price tag and should have been well-received by sixgunners. Unfortunately, it was not to be.

THE STI TEXICAN

Why is the STI Texican in a chapter mainly about Hartford Armory? Well, the Texican was not manufactured in Texas by STI International, but actually in Connecticut by Hartford.

Hartford Armory offered the .45 Colt 1875 Remington with the full underbarrel web (bottom) as well as the 1890 Model (top) with the abbreviated web.

The Hartford Armory has uniform .452-inch cylinder throats.

STI International has long been known for producing high-quality semiautomatics and joined the single-action revolver market by jumping in right at the top. The first, and possibly only run of Texicans were 5½-inch .45 Colts. These sixguns were equal in quality to the Hartford Armory Remingtons. There were no castings in the Texican – all parts were either forged or made from 4150 chrome moly bar stock. Barrels were made from Green Mountain blanks with a 1:12 twist and air gauged to .0002-inch tolerance along with a chamber throat to barrel bore alignment less than +/- .001 inch.

The mainframe, loading gate and hammer were all color casehardened by Doug Turnbull, and the specially designed pawl rides on a fixed pivot and is expected to have three to four times the life expectancy of other traditional pawl springs.

I found the fitting and polishing of the Texican to be exceptional. Running my finger from the bottom of the cylinder down the mainframe to the trigger guard resulted in no perceptible feel of where the two parts meet. This is a sure sign of great fitting and finishing. Flat surfaces are *flat*. There are no dished-out screw holes.

There is a long list of items to be attended to in producing an accurate single-action revolver. These include placement and alignment of chamber pilot holes, chambers in relation to pilot holes, the cylinder base pin hole and the two holes in the frame which accept the base pin, cylinder stop notches, threaded portion of the frame and threads on the barrel, barrel bore centerline and outside diameter of the barrel, the cylinder bolt notches and the cylinder bolt itself. Then there is the placement of the cylinder bolt in the window in the bottom of the frame, tension on the pawl when the sixgun is at full cock and the chamber throats. It is neither simple nor easy to produce a quality single-action revolver.

The first thing I did to test the Texican's tolerances was to measure the chamber throats. Using a set of plug gauges, I found all six to be perfectly reamed to .452 inch. Then enlisting the help of my engineer friend, Denis Fletcher, who

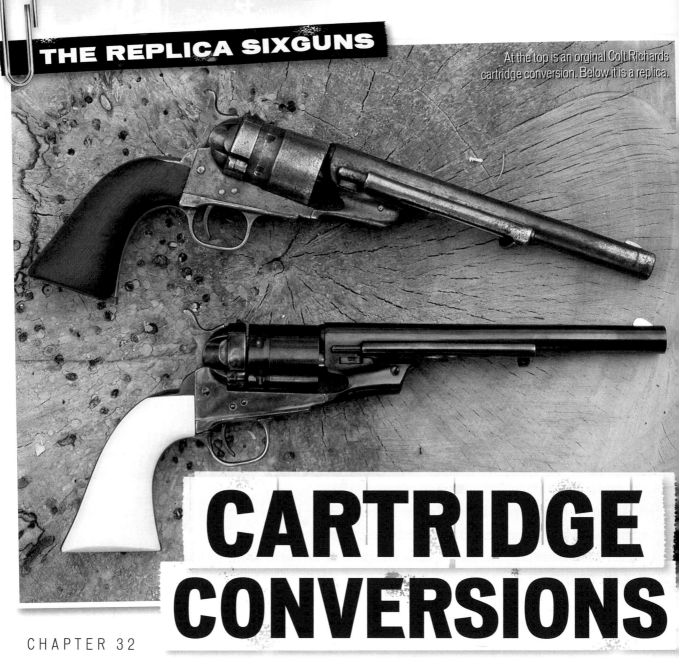

THE REPLICA SIXGUNS

At the top is an orginal Colt Richards cartridge conversion. Below it is a replica.

CARTRIDGE CONVERSIONS

CHAPTER 32

Sam Colt is generally credited with producing the first practical single-action revolver. That first effort was the Paterson of 1836, which was followed by the 1847 Walker, the 1st, 2nd and 3rd Model Dragoons and the 1851 Navy.

Colt may have passed on to his reward in 1862, but he lived to see his factory acquire a lucrative contract to produce .44-caliber Model 1860 Army percussion revolvers for the Union Army during the Civil War and the frontier expansion which followed.

Meanwhile the folks over at Smith & Wesson were producing their seven-shot, tip-up little .22 revolver and planning bigger things. Sam himself was gone, but the Colt factory stayed the course producing percussion sixvolvers.

But when S&W introduced the first cartridge-firing, big-bore revolver in late 1869, the U.S. Army — which had been using Colt 1860 Army Models — ordered them almost immediately. Colt had evidently struck out on this one, and it would take some major maneuvering to get back into the single-action ball game. When Colt did fully recover, it was with the legendary Single Action Army, but the company had to cross a couple of bridges to get from the 1860 Army to the 1873 Peacemaker.

ENTER THE CARTRIDGE CONVERSIONS

During the late 1860s, the Thuer Conversion was performed on approximately 5,000 Colt cap-and-ball sixguns by altering the cylinder of percussion revolvers to allow a tapered cartridge to be inserted from the front end. It was less than satisfactory and short lived. When

Ruger's Old Army is stronger than any conversion repro — and this one of John's is capable of excellent accuracy.

S&W changed the rules about sixguns, Colt was left with thousands of parts on hand, and it fell to Charles Richards to convert them into cartridge-firing sixguns. The backs of the cylinders were cut off and fitted with a backplate conversion ring or completely new cylinders were fitted. (Colt 1860s with the Richards conversion are easily recognized by the ejector rod extending past the back of the ejector rod housing about an inch.)

Enter William Mason, Colt's factory superintendent. Richards conversions were alterations on 1860 Army Models, and the Richards-Mason went a step further, providing a completely new barrel and longer ejector-rod housing. They are easily distinguished from the Richards conversions by the web shape under the barrel and a regular cylinder with no conversion ring. Without the conversion ring, however, the rear sight had to be moved back to the original place on the hammer as on the original 1860 Army. The original Colt cartridge conversions were chambered for rounds that used a heeled-type bullet, or a bullet whose base was smaller in diameter than the rest of the projectile.

To keep things simpler for today's shooters, the replica cartridge conversions have been modernized. Those based on the 1851 Navy are chambered for standard .38 Specials, or the .38 Long Colt (which I prefer), while the 1860 Army Conversion uses the .44 Colt. Today's .44 Colt, with properly headstamped brass available from Starline, is simply the .44 Special trimmed back from 1.16 inches to approximately 1.10 inches. Because the diameter of the cylinder of the 1860 Army is too small to accept six .44 Special .514-inch diameter rims, the rims are also trimmed.

One more step was necessary before William Mason would design one of the greatest sixguns of all times, the Colt SAA. While the Thuer, Richards and Richards-Mason were true conversions on existing cap-and-ball revolvers or built from parts at the factory, the 1871-72 Open-Top was Colt's first big-bore, single-action cartridge revolver, a totally new design with new parts that would *not* interchange with the percussion models or their conversions. All original Open-Tops were in .44 Rimfire, and when the 1871-72 was unsuccessfully submitted to the army for testing, Colt's

Mason was sent back to the drawing board to come up with a stronger gun and a more powerful chambering. The result was the solid-frame Colt SAA — still in .44 Rimfire. But when the army asked for a larger, centerfire caliber, it was chambered in .45 Colt (and the rest, they say, is history).

Colt's transition from the 1860 Army cap-and-ball revolver to the Single Action Army was bridged by the Thuer, Richards and Richards-Mason conversion, and the 1871-72 Open-Top. They were only produced for a very short time but represent an important part of sixgun history.

The Colt cartridge conversions and the Open-Top helped move Colt into what was the modern age in the last part of the 19th century. Thanks to the revived interest in single-action sixguns of all types, mainly due to Cowboy Action shooting, three of the four transition revolvers (prototypes of the Thuer conversion were made but never brought to production) still exist in replica form. Unlike the originals, they are safe for use with smokeless powders.

My wife bought an original 1860 Army Richards conversion. The finish on it is long gone and the one-piece walnut stocks have a chip out of each corner, however it is mechanically solid with excellent rifling. These guns were made to take a .44 Colt cartridge using a heeled bullet.

The chamber mouths are .451 inch and the barrel is also .45 caliber as a heeled bullet in a .44 case is basically a .45. Rapine offers a hollowbase .44 bullet mould which I have tried in the Colt cartridge conversion loaded over 25.0 grains of Goex FFg black powder. Twelve rounds at 15 yards result in a pattern measuring 1½ feet in diameter with all bullets hitting the target sideways. Moving up to 7 yards finds all bullets hitting very close to point of the aim with four straight on, one starting to tip and one totally keyholed. Obviously, they didn't stabilize in the oversized barrel originally rifled for roundballs.

Loading for these old sixguns is certainly *interesting*, especially when you're trying to make .44 bullets work in what is actually a .45 — dimensionally speaking.

Cap-and-ball replicas have been available for all of my adult life, and they have continued to increase both in quality and quantity. In addition, conversion cylinders are now available for nearly all the replicas as well as the Ruger Old Army. All of these conversion cylinders are for use *only* in steel-framed revolvers. Brass sixguns are not strong enough. Period. Walt Kirst offers the Kirst Cartridge Konverter For Percussion Revolving Pistols, with the first of these consisting of a five-shot

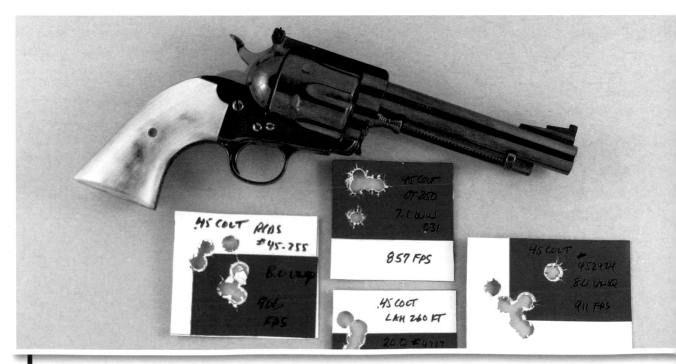

Cowboy Action loads — like these from Black Hills — are a safe bet for .45 Colt loads in 1858 Remington conversion cylinders.

The Kirst .45 ACP cylinder for the 1858 Remington holds six rounds. But don't carry loaded "all the way around."

replacement cylinder and a conversion ring for Remington percussion replicas. Although the Remingtons are called .44 caliber, just as with the above-mentioned Richards conversion, the bore diameters are actually the same as found in .45 Colt sixguns. This allows the Remington to be converted to fire .45 Colt ammunition assembled with black powder or loaded to black-powder levels.

THAT EXTRA CYLINDER

All sensible users of traditional single-action sixguns carry them with five rounds and an empty chamber under the hammer. Kirst provides his Safety Version of the Kirst Cartridge Konverter for the 1858 Remington. This is a five-shot cylinder, however it has a larger area between two of the chambers to allow for the hammer to be placed in a safe position thus making the Kirst Remington conversion cylinder safe to carry fully loaded with five rounds. For the Remington percussion pistols, Kirst offers another .45 cylinder, a six-shot version chambered in .45 ACP. The .45 ACP is rimless and there is enough room for six rounds in the Kirst-made Remington cylinder. With this conversion, "ACP" becomes "Action Cowboy Pistol." Both cylinders work fine with standard smokeless or black-powder loads.

Belt Mountain offers a replaceable base pin for the Ruger Old Army for use with cartridge conversion cylinders (left). Ruger Old Army and 1858 Remington .45 Colt conversion cylinders — one nickeled, one blued, with their respective back plates.

To use the Kirst cylinder, first place the hammer in the half-cock notch, extract the base pin and remove the original percussion cylinder. Then lift the conversion ring from the back of the Kirst cylinder, insert the cartridges and replace the conversion ring. Once the replacement cylinder is loaded, put it in the revolver with the firing pin at the top and the squared-off portion at the bottom. Then replace the base pin to make your percussion revolver a cartridge-firing sixgun. As you fire it, the cylinder rotates each time the hammer is cocked, while the conversion ring with the built-in firing pin stays in a fixed position.

Kirst offers a drop-in .45 Colt cylinder for the Ruger Old Army. Unlike the .45 Colt Remington cylinders, this version is a traditional six-shot cylinder offered in blue and also nickel (to match stainless-steel finishes). The Ruger cylinder easily dropped into both a first-year production Old Army as well as the last-produced 5½-inch version. If the conversion cylinder is used in the Ruger Old Army, the rammer assembly is not needed and can be removed. But this also does away with the base pin. The answer from Belt Mountain Enterprises is a special new base pin for the Old Army to replace the original base pin/loading lever arrangement. This Belt Mountain pin has a large knurled head for easy removal. On the 5½-inch Old Army, the locking latch under the barrel is easily removed — it's held on by a screw (the 7½-inch barrels have latches in a dovetail). So I simply remove the latch when using the shorter barrel and the Belt Mountain base pin, and leave it in place on the longer barrels. Both the Remington 1858 and Ruger Old Army shoot

Whether with John's .45 Colt handloads or suitable Winchester factory ammunition, this 1858 Remington shoots quite well indeed.

to point of aim with Kirst .45 Colt cylinders and standard loads.

In addition to Remington and Colt conversions, Taylor's & Co. also offers six-shot .45 Colt conversion cylinders for the Ruger Old Army. These cylinders became available at about the same time Ruger announced the Old Army with a 5½-inch barrel. They exhibit excellent workmanship and are well worth the going price. The cylinder is a two-piece affair with a typical bored-through cylinder and removable back plate with six firing pins resembling percussion nipples. A hole in the back plate lines up with a pin on the back of the cylinder to lock the plate in place after five cartridges are loaded in the cylinder. One of the firing pins is a different color, so it is always easy to locate the empty chamber. Once you load the cylinder and replace the back plate, put it back into the Ruger frame and replace the the base pin. You're now ready to shoot metallic cartridges.

Conversion cylinders are not cheap, but they are less expensive then buying a new sixgun. Percussion sixguns can be used with black powder and roundball, black-powder cartridge loads or sensible smokeless loads. And they shoot exceptionally well. I'd call that a bargain.

Currently Taylor's and Co. offers six-shot .45 Colt cylinders for the Colt Walker and Dragoons, Ruger Old Army and 1858 Remington while the 1860 Army gets a five-shot cylinder. Both the 1858 Remington and 1860 Army Kirst cylinders are five-shot affairs, while the Walker, Dragoons and Ruger Old Army cylinders all carry six rounds.

The Old Army is of modern design and capable of handling heavy loads. However, replicas of all the original percussion sixguns of the mid-19th century are not that strong. Make sure you keep any loads at the level of factory Cowboy Action cartridges or less. ◎

SEMI

AUTO PISTOLS

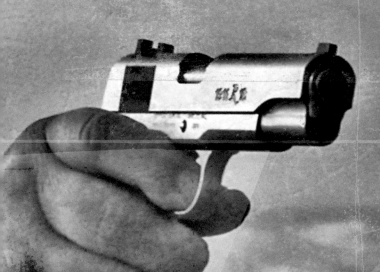

SEMIAUTO PISTOLS
AND THEIR
CARTRIDGES

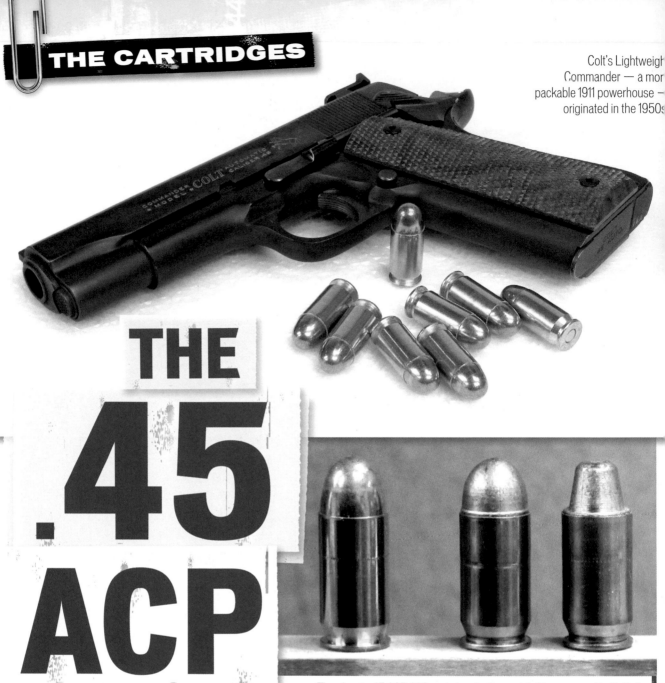

THE CARTRIDGES

Colt's Lightweight
Commander — a more
packable 1911 powerhouse —
originated in the 1950s

THE
.45
ACP

The classic .45 ACP 230-grain hardball round (left), compared to Taffin's
pet handloads with 225-grain RN and 200-grain SWC bullets.

CHAPTER 33

In 1873 the U.S. government officially adopted the .45 caliber as the military standard for both rifles and handguns. For the issue Colt Single Action Army, the cartridge was the .45 Colt. Both gun and cartridge served well during the frontier days, but by the 1890s the move was made to a smaller caliber — the .38 Long Colt, chambered in the company's new Model 1892 double-action revolver.

Militarily speaking, the new handgun was possibly a step forward. The cartridge, however, was not. The .38 caliber proved inadequate in the Philippine Campaign, and the army began to seriously look for a new chambering.

A COMBO FOR THE AGES

Then John Browning and Colt entered the picture with a new semiauto pistol, the Colt Model 1905, firing a 200-grain .45-caliber bullet. Within six years the Model 1905 had been modified to become the Model 19ll, one of the most successful handguns of all time. It fired a 230-grain round-nosed, .45-caliber bullet at 850 fps. The cartridge itself was — and still is — called the .45 ACP (Automatic Colt Pistol). Both gun and cartridge would eventually serve the U.S. military well in two world wars, Korea, Vietnam and various brushfire conflicts around the globe.

In the 1980s the U.S. government once again officially

.45 ACP

THE CARTRIDGES

OT200RN
4.0 Bull

The .45 ACP is supremely useful in revolvers, like these S&W 2nd Model Hand Ejectors.

SEMIAUTO PISTOLS AND THEIR CARTRIDGES

THE BOOK OF THE .45

dropped the .45 in favor of a smaller caliber — this time the 9mm Parabellum. And once again the smaller caliber has been found wanting in some circumstances, causing select units to return to the .45 ACP. History seems to always have a way of repeating itself. (As this is being written, Colt has received a contract to build 20,000 special combat 1911s for the Marines).

The .45 ACP is certainly one of the most popular handgun cartridges ever, probably second only to the .38 Special/.357 Magnum. And it is virtually impossible to separate the cartridge from the gun — the Colt Government Model in all its variations. From its introduction in 1911 until well into the 1970s, the Colt was pretty much the only factory-new .45 semiauto available.

A FLOOD OF FORTY-FIVES

To Jeff Cooper goes much of the credit for making the 1911 the No. 1 fighting handgun. There was a time, 40 years ago or so, when only two types of 1911s were encountered, namely the original Colt and military surplus versions built by several manufacturers for use during two world wars.

While the 1911 was becoming more and more popular, polymer-framed auto pistols also began to appear, first in 9mm and then in .45 ACP. In my lifetime I have seen more than 50 different manufacturers produce 1911s, and today we also have a proliferation of polymer-framed pistols from such manufacturers as Smith & Wesson, Springfield Armory, Taurus and even Ruger who not only offer their versions of traditional 1911s but polymer-framed .45 ACPs as well.

ME AND MY ACP

I've *always* had a .45 ACP it seems. During the late 1950s and early '60s, it seemed that everyone had a surplus 1911. If I remember correctly, these were sold through the DCM for $7.50 to $15. In the early '70s I fell heir to both a new, unfired Colt MK IV Series 70 and a Lyman four-cavity mold dropping Lyman #452460 bullets — a 200-grain SWC designed specifically for the .45 ACP. So I figured it was time to get serious.

My first handload using the above-named bullet and 3.5 grains of Bullseye was put together for use at an indoor range. The first five offhand shots out of that fixed-sight Colt

· 213 ·

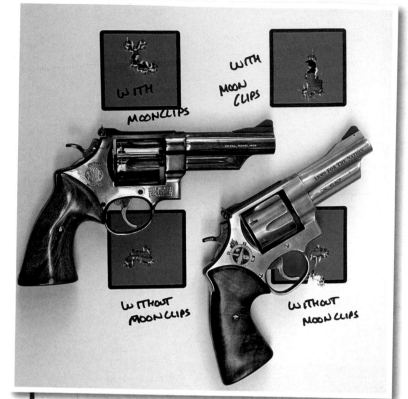

A newer generation of S&W .45 ACP revolvers includes its Model 25-2 (left) and a Jerry Miculek favorite — the Model 625 (right).

gave me a group that would have done an accurized pistol proud. Four shots were in one ragged hole, with the fifth less than 1 inch away (so much for the "inaccuracy" of an out-of-the-box Colt 1911.

When metallic silhouette shooting became popular during the 1980s, I found myself shooting less and less .45 ACPs and more and more heavy .45 Colt loads, as well as the .454 Casull, and of course, the .44 Magnum. But as more and more models of semiautos chambered in .45 ACP began to arrive in the 1990s (and have continued to proliferate), I've gone back to the .45 ACP more and more. In fact, in the last 10 years I've probably tested more .45 ACPs than anything else.

Taffin's most-used bullets in reloading the .45 ACP are all 200-grain SWCs from H&G and RCBS bullet molds, plus Oregon Trail LaserCast SWCs.

During the past 30-plus years, I have found myself spending a large part of my time testing various handloads from sixguns and leverguns — all of which called for spending a lot of time by myself in the desert and mountains. As I looked at some of the older pictures, I often see myself with a holstered sixgun while I am testing semiautomatics. Oddly enough, I also see myself wearing a Government Model while testing sixguns! During these trips I would also fire several rounds of .45 ACP along with the many rounds fired through whichever particular sixgun I happened to be testing at the time. What I am saying is, I think enough of the .45 ACP to bet my life on it.

AN ELUSIVE IDEAL

I have spent much of my shooting life in search of the "perfect packin' pistol." I'll never find it. In fact, I never *want* to find it. I just want to get closer and closer, as the joy is in the searching. The .45 ACP, especially in several iterations of the 1911, certainly comes close though. When it comes to versatility, the .45 ACP is way up close to the top.

What other handgun cartridge can be put to so many different uses, do them all so well and be chambered in so many different handguns? How many cans of Bullseye powder are still expended every year by target shooters? How many thousands of shooters use it for various forms of combat shooting every year? How many shooters try to emulate Jerry Miculek when shooting full-moon clips of .45 ACPs through S&W sixguns? How many people — like me — carry a .45 ACP for self-protection? And don't forget that the cartridge can also be used as a short-range hunting load. That's a whole lot of uses for a 100-year-old cartridge.

The .45 ACP sixgun has several advantages over a semiauto. Heavier loads can be safely used, brass is not scattered all over the landscape, longer-than-standard loads (which will not fit in a magazine) work just fine in a

.45 ACP

Using auxiliary cylinders in .45 ACP increased the utility of single-action sixguns, such as the Freedom Arms Model 97 and Model 83, Ruger's Old Model Blackhawk and Colt's New Frontier.

sixgun cylinder, as do light loads which will not cycle a semi-auto. At about the time I got my first military surplus 1911 (for less than $20!) back in the mid-1950s, bullseye shooters were running a lot of .45 ACPs through Smith & Wesson's Model 1950 and 1955 target revolvers.

But gunsmiths started working with the 1911 by tightening and tuning, fitting adjustable sights and giving it a crisp, creep-free trigger pull. It wasn't long before the world's best combat pistol also became a superb target gun. We soon had two distinct types of 1911s — loose ones for combat and tight ones for target shooting. Everyone knew the two could never mix.

Almost everyone that is. Today we have .45 ACPs on the 1911 platform with slides hand-fitted to frames so tightly there's no perceptible play. They may feel like target pistols; however, those from such custom 'smiths as Bill Wilson, Ed Brown or Les Baer (to name a few) are totally reliable at the same time. Even non-custom factory produced 1911s are also very tightly fitted, yet still work perfectly when quality ammunition is used.

HANDLOADING

Handloading for the .45 ACP is not quite the same as for such sixguns as the .357 Magnum, .44 Magnum and .45

Colt. Anything that fits a revolver cylinder will normally work satisfactorily — light loads, medium loads, heavy magnum loads. The parameters of the .45 ACP — in a semiauto — are much more narrow. If it's too light a load, the action won't function. Try to make a magnum out of it and more serious problems can result. Changing recoil springs adapts the 1911 to lighter and heavier loads, and there have been various attempts to "magnumize" the .45 ACP using different — although somewhat similar — cartridges.

However, here we are talking about the standard .45 ACP. I like to stay around 700-800 fps for most plinking loads, using 185- to 230-grain bullets. I go to 900-1,000 fps with 200-grain lead SWCs for what could be called "serious work." When jacketed bullets are called for, 185 grainers can be safely driven to 1,100 fps. Reloading the .45 ACP requires dies that will allow a tight friction fit on the bullet since semiauto cartridges are not given a heavy roll crimp as found on sixgun loads. At the same time, you'll need dies that will expand the case mouth enough to prevent the shaving of lead bullets when they're being seated.

I have three favorite cast bullets for the .45 ACP, especially for use in the 1911. All are in the 200-grain weight range and are of semiwadcutter design. There was a time when it was

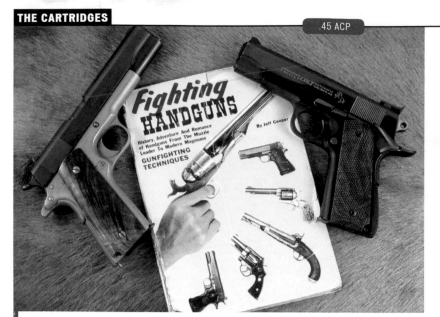

Col. Jeff Cooper's *Fighting Handguns* was one of his earlier efforts in promoting the virtues of the 1911 — and the .45 ACP.

also necessary to have a gunsmith work over 1911s to make them capable of reliably feeding SWCs. That time, however, has long passed — it is a rare 1911 from any current manufacturer that isn't set up for 100 percent SWC reliability.

This was certainly not always the case. When I started, more often than not, the only bullet that could be counted on to feed and function in a 1911 was the 230-grain FMJ hardball load. In fact, the 1911s I purchased in the late 1960s and 1970s had to be worked over before they would reliably feed anything else.

While Jeff Cooper started beating the drum for the .45 ACP, several other gunwriters not only said the 1911 was not dependable, but also hung this same albatross around the necks of other semiautos. This myth did have some foundation, however it was busted decades ago. Today's crop of semiautos in general — especially the .45s — are exceptionally dependable with JHPs and cast bullets. Some can be cranky with JHPs featuring very large cavities. I'd say about 1 in 10 I've tested in the last two decades would fall into this category. But any of the quality .45 ACP semiautos — whether 1911s or one of the newer polymer-framed guns — are just as reliable as any revolver. I would not hesitate to choose any of them for self-defense.

I've always been one to carefully sort brass for reloading by headstamps. Whether loading for sixgun or rifle, I would not think of mixing one brand of brass with another. But I'm not sure anymore this is necessary for most purposes. What changed my mind was a box of .45 ACP reloads of mixed brass from Black Hills Ammunition. After testing a dozen or

Some Taffin 1911 favorites (from top): A Clark Custom Commander, a Wilson Professional and Colt Commander.

The standard Colt Series 70 .45 ACP leaves nothing to be desired when it comes to accuracy.

OT 200 SWC
5.5 BULLSEYE
880 FPS

Taffin's grandson, Jason Michael Seals, having a ball with one of grandpa's several 1911s.

so different factory loads, I was stunned to find those bargain-priced reloads outshot everything else. Now, unless I'm working on a special project, none of my brass gets sorted by headstamp. My everyday shooting loads are diversity at work.

Today most of my .45 ACP reloads are assembled on the RCBS Pro-2000 Progressive Press with two sets of dies, Lyman and RCBS, in two separate die plates. With this setup I can load enough rounds in one pleasant afternoon to fill a .50-caliber ammo can. Although I no longer pay any attention to the headstamps, I do check the overall length carefully to make sure rounds will fit my magazines. I also like to load SWC bullets with just a kiss of the front shoulder protruding from the case; for scientific purposes, a kiss is about the width of two human hairs, maybe a little more. This works for most semiautomatics; however, some are chambered so tightly bullets must be seated with the shoulder flush with the end of the case.

My early experiments with cast bullets — before I started casting my own — were with 230-grain commercial hard-cast, roundnose bullets, which basically duplicated the weight and shape of FMJ hardball.

About 35 years ago, I stumbled upon a full-house load used by Jeff Cooper — a 215-grain SWC over 7.5 grains of Unique for close to 1,100 fps from a 1911s 5-inch barrel. For my use, I cut the bullet weight to 200 grains by using the Lyman mold for the #452460 SWC. Later I used the same

weight bullet with a slightly longer nose from the H&G #68 mold. I am also very fond of the RCBS version which is #45-201. By running two double-cavity molds simultaneously, the RCBS bullets pile up quickly.

For all of these bullets I mostly use pure type metal, which is not so easily found these days. However, I certainly have enough to last the rest of my shooting life.

The jacketed version of this bullet is Speer's 200-grain TMJ. I also cut the powder charge to 7.0 grains of Unique, which gives me 1,050 fps. This remains a very powerful load.

Today we have many different .45 ACP bullets available. I still cast my own from both the Lyman, RCBS and H&G molds, but I'm more likely to use the Oregon Trail version as well as its 200- and 230-grain RN and 225-grain FN. That gives me four choices of commercial cast bullets covering just about any application I need.

When the task at hand calls for jacketed bullets, Hornady, Sierra and Speer all offer excellent choices from 185 to 230 grains in both JHP and FMJ versions. JHP bullets for the .45 ACP are basically state-of-the-art today, with wide,

SEMIAUTO PISTOLS AND THEIR CARTRIDGES

THE BOOK OF THE .45

Classy carry: Taffin's ivory-stocked and engraved Colt Series 70 with leather by El Paso Saddlery.

deep cavities to guarantee expansion. For those who do not reload, of course, there is a near-endless supply of excellent factory ammunition available.

Two bullets — not normally thought of as .45 ACP bullets — work very well in all .45 semiautos I have tried them in. They are Elmer Keith's old sixgun bullets that he designed long before I was born. These are #454424, specifically for the .45 Colt (255 to 260 grains) and the #452423 for the .45 Auto Rim (230 to 240 grains). Both feed through most actions when they are seated with about .03 inch of the front shoulder exposed, and the .45 Colt bullet is particularly businesslike-looking in the .45 ACP cartridge. Using 6.5 grains of Unique with this bullet gives a load that is slightly faster than hardball and *definitely* hits with more authority.

The .45 ACP can be had in "back-to-basics" GI-type pistols such as this no-frills Auto-Ordnance 1911.

NO END OF CHOICES

Over the next few chapters, I will be looking at a sampling of 1911s and polymer-framed pistols currently available. Of course, there are many excellent examples which will not be covered simply because I haven't yet had the opportunity to use them.

When it comes to .45s on the 1911 Government Model platform, we have dozens upon dozens of choices and new manufacturers continue to enter the market.

As I've mentioned, my first military surplus 1911 served me well for many years. It has been replaced many times over by everything from a circa 1914 Commercial Model to highly customized Commanders by Jimmy Clark and Bill Wilson. In between have been 1911s from Colt, Auto-Ordnance, Kimber, Springfield Armory, Para-USA, USFA, Dan Wesson, Taurus, Smith & Wesson, and just recently, Iver Johnson.

In the early 1950s, the standard Government Model was given a shorter barrel and the alloy grip frame to become the Commander which was soon offered in a steel frame as well. Several companies have vied with each other to see who could make the smallest 1911, and even double-action versions have been offered. Whatever one desires in a 1911 is readily available. It is second only to the AR-15 in the number of add-on and custom parts being offered.

I have no idea how many thousands of rounds of .45 ACP I have run through several dozen 1911s over the past half-century. I do know there is a 5-gallon bucket of empty brass in the loading room waiting to be refilled.

We could argue for days on end about who is putting out the best 1911 today, however Colt has been making them for a century now with today's Government Models being some of the finest ever offered. Several years ago, a friend came up to me at church and said he was settling an estate and he had a Colt .45 for sale for $100, at which point I interrupted him and said I would take it.

"Don't you want to know anything about it?" he asked.

"No," I said. "If it's a Colt at that price, I'll take it sight unseen."

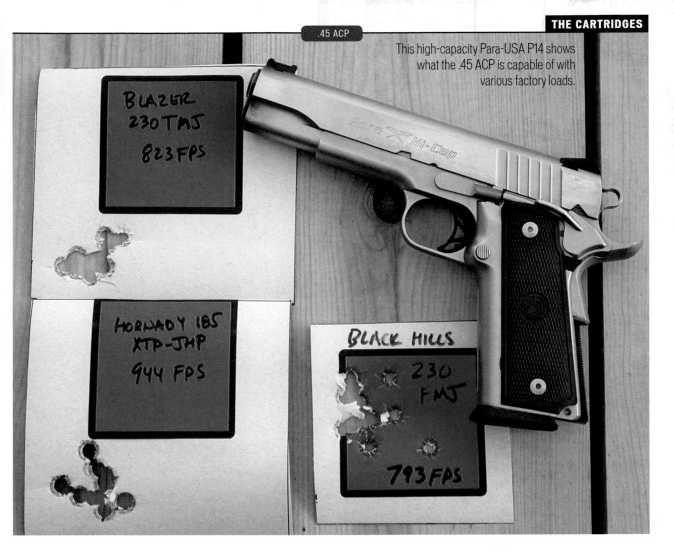

This high-capacity Para-USA P14 shows
what the .45 ACP is capable of with
various factory loads.

In the early days of *Guns Magazine*, Kent Bellah taught me the idea of "a pair and a spare," that is, if you have a good gun, make sure you have backups. (Clint Smith says the same thing today.) My "pair and a spare" of Colts are somewhat mismatched, consisting of two Series 70 Government Models, one an everyday working blued model with ivory grip panels, the other engraved, ivory stocked and satin nickeled. The third member of the trio is a recent production Colt Combat Elite, a superb pistol by anyone's standards.

Several companies have gone back to the original roots of the 1911 by offering their versions of the original pre-World War I 1911s. Those I shoot on a regular basis are the Auto-Ordnance 1911, Iver Johnson 1911A1, Para-USA GI Expert, Springfield Armory Mil-Spec and USFA 1911. Just recently I have added the Colt Anniversary Model to the group.

Back around 2000, I attended the Springfield Armory Seminar in Mississippi and came away with two excellent .45s, the full-sized TRP and the V10 Ultra Compact, the latter being much smaller than a Commander. The number one producer

of .45s is Kimber; its Custom CDPII is a full-sized 1911 with an alloy frame. It not only shoots very well but it also packs easily. Kimber's Compact Aluminum, like the V10, has a 3-inch barrel and short grip frame making it very easy to conceal.

Two relative newcomers to the 1911 scene are Taurus and Dan Wesson. The Taurus really shook up the market by offering a 1911 with all the custom features normally found on more expensive guns, and did it for under $600. Dan Wesson made some of the best long-range revolvers ever offered, but the company discovered it could produce 1911s with less machine time and sell them for more money. Its Patriot is an excellent 1911. Then there is the "Magnum .45," the .460 Rowland which only requires a conversion kit to turn any modern .45 into the equivalent of a 4-inch .44 Magnum.

So many choices makes picking favorite 1911s pretty hard, so I will take the easy way out and choose my Colts, especially the Gold Cup and the engraved Series 70.

But with all the .45 ACP pistols out there, if anything, the cartridge is destined to become even more popular. ◎

THE .45 WINCHESTER MAGNUM

A cast of cast-bulle[t]
handloads: .45 GAP, .45 ACP, .45 WinMag

CHAPTER 34

The idea simply had to come to fruition. After all, other standard cartridges had been lengthened and "magnumized." The .38 Special was lengthened to become the .357 Magnum in 1935. The .44 Special was lengthened to the .44 Magnum in 1955. Each became one of the most popular sixgun cartridges of all time.

But what about semiautos? Mainly, *the* semiauto cartridge? The .45 ACP had been around since well before World War I, but no one had lengthened it until 1979 — when Olin was convinced to stretch the legendary service round to create the .45 Winchester Magnum. It was to be used in Wildey Moore's big gas-operated pistol. But while the .357 and .44 Magnums have been tremendous successes, the .45 WinMag has mostly been offered only in one factory loading, featuring the familiar 230-grain hardball.

Exceptions now include Black Hills' 250-grain JHP load and Winchester's 260-grain JHP. The reason for the relatively small selection is quite simple. The promised

In John's opinion, the Dan Wesson Model 460 (shown in action on the opposite page) is an outstanding double-action revolver platform for the .45 WinMag–scoped or unscoped.

semiautos chambered for the .45 WinMag did not immediately materialize, and when they did, they didn't last long. The original Wildey pistol itself has been an on-again, off-again proposition for years.

OTHER OPTIONS

The .45 WinMag did find a home in the Thompson/Center Contender, and my photographer Joe Penner swears by his as a superbly accurate handgun. The .45 WinMag also found a semiauto home in LAR's Grizzly and the AutoMag III from IAI. It is impossible to look at the cartridge without first looking at its most prevalent platform, the Grizzly — which looks like a Government Model on steroids. It seemed intimidating to me, at least at first, and I've shot 'em all — all the big ones from every make and style of .44 Magnum through the .454 Casull and the .475 and .500 Linebaughs on up. All guns generate considerable recoil, but none put me on the defensive like the Grizzly.

The problem isn't recoil. The problem is grip shape. To allow the Government Model grip frame shape to accommodate magnum-style cartridges, it must be made much wider from front to back. This does not mate well with short, stubby fingers. I felt that I did not really have a secure hold on the Grizzly as I began to test-fire it, and actually felt

that I would not be able to hold on. But the more I fired it the better it felt. Soon I didn't notice the grip girth.

The .45 WinMag Grizzly operates and strips like a Government Model (conversion kits were available in 10mm and the bottlenecked .357/.45WM). LAR also offered a compensator that replaced the standard bushing and definitely reduces felt recoil. (I refer to the Grizzly .45 WinMag in the past tense, as it is no more.) Custom revolver 'smith Gary Reeder holds the Grizzly in very high regard as a hunting handgun; in fact, it is probably the best semiauto ever offered for hunting.

RELOADING

The .45 WinMag case is ³⁄₁₀ inch longer than the standard .45 ACP and — theoretically at least — can be reloaded with .45 ACP dies. I use an RCBS .45 WinMag 4-die set that includes a taper-crimp die, which I consider mandatory for reloading any heavy recoiling semiauto. I *say* I use the RCBS 4-die set, but it's not quite so simple. Actually, two additional dies are needed to successfully load for the .45 WinMag.

The brass takes a considerable beating when fired in the Grizzly. Ejected empties come flying out, leaving brass skidmarks across the top of the slide, and unless caught with some type of brass catcher, will wind up 55 to 60 feet behind the shooter. When retrieved, the brass is

Target shot with the Wildey .45 WinMag using Winchester 260-grain JHPs. The knurled ring just forward of the receiver is the gas regulator.

too crooked to enter the .45 WinMag sizing die, so all brass must then be run through a .45 Colt carbide sizing die. After this is done, the .45 WinMag brass is ready to be run through the 4 RCBS dies to produce a loaded round.

The .45 WinMag is definitely a reloader's cartridge, as the factory 230-grain roundnose FMJ bullet is really only good for, ah, ... I really can't *think* of anything. Muzzle velocity of the factory Winchester hardball clocked 1,392 fps from the 6-inch barrel of the Grizzly (compared to 1,450 fps with a 240-grain .44 Magnum JHP from a 7½-inch Ruger Bisley).

almost hopelessly out of round. So much so that it won't enter the .45 WinMag sizing die.

To reclaim the brass, I first use a NexPander tool. It was at one time available from NEI and is a valuable addition to any reloading bench. The NexPander is a cylinder approximately 3 inches long by .900 inch in diameter with a tapered pin on each end. One tapers from approximately .500 to .350 inch and the other about .350 to .200 inch. It is used, as its name implies, to expand case necks by simply tapping the bottom of the brass on the bench as the tapered pin enters the brass. It is also invaluable for rounding out misshapen case mouths.

Once the case mouths are "NexPanded," the brass is ready for standard handling. *Almost.* The mouths are still

John does a bit of long-range plinking with the LAR Grizzly in .45 WinMag — an ideal tool for the job.

JACKETED HOLLOWPOINTS

I consider the factory round as maximum. Any attempt on my part to exceed this velocity with Sierra 240-, Hornady 250- or Speer 260-grain JHPs resulted in much higher pressures — at least this appears so from reading the flattened primers. I would definitely consider 1,400 fps as absolute maximum with this bullet-weight range when used in the LAR Grizzly.

I found the optimum powders to be Hercules Blue Dot and Herco, Accurate Arm's AA #7 and AA #9, and Hodgdon's H110. I assembled all my loads in Winchester brass using CCI #350 Magnum primers. My loads with Sierra 240-grain JHP used 15.5, 16.5 and 17.5 grains of Blue Dot for muzzle velocities of 1,255, 1,325 and 1,400 fps. With 17.0 grains of AA #7, I got 1,320 fps. With 13.0 and 13.5 grains of Herco I averaged 1,260 and 1,285 fps, respectively. With 25.0 grains of H110, I got a maximum load at 1,380 fps.

Going up to the 250-grain Hornady JHP, the most accurate and best loads were with 16.5 and 17.5 grains of Blue Dot for 1,330 and 1,415 fps; 25.0 grains of H110 yielded 1,375 fps. Milder loadings — which showed excellent accuracy with the 250-grain Hornady JHP — used 17.5 grains of AA #9 (1,040 fps) and 21.0 and 22.0 grains of H110 (1,085 and 1,170 fps, respectively).

Speer's 260-grain bullet proved to be the most accurate JHP in the Grizzly. With 15.5 and 16.5 grains of Blue Dot, I got 1,235 and 1,305 fps. With 16.0 and 17.0 grains of AA #7, I got 1,155 and 1,235 fps. Using 12.5 grains of Herco yielded 1,185 fps, and 25.0 grains of H110 produced 1,375 fps. Actually, 25.0 grains of H110 proved to be an excellent load for all three bullets. But again, consider this a maximum load. Blue Dot is an excellent powder for use in the .45 WinMag. Any of these three bullets are excellent for hunting.

Despite a checkered production life, the Wildey Survivor once again offers big-bore magnum power in a semi-auto pistol.

CAST BULLET MENU

Switching to cast bullets for the .45 WinMag, Oregon Trail's 255-grain SWC .45 Colt bullet works quite well. Top loads turned out to be 18.5 grains of AA #9 (1,215 fps), 12.5 grains of Herco (1,245 fps) and 22.0 and 23.0 grains of H110 (1,275 and 1,340 fps, respectively). All would work fine on medium-sized game at reasonable ranges and put the .45 WinMag right alongside a heavy-loaded Ruger .45 Colt, and not too far behind a .44 Magnum.

Surprisingly, at least to me, is the fact the .45 WinMag works fine with the NEI 310-grain .45 Colt Keith bullet. I didn't try to push this one real hard but did go to 1,185 fps with 19.5 grains of H110. A better heavyweight proved to be the 300-grain Freedom Arms/Lyman #454629GC flatnose. Accurate, powerful loads using this gas-checked bullet were assembled with 16.5 grains of AA #9 (1,130 fps) and 17.5 and 18.5 grains of H110 (1,085 and 1,130 fps).

All are equivalent to loads I use with the same bullet in the .45 Colt for use in my Ruger Bisley, Ruger Blackhawk and Freedom Arms .454 Casull. They are perfect close-range hunting loads and excellent long-range plinking loads out to 800 yards. They may take a few seconds to get out there, but they do raise a lot of dust when they hit.

The .45 WinMag is definitely in the true magnum class, and the Grizzly does make a fine hunting pistol when properly handloaded. Today, I mostly shoot the cartridge in my

TEST-FIRE: WILDEY MAGNUM SURVIVOR .45 WIN MAG (8-INCH BARREL)

LOAD	VELOCITY	4 SHOTS, 25 YARDS
Black Hills 250-gr. JHP	1,407 fps	1 ½"
Cor-Bon 230-gr. FMJ	1,471 fps	1 ½"
Winchester 260-gr. JHP	1,353 fps	7/8"
Sierra 240-gr. JHC/23.0 gr. H110	1,201 fps	1 ¾"
Hornady 250-gr. JHP/23.0 gr. H110	1,243 fps	1 ½"
Speer 260-gr. JHP/23.0 gr. H110	1,244 fps	2"
Speer 260-gr. JHP/16.5 gr. Blue Dot	1,421 fps	1 ⅜"

sixguns, as I have an auxiliary .45 WinMag cylinder for a Freedom Arms 4¾-inch .454 Casull. I also have one of the very rare Dan Wesson Model 460s which, while built mainly for the .460 Rowland, also handles the .45 WinMag.

THE ORIGINAL ITEM

The first semiauto .45 WinMag, the Wildey, had a brief moment of fame in the movies. A little background is necessary here. Those shooters who have been around more than four decades will well remember the frustration in trying to find an S&W .44 Magnum in the early 1970s. Demand far exceeded supply, thanks to a Clint Eastwood character by the name of Dirty Harry.

When Dirty Harry uttered those now famous words,

John relaxes after a session with the Wildey Survivor. Its weight and gas operation make it surprisingly soft shooting.

Wildey Moore first began producing them in the 1970s. I first met him at an NRA Show in the late 1980s when I had begun volunteering with Hal Swiggett and the Outstanding American Handgunner Awards Foundation. In fact, Wildey donated pistols to be given away at our annual banquet. Then suddenly it seemed as if Wildey disappeared. The bank holding the mortgage went under, and Wildey's company was under the control of the FDIC, which put a squeeze on the cash flow.

By the mid-1990s the company was purchased back from the FDIC, resulting in another cash-flow problem, restraining advertising, promoting and traveling. But Wildey (www.usafirearmscorp.com) offered the Survivor chambered in .44 AutoMag, .475 Wildey Magnum and .45 WinMag.

"Make my day," he definitely made Smith & Wesson's day, as the company could sell every .44 Magnum it could turn out. Other movies, on a somewhat smaller scale, have also affected sales of firearms. Some of my favorites include the *Death Wish* series starring Charles Bronson.

Bronson starts out on small scale with a .32-caliber revolver; however, by the third and final episode, his character, Paul Kersey, has definitely moved to the top of the food chain. Bronson wages one of the longest gunfights ever filmed (at least until *Open Range* came along in 2003), using what he calls "my friend Wildey," a semiauto Wildey Survivor.

The Survivor is reminiscent of Harry Sanford's AutoMag, which arrived five years earlier than the Wildey. Both are very large, stainless-steel semiautos equipped with vent-rib barrels. Striking differences that you'll immediately notice are the larger trigger guard and double-action trigger of the Wildey, as well as the grooved ring on the barrel in front of the receiver. The patented gas system is an air/hydraulic piston powered by the gasses through six small holes in the barrel. It is this piston, forcing the slide rearward that ejects a fired case. The ring you may have first noticed is the gas regulator, which is used to adjust the amount of force the piston provides and is adjustable to accommodate the loads being used.

The single-action option: This Freedom Arms sixgun has four cylinders — .454 Casull, .45 Colt, .45 ACP and .45 WinMag. Now that's versatility!

John got impressive results using a series of FMJ handloads with the LAR Grizzly.

AN EASY RETRIEVE

One of the less enjoyable things about shooting a semiauto is having to pick up the brass. I've tried several things, including parking the pickup so the brass would wind up in the bed.

But in setting the gas regulator of the Wildey, I discovered a better way.

This JHP lineup shows (left to right): the .45 GAP, .45 ACP, .45 Rowland and .45 WinMag.

The directions for setting the regulator say to insert an empty magazine into the pistol and single load cartridges into the ejection port. Turn the gas regulator clockwise one click at a time, firing one round after each adjustment until the slide stop lock engages. Then fire a full magazine to check for the proper adjustment. If cartridges are not fully ejected, open the gas regulator another click until the operation is perfect. If you want the pistol to function as a single shot, just turn down the gas regulator until it doesn't cycle automatically.

But you can also set the regulator so the slide locks opened and the fired case remains in the ejection port. It's then a simple matter to turn the pistol sideways to drop the fired case into a container. No fuss, no muss, no shagging brass.

The Wildey can be had with interchangeable barrels (5 inches all the way up to a rifle-length 18 inches, which can be used with a forearm and buttstock). The same mainframe can be used for all chamberings. There are no screws holding the grips to the grip frame. Those fully checkered walnut grips are held on by springs on the inside of the grip panel, making for a very smooth appearance.

The Wildey is a traditional single/double action. Push a cam lever on the left side of the gun down to drop the hammer and place the pistol in a safe condition. For firing, push the lever up. The Wildey may then be fired by using the double-action trigger or by cocking the hammer.

I definitely prefer the single-action mode, because my trigger finger just barely reaches the trigger when it's set in the double-action mode. It is much easier to reach the trigger when the hammer is cocked and the trigger is farther rearward. Because of the checkering of the grips, I expected some resulting discomfort when firing. There was none.

The Survivor recoils, to be sure. However, it is not punishing thanks to the gun's 4-pound weight, gas operation and the wide beavertail-style grip frame. Although the .45 WinMag is in the same league as the .44 Magnum, it is definitely more comfortable to shoot in the Wildey Survivor than the .44 Magnum is in *any* revolver.

I test fired the Survivor with three factory loads and six handloads, using both Hodgdon's H110 and Alliant's Blue Dot. Although six handloads were used, only four are included in the accompanying chart, as for some unknown reason the 240- and 250-grain bullets simply would not shoot with the Blue Dot. Why? That's one of the things that keeps handloading so interesting, and also why it is a good idea to never load a large batch of ammunition until it is thoroughly tested in the handgun in which it is going to be used. Once the gas regulator was set properly, the Wildey functioned perfectly.

Wildey offers a large line of accessories for its Survivor, including ammunition, brass, Lyman reloading dies and scope mounts. A pistol this big is not all that easy to carry comfortably; however, Wildey offers both leather and nylon holsters to be worn strong-side or crossdraw, as well as shoulder versions. I decided long ago the only way to carry a large pistol — short of a sling — was in a quality shoulder rig. This also places the handgun out of the way when working your way through heavy brush.

Although the test gun was a polished stainless-steel Survivor with a round trigger guard, three other models were available — the Survivor Guardsmen (same gun with a square trigger guard), the Hunter and Hunter Guardsmen (round and square trigger guards, respectively), both finished in matte stainless-steel. ◉

THE CARTRIDGES

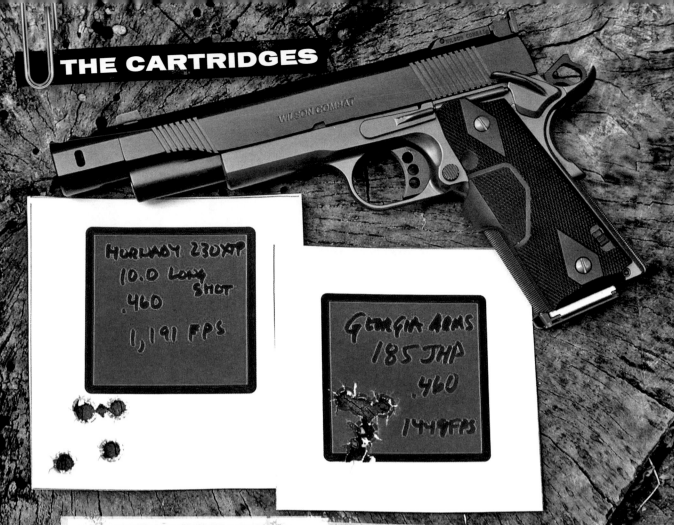

HORNADY 230XTP
10.0 LONG SHOT
.460
1,191 FPS

GEORGIA ARMS
185 JHP
.460
1449 FPS

THE .460 ROWLAND

The Wilson Combat Custom Hunter in .460 Rowland (shown above) combines excellent accuracy with hog-stopping power — all combined in the familiar 1911 format.

CHAPTER 35

The Model 1911 in .45 ACP remains the epitome of what a fighting handgun should be. But for hunting it is somewhat wanting when it comes to anything bigger than large varmints. Yes, I know some have used it for hunting critters such as wild hogs, but use it often enough for such endeavors, and eventually the wrong hog will take a hit in the wrong place and not be real happy about it!

Wouldn't it be great if we could have a standard-sized 1911 that would deliver a .44 Magnum payload with no more recoil than a .45 ACP? Think I'm dreaming? *Wrong.*

BIRTH OF A BLASTER

The dream was realized in the 1990s with the .460 Rowland, a cartridge which can be handled by any standard 1911 using a drop-in kit from Clark Custom Guns. The concept itself comes from Johnny Rowland, who hosts the *Shooting Show* out of Louisiana. I hunted with Rowland during the Fourth Annual HHI World Championship Hunt and Competition at the YO Ranch in the late 1990s and found him to be a grand guy to be around, and a dedicated handgun hunter as well.

Five months later I found myself at the SHOT Show, talking with Rowland at the Clark booth. He was all excited about the cartridge and showed me a couple of revolvers that had been rechambered to it — a Ruger Blackhawk and a Smith & Wesson Model 625. I came away with a drop-in kit from Clark and set about putting a .460 Rowland together on a 1911 platform.

What then is a .460 Rowland? It is simply a .45 ACP case that has been stretched and strengthened. Starline makes the brass, headstamped ".460 Rowland," that is ¹⁄₁₆ inch longer than the standard .45 ACP (standard .45 ACP reloading dies work) with a beefed-up interior. It will not chamber in guns designed to handle the .45 ACP, and .45 ACPs will not properly chamber in semiautos designed for the .460 Rowland (they can't headspace on the case mouth but will drop too far into the chamber). Double-action sixguns chambered for the .460 Rowland *will* accept .45 ACP rounds from half- or full-moon clips. *Caution*: Some of the early 1917 revolvers dating back to World War I are chambered straight through, and although they may accept the .460 Rowland, the results could be disastrous.

A SPRINGFIELD BUILD

To put a .460 Rowland together using the kit, I took the Springfield Armory 1911 mainframe off a Springfield Armory Single Shot pistol and ordered the parts to complete the gun from Brownells. I needed a slide along with several inner parts, such as a firing pin, firing-pin stop and barrel-link pin. For the sights I chose a BoMar adjustable

Cor-Bon offers two excellent factory loads for the .460 Rowland — a 185-grain JHP and a 230-grain JHP.

rear sight and a Clark post front sight. The slide proved to be very tight on the frame, it took a little work to loosen it up so it would work before I delivered everything to Mike Rainey (now at Buckhorn), who cut dovetails in the slide and installed the sights. A pair of Herrett's cocobolo grip panels completed the package.

If you start with a completed 1911, it's only necessary to change the barrel and replace the standard spring with the 24-pounder found in the drop-in kit to come up with a .460 Rowland. Standard 1911 magazines will work with the cartridge.

In addition to drop-in kits being available from Clark Custom Guns, completed guns are also offered, including a Kimber Convertible with barrels for both .460 Rowland and .45 ACP. They also offer converted S&W M625s and Ruger Blackhawks originally chambered in .45 ACP.

As I mentioned earlier, Starline has the brass, and factory ammunition is available from Georgia Arms. The latter also offers another great idea for Rowlands, the .45 DA cartridge which is nothing more than the .45 Colt with a larger rim for positive extraction from double-action sixguns. It

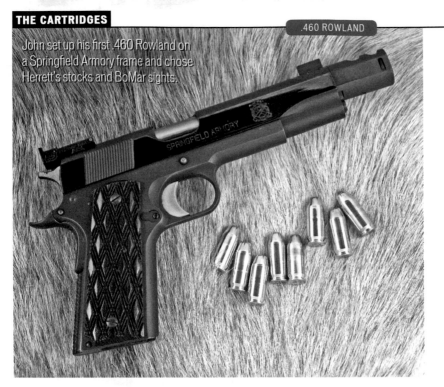

John set up his first .460 Rowland on a Springfield Armory frame and chose Herrett's stocks and BoMar sights.

grain JHP at 1,340 fps. These are published figures. When fired in my completed .460 Rowland, the 185-grain load does 1,530 fps (and drops five shots into ⅝ inch at 15 yards), the 200 does 1,436 fps, and the 230 clocks out at 1,330 fps. For a comparison with .44 Magnum loads, I fired the Federal 180-grain JHP from the 5-inch barrel of an S&W Model 629 and got 1,564 fps. Hornady's 200-grain XTP .44 Magnum loading clocked out at 1,350 fps, while Black Hills' rendition of the 240-grain JHP load came in at 1,247.

works in any sixgun chambered for .45 Colt which does not incorporate recessed case heads in the cylinder.

.44 MAGNUM COMPARISON

Factory loads for the .460 Rowland include a 185-grain JHP at 1,550 fps, a 200-grain JHP at 1,450 fps and a 230-

For all practical purposes, the .460 Rowland with its 5-inch barrel equals, or surpasses, the .44 Magnum from a 5-inch sixgun — so we basically have .44 Magnum performance in a standard-size 1911. But what about recoil? The Clark Drop-in Kit features a built-in compensator that works. Really works. With it in place, the felt recoil of the

John shoots the Wilson Combat Custom Hunter .460, his one-handed grip testifying to its manageability.

SEMIAUTO PISTOLS AND THEIR CARTRIDGES

The Model 1911 in 45 ACP remains the epitome of what a fighting handgun should be. But for hunting it is somewhat wanting when it comes to anything bigger than large varmints.

The .460 Rowland is equal to the .44 Magnum in a short-barreled sixgun and works well with a variety of bullet configurations (examples below).

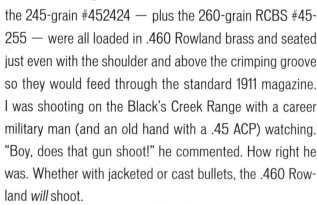

.460 Rowland to me is less than that of standard .45 ACP. It's a different kind of recoil, coming straight back rather than twisting, so it affects me less.

Many hunting applications call for hard-cast bullets, so it was only natural that I turned to my stock of Keith-style .45s to see what could be accomplished with the .460 Rowland. Two bullets from Lyman molds, the 230-grain #452423 and the 245-grain #452424 — plus the 260-grain RCBS #45-255 — were all loaded in .460 Rowland brass and seated just even with the shoulder and above the crimping groove so they would feed through the standard 1911 magazine. I was shooting on the Black's Creek Range with a career military man (and an old hand with a .45 ACP) watching. "Boy, does that gun shoot!" he commented. How right he was. Whether with jacketed or cast bullets, the .460 Rowland *will* shoot.

Giving myself and the pistol a break, I shot seven-shot groups and counted five. One of the reasons for this, is my particular gun has a common semiauto ailment. It puts the first shot an inch or so away from subsequent ones. Taking

this into consideration, Hornady's 200-grain XTP over 17.5 grains of AA #7 (1,455 fps) shoots into one inch, while the 230-grain XTP over 15.7 grains of AA #7 has a muzzle velocity of 1,335 fps and does even better at ⅞ inch for five. With cast bullets it's the same story, second verse. The 230-grain #452423 over 13.0 grains of AA #7 at 1,160 fps groups in 1⅛ inches, while the 245-grain #452424 and the 260-grain #45-255 are at 1,130 fps for ¾ inch and 1,120 fps and ½ inch, respectively, both over 13.0 grains of AA #7.

In reloading for the .460 Rowland, I've learned several things. Accurate Arms #7 is my top-performing powder, however Hodgdon's new Long Shot also does well. Bullets must be of the right construction for .460 Rowland speeds

THE BOOK OF THE .45

TEST-FIRE: BRAKED WILSON COMBAT HUNTER

LOAD	MV	BEST 20 YD. GROUP (5 SHOTS)
Cor-Bon 185-gr. JHP	1,475 fps	1 5/8"
Cor-Bon 230-gr. JHP	1,303 fps	1 1/2"
Georgia Arms 185-gr. JHP	1,449 fps	7/8"
Hornady 200-gr. XTP/10.0 gr. LS	1,133 fps	1 1/2"
Hornady 230-gr. XTP/10.0 gr. LS	1,191 fps	1 1/4"
Sierra 185-gr. JHC/11.0 gr. LS	1,305 fps	1 3/4"
Speer 185-gr. GDHP/11.0 gr. LS	1,275 fps	1 7/8"
Speer 200-gr. JHP/11.0 gr. LS	1,106 fps	2"

TEST-FIRE: STANDARD WILSON COMBAT HUNTER

LOAD	MV	BEST 20 YD. GROUP (5 SHOTS)
Cor-Bon 185-gr. JHP	1,465 fps	1 5/8"
Cor-Bon 230-gr. JHP	1,252 fps	7/8"
Georgia Arms 185-gr. JHP	1,418 fps	1 3/8"
Hornady 200-gr. XTP/10.0 gr. LS	1,160 fps	1 3/4"
Hornady 230-gr. XTP/10.0 gr. LS	1,143 fps	1 3/4"
Sierra 185-gr. JHC/11.0 gr. LS	1,245 fps	1 1/8"
Speer 185-gr. GDHP/11.0 gr. LS	1,242 fps	1 5/8"
Speer 200-gr. JHP/11.0 gr. LS	1,150 fps	1 1/8"

and pressures. Care should be exercised in selecting any .45 bullets for muzzle velocities in the 1,000-fps range.

Speer's Gold Dots that are designed for the .45 ACP are too soft for the .460 Rowland at top-end pressures.

WILSON STEPS IN

In addition to building superb semiautomatic pistols, Bill Wilson is also a passionate handgun hunter. That presented a minor problem of sorts. Those beautiful semiautos were simply not as good a choice for hunting large critters as a .44 Magnum sixgun. Now semiautos designed with the handgun hunter in mind have been available for decades. But the AutoMag, LAR Grizzly and Desert Eagle are much larger and heavier than the standard 1911. Wilson wanted a

TRITON 240 JHP 1733 FPS

Obviously, John was quite pleased with the accuracy level of his .460 Rowland Springfield Armory "build."

1911 sufficiently powerful for hunting big game. The answer came with Johnny Rowland's .460 Rowland.

The Wilson Combat Hunter is not a conversion. It's built from the ground up as a .460 using, of course, Wilson Combat parts. The frame and the slide are custom fitted to match perfectly with the frame rails. The hammer is a Wilson Ultralight, the grip safety is a Wilson High Ride Beavertail, the ejector is an Extended Ejector, the thumb safety is an Extended Tactical and the trigger is an Ultralight. (Wilson Combat advertises the trigger pull to be from 3½ to 3¾ pounds; my two test guns came in at 3½ and 4 pounds).

The magazine well is contoured for easy magazine insertion. The heavy 5½-inch barrel is hand-fitted and features a supported chamber, polished barrel throat and polished feed ramp. The slide features cocking serrations both front and rear, and the ejection port is lowered and flared. As you might imagine, the .460 Rowland places a lot more stress on a 1911 than the standard .45 ACP; heavy-duty springs and the Shok-Buff help to tame that stress.

The rear sight is a Wilson Lo-Mount adjustable and is matched up with a serrated and forward-tapered front post. Both sights are all black and square, presenting a beautiful sight picture. But that's not all. Since hunting situations for bear and hogs often take place in dim light, Wilson provides — as standard — Crimson Trace LaserGrips. They feature an easy to operate on/off switch at the bottom of the left-hand grip. When they are "on," the middle finger of your shooting hand naturally presses an activation switch

Wilson Combat offers the Custom Hunter .460 with — or without — a compensator.

on the front of the grip. The Combat Hunter is dehorned for comfort — the pistol is smoothed out so that the only sharp edge to be found anywhere is on the top of the front sight. Because things can get slippery real fast in bad weather, the pistol features 30 LPI checkering on the front strap and flat mainspring housing, which works well with the molded-in checkering found on the LaserGrips. The Wilson Combat Hunter is finished in Armor Tuff with a gray frame mated up with a black slide. Shooting the .460 Combat Hunters, one regular and one ported, proved to be most enjoyable.

For test-firing I had factory loads from both Georgia Arms and Cor-Bon. Wilson Combat guarantees one-inch groups at 25 yards. I am nowhere near as steady as I used to be, and I did my test-firing at 20 yards; however, I came in at under one inch using the ported model and Georgia Arms 185-grain JHPs at 1,450 fps. When I

switched to the standard model, Cor-Bon's 230-grain JHPs at 1,250 fps did just as well. After Bill gave me some loading information using Long Shot powder from Hodgdon's, I cut his loads just slightly and had excellent results using JHPs from Hornady, Sierra and Speer.

The standard barreled version puts out more felt recoil than a standard 1911 chambered in .45 ACP; however, the braked version proved to be no worse in felt recoil than any 1911. Anyone planning to do a great deal of shooting with full-power .460 Rowland ammunition might well consider this. ◉

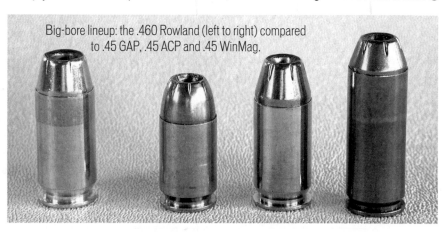

Big-bore lineup: the .460 Rowland (left to right) compared to .45 GAP, .45 ACP and .45 WinMag.

THE CARTRIDGES

This now-discontinued Springfield Armory XD in .45 GAP holds 10 rounds in its double-stack magazine.

THE .45 GAP

John tries his hand – well, just one of 'em thi time — with the compac Glock Model 38

CHAPTER 36

American pistoleros can be a tough crowd to please and are not always kind to new cartridge introductions. Try to find a 9x21, 9x23, 9mm Magnum, 10mm Magnum, .38 Casull or .41AE chambered semiauto. Some do manage to hang on, however. The excellent 10mm has been resurrected and is now chambered in pistols offered by Colt, Glock and Kimber. Wildey offered the .44 AutoMag and .45 WinMag, while the .50AE is still found in the Desert Eagle.

SHORTER STUFF

Shooters seem to treat .45s kinder than most offerings. In 1905 John Browning developed the .45 ACP chambered in a new semiauto which soon evolved into the legendary

A shorter solution: The .45 GAP (left) and .45 ACP (right) with both 200-grain FMJ and cast SWC bullets.

Two makers, four .45s: At left are a Glock .45 ACP (top) and .45 GAP (bottom). At right are a Springfield Armory .45 ACP (top) and .45 GAP (bottom).

1911. It is now more than a century later and the 1911 — and its .45 ACP cartridge — still remains a semiauto combination by which all others are judged.

In the 1980s the 10mm was introduced as a cartridge to take over from the .45 ACP. It obviously did not. Although it featured a 200-grain bullet at 1,200 fps, it was too much for most shooters to handle.

During the 1980s many new semiautos were offered chambered in 9mm, so it only seemed natural to come up with a shorter, less powerful round than the 10mm to fit in all those 9mm pistols. The result was the highly successful .40 S&W.

Reams of paper have been exhausted arguing the merits of various semiauto cartridges. When I was a kid, it was always the 9mm versus the .45 ACP. After 1990 it became the 9mm versus the .40 S&W and the .40 S&W against the .45 ACP. Although the .45 held the edge in power, the .40 could be found in a smaller package, allowing high-capacity magazines in a reasonably sized grip frame.

Some shooters have a difficult time reaching the trigger on a 1911, while a high-capacity double stack is either very bulky or makes things impossible for the same shooters to reach the trigger. But a smaller double stack would solve the problem. Since powder development is eons away from where it was in 1905/1911, the prospect of actually shortening the .45 ACP looked to be within reach.

FILLING A GAP

The goal of putting a new cartridge with the power of the .45 ACP in a semiauto the size of .40 S&W resulted in the .45 GAP. GAP stands for "Glock Automatic Pistol," however it can also be regarded as filling in a real "gap."

The .45 GAP was suggested by Gaston Glock and developed by Speer. The GAP– with its case length of .755 inch

— is shorter than the ACP by .143 inch, .095 inch shorter than the .40 S&W, and about the same length as the 9mm.

Although the GAP may appear to be simply a shortened ACP, it definitely is not, and ACP brass cannot be used to make GAP cases. Not only is the GAP shorter than the ACP, but it also has a slightly rebated rim, the extraction cannelure has a different angle and the internal wall profile differs quite markedly to allow the seating of bullets in the shorter case. In addition, the .45 GAP uses Small Pistol primers, not the large primers found in the .45 ACP.

The .45 GAP was originally designed to fit the medium-sized Glock 37. It was also offered by Springfield Armory in its XD (no longer cataloged), and both Springfield Armory and Para-Ordnance offered miniaturized 1911s chambered

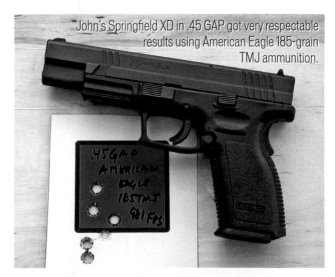

John's Springfield XD in .45 GAP got very respectable results using American Eagle 185-grain TMJ ammunition.

The trio of .45 GAP factory loads John used in his rangework included American Eagle 185-grain TMJ, Winchester 185-grain Silvertip and Winchester 230-grain JHP.

for it. My experience with the .45 GAP is with the Springfield XD and the compact Glock 38. (Glock also now offers the sub-compact Model 39.) At least two dozen law-enforcement agencies adopted the .45 GAP, including the New York State Police, the Pennsylvania State Police, the South Carolina Highway Patrol and the Georgia State Police.

However, I do not know what the situation is currently. During my lifetime I have seen the switch from the .38 Special to the .357 Magnum, and the 9mm to the .40 S&W. In recent years more and more agencies have gone to the .45 ACP, so it will be interesting to see the future of the .45 GAP, or if it even *has* a future. It is a tough, perhaps impossible, battle to push the .45 ACP aside. That

Would the sub-compact Springfield EMP be the perfect 1911 platform for the .45 GAP? John thinks so.

may be why you rarely hear about the GAP all that much anymore since its 2003 introduction.

SAAMI specs for the .45 GAP give a maximum of 23,000 psi, which is the level for a +P .45 ACP. Factory loads for the GAP are basically offered with the same weight bullets as the ACP, which means up to 230 grains.

I had three factory loads at my disposal. The first was the American Eagle 185-grain TMJ, which clocked out at 1,030 fps from the Springfield Armory XD and 940 fps from the Glock. Next was Winchester's 185-grain Silvertip (995 fps and 890 fps, respectively). Then there was Winchester's 230-grain JHP (885 fps and 860 fps). The Winchester Silvertips proved to be the most accurate in both guns, with five-shot groups of 1½ inches at 50 feet.

For reloading, I used Starline brass, Hornady's 185- and 200-grain XTPs and Sierra's 185-grain JHCs and 200-grain FMJs. All loads were ignited with CCI's #500 Small Pistol primers. One cast bullet load was assembled with Oregon Trail's 200-grain SWC with 4.5 grains of Hodgdon's Tite-Group. This resulted in an excellent practice load at over 900 fps. For other powders in addition to TiteGroup, I used Hodgdon's Universal and LongShot, plus Alliant's Power Pistol and Unique.

RUNNING GAP GUNS

I spent time one summer shooting a pair of .45 GAPs, as well as comparable pistols chambered in .45 ACP. From Springfield Armory came a pair of XD Tacticals, one in .45 ACP and the other in .45 GAP. From Glock I had a Model 21SF .45 ACP and a compact Model 38 chambered in .45 GAP. I have been a fan of the 1911 and the .45 ACP for more than a half-century. There is such a traditional aura around John Browning's original cartridge and 1911 platform that in some circles it is almost heretical to suggest any changes to either one. But in the past two decades, we've seen many non-1911 .45 ACP's offered that have been well received by the shooting public as well as law enforcement. Glock just took things a step farther by also changing the cartridge.

Neither the Glock nor the XD will win any beauty contest when stacked up against an ivory-stocked, engraved 1911.

John's efforts at the reloading bench showed that this Glock Model 38 was more fond of the 200-grain Hornady XTP (right) than the 200-grain Sierra FMJ (left).

TEST-FIRE: .45 GAP

	SPRINGFIELD ARMORY XD		GLOCK MODEL 38	
FACTORY LOADS	MV	5 SHOTS, 50 FT.	MV	5 SHOTS, 50 FT.
American Eagle 185-gr. TMJ	1,028 fps	2 ¼"	942 fps	2 ⅛"
Winchester 185-gr, Silvertip	997 fps	1 ¾"	893 fps	1 ¾"
Winchester 230-gr. JHP	885 fps	2"	862 fps	2 ½"
HANDLOADS	MV	5 SHOTS, 50 FT.	MV	5 SHOTS, 50 FT.
HORNADY 185-GR. XTP				
4.5 gr. Hodgdon TiteGroup	888 fps	2 ½"	855 fps	1 ½"
6.0 gr. Hodgdon Universal	939 fps	2 ¼"	839 fps	1 ⅝"
7.0 gr. Hodgdon LongShot	986 fps	2 ⅜"	895 fps	2 ¼"
6.0 gr. Alliant Power Pistol	819 fps	2"	749 fps	2 ½"
6.0 gr. Alliant Unique	918 fps	1 ⅞"	834 fps	2 ½"
HORNADY 200-GR. XTP				
6.0 gr. Hodgdon Universal	967 fps	1"	953 fps	2"
6.5 gr. Hodgdon LongShot	921 fps	1 ½"	883 fps	2 ½"
6.0 gr. Alliant Power Pistol	840 fps	1 ⅜"	787 fps	1 ¼"
6.0 gr. Alliant Unique	826 fps	1 ¾"	750 fps	2"
SIERRA 185-GR. JHC				
6.0 gr. Hodgdon Universal	966 fps	1 ⅜"	902 fps	2 ⅜"
7.0 gr. Hodgdon LongShot	986 fps	2 ⅞"	895 fps	2 ¼"
6.0 gr. Alliant Power Pistol	814 fps	1 ⅝"	798 fps	1 ½"
6.0 gr. Alliant Unique	950 fps	2 ½"	880 fps	2"
SIERRA 200-GR. FMJ				
6.0 gr. Hodgdon Universal	936 fps	2 ½"	849 fps	1 ¼"
6.5 gr. Hodgdon LongShot	865 fps	1 ⅜"	807 fps	1 ⅝"
6.0 gr. Alliant Power Pistol	802 fps	1 ⅞"	735 fps	2 ¼"
6.0 gr. Alliant Unique	804 fps	2 ¼"	727 fps	2 ½"
OREGON TRAIL 200-GR. SWC				
4.5 gr. Hodgdon TiteGroup	938 fps	2 ¼"	913 fps	2 ½"

However, when the shooting starts, I would feel most comfortable whether my hand is wrapped around a 1911, Glock or XD. And I wouldn't feel the least bit handicapped if the .45 happened to be a GAP instead of an ACP. I like the idea of the .45 GAP, and I also like the slightly smaller grip frame the shorter cartridge allows.

One of the great attributes of the 1911 is how easily it tucks into the waistband and stays in place. This is not so with either the Glock or XD. For concealment use with these, you need an inside-the-waistband holster. For the Glock 38, my choice turned out to be one of CrossBreed Holsters' Super Tuck Deluxe rigs. There are several things special about the design of this holster. The holster body itself is made of Kydex, which is molded to hold the gun securely, while allowing for a smooth draw. The rigidity also allows the gun to be easily reholstered. The part of the holster that rides against the body is leather, which makes it much more comfortable for extended periods of wear than would be afforded by a Kydex backplate. This is an excellent design and can also be adjusted to ride higher or lower on the belt. Good stuff!

Does the .45 GAP have a future? I'd like to see it chambered in the excellent little 1911-style EMP from Springfield Armory. Now offered in 9mm and .40 S&W, perhaps the EMP would also work well as a .45 GAP. Very small and easy to conceal, it could well be the ideal traditional platform for the .45 GAP. ◎

The .45 GAP Glock Model 38 carries easily in the Crossbreed Holsters Super Tuck Deluxe. It's a packable powerhouse for sure.

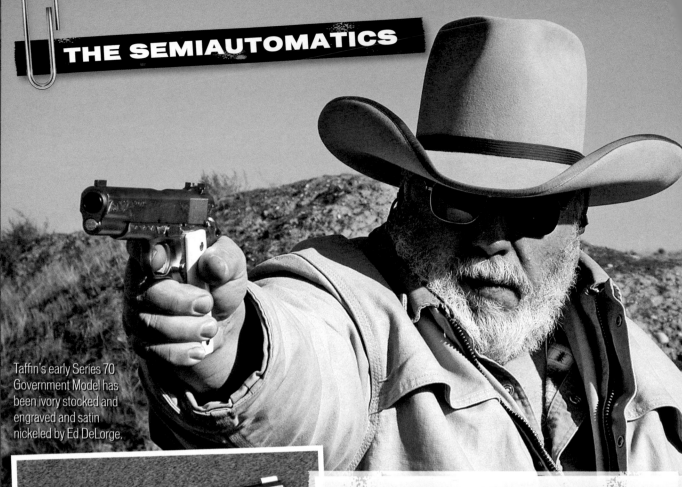

Taffin's early Series 70 Government Model has been ivory stocked and engraved and satin nickeled by Ed DeLorge.

THE COLT GOVERNMENT MODEL

CHAPTER 37

It's 1911. Glenn Curtiss flies the first successful seaplane. The Indianapolis 500 is run for the first time. The Mexican Revolution starts. Jack Johnson is boxing's heavyweight champ, and the Philadelphia Athletics beat the New York Giants four games to two in the World Series.

Unless you live in a large city, chances are pretty good the closest thing you have to indoor plumbing is a hand pump in the kitchen and a door on the outhouse. Electricity is something you see every time there's a thunderstorm. The town banker has an automobile that no one else has the foggiest idea how to drive or even start.

For years you've been shooting grandpa's .45 Colt Single Action Army with black-powder loads. However, your older brother in the military manages to provide you with a glimpse of the future, as the U.S. Army has just tested what has become known as the 1911 Government Model.

Fast-forward 100 years: Electricity is everywhere. Virtually everyone now has air conditioning, not only in the home but in their cars as well — cars built to travel safely on highways at 75 mph or more. Almost everyone has flown on

COLT GOVERNMENT MODEL

Made for the hot stuff: Colt's Rail Model features combat sights and a rail for mounting a flashlight.

commercial airlines at 500 mph, and we have instant communication — via radio, television and the Internet. Everything has changed dramatically.

Well, almost. State-of-the-art when it comes to a defensive handgun is the very same Government Model of 1911. John Browning's design for the ultimate defensive handgun was so far advanced it is still No. 1 more than a century later.

FORGED IN COMBAT

Two events baptized the 1911 prior to our entry into WW I. First, we experienced our first Muslim jihad in the Philippines. Then in 1916 General Pershing led the Punitive Expedition into Mexico. In both cases our troops used the .45 semiauto that Browning had finalized for adoption by the U.S. Army. With the coming of the Great War, young American men who had never been off the farm saw the world. After they'd "seen the elephant," our society would be forever changed in many ways.

Before the war, the No. 1 hunting rifle was a lever-action .30-30. The handgun? Those who did not stick with the Colt SAA gravitated toward the relatively new double-action .38s from Colt or Smith & Wesson. But things changed when the men came home. They had discovered bolt-action rifles and semiautomatic pistols.

The 1911's .45 ACP cartridge was designed to be every bit as effective — but in a more modern platform — than the old .45 Colt in the Single Action Army. The fact both the .45 ACP and the 1911 remain top choices a century later, in spite of all the "improvements" since they were introduced, attests to just how good both really are. John Browning's Colt 1911, though old in years, is still the first choice for many needing a serious sidearm.

After the Great War, the 1911 became more and more popular. Up to that point, for example, most Texas Rangers carried Colt SAAs. Now many of them switched to the newer .45.

This is what the Colt Combat Elite is all about. Accurate, rapid-fire delivery of big-bore bullets when the chips are down.

I can remember seeing several pictures during the 1950's of Rangers such as Bob Crowder and Clint Peoples wearing a pair of 1911s in floral-carved holsters on a matching belt. The Texas Rangers were way ahead of the curve, but generally speaking, law enforcement was slow to adopt the .45. Some of the smaller departments allowed it, but most stayed with the tried-and-true .38 Special or, if they

John's respect for the .45 ACP covers everything from the latest high-tech JHPs (left) to his own homebrewed cast SWCs (right).

were really forward-looking, a .357 Magnum. One group was definitely *not* slow in adopting the .45. They were the gangsters of the Roaring '20s and were not bound by any departmental rules. All they wanted was the most firepower they could get.

MYTH AND LEGEND

From the very beginning, the 1911 was burdened with two myths. First, it was reported anyone hit anywhere with a .45 hardball round would be totally incapacitated and knocked off his feet. The second said it was impossible to hit the broad side of a barn from the inside — using a 1911.

There may have been some validity to the inaccuracy myth, though it was highly exaggerated. Military semiautos needed to be loosely constructed so they would work under all conditions, and the original sights were very small, as they were on most handguns of the period.

Credence to the inaccuracy of the 1911 is provided by no less than John Henry FitzGerald, who was the face of Colt between the world wars. He had this to say:

"In 1919 at Caldwell, New Jersey, the .45 automatic came into its own. In the earlier years of its existence the comments and criticisms were these: sights not being attached to the barrel, short distance between sights, slide loose on receiver, trigger pull not right, etc. These all retarded its popularity, but only for a short time. A few shots from a properly sighted .45 automatic will convince the most skeptical that it is a wonderful arm and very accurate, extremely so if fitted with the .45 Colt Match Barrel ..."

THE COOPER FACTOR

I believe everything happens for a reason. In 1958 I was still a teenager and, being the dutiful son, drove my mother to the grocery store on Saturday morning. It was too cold to sit out in the car, so I ventured into the store, hoping against hope of finding anything interesting. As I looked at the rack of reading material inside, my eyes fell on a paperback with a yellow cover and the stunning title of *Fighting Handguns*. The book (along with Elmer Keith's *Sixguns*) was destined to have a large effect on my life.

The author of *Fighting Handguns* was a man I had never heard of, one Jeff Cooper. I didn't know at the time, of course, he would become a friend 35 years later. And I certainly had to way of

Chopped 'n channeled: Colt took the miniaturization process a step beyond the Commander with the Mk IV Series 80 Officers Model. The barrel length? Three-and-a-half inches.

BULL-X
230 RN
6.5 UNIQUE
855 FPS

This type of accuracy — here from the Colt Combat Elite — is really above and beyond what is needed in a defensive pistol.

knowing I would present him with the Outstanding *American Handgunner* Award. Nobody at the time knew what an impact he would have on the defensive use of the pistol. It was Cooper who picked up — and actually *lit* — the torch for the .45 Government Model of 1911, and would do for it what Elmer Keith did for the .44 sixgun. Writing in 1958, Cooper said:

"This rugged old bruiser has been sworn at by generations of US Servicemen, and has baffled regiments of target shooters, but I'm going to stick my neck way out and say flatly that it is the finest fighting sidearm ever produced up to now. It's a long way from ideal, to be sure, but there isn't anything better around to supersede it ... But as something handy to wear in situations where some uncouth characters may try to brain you without notice, it's tough to beat."

At about the same time Cooper started writing, a handful of pistolsmiths also discovered what the 1911 was actually capable of. Now, 50-plus years later, I will stick *my* neck out and say nothing has changed.

The original compact: Colt's Combat Commander is an all-steel variant of the original alloy-framed Commander. This one has been highly customized by Jimmy Clark.

TWEAKING A CLASSIC

For nearly 20 years, the only chambering for the 1911 would be the .45 ACP. However, by the late 1920s it was obvious law enforcement needed better tools than the standard .38 Special revolvers they were carrying at the time. Colt — using its 1911 — came up with the .38 Super, whose 130-grain bullet at about 1,300 fps gave peace officers something which would penetrate car bodies.

By this time, however, the original 1911 had become the 1911A1 with some changes. The grip tang was made longer to help prevent hammer bite. For those who had complained the 1911 had a tendency to shoot low, the flat magazine housing was given an arched profile to naturally

raise the pistol in the hand. Finally, the trigger was shortened to be more easily reached.

In 1933 Colt introduced the National Match in both .45 ACP and .38 Super. The 1950s saw the introduction of the first lightweight version. The original Commander used an alloy frame and was chambered in .45, .38 Super and 9mm. It was soon joined by a steel-frame version known as the Combat Commander. Both versions featured a shorter 4¼-inch barrel compared to the standard 5-inch length.

In 1957 the Gold Cup National Match version arrived chambered in .45 ACP and .38 Special. In 1970, with the introduction of the Series 70 pistols, Colt went to a collet barrel bushing, designed to provide a tighter lockup, resulting in better accuracy. However, the "fingers" of the collet bushing didn't hold up to repeated pounding and was soon dropped.

In 1983 the Series 80 version arrived with an internal

firing-pin safety. Two years later Colt began producing 1911s in stainless steel.

OPTIMUM AMMUNITION

In regards to the legendary power of the .45 ACP, Cooper once said:

"In the hands of a man who knows how to use it the .45 auto is a terrible weapon — very quick, very powerful, very accurate, and completely reliable. To get its full potential it must be handloaded with Keith-type semi-wadcutter bullets. But even with service loads it's no slouch."

Much has changed since those words were written more than 50 years ago. Today we have a nearly endless list of highly effective JHP loads available, so the Keith-type SWC may seem out of date. However, when I reload for the .45 ACP, it is still my No. 1 choice — be it a commercial cast bullet from Oregon Trail or one dropped from either Hensley & Gibbs or RCBS mold blocks.

Not only has the 1911 .45 been the combat pistol by which all others are judged for the past century, it also has served in another capacity. In the 1950s several talented gunsmiths turned it into a first-class bullseye pistol.

COLT AND THE 1911

I well remember the title of the article appearing in *GUNS* in the late 1950s. It was "Can Colt Come Back?".

Double the fun: John proves that, yes, you can "go Western" with the 1911.

Over the years we have all seen Colt's catalog shrink as such familiar revolvers as the Official Police, Detective Special, Cobra, Diamondback, King Cobra, Anaconda and even the Python were dropped.

Colt management had its ups and downs, and the few handguns which were left quite often simply did not live up to the Colt name. For too many years it was difficult to even reach a live body at Colt.

Now, I am happy to report Colt is back. The trip back has not been short nor has it been easy. Today we have a long list of custom gunsmiths as well as manufacturers turning out superb 1911s. To get back in the game, Colt has had to face some stiff competition. The good news is it is doing it. I recently received three new 1911s directly from Colt, and I must say I am definitely impressed. They are very well put together, with a tight slide-to-frame fit, while at the same time they operate very smoothly. Let's take a closer look at today's Colt 1911s.

Most shooters are familiar with the standard exterior safety features of the 1911, namely the grip safety and the thumb safety. On newer Colts there is also an internal safety-stop on the hammer which is designed to engage the sear should the hammer be allowed to fall forward as it is being cocked (preventing any type of uncontrolled automatic fire).

There is also a disconnector to prevent any possibility of the pistol firing unless a round is fully chambered and the slide is completely forward. The firing pin is shorter than its housing and is held to the rear by a spring; it cannot protrude through the face of the slide unless a hammer blow overcomes the spring force and the pin's inertia.

There is also a firing-pin lock to minimize the possibility of discharge if the pistol should be dropped or receive a sharp blow to the muzzle. Basically, all these things make a single-action semiauto as safe as possible.

However, the backstrap has the original 1911 straight mainspring housing matched up with the long trigger I prefer. It also has the

This updated incarnation of the 1911 is the Colt Combat Elite, designed from the ground up as a full-on, full-size fighting handgun.

flat-bottomed magazine with no pad attached. I'm sure pads have their place in competition, but I prefer the old style.

With all the changes and custom features added to the 1911 over the years, there is still nothing wrong with the standard Government Model. Holding one in your hand is like being transported back to the time of the American Expeditionary Force — the doughboys of WW I.

One major change for the better is the improved sights. The originals were very tiny and hard to see. On the 21st-century version they are larger, with a square-notch rear and a sloping-post front. In addition, the new sights are of the white-dot style with one dot for the front sight and one on each side of the rear. The rear blade is set in a dovetail and is adjustable for windage. However, as it came from the factory, my current stainless 1911 is basically dead-on with most loads, matching perfectly with my eyes and hold.

Trigger pull on this stainless model weighs out at 4⅝ pounds on my RCBS scale, with no discernible creep. The slide/frame fit is tight, with just a very slight side-to-side movement. Vertical serrations on the back of the slide aid in cocking. There are also vertical serrations on the flat mainspring housing. The grip panels are checkered hard rubber.

Shooting it is pure pleasure. My average for 10 different loads from 185 to 230 grains was 1⅝ inches for five shots at 20 yards. Best results were with the Black Hills 230-grain JHP +Ps that clocked at 971 fps with a one-inch group, and the Federal 230-grain Hydra-Shoks for 884 fps and just slightly over an inch even.

The stainless Series 80 Government Model is basically plain-Jane; however, the next one I shot, the stainless Rail Model, has all kinds of extras. It has the same brushed stainless steel finish as well as the flat mainspring housing and long trigger and, of course, the same interior features and .45 ACP chambering. But all similarity ends at this point. This pistol is designed for serious self-defense. Slide-to-frame fit is absolutely perfect with no movement whatsoever, yet the slide moves very smoothly on the rails. Sights

This Colt Lightweight Commander (top) and Series 70 Government Model (bottom) go back more than 40 years, making them today's classics. John obviously couldn't resist swapping out the grip panels on the Government Model.

Grips are double-diamond checkered and appear to be rosewood. An extra added feature — from which the pistol's designation comes — is the machined-in rail found in front of the trigger guard to accept a light or laser.

To state it simply, this is a real shooting machine! Even with the trigger pull of 5½ pounds, it shoots superbly. With the same 10 factory rounds as used in the standard .45 Government Model, this pistol averaged 1¼ inches for the 10 different loads with weights varying from 185 to 230 grains. I got groups under one inch with both the Cor-Bon 200-grain JHP +P at 1,055 fps and the Federal Hydra-Shok 230-grain JHP at 890 fps.

are the fixed combat style of the three white-dot variety, both being set in dovetails. The rear has a locking setscrew and is set low in the slide. It's melted so there are no sharp edges to catch on clothing. The slide has deep diagonal serrations both front and rear for easy cocking.

The thumb safety is ambidextrous. The aluminum trigger has three weight-lightening holes bored through from side to side and is matched up with a Commander-style hammer. The grip safety is the beavertail style, hollowed out at the top to allow it to a ride high and not interfere with the hammer.

As John M. envisioned it: To celebrate the 100th Anniversary of 1911, Colt went back to basics to produce the 1911-2011 Model.

A FACTORY-PRODUCED TARGET 1911

Colt's Gold Cup — designed to be a factory-produced target pistol — was introduced in 1957; however, it would be in the 1990s before I ever had one. Normally I do my best to bring down the price on any used gun I'm trying to buy, and if things really get serious I turn my wife, Diamond Dot, loose. (She has no shame when it comes to bargaining.)

In 1932 Colt had introduced a 1911 specifically designed for target shooting called the National Match. Not only was it more tightly fitted than a standard 1911, it also had a match barrel and a match trigger. The original National Match pistols had fixed sights, but in 1935 Colt offered it with the Stevens adjustable rear. It was difficult to adjust for windage and elevation, but was a great improvement over the fixed sights.

When the Gold Cup came along, it featured cutouts in the slide interior to reduce weight and allow for better cycling with light target loads, an Accurizor bushing with fingers for more consistent lockup and was also fitted with a special Micro rear sight. The Micro was replaced by the Colt Eliason rear sight in 1965. It was soon discovered the cutouts were a mistake, and the rear sight was not as rugged as it needed to be, often shearing the pin holding it to the slide.

The Gold Cup was upgraded to the Series 70 without

the cutouts and with a collet-style bushing to improve lockup; however, the rear sight was still the same. When Colt fell on hard times in the waning years of the last century, many of the classic Colt designs, including the Gold Cup, disappeared.

But the Gold Cup is now back better than ever as the Series 80 Gold Cup National Match, which has a beautiful bright blue finish with the rounded top of the slide featuring a matte finish to cut down on glare. The adjustable sights consist of a plain, flat-black post front set in a dovetail, matched up with a sturdy rear sight. It's much like a BoMar, although it's marked "Colt" on the left side.

Colt's stainless-steel stable includes (from top) the Government Model, the Combat Commander and the Rail Model.

The back of the rear sight is slanted backwards and serrated to cut down on glare. The rear notch is cut to allow just the right amount of daylight to show on both sides of the front post. Adjustment screws are large and the directional arrows are clearly marked. Finally, the sights are set deeper in the slide than on older 1911s with adjustable sights.

When I get groups with my handloads using cast bullets from Lyman and RCBS going into ⅝ and ⅞ inch for five shots at 20 yards, I have to admit things are about as good as they're going to get with me doing the shooting. It took more than three decades for me to come up with my first Gold Cup. This second one is not going to get away.

A LIGHTER GOVERNMENT MODEL

One of the latest 1911s from Colt is the Lightweight Government Model. However, it's full-sized (not Commander-size) with the standard 5-inch barrel. I don't recall Colt ever offering such a version in the past. I'm sure some have mated up Commander alloy frames with standard Government Model slides and barrels to come up with a custom full-size lightweight, but this is a catalog version. The slide and barrel of the Lightweight are steel, of course, with the

slide finished in bright blue on the sides and matte blue on the top. The alloy frame has a dark black-matte finish. The slide is tightly fitted to the frame with virtually no play — as is the case between the barrel and bushing.

THE COMBAT ELITE

I did a comparison of the new Government Model Lightweight and the Combat Elite. Except for the ambidextrous safety on the Lightweight — and the weight difference — they are virtually identical. Weighing them on my postal scale, I found the Combat Elite registers 37 ounces (unloaded), while the Lightweight comes in at 29 ounces. The Combat Elite has all the features you'd want in a carry/self-defense pistol. The stainless steel frame is matched up with a blue steel slide, and the pistol has the best-looking factory grips I've ever seen on a Colt 1911. They're rosewood, with a diagonal line separating checkering to the right of this line from a smooth finish to the left. In the center, "Colt" is carved into each grip panel. Although I normally add custom grips to any 1911 I come up with, these are too nice to swap out.

Both versions were fired with standard hardball to compare felt recoil. There was definitely an obvious difference; however, the more I fired the Lightweight the less I seemed to notice. When I finished up with 200-grain bullets (at 1,060 fps) it hardly registered at all.

Both front and rear sights on both guns are set in dovetails. The Novak rear is adjustable for windage by tapping it in the slot, then locking it in place with a setscrew. With most of my loads, and my shooting style, the sights were already in near-perfect alignment for windage and elevation. The sights are of the three-white dot variety which, in my hands, are a little more difficult to use when trying to shoot tight groups on paper. But they are perfect for what this Lightweight .45 is designed for, namely self-defense. White dots pick up much quicker for me in such a situation than trying to align black on black.

Controls consist of a beavertail grip safety with memory bump, a standard slide lock on the left side and an ambidextrous thumb safety. Personally, I am not a fan of ambi thumb safeties (which is easy to say since I'm right-handed), and I find the right-side version of this one has quite a bit of play in it. The magazine release is found in the normal position on the left side behind the trigger and is rather stiff to operate. The mainspring housing is serrated and flat (thank you!) and a pair of flush-seating eight-round magazines are provided. The grip panels are excellent, being of the double-diamond checkered style. With their reddish color, they set off the matte frame quite nicely. The grip frame is also relieved at the rear of the trigger guard to allow the highest possible grip.

The hammer is Commander-style, while the serrated lightweight trigger has three holes drilled from side to side. When I started shooting the Lightweight, the trigger felt somewhat creepy; however after several hundred rounds it has definitely smoothed out, and I no longer feel what may have been a small metal shaving or something similar. Whatever the case, it is now smooth and measures out just under six pounds. So the only thing I need to do to turn this into a perfect packin' pistol is have my gunsmith Tom at Buckhorn bring it down to four pounds — which is about as light as I will deliberately go with a semiauto not designed exclusively for bull's-eye shooting.

My most-favored handload for the .45 ACP over the years has been one recommended by Jeff Cooper — 7.5 grains of Unique under a 200-grain H&G #68 SWC hard-cast bullet. For my current use, I've dropped it to 7.0 grains of Unique, and I use both his recommended bullet as well as the RCBS #45-201, which are virtually identical. Shooting the latter through the Lightweight gave the best results with a 1⅛-inch group while clocking out at 1,060 fps — a great combination of accuracy with about as much power as you should expect from a standard .45 ACP 1911.

A WORTHY TRIBUTE

When the decision-makers at Colt decided to commemorate the 100th Anniversary of the 1911, they had a choice. They could follow the original pattern or they could include 100 years of "improvements." Thankfully, they decided to stick with the original.

Colt describes the result like this:

"This firearm is a WWI reproduction of the Colt M1911 pistol and does not contain a firing-pin safety mechanism as found in our Series 80 models."

In other words, shooters are expected to be as smart as they were 100 years ago.

My first reaction to the 100th Anniversary Model was as if I had stepped back

Dead-stock GI: This WW II-era 1911A1 was produced by Colt in 1944. Note the arched mainspring housing.

The author of Fighting Handguns was a man I had never heard of, one Jeff Cooper. I didn't know at the time, of course, he would become a friend 35 years later.

into history. Everything looks exactly — well at least 99 percent so — as my circa-1914 commercial Colt 1911. Most of the Colt 1911s I experienced in my early shooting years were war surplus with a Parkerized finish. (The originals had a nicely polished finish.) The Anniversary Model is polished and finished in a deep blue-black Colt calls "black oxide." Grip panels are double diamond, nicely checkered walnut with a somewhat light tan finish with some grain pattern; very attractive and these grips will not receive the treatment of most coming into my hands, meaning they will *not* be replaced.

John's prize Gold Cup dates back to 1968 and has been fitted with a BoMar full-length sight rib. It can bring out what most loads are capable of.

The sights of the Anniversary Model are exactly as found on my 1914 Colt, with a very small front blade matched up with a tiny "U" in the rear sight which is set in a dovetail for easy windage correction. Controls also mirror 100-year-old technology, with no extension on the thumb safety or slide stop, and of course, no beavertail grip safety.

The mainspring housing is flat and smooth, just as it was on the original and is matched up with a long trigger. The trigger pull is smooth and measures four pounds, which for me is just about right for a 1911. There are no serrations or checkering on the front strap. Any doughboy of 1917 would feel right at home taking up this new/old Colt.

It would be no great chore for my gunsmith to change out the sights and replace them with the big, black square sights I prefer; however, modernizing this 1911 would destroy its charm. I'll leave things exactly as they are, and every time I shoot this pistol, my mind, soul and spirit will transport me back to another time.

I find it quite interesting to see the best shooting load factory-wise is as close to the original 100-year-old load as I can find — Winchester's 230-grain FMJ at 822 fps. Right along with this load is the RCBS #45-201 200-grain SWC over 7.0 grains of Unique for 1,040 fps. Both loads shoot into 1⅛ inches. The Colt 1911-2011 is a fitting tribute to John Browning's immortal design. ◎

Colt's current Gold Cup National Match proved its mettle with a variety of factory loads.

THE SEMIAUTOMATICS

Taffin's Wilson Combat 1911s compared: Bottom left is John's prized .38 Super, followed clockwise by the .45 Carry Comp, the .45 Professional and the .45 Sentinel.

WILSON COMBAT .45s

CHAPTER 38

Today, we have access to superb firearms shooters could only dream about in the pre-WW II era. One of the reasons for this state of affairs is Bill Wilson,

John used Speer 230-grain Gold Dot ammunition — one of his preferred carry loads — to punch this impressive group with the .45 Professional.

whose Wilson Combat catalog is filled with the stuff of which dreams are made. Of all the skilled craftsmen turning out 1911s today, I have had more experience with Wilson's guns than any others.

WILSON COMBAT SENTINEL

My experience with Wilson 1911s goes back to 1988, when he built a .45 ACP Comp Gun for me to use in the Masters Tournament that year. It shot a whole lot better than I could hold. Since then, I've used a Classic .38 Super, a .45 ACP Professional and a .45 ACP Carry Comp. However, my latest pleasant experience has been with the .45 ACP Sentinel. Gunwriters can turn out endless articles about the superiority — or lack thereof — of the 1911 chambered in .45 ACP. I happen to believe the 1911/.45 ACP combination has never been surpassed when it comes to a pure fightin' handgun. Equaled? Maybe. Surpassed? *Never.*

The Sentinel proved its accuracy potential with three Winchester factory loads. That heavy tapered bushingless barrel (inset) had a lot to do with it!

WINCHESTER 230 JHP 774 FPS

WINCHESTER 230 FMC 745 FPS

WINCHESTER 185 FMJ 829 FPS

The Sentinel uses a heavy tapered barrel with no bushing. The sights are Wilson's Tactical Combat, with both the front and rear set in dovetails for easy windage adjustment. It has an extended ejector for positive operation, a high-riding beaver-tail which, when combined with a skeletonized Commander-style hammer, removes all possibility of the shooter being bitten on the back of the hand. To further add to shooter comfort, the entire pistol has been dehorned – there are no sharp edges anywhere. The front strap is checkered 30 LPI to aid controllability and is matched up with checkered Micarta stocks sporting the Wilson Combat insignia.

The Sentinel trigger is a Wilson Combat Competition Match version with the well-recognized three holes drilled laterally. The trigger pull itself is set just about perfect for me at an even four pounds – plenty light for a self-defense sidearm. The entire pistol is finished in an all-black Armor-Tuff polymer coating.

Wilson's Sentinel is a "4 figure" .45. For that price you expect — and have a right to expect — total reliability right out of the box. That is exactly what the Sentinel delivers. I used 13 different .45 ACP loads — from six different manu-facturers, spanning three bullet weights — in mine. From the very first round I experienced total reliability with every-thing — JHP, FMJ, 185, 200 or 230 grains. It made abso-lutely no difference.

From the very first round the Sentinel could have been pressed into immediate duty. It was dead on for elevation and — with my eyes and hold — shot an inch to the left, which is easily corrected by loosening one screw and tap-ping the rear sight to the right. At no time did I experience a failure to feed or eject. This little pistol can be counted on to put a bullet exactly where desired in a self-defense situation.

As .45 ACPs go, the Sentinel is very small, yet it main-tains a six-round magazine, making it a seven-shooter when carried cocked and locked with one in the chamber. One

Bill Wilson considers the .45 Sentinel to be the smallest practical 1911 design to still offer complete functional reliability.

of the problems inherent in making a design smaller and more compact is the loss of reliability. Wilson considers the Sentinel the smallest possible rendering of the 1911 while still maintaining total reliability. The Sentinel's barrel length is 3⅝ inches, overall length is only 7¼ inches, and overall height is 5 inches. Unloaded, the pistol weighs 29 ounces, which goes up to 35 ounces fully loaded. I also found it very easy to control without bothersome felt recoil. And even with the short barrel, both Black Hills and Remington 185-grain JHPs clocked out at 925 fps.

Taffin's .45 Professional carries concealed and secure in this holster by Milt Sparks. Always fond of grip-switching, John couldn't resist these Herrett's skip-checkered panels.

How does the Wilson Combat Sentinel shoot? Because of its small size and short barrel, I test-fired it at a self-defense distance of seven yards, shooting five-shot groups. Since it wears the name "Wilson Combat" and carries a high-dollar price tag, I expected it to shoot very well. It did. With everything tried, from 185 grains to 230 grains, both JHPs and FMJs from Black Hills, Cor-Bon, Hornady, Remington, Speer and Winchester, groups averaged ¾ inch or less.

Wilson Combat began in 1977, and in 1996 Bill began building his own frames. A year after starting with his own frames, his company began producing leather goods, holsters, belts and magazine pouches while working with some of the nation's top holster makers to produce more practical, user-friendly rigs. Wilson Combat holsters are designed primarily for concealed carry, with safety and comfort as the primary concern.

The test holster sent along with the Sentinel is constructed of sharkskin and rides high and tight with total comfort and security. Wilson Combat pistols are provided with a padded nylon carry case with a pair of 6 x 6-inch pockets for gear, plus seven magazine pouches along the front of the bag. Everything is kept secure with zippers and Velcro.

From the leather: John got excellent rapid-fire results at 15 yards (inset) with the Wilson Combat Carry Comp .45.

THE COMBAT PROFESSIONAL

Moving up the size scale, we come to the Wilson Combat Professional .45 ACP, which is basically the same size as the Colt Commander. My original Commander was, and is, a good pistol. It did, however, need help to make it usable. That help consisted of high-visibility fixed sights, a beavertail grip safety and polishing of the ramp to allow it to handle anything other than hardball. In today's dollars, that 1968 Colt cost me more than the price of the Wilson Professional Model — which needs absolutely nothing to make it right, except possibly custom grips which are designed more for show than go. The Professional Model is a "go" from the beginning. Since it is now my personal pistol, I have fitted it with skip-checkered grips from Herrett's. These are quite attractive and also provide a secure hold.

Operating a perfectly tuned 1911 is almost a sensual experience. Just work the slide. Most will feel somewhat like driving over a rough road. Working the slide of the Professional Model will bring you tears of joy. The slide just, well, *slides* like it should, smoothly, tightly, with no play and no rough spots. The mating of the frame to the slide is so perfect if the tolerances were any closer, the pistol would be too tight to function.

For years, probably decades, the common perception was you could have a loosely fitted .45 for perfect function or a tightly fitted target model for dedicated paper punching.

This target, fired from a rest at 20 yards with the Wilson Combat Carry Comp, proved the pistol's affinity for Hornady's 185-grain XTP ammunition.

HORNADY 185
.45ACP   XTP
867 FPS

Here's an up-close look at the compensated barrel of the Combat Carry Comp.

Bill Wilson proved it is possible to combine function and fitting in the same high-quality 1911. Even though it's probably impossible to love an inanimate object, if love cannot be achieved between man and metal, I certainly get as close to that feeling as possible with this pistol.

The Professional Model has a barrel length just over four inches. The weight is a gnat's hair under 36 ounces according to my postal scale. The trigger pull — which is guaranteed to be between 3¼ and 3¾ pounds — comes

in at 3⅝ pounds. Features include the Wilson Combat High Ride Beavertail grip safety, the Extended Tactical thumb safety, the Ultralight Trigger and matching Commander-style Ultralight hammer. Then there's the 30 LPI checkering on the front strap and mainspring housing. The fine-line checkering matched up with the checkered grip panels allows for a secure hold. The ejection port has been lowered and flared, and the rear of the slide has serrations for easy cocking.

For ease of both shooting and holstering, the Professional Model has been dehorned. The magazine well has been beveled for quick and easy insertion of magazines. Two, eight-rounders are furnished, each with a pad at the bottom for painless application of the palm to seat them securely — these pads also serve well in competition if empty magazines are allowed to hit the ground. For my concealed-carry use, I opt for a standard flat-based magazine, both for looks and a slight increase in ease of concealment. For spares I carry two padded magazines in a carrier on the offside.

HANDGUN GUY BILL WILSON ON
BILL WILSON

My Dad was a watchmaker for over 40 years and ran a jewelry store since the early 1950's. His dream was always for me to follow in his footsteps and become a watchmaker and eventually run the family jewelry store.

Dad always liked guns (as a collector) and had them around, but never was interested in shooting. At any rate, he talked me into going to watchmaking/jewelry making school in Okmulgee, Oklahoma, which I attended in '73 and '74. I really had very little interest in it, but managed to do fairly well with a 3.4 average. Some parts of this training were very helpful in working on guns, such as making clock parts from scratch including heat treating and jewelry making which requires a lot of silver-solder work. I remember one test we had where we had to file a common nail into a perfect square by hand. To pass it had to be within a thousandth or so of being perfectly square. This precision use of hand tools easily transferred over into my gun work.

I graduated watchmaking school (I also had several good basic business classes, too) in '74 and moved back to Berryville to work with Dad in the jewelry store. As an incentive to get me in the jewelry business, he agreed to let me set up part of the store as a gun shop (big mistake on his part). We set it up as a normal small-town gun shop and I also did some commercial reloading. As time went on I did less and less watchmaking and more and more gun stuff.

Somewhere around '76 I started shooting. Soon I was shooting in the upper 580's, low 590's, which wasn't too bad for the local boys. Problem was when I started beating the cops every time, they revoked my "associate member" status in the LE club, so PPC was out. I got into shooting pins next (still with wheelguns) and did a lot of this in the late '70's early '80's. The PPC and pin shooting with revolvers is what really got me interested in gunsmithing. I started doing action work on revolvers.

Somehow I learned about IPSC about the time of the Columbia Conference in '76 and in Sept '76 shot my first IPSC match at MPPL in Columbia with a 6" Colt Python. Shot my 2nd match with a Browning Hi-Power and finally had my first .45 for the 3rd match. I was hooked! This soon led to me working on my own gun to make it more suitable for IPSC. I customized 2 or 3 for myself. Eventually some of my buddies were asking me to work on their guns too. As I said before, the hand skills were there. All I had to do was learn the technical stuff as to what made them work.

Sights on the Professional Model consist of Wilson Tactical Combat sights made up of a low-riding rear (with no sharp edges) and a post front. Both are set in dovetails. These sights can also serve well as night sights, thanks to the three tritium dots. The finish is Armor-Tuff, a chemical and heat-resistant, thermally cured finish that provides a satin matte surface. It also has antifriction characteristics and is available in matte black, as on the furnished test model, matte silver or even matte olive drab.

Before it is applied, the pistol is blasted with fine-grit media, and the surface is prepped before being sprayed, then thermally cured. Armor-Tuff passes some unbelievable testing consisting of 1,000 hours of saltwater spray and 1,000 hours of saltwater immersion. Wilson Combat guarantees Armor-Tuff surfaces will never rust when subjected to normal use. It can also stand 24-hour immersion in just about any type of gasoline, paint remover and several acids. On top of all this, Armor-Tuff is not affected at temperatures from -250 F. to +500 F., which means no matter how hot or cold it gets, nothing will affect it. This finish also contains molybdenum disulfide, which is another way of saying those contact surfaces are *slippery*.

Other things making the Wilson Professional Model work so well include the polished Wilson Bullet Proof extractor matched up with a Wilson Tactical extended ejector, Wilson Heavy Duty recoil springs with Shok Buff, hand-fitted stainless-steel match barrel and a polished feed ramp and barrel throat.

The Professional Model was test-fired at 20 yards from a rest. Even though the magazine capacity is eight, I still prefer to load seven. My groups are for the best six out of seven shots, allowing me one throwaway round (which minimizes my stress!). Factory rounds of 185-, 200- and 230-grain weights (with muzzle velocities from 685 to 1,040 fps) were fired, with groups averaging just under 1½ inches. Expect someone with younger eyes to improve on this performance; however, I am more than satisfied with the results.

Even more important than the groups fired from a rest is how well the Professional Model performs from the leather on a silhouette target. Firing two-handed from the standing position as fast as I could align the sights resulted in all 7 shots staying within the 9- and 10-ring of a B27 reduced-size silhouette target at 50 feet. I can certainly protect me and mine with this type of performance. In the real world I carry the Professional Model loaded with Speer's Gold Dot 230-grain JHPs. With this load I can put 6 shots into a 1¼-inch group at 20 yards.

COMBAT CARRY COMP

Moving up the line we now come to Wilson's full-sized 1911, the Combat Carry Comp .45 ACP. I used 11 different loads in mine, 10 of which were JHPs, weighing from 165 to 230 grains, both standard and +P versions. No matter what I put in the magazine, the Carry Comp fed and fired everything flawlessly. (With its price tag it had better be perfect, and it is.) Wilson's competition 1911 in the 1980's was dubbed the AccuComp. To come up with the Carry Comp, Wilson basically blended the Professional and the AccuComp — the Carry Comp having the same compensator at the end of the barrel as found on those early competition guns.

The Carry Comp was easy-shooting with all loads tested. I did nothing to break it in except shoot it right out of the box. This appears to be one 1911 you could buy, load, strap on and be ready to go. However, a wise man would definitely shoot it first to check it for function, reliability, accuracy and point of impact.

The Wilson Combat Carry Comp is offered only in .45 ACP — the one semiauto cartridge that has never really

The Wilson Combat Carry Comp .45 with matte black slide and matte olive drab frame features a Commander-style hammer, High Ride Beavertail and Tactical Night sights (inset).

been surpassed for its purpose. It has a barrel length of 4½ inches, an overall length of 8¼ inches, an overall height of 5¼ inches, an empty weight of 38 ounces, and a magazine capacity of seven rounds. It is built on a Wilson Combat slide and frame and is guaranteed to function 100 percent of the time right out of the box. It is quite attractive as it is two-tone, with a matte black slide on an olive drab receiver, both of which have Armor-Tuff fin-

Blast from the past: John's first experience with a Wilson Combat .45 goes back to 1988 and this Accu-Comp. The competition-grade rig is by Ernie Hill.

ishes. The sighting system consists of Tactical Combat night sights with the rear being "melted." Two white dots match up with a front post featuring a third white dot. Both sights are set in dovetail slots and are adjustable for windage. In addition to the melted rear, the entire pistol has been dehorned.

The grip safety is a Wilson High Ride Beavertail, while both the front and back strap have been checkered 30 LPI. The hammer is a Skeletonized Ultralight machined from S-7 steel bar stock.

Other custom features include a Duty Recoil spring mated with Shok Buff buffers and a Bullet Proof firing pin and extractor. The slide-to-frame fit is custom and the pistol has a crisp, creep-free trigger with a measured four-pound pull. The ejection port is lowered and flared. The throated barrel is a hand-fitted Tactical Tapered Cone with a polished feed ramp. The rear of the slide features cocking serrations for easy racking.

The Wilson Combat .45 ACP Carry Comp shoots like a dream. Examples? With five shots at 20 yards using Cor-Bon 200-grain JHP +Ps (966 fps), I got a 1⅛-inch group. With Cor-Bon's 230-grain JHP +P (924 fps) I got a 1¼-inch group. Hornady's 185-grain XTP (867 fps) yielded 1⅜ inches. Speer's Gold Dot 230-grain JHPs (809

fps) punched 1⅛-inch clusters. That's the type of performance you should expect from a serious custom 1911.

Wilson pistols are expensive, as are all other custom sixguns and semiautos from top-of-the-line custom pistolsmiths. John Linebaugh addressed the issue years ago when someone asked him about buying a self-defense handgun for his wife. "How much should I spend?" was the question. "How much is her life worth?" was his answer. That reply still stands. ◎

All dressed up with somewhere to go. The .45 Sentinel comes with a range bag. That custom sharkskin holster is extra.

THE SEMIAUTOMATICS

Stainless and blue by the Big Green: A pair of R1s ready to go.

RETURN OF THE REMINGTON 1911

CHAPTER 39

A while back I got a message from my niece back in Ohio telling me they were tearing down my old high school — just the latest in a long line of things disappearing from my past. The first house I lived in was leveled decades ago. The first company I worked for disappeared ages ago. Seems there is no "back" to go to anymore!

But one bright spot where we can actually go back to is found with firearms. Some models — made long before I was born — still exist. Companies continue to look backward as they go forward, resurrecting tried-and-true designs. Now a familiar name in 1911s is back with the Remington R1. Remington is the oldest American firearms

company, going all the way back to 1816 when Eliphalet Remington forged his first rifle barrel. He was later joined by his sons to become E. Remington & Sons and began the long line of quality firearms with both percussion and cartridge sixguns, single-shot rifles, and eventually some the finest repeating shotguns and rifles ever produced.

EARLY 1911 EFFORTS

During WW I Remington Arms-UMC began producing .45 ACP 1911s for the war effort. The original order issued after Christmas in 1917 called for 150,000 pistols from Remington to be built in the new Remington plant in Connect-

Three options (left to right): R1, R1S
and the upgrade R1 Carry.

TEST-FIRE:

LOAD	VELOCITY	R1	R1 STAINLESS	R1 CARRY
Black Hills 230-gr. FMJ	799 fps	1½"	2"	1⅛"
Black Hills 230-gr. JHP +P	953 fps	1⅜"	1"	1¾"
Black Hills 185-gr. JHP	1,013 fps	1"	1⅜"	1½"
Remington 230-gr. FMJ	848 fps	1¼"	1"	1"
Lyman #452460/7.0 gr. Unique	1,074 fps	1½"	1"	¾"
Oregon Trail 200/6.0 452AA	1,071 fps	1½"	1⅝"	1⅛"
Groups are 5 shots at 20 yards.				

icut, however problems developed quickly, some due to incomplete and/or inaccurate drawings. Instead of using drawings, Remington had to start with original Colt pistols and work backward. Three months later the order was increased to 500,000 pistols. But with such a late start, the company had only produced just over 13,000 pistols by the ending of hostilities in November 1918, and then another 8,000 afterward.

During WW II the name Remington once again appeared on 1911s, however it was Remington Rand the typewriter company. There are those who have said this had nothing to do with the Remington we normally associate with firearms. Not *quite* true, however. Early on, the "original" Remington had added a typewriter division. But in 1886 the typewriter group had separated to become the Remington Typewriter Company, which was then sold off to Rand in 1927 to become Remington Rand.

In 1942 the United States government moved tools and machinery into the Remington Rand operation changing

This is target-pistol performance from the working-grade R1S, using one of John's pet handloads (left) and good, old Remington hardball (right).

John reacquaints himself with the pleasures of a Remington-made 1911.

The Remington R1 is a traditionally styled 1911 with a magazine capacity of seven rounds.

As an essential upgrade, the Remington R1 Carry features excellent Novak/Trijicon sights.

them from building typewriters to 1911s. Just under 900,000 were produced for the war effort. My first .45 ACP 1911 was marked Remington Rand and was purchased sometime in 1956/1957 beginning my experiences with the 1911. I should've held on to it.

RESURRECTION, REISSUE

Now, thanks to Remington I can go back and once again shoot a 1911 with Remington marked on the slide.

It is not a Remington Rand, of course. Remington has issued several versions of the .45 ACP 1911 in blued and stainless versions. The original 21st-century version of a Remington 1911 coincided with the 100th Anniversary of the original Colt 1911 and was given the model designation "R1." It is a 1911, not a 1911A1. Well, *almost*.

The original 1911 was "upgraded" in the early 1920s to become the A1 version. Three basic changes were made. What came to be known as the "short trigger," was replaced by a longer one. The flat mainspring housing/backstrap was given an arch which helped combat the tendency of the original 1911 to shoot low in the hands of most shooters. The new arch raised the muzzle and seemed to solve the problem for many; however, I still prefer the original flat configuration. Another problem of the original 1911 concerned "hammer bite." As the gun recoiled and the hammer came back, it could catch a piece of skin in between your thumb and trigger finger. The tang on the grip safety was lengthened slightly to prevent this. Today, most 1911s feature the beavertail style of grip safety to protect your hand.

The Remington R1 reflects all of these basic changes, along with a few others. The original small issue sights have been upgraded. Both the front and rear sight are now big where the originals were little. The front-slanting post and wide, square-notch rear feature three dots. Normally I prefer all-black sights; however, as I have gotten older these three-dot sights are much easier for me to pick up quickly. And both front and rear are set in dovetails for easy windage adjustment — the rear locks in place with a setscrew.

One thing most of us will remember from the government surplus 1911s we may have had as kids is how easy they were to take down. This new Remington operates the same way, however barrel-to-bushing fit is much tighter and the bushing wrench included with each R1 is necessary. All versions have five-inch stainless steel barrels. Slide-to-frame fit is also very tight with no perceptible play. Yet the slide is quite easy to operate by grasping the serrations below the rear sight on both sides of the slide.

I experienced flawless feeding and functioning except for some +P ammunition with large hollow-points, which not only refused to feed in each R1 but also in another manufacturer's guns. The problem seemed to be ammunition, not firearm. With other loads, no problems occurred and ejection was certainly enhanced by the lowered and angled ejection port.

The flat mainspring housing is serrated, while the front strap is smooth just as on the original model. One of the main sticking points with me on most handguns is the grips. I probably replace 90 percent of them, whether we are talking single- or double-action sixguns or 1911s.

This was not the case here. These grips are excellent — nicely checkered and figured walnut of the double-diamond pattern. The combination of the serrations on the backstrap and the checkering on the grips provides an extremely secure hold.

Controls include a memory bumpless grip safety, standard thumb safety and slide lock, along with the standard-size magazine release button on the frame behind the trigger. Magazines eject "right now" and very easily. I only dropped one mag before I learned to catch them – a good thing if the R1 has to be quickly reloaded in a serious situation.

The left side of the slide is marked "Remington" while the right side says "1911R1." There is one strange marking found on the pistol as well as in the owner's manual. That marking — found above the front of the trigger guard on the side of the receiver — are the letters "ERPC." The same

The Remington name (inset) is back on the 1911. This stainless R1S proved to be very accurate with "house-brand" 230-grain hardball.

four letters are found on the lockable plastic pistol box each R1 comes in. And when reading the manual it sounded like the R1 was produced not by Remington but by this rather strange sounding "4-letter" company. So I contacted Remington and asked about it. Turns out that "ERPC" is the legal entity for Remington's handgun line — not some strange European trade association.

Almost any company producing a quality 1911 at a reasonable price is going to be successful. In fact, some companies have been so successful at it they have cut back on other products to produce more 1911s. Remington has been successful enough to be able to expand its line with additional models. The next R1 is a dead ringer for the original, except the right side of the slide is inscribed "1911R1S." That extra "S" stands for stainless steel. Everything about this pistol has been done in stainless steel except for the same excellent white-dot sights. Grip panels are also identical. Both versions come in the same bright green box along with a pair of flat-bottomed seven-round magazines.

The slide-to-frame fit on the R1S is every bit as tight as the blued R1, slide operation is just as easy and functioning

SEMIAUTO PISTOLS AND THEIR CARTRIDGES

THE BOOK OF THE .45

The R1 Carry was evidently fond of John's potent handloads, using Lyman and Oregon Trail cast bullets.

equally flawless. The finish on the blued version is somewhat subdued (actually it's a satin black oxide). The stainless pistol is brushed satin matte rather than high polish. Trigger pulls, measured with the Brownells Trigger Pull Gauge measure out at 4½ pounds on the blued version with no creep, while the stainless version's trigger broke at a most satisfying 3 pounds.

CUT FOR CARRY

So much for the standard versions; now let's move up to the upgraded example. This one is marked with "Carry" on the right side of the slide, directly below the ejection port. This gem of a 1911 has all the little niceties many of us want in a concealed-carry gun. The sights consist of a front post (a Trijicon, complete with a night-sight dot) matched up with a low-riding, square-notch Novak rear. Both are set in dovetails and adjustable for windage with a locking setscrew on the rear. There are no sharp edges on the sights to catch on clothing. In fact, the entire pistol's sharp edges have been removed wherever possible.

Controls consist of an ambidextrous and extended thumb safety which operates easily but is not so loose as to be inadvertently pushed off. The beavertail grip safety has a memory bump. The slide stop is a standard one. The slide is easily operated, as there are six rather large and deep slanted serrations on both sides of the slide below the rear sight.

The hammer is skeletonized and fits deeply in the top of the beavertail when this pistol is cocked. The aluminum hammer is of the long style, has three holes and is fitted with a backlash adjusting screw. The trigger pull measured right at 4 pounds with no discernible creep. The flat mainspring housing, the front strap, and the memory bump on the beavertail grip safety are all finely checkered. Grips are about as good as grips get, this side of ivory. They appear to be of a deep red cocobolo with dark brown stripes. They are a combination of smooth and checkered, with a diagonal line running from the front top of the grip panel down to the rear back part. The front half is nicely checkered while the back half is smooth. I believe the idea here is the smooth part helps to start your grip in the proper fashion while the

R1 Carry features include a skeleton-ized trigger and hammer, a beavertail grip safety with "memory bump," and a distinctively-patterned set of grip panels.

Not true blue: The R1 and R1 Carry both sport no-nonsense black oxide finishes.

checkering secures it once your hand is in place. Finish is the same subdued satin black oxide found on the original R1.

Slide-to-frame fit is tight with no play whatsoever; however, you should have no problem working the slide to chamber a round. Functioning, as with the other R1s, was perfect.

RANGE WORK

The three R1s arrived three days before Thanksgiving (just in time to be included in this book). Even though the wind was punishing and the temperature was in the low 50s, I was able to do considerable shooting with all three without suffering too badly.

I chose eight different .45 ACP loads — six factory and two handloads. As mentioned earlier two of these loads were very heavy +P+ loads, and it only required a few rounds to find they would not work, as their large hollowpoints would not feed. So I wound up going with three loads from Black Hills — 230-grain FMJ, 230-grain JHP +P and 185-grain JHP. I also had some Remington 230-grain FMJ, plus my handloads consisting of the Lyman 200-grain #452460 loaded over 7.0 grains of Unique and the Oregon Trail 200-grain SWC ahead of 6.0 grains of WW452AA.

With the original R1, the most accurate load proved to be Black Hills' 185-grain JHP (five shots in 1 inch at 20 yards,

with a muzzle velocity averaging just over 1,000 fps). This was followed by Remington's 230-grain FMJ MC at 850 fps, which gave me a 1¼-inch group. Then came the Black Hills 230-grain JHP +P (950 fps and 1⅜ inches).

Switching to the stainless steel R1 saw the Remington FMJs deliver five shots in a nearly unbelievable ½ inch, while both the Black Hills 230-grain JHP +P and my Lyman #452460 handload shot 1-inch groups, with the latter clocking out at 1,075 fps. The R1 Carry shot this same Lyman handload into ¾ inch. With the Remington FMJ, the Carry put five shots in 1 inch. The Black Hills 230-grain FMJ and the Oregon Trail handload (at 1,071 fps) both grouped into 1⅛ inches.

The bottom line on these Remington R1s? Suffice it to say all are excellent-shooting .45s. ◎

Remington R1s ride well in belt slides by Rudy Lozano of Black Hills Leather.

THE SEMIAUTOMATICS

The USFA Models 1910 and 1911 rest on early advertising for the Colt .45 ACP. The Model 1910 sports the distinctive hammer of the original Colt Model 1905.

UNITED STATES FIRE ARMS GOVERNMENT MODELS

CHAPTER 40

From its inception in the early 1990s, United States Fire Arms Patent Company had two goals. One was to emphasize the history of great firearms. The other was to eventually produce all American-made products. It started by using Italian parts which were finished into assembled sixguns in this country. The company ultimately changed its name to United States Fire Arms and achieved its goal of producing American-made sixguns. Beautifully finished sixguns, I might add.

This philosophy eventually carried over to the 1911 Government Model. But first let's look back at an often-forgotten part of history USFA highlighted with the guns

The Model 1910 combines traditional panache with eye-popping accuracy. And those fixed sights were out-of-the-box on the money for John.

it produced. Specifically, the history of our southwestern border country around the time of the Mexican Revolution.

VIOLENT UPHEAVAL

It was a time of great violence. Pancho Villa and others like him were fighting against Mexico's federal troops.

Bloodshed was normal and the violence spilled over into our Southwest as Villa and his army raided Columbus, New Mexico. The United States retaliated with the Punitive Expedition led by Black Jack Pershing, who would soon command the United States forces in the Great War.

It was a time of transition. The horse was being pushed aside by the automobile and the airplane. The Winchester levergun was giving way to the bolt-action Springfield. And, of course, the legendary Colt Single Action Army was being challenged by the relatively new .45 ACP Model of 1911. For many men — outlaw and peace officer alike — the old days were gone or rapidly going. The era has been well captured in several movies such as *The Professionals*, *Bandido*, and above all, *The Wild Bunch*.

In Sam Peckinpah's classic, *The Wild Bunch* — Pike, Dutch, Angel and the Gorch Brothers (played admirably by William Holden, Ernest

Borgnine, Jaime Sanchez, Ben Johnson and Warren Oates) escaped to Mexico after a botched bank robbery and found themselves smack dab in the middle of the Mexican Revolution, around the time when World War I was underway in Europe.

Now they were faced with a decision, and the result was some of the most violent scenes ever filmed. The town they

USFA's traditional SAA sixguns and period-1911s mirror the era brought to life in *The Wild Bunch*, and were both carried by members of the gang portrayed by (left to right) Ben Johnson, Warren Oates, William Holden and Ernest Borgnine.

SEMIAUTO PISTOLS AND THEIR CARTRIDGES

THE BOOK OF THE .45

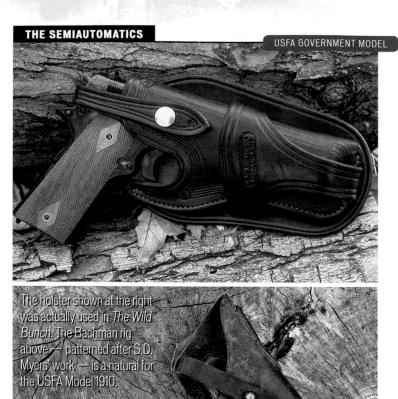

The holster shown at the right was actually used in *The Wild Bunch*. The Bachman rig above — patterned after S.D. Myers' work — is a natural for the USFA Model 1910.

HARDWARE TRANSITION

Paralleling the political upheaval of that tumultuous time was a revolution in small arms as well. Since 1836 the defensive firearm of the 19th century had been the single-action revolver in general – the Colt SAA in particular. Beginning in the 1890s, semiautos began to appear. John Browning turned from rifles to handguns with the result being the Colt 1905, the short-lived Colt Models 1907 and 1910, and ultimately the Colt Model 1911. The Colt SAA sixgun and the Colt 1911 would be "in-house" rivals for quite some time.

The Texas Rangers were probably the last official law enforcement group to give up their single actions, and by the 1950s many of them, such as Clint Peoples and Lone Wolf Gonzualles, were carrying a pair of 1911s. William Holden's *The Wild Bunch* character, Pike Bishop, carried both — the Colt SAA .45 in a hip holster and the .45 ACP Model 1911 in a shoulder holster — a perfect example of blending the old and the new.

found themselves in was under the control of a malevolent, self-appointed general Mapache (who was being courted by representatives of the Imperial German government). The American outlaws, knowing full well what the eventual outcome would be, basically destroyed the General's Mexican forces and all lost their lives in the process.

One of the greatest lines ever uttered in western movies comes at the end, with the meeting of Robert Ryan's character (Deke Thornton) and Edmund O'Brien's (Freddie Sykes). Thornton is an ex-member of the gang, and Sykes, having been recovering from wounds, had missed the final carnage. Sykes proposes that Thornton join his Mexican gang to continue the fight. "It's not like it used to be," Sykes says. "But it'll do."

All of us in our turn can apply the same message to our lives. Mine is certainly not like it used to be, but it will have to do. If I can't do all the things I enjoy, I can at least *enjoy* all of things I do.

A CLASSIC APPROACH

It is most interesting to see Colt only producing two handguns, the same two marking the time of *The Wild Bunch* — the Single Action Army (plus the target-sighted New Frontier) and the 1911. USFA, however, not only offered a Single Action Army and the Model 1911 as they were configured in the early 1900s, but as an added bonus they made Browning's transitional Model 1910 as well.

A USFA sixgun features a beautifully case-colored mainframe and hammer in what is described as "Armory Bone Case." The rest of the gun is deep, dark Dome Blue. Grips furnished as standard are checkered hard rubber with a "US" molded into the top. These stocks are so perfectly fitted to the frame – and feel so good in the hand – I was very hesitant to change them. Nevertheless, my habit

John loves all things traditional relating to 1911s, and he very much enjoyed his range time with the USFA Government Models.

of grip-swapping proved too strong to resist, and I installed Eagle Grips' Ultralvory stocks.

I have been shooting traditional single actions for nearly six decades and very few of them came perfectly sighted, perfectly timed, with perfectly fitting grips, and with the desired trigger pull. The USFA .45 Colt sixgun is an exception which could only be improved by smoothing and polishing the interior parts with a stone. Any of the characters in *The Wild Bunch* would have been happy to have it in his holster.

TRADITIONAL AND TRANSITIONAL

USFA normally reached back into 19th-century history for all of its firearms, however in 2005 its newest offerings showed the company progressing into the 20th century, but just barely. Browning designed the Model 1900 chambered in .38 ACP and then three years later the Model 1905 came forth in .45 ACP. Approximately 6,000 Model 1905s were produced.

It is easy to see the ancestry of the 1911 in the 1905, how-

Both the USFA Model 1910 and Model 1911 shot exceptionally well for John.

ever it was necessary to make changes to suit the military. Approximately 200 Model 1905s were modified to the 1907 Contract Pistols and they were then further altered to become the Model 1910. With the final changes suggested by the military, the 1905/1907/1910 became the "Model of 1911 U.S. Army" as marked on the right side of the slide of the USFA Model 1911. The Model 1910 as offered by USFA is a dead ringer for the Model 1911 *except* for one obvious difference — the 1905-style hammer and the slide markings — plus a very slight difference in the finish.

The right side of the slide of the Model 1910 is marked "USFA Automatic" and "Calibre 45 Rimless Smokeless." This latter description is very apropos for the time period represented, as is the "United States Property" stamp found on the left side of the Model 1911. Although both models represent military .45s, they deviate in two ways. First, they are beautifully finished in a deep, dark black-blue reminiscent of the old Colt Royal Blue and the Smith & Wesson Bright Blue finishes of the

TEST-FIRE: USFA GOVERNMENT MODEL .45s

LOAD	MV	USFA M1910	USFA M1911
Black Hills 185-gr. JHP	1,105 fps	1 ½"	1 ⅛"
Black Hills 200-gr. JHP	942 fps	1 ⅝"	1 ½"
Black Hills 230-gr. JHP	828 fps	1 ⅜"	1 ½"
Black Hills 230-gr. FMJ	791 fps	1"	1 ¼"
CCI Blazer 200-gr. TMJ Match	949 fps	1 ½"	1 ¼"
CCI Blazer 200-gr. JHP	952 fps	3/4"	1 ⅛"
Hornady 185-gr. XTP	972 fps	1 ½"	1 ¼"
Hornady 200-gr. XTP	898 fps	1 ¼"	1 ¼"
Hornady 230-gr. XTP	892 fps	1 ⅛"	1 ⅜"
Winchester 185-gr. FMJ	876 fps	1 ¼"	1 ⅜"
Winchester 230-gr. FMJ	797 fps	1 ¼"	1 ⅛"

Groups are six shots at 20 yards.

1950s. The Model 1905 is also set off nicely with carbona blue (aka "Fire Blue").

The second major difference found in these USFA .45 semiautos — as compared to military originals — is in their fitting. There is absolutely no play between slide and frame. They are in fact fitted as nicely as any of the current 1911s offered by several top-quality makers.

I have shot both with a large variety of factory .45 ammunition; however, since we are looking mainly at the time era for World War I, I concentrated on ammunition which would have been used during the appropriate period – namely 230-grain hardball. USFA did stay with the military on one note. The trigger pulls for both .45s are set at an even six pounds. In 1911 the cavalry had not yet switched from horses to wheels, so the heavier trigger pull was an asset. This, for me at least, did not interfere with my ability to shoot them well.

The USFA Government models mate up well with period-correct leather by Rick Bachman.

HIGH PERFORMANCE STANDARDS

The question always comes up as to why factories don't sight in fixed-sighted sixguns. Actually, they do, but everyone doesn't see the sights the same, or hold the same, or use the same ammunition. I struck pay dirt with this USFA Single Action. Not only is it dead on for windage, it shoots most of my .45 Colt loads right to point of aim for elevation. The original black-powder loads used a 255-grain bullet at approximately 850 fps. Using Oregon Trail 255-grain cast bullets in front of eight grains of

For the most part, John relied on traditional 230-grain hardball loads to test the USFA 1911's.

Unique duplicated the original load, placing five shots in ¾ inch at 50 feet — great shooting by any single-action standard!

My first firing of the USFA Government models was accomplished using two factory hardball offerings from Black Hills and Winchester. Shooting was done at 20 yards using a full magazine of seven rounds with the best six measured. Muzzle velocity of the Black Hills 230-grain FMJ clocked out at 830 fps with the Model 1910 grouping its shots in 1⅜ inches and the 1911 going into 1½ inches. Winchester's 230-grain FMJ clocked out at 800 fps with groups of 1¼ inches and 1⅛ inches, respectively. Except for the obvious differences in the hammer and the markings on the slide, these two .45s are peas in a pod. Even their serial numbers are only 28 digits apart.

RIGGED FOR REALISM

Great guns deserve great leather, so it was natural to turn to Rick Bachman of Old West Reproductions for period style leather. Rick has long offered authentically styled leather for frontier-era sixguns. In fact, I believe he was the first to specialize in authentic Old West leather with his business dating back to 1978, when he started crafting holsters and belts patterned after the real thing in his extensive collection of western memorabilia. Now he does the same style leather for semiautos.

Rick's holsters are patterned after the likes of the Moran

Brothers, F.A. Meanea, E.L. Gallatin, J.S. Collins, all names well-known to students of authentic leather, and probably the most well-known of all, S. D. Myres of El Paso, Texas. The leather pictured for the 1910 and 1911 are patterned after the work of Myres. Sam knew many of the old-time gunfighters on both sides of the law. For the 1910/1911 USFA .45s, Rick crafted a Model 110 Border Patrol carved in the S.D. Myres pattern and a Model 115 Jock Strap, a design which was very popular for single-action sixgun use more than a century ago. His work is some of the best to be found with exquisite attention to detail, authenticity, craftsmanship and the finest possible leather obtainable from Hermann Oak.

Unfortunately, as this is written, USFA is gone. This is a shame, as in the sea of 1911s, they were definitely of exceptional quality. Maybe history will repeat itself and USFA will return. Maybe. ... ◎

THE SEMIAUTOMATICS

A whole lot of .45 ACP "throw weight": The Para-USA P-14 has a capacity of 14+1 rounds.

PARA-USA .45s

CHAPTER 41

Para-USA is a perfect example of what diversity should look like. More than a quarter-century ago, an engineer whose family had fled communist Hungary and a lawyer who was the son of Greek immigrants started a company in Canada producing a Dye Marking Tactical Machine Pistol. The engineer was Ted Szabo. The lawyer in charge of paperwork and marketing was Thanos Polyzos. They soon came up with the idea of offering a kit for the 1911 consisting of a high-capacity frame with a double-stack magazine. These could be fitted to any 1911 single stack.

The kits sold so well Para-Ordnance expanded its operation to include complete pistols with a long list of both double stack and single stack 45s. In addition to the standard 1911s, Para soon began offering compact and subcompact versions.

Tragically, in 2007 — at way too young an age — Ted Szabo passed away. Polyzos then decided it was time to move production of America's iconic pistol from Canada to the United States. The machinery, as well as many employees, was relocated to Charlotte, North Carolina, and Para-Ordnance became Para-USA — a completely American company.

Hardly a day goes by when we do not read of a major company relocating outside the United States, so it's refreshing to see the opposite occur. There are many shooters who simply will not buy firearms not produced in

This shows the difference between single-stack and double-stack Para-USA magazine wells. John does not feel the size of double-stack grips hinders his shooting at all.

The Super Hawg is a Para P-14 with a 6-inch barrel and slide, and an obvious affinity for hot 185-grain JHPs.

COR-BON 185 JHP+P 1175 FPS

These targets shot at 20 yards with the Para SSP indicate that it is pretty fond of 185- and 200-grain bullets.

BLACK HILLS 185 JHP 1037 FPS

.45 ACP BLACK HILLS 185 JHP 1,023 FPS

.45 ACP BLACK HILLS 200 JHP 921 FPS

.45 ACP HORNADY 185 XTP-JHP 965 FPS

the U.S. This move by Para-USA not only got it out from under Canadian regulations, but it also expanded the company's market considerably.

Let's take a look at some of Para-USA's offerings I've used.

DOWN TO CASES

The SSP Para 1911 is a basic, single-stack, single-action 1911 with several worthwhile modifications. First off are the low-riding combat style sights with a drift-windage adjustable rear which locks in place with a setscrew. The back of the sight slopes forward and is serrated to cut glare. On each side of the square notch are white dots which contribute to an easy-to-acquire sight picture in conjunction with the red fiber-optic insert on the dovetailed front post.

For ease of operation and comfort, the SSP has an extended thumb safety, competition trigger matched up with a skeletonized competition hammer, and a beavertail grip safety to eliminate hammer bite. The backstrap is finely checkered and is of the original flat 1911 style rather than later arched 1911A1s. The arched version was introduced to naturally raise the barrel when shooting, as the 1911 seems to point low for many shooters. Personally, I prefer the looks and feel of the original version.

On the slide are six large grooves on both sides in front of the rear sight as a gripping surface for manually operating the slide. The Para SSP features a 5-inch ramped stainless steel match-grade barrel, a full-length guide rod and a Para Power Extractor which delivers 50 percent more gripping surface to the rim of the cartridge for positive extraction.

Everyone has a different idea of what a "perfect pistol" should be. There are two things on the SSP I have changed to get closer to the ideal — my totally subjective concept of perfection, that is. The trigger pull measured 6 pounds on my RCBS trigger-pull gauge. I wanted it closer to 4 pounds, so that was my first order of business.

Next, anyone who has read me knows of my obsession with custom grips. The SSP comes with beautifully checkered cocobolo grip panels; however, the effect — in my opinion —

The Para-USA SSP 1911 is a stainless steel single-stack .45 with a combat-style rear sight and fiber-optic front sight. Naturally, John stuck on Herrett's replacement stocks.

is spoiled by the large gold medallions. Rather than enhancing the looks of this grand 1911, they distract. So I solved the "problem" by exchanging the factory grips for a pair of Herrett's checkered cocobolo panels. Herrett's also offers stocks composed of other exotic woods for the 1911.

The Para SSP delivered more than adequate combat accuracy at 15 yards. Loads performed exceptionally well — Black Hills' 200-grain JHP (five shots in ¾ inch) and Winchester's 230-grain FMJ (coming in at 1¼ inches). Any pistol

chosen for self-defense, competition or hunting should be thoroughly tested for reliability with any ammunition you might use. For whatever reason, this SSP will not feed CCI's Blazer 200-grain JHPs. When loading semiwadcutter cast bullets for use in a 1911, I prefer to allow a small amount of the shoulder exposed above the rim of the cartridge mouth. Para-Ordnance .45s have tight chambers, requiring full-shoulder bullets to be seated flush — or nearly so — with the case mouth.

GOING HI-CAP

Everything found on the SSP Para 1911 is also on the P14-45 Hi-Cap, plus one major addition — the high-capacity feature. The Hi-Cap carries a 14-round magazine, which with a chambered round, results in a 15 shooter. Para has managed to do this without making a bulky grip frame. In fact, I find this wider grip even more comfortable than the single-stack version. The pad of my trigger finger falls naturally on the trigger. With a fully loaded Hi-Cap and two extra magazines, you have easy access to the firepower of nearly a full 50-round box of .45 ACP cartridges.

My Hi-Cap came with a smooth 4-pound trigger, just the way I like it. And I have no complaints about the grips. To cut down on girth, the slimmest possible panels

John feels that the PDA LSA may be the right combination of .45 ACP power and compact dimensions. It proved itself on silhouette targets as well as bullseye.

are utilized and the front of the panels are actually flush with the grip frame itself. These synthetic panels are checkered (no gold medallions!), and I can live with them quite well.

In my original test-firing of the Hi-Cap .45, I tried 10 factory loads, all of which were fired for accuracy with 9-shot groups at 15 yards. All loads exhibited more than adequate combat accuracy, with three loads placing all shots right at an inch. These three are CCI's Blazer 230-grain FMJ, Hornady's 185-grain XTP-JHP and Hornady's 230-grain +P XTP-JHPs. The latter clocks out at nearly 875 fps, while the 185-grain XTP is right at 950. Either of the three would be an excellent choice for self-defense.

John tries his hand — well, one of 'em — with the SSP in one of his favorite wide-open shooting venues.

LIGHT DOUBLE ACTION

One of the "problems" associated with the 1911 from the very beginning has been how it should be carried. Choices include hammer down on an empty chamber (which, of course, requires racking the slide to chamber a round) or cocked and locked with a round in the chamber and the thumb safety engaged. The presence of a cocked hammer makes some uninformed observers nervous. If I recall correctly, at one time it was possible to get a conversion kit which allowed the carrying of a round in the chamber with the hammer down and then as one pressed on a lever the hammer would be cocked and the 1911 ready for firing.

Para-USA has come up with a much better way, and that way is the Light Double Action. The LDA is the same basic 1911 as the SSP, except it's a double-action-only .45 and a mighty fine DAO at that. When a round is chambered, the double-action trigger is activated; however, the hammer remains flush with the back of the slide. When you fire the LDA SSP, the trigger recocks itself. However, the hammer remains in the down position. So in essence the LDA works the same as a double-action revolver (only easier). Try to

find a dependable double-action revolver with a 6½-pound DA trigger pull as found on this LDA. Para-USA is able to accomplish this because the trigger only performs the function of cocking the hammer and firing, without having to rotate a large, heavy cylinder. Even though the trigger in the cocked position is forward in the trigger guard, I have no problem reaching it with the pad of my trigger finger.

I tested the LDA with 5-shot groups at 15 yards. For some reason, it would not feed Black Hills' 200- or 230-grain JHPs reliably. This is strange, as Black Hills uses the same XTP bullets loaded by Hornady. As mentioned earlier, Para-USA's pistols are tight-chambered and the brass used by Black Hills may be slightly thicker than the Hornady version. However, the

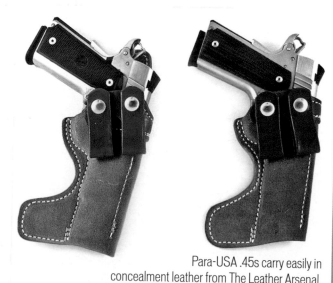

Para-USA .45s carry easily in concealment leather from The Leather Arsenal.

The LDA (bottom) is basically the SSP with a double-action trigger.

It may be a tribute 1911, but Para-USA's G.I. Expert shoots better than practically any original surplus Government Model.

Black Hills 185-grain JHPs chambered with no problem and produced some of the best groups.

All three of these Para-USAs come with matte stainless steel grip frames and highly polished slides. The LDA does not have the flat backstrap, but instead features the arched A1 type. I also replaced the factory grips on the LDA with very attractive diamond-pattern Herrett panels of bubinga wood. All Para-USA 1911s are supplied with two magazines and a high-impact pistol case. For carry, I turned to Elmer McEvoy of The Leather Arsenal. Elmer is former LEO and learned his leatherworking skills from the master himself, Milt Sparks. (Elmer is recommended by none other than Mas Ayoob.) My two concealment holsters of his are both inside-the-pants style. They're lightweight, with two straps fitting over the belt. There is a stabilizing tab at the bottom,

and holsters have the smooth side inside. This helps protect the finish of the gun. Having the rough side out makes the holster cling to your pants and body when you are drawing the pistol.

DOWNSIZING DEFENSE

My personal LDA is a standard-sized 1911; however, the latest Light Double Action version from Para-USA is quite different. Known as the PDA, this miniaturized 1911 features an abbreviated grip frame holding a six-round magazine. The alloy frame is matched up with a steel slide and a 3-inch tapered, match-grade barrel. A friend's reaction when I showed him the PDA was, "Oh my, look how easily this slips into my pants pocket." Call it the smallest possible big gun or the largest possible small gun, it is as easy to pocket as a five-shot, small-framed .38 revolver.

If there is a drawback to the PDA, it's the heavy spring which requires quite a bit of effort to pull back the slide, so I'd never carry this pistol with an empty chamber. With an empty magazine in place, rack the slide backward until it locks, remove the magazine and load six rounds, pull back the slide and let it go forward, and it's ready to go. The magazine can then be removed and topped off with an extra round. There is an ambidextrous thumb safety for extra security when carried with a round in the chamber. The three-dot Trijicon sights on the PDA LDA are excellent. The low-riding, snag-free rear is adjustable for windage and can be locked in place with a

Para-USA's salute to the original 1911 is the GI Expert. It comes with two magazines and rubber grip panels. Again, John added replacement grip panels by Herrett's.

setscrew. Both the frontstrap and backstrap feature fine-line checkering, while the slim grip panels are a most attractive rosewood color with a pebble-grained surface. Shooting the PDA was a lot easier than I expected a 21-ounce .45 would be. All shooting was done at a "self-defense" distance of seven yards with one-hole groups being common.

UPDATED GI 1911

With the celebration of the 100th anniversary of the 1911 in 2011, many companies brought out a no-frills version reminiscent of the original. For Para-USA, it is the GI Expert, advertised as an entry-level 1911. Para-USA says it "feels like an old friend, the one that the company armorer worked over for you to earn your Expert Marksman's badge. Using the new millennium technology Para has built you a production .45 that is silky smooth with a crisp, clean trigger that makes you the best shot you can be."

Okay, there's a little hype there, but not much. It *is* silky smooth with an excellent five-pound trigger pull. The slide is tightly fitted to the frame with no perceptible movement. The excellent sights are of the three-dot variety. I would prefer all-black, however they are much improved over the very small sights found on 1911s a century ago. Both sights are set in a dovetail making them drift adjustable for windage, and for my eyes and hold, shot less than an inch low for most loads tested.

Not only are the sights better than the original, the barrel is of premium stainless steel fitted to a steel bushing; no guide rods here. Both the trigger (serrated on the face) and Commander-style hammer are skeletonized. The mainspring housing is the flat style I prefer; it is grooved while the front strap is smooth. Perpendicular grooves are also on both sides of the slide below the rear sight to provide a grasping surface for working the slide.

For my everyday use, I replaced the plastic grips with Herrett's Tactical Ovals of fancy walnut. They're not as flat as most factory grips and help to fill in the hollow of my shooting hand for better control. They also look a whole lot better than plastic grips. Also, I have never been a fan of magazines with padded bases and much prefer to use stan-

At combat yardage, the Para P-14 was pretty much on the money.

dard flat-base ones, even if it means giving up one round. Some old habits are just hard to change ...

The Para GI Expert performed perfectly with no feeding problems whatsoever. The best factory loads for mine were Black Hills 230-grain JHP at 876 fps and the Buffalo Bore 200-grain JHP at 1,019 fps. Both went into 1⅜ inches at 20 yards. Both of my cast bullet loads using the RCBS #45-201 bullet group right at 1½ inches with 5.0 grains of Bullseye yielding just under 900 fps, while 7.0 grains of Unique clocked just over 1,050 fps. *Note: Para was purchased by Remington and then replaced with the Remington R1.* ◉

John found the SSP to perform well with most factory ammunition.

THE SEMIAUTOMATICS

Evolution of the double-action S&W .45 semiauto (from bottom left clockwise): Model 4506, 4516, CS45 and M&P.

SMITH & WESSON'S .45 SEMIAUTOS

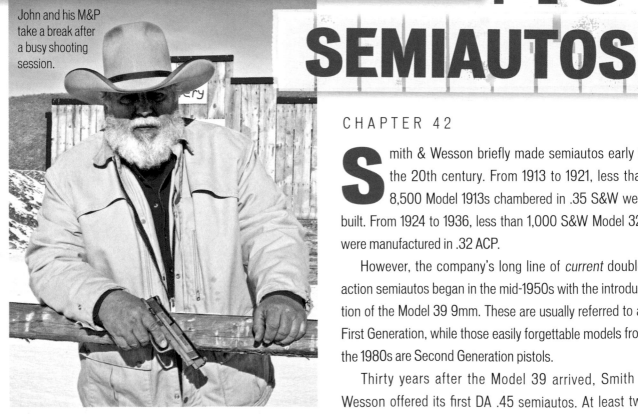

John and his M&P take a break after a busy shooting session.

CHAPTER 42

S mith & Wesson briefly made semiautos early in the 20th century. From 1913 to 1921, less than 8,500 Model 1913s chambered in .35 S&W were built. From 1924 to 1936, less than 1,000 S&W Model 32s were manufactured in .32 ACP.

However, the company's long line of *current* double-action semiautos began in the mid-1950s with the introduction of the Model 39 9mm. These are usually referred to as First Generation, while those easily forgettable models from the 1980s are Second Generation pistols.

Thirty years after the Model 39 arrived, Smith & Wesson offered its first DA .45 semiautos. At least two dozen have been offered since. However, my experience has been limited to only three.

THE MODEL 4506

The first was the Model 4506, introduced in 1988. It has a 5-inch barrel, stainless steel slide, and 8-shot magazine. It is big, weighing in at 45 ounces and bulky. I use it mostly for open carry. Just like the Ruger P-90

S&W's Third Generation Model 4506 is a large, heavy-duty .45 ACP. John replaced the factory grips — naturally — with a set of Hogue stocks.

from the same era, it's a heavy-duty .45 which will stand up to rugged use. The Model 4506's Novak-style sights are fully adjustable and of the three-dot type. They are simply all-around excellent for quick defensive shooting.

The pistol has an ambidextrous safety requiring an upward push to put it in the "fire" position. The double-action trigger is easy to reach and is quite smooth with no discernible creep. At the time S&W offered the Model 4506, hooked trigger guards were in fashion, though I have never quite understood what function they perform. The magazine release is on the left side in front of the grip, and there is no way I can reach it without shifting my hold. The factory wrap-around grip is checkered synthetic, which I immediately replaced with a set of exotic wood panels from Hogue.

Functioning with my Model 4506 has always been 100 percent reliable – no jams, stovepipes or failures to feed with any ammunition tested. My average group sizes at 25 yards with factory ammunition are slightly under 2½ inches. However, Cor-Bon's potent 185-grain +P JHPs shave an inch off the average, while clocking out at more than 1,100 fps.

VARIATIONS ON THE THEME

At the 1990 NRA Show, Smith & Wesson unveiled the newest of what was then its Third Generation — a compact version of the Model 4506 called the 4516. It was S&W's answer to the need for a compact .45. Fully loaded, full magazine plus one in the chamber, the 4516 holds 8 rounds and weighs 39½ ounces. So it's not exactly a lightweight!

The Smith & Wesson was a totally new design at the time and was made to fit the average hand and also allow easy access to the double-action trigger, which by the way is better than that found on many double-action sixguns. The grip supplied on the 4516 is a synthetic wrap-around style that fits my hand quite well. It is fitted with an ambidextrous decocking lever and no grip safety, although it does have a magazine disconnect.

There are two schools of thought on the magazine-disconnect issue. Some say it prevents negligent discharges after removing the magazine and forgetting about the round in the chamber. Others say it renders the pistol useless if the magazine is lost.

Using three different Black Hills factory loads, John's Dark Earth M&P45 demonstrated excellent accuracy.

Double-action .45 semiautos from the early 1990s include (left to right) the Beretta Cougar, S&W's Model 4516 and 4506 and the Ruger P90.

Sights on the Smith & Wesson 4516 are also Novak-style — a low-profile, non-snag rear with two white dots teamed with a white-dot post front. I like white dots on a defensive pistol as they help me in acquiring the sights quickly.

Recoil of the Model 4516 is considerably less than a full-size Government Model .45. The top of the backstrap of the 4516 is quite broad. Its spurless hammer is flush with the frame when in the down position. The accuracy I got with this 3¼-inch barreled pistol is astounding when you consider it is designed as a quick-handling defensive sidearm.

I have had mine for more than 25 years and have used it with 30 different loads, both factory and handloads, using jacketed and cast bullets. Most of my 5-shot 25-yard groups have been in the 2½-inch range, which is excellent

for such a short-barreled gun in my hands. The best factory load for my Model 4516 is a three-way tie between CCI Blazer 200-grain JHPs, and Hornady and Winchester 230-grain FMJs — all going into 2¼ inches at 25 yards.

My 4516 is no slouch in the cast-bullet accuracy department either. Results with RCBS #45-201 in front of 7.0 grains of Unique come in at 1¾ inches, clocking a satisfying 968 fps.

The Model 4516 may be long gone from production, but it remains an excellent .45.

LITTLE BIG CHIEF

Both the 4516 and the 4506 were dropped from the S&W catalog in 1999. The year before they were dropped, the company introduced the double-action, semiauto Chief's Special in a .45 ACP version, Model CS45. (It borrowed its name from the original

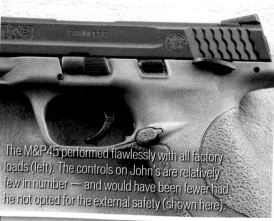

The M&P45 performed flawlessly with all factory loads (left). The controls on John's are relatively few in number — and would have been fewer had he not opted for the external safety (shown here).

Chief's Special, which was the first .38 Special J-frame revolver.)

More compact than the 4516, this satin stainless pistol also has a bobbed hammer, 6-shot magazine and 3¼-inch barrel. But it's even better for concealed carry, at least subjectively speaking. I liked it so well I purchased a pair of them – one went to my son on his 45th birthday. The other one remains always within reach.

THE DAO M&P

Smith & Wesson's latest line of double-action semiautos is quite different from the 4506/4516/CS45 style. They're striker-fired double-action-*only*. The current M&P .45 is a polymer-framed pistol with a capacity of 10+1 rounds and a barrel length of 4½ inches.

The M&P name goes back to 1899, which is when the first K-frame – the Military & Police revolver – was introduced. Until very recently, the term M&P made most shooters think of a 4-inch double-action .38 Special revolver. No more!

Since it is available in other chamberings, the biggest version of the M&P is dubbed the M&P®45, and is available with a black or Dark

The Model 4506 is no slouch in the accuracy department (below). John found it very comfortable to shoot.

FED 185 JHP
S&W
4506

Earth-colored frame. Since polymer-framed pistols with integral grip panels can't be fitted with custom stocks, the colored frame is the next best option, at least for me. My Dark Earth M&P45 is matched up with a stainless steel barrel and slide, with the latter being coated with black Melonite, an almost-indestructible finish.

The backstrap design is rather ingenious as it is easily removable by rotating the handle of the frame tool one-quarter turn and pulling it out of the frame. The contoured handle of this tool blends in neatly with the bottom of the backstrap and the base of the magazine. Once it is removed, access to interchangeable backstraps is allowed. Three sizes are provided: small, medium and large. I use the small one; it feels very good to me, and I can easily reach the trigger with it.

The grip frame is especially comfortable, not the least bit bulky, with a width just over one inch. The pebble-grained surface feels good in the hand while providing a secure grip.

My particular M&P45 came with an ambidextrous safety. Models are also available without an external safety. Instead of being pushed up to fire as on the 4506, 4516 and CS45, the M&P45 has a "1911 feel" and operates the same way — up for "safe," down for "fire." This not only seems more natural, it's also much easier for me to operate than those that are "backwards." There's also an inconspicuous loaded-chamber indicator which is a very small hole at the top of the slide/ejection port. Some folks become very upset at the thought of a loaded-chamber indicator; however, this one is barely detectable unless you know what to look for.

The front sight consists of a dovetailed, forward-sloping square post with a white dot. The Novak Lo-Mount Carry

The CS45 has a magazine capacity of six. John found the accuracy (right) to be exceptional for a short-barreled concealed carry pistol.

rear — also mounted in a dovetail — is a square notch with a white dot on each side. It is adjustable for windage by loosening a locking screw and tapping the rear sight in the direction you want, then tightening the locking screw. For my eyes and hold, most loads shot to point of aim for elevation. Only a very slight adjustment was needed for windage.

There are four controls located on the left side of the frame. Three of these are right below the slide — takedown lever, slide lock, and if the M&P45 is so equipped, the thumb safety. The latter is ambidextrous, so it's also found on the right side. The magazine release is found behind the trigger at the juncture of the trigger guard and front strap — it's easily reached with the thumb of the shooting hand and the magazine drops easily and freely when it is pushed

Two targets fired with John's S&W 1911 show a definite preference for CCI Blazers in both 200- and 230-grain persuasions.

in. It is also reversible and can be placed on the right side for southpaws, or for those who use their trigger fingers instead of their thumbs to release the magazine.

The trigger on the M&P is hinged in the middle, and it will not fire unless the bottom part is pressed rearward. The trigger travels approximately .300 inch, and there's a built-in trigger stop which contacts a stop molded into the trigger guard as the M&P is fired. The trigger is rated at 6.5 pounds on the spec sheet, but I couldn't get it to register on my RCBS Trigger Pull Scale, which goes up to 8 pounds. Whatever the pull is, I did find the pistol comfortable and easy to shoot.

Over the past couple of years, I have fired more than 20 different factory loads through the M&P45. It not only shoots accurately and to point of aim, but operation is also flawless. The most accurate load tried to date is the Hornady 230-grain FMJ at 820 fps. It delivered a five-shot group of one inch. Following right behind with 1⅛-inch groups were Black Hills' 230-grain JHP (835 fps), Black Hills' 230-grain FMJ (790 fps), Speer's Gold Dot 200-grain JHP+P (1,040 fps) and Speer's 230-grain Gold Dot JHP (830 fps). These are excellent results from a self-defense handgun. Actually, it's pretty hard to find a load which will *not* perform satisfactorily in the M&P45.

One useful accessory for the M&P45 is the LaserMax Unimax Green Laser Sight. This compact unit mounts on the pistol's integral Picatinny rail underneath the barrel and is activated by an ambidextrous switch. The reason for

When S&W finally decided to offer a 1911, it did things right. John did add aftermarket stag grips on his.

green? Red tends to wash out in all but low-level light, while green is more easily visible in daylight. The Unimax mounts easily, is held securely by one transverse screw and adjusts for windage and elevation using the provided tool.

THE S&W 1911

Smith & Wesson first entered the .45 ACP market in 1917. Because of the shortage of 1911 Government Models, both S&W and Colt altered their 2nd Model Hand Ejector and New Service revolvers to handle the .45 ACP cartridge using half-moon clips.

It would be the 21st century before S&W produced a 1911. But when they did, they did it *right*.

I first saw the SW1911 at the 2003 SHOT Show. This excellent .45 ACP is satin-finished stainless steel with the standard five-inch barrel and a magazine capacity of eight. The sights consist of a white dot front matched up with a white dot Novak Lo Mount rear. Factory grips are checkered black rubber (which I quickly replaced with stocks made from elk antlers). Other features include an extended beaver-tail grip safety, extended thumb safety, external extractor and skeletonized trigger and hammer. Since the arrival of

The M&P45 comes with three back straps. John prefers the smallest. The green LaserMax — which mounts on the integral rail–is an excellent addition for the pistol.

this first 1911, Smith & Wesson has offered a long list of other variations.

When I started shooting seriously back in the 1950's, I never dreamed Smith & Wesson would someday offer .45 ACP semiautos. My three Third Generation examples are definite keepers. Now they've been joined by the M&P and SW1911. ◉

The compact version of the Model 4506 is the Model 4516. John first encountered it at the 1990 SHOT Show. He's still shooting one (right).

THE SEMIAUTOMATICS

A slimmer, sleeker, sexier .45: The difference in size is obvious when comparing the Ruger P345 (left) to the P90.

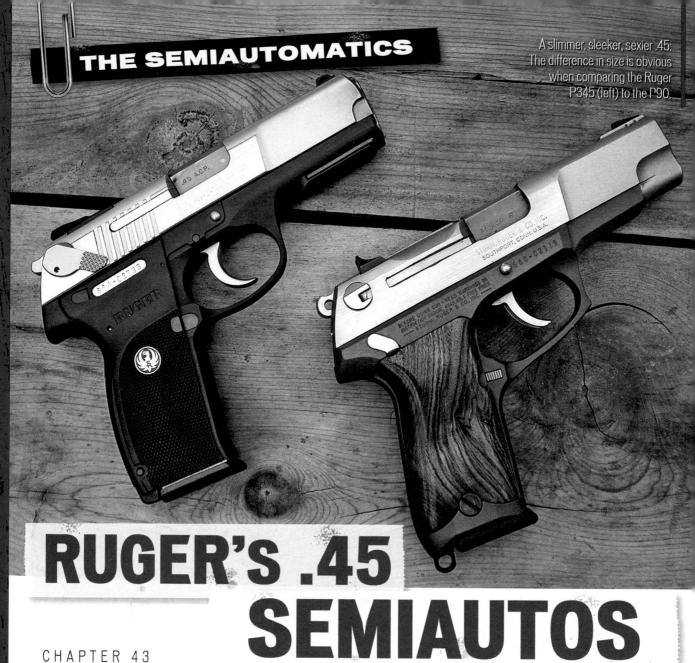

The Ruger P345R, thanks to its integral rail, accepts lights and laser sights, making it a natural for the nightstand.

RUGER'S .45 SEMIAUTOS

CHAPTER 43

Anyone taking anything more than a cursory look at the 9mm Ruger P85 for the first time in the mid-1980s knew it was destined for greater things. At a time when everyone else was trying to see how compact they could make a 9mm, Ruger was offering a large-framed — almost clunky — one. When placed next to any other 9mm of the era, the P85 made it look as if the engineers at Ruger had a lot of extra metal at their disposal and didn't quite know what to do with it.

Neither Bill Ruger nor his company have ever been known for making mistakes, so the reason for the large-size 9mm just had to be to provide a platform for larger calibers later. And "later" soon arrived with the P90 in .45 ACP.

This, of course, was not the first .45 ACP handgun from Ruger. For more than 20 years, off and on, they had been offering the Blackhawk .45 Colt with some models available as Convertibles with extra .45 ACP cylinders. But while the .45 ACP

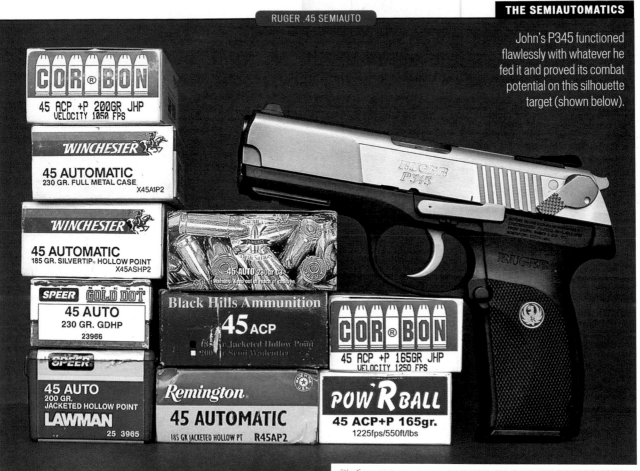

John's P345 functioned flawlessly with whatever he fed it and proved its combat potential on this silhouette target (shown below).

shoots fine through sixgun cylinders, it was meant for semi-autos. Now Ruger had finally given the grand, old cartridge the platform it deserved.

THE P90

The initial Ruger .45 semiauto was assigned the model number of KP90DC, ("K" denoting stainless, "DC" denoting decocking lever). The Ruger P90 came in stainless steel with the grip frame being cast of A356T6 aluminum alloy and given a hard coating to resist corrision. The 4½-inch barrel, the slide and most parts are of 400 series stainless steel.

Before the P90, my only previous experience with Ruger centerfire semiautos had been with one of the original 9mm P85. I'd used it for the previous five years both as a carry gun in my vehicle and a competition gun for standard law-enforcement qualification courses.

When I picked up the P90 for the first time, it felt lighter in weight and slimmer in the grip area than the P85. I was surprised to find that the .45 is actually one ounce heavier than the P85 — 34 ounces, opposed to 33 — and the grip frames are exactly the same.

It's difficult for me to engage and disengage the P85's safety without shifting my grip, and I have no doubt this was the reason it was not more popular in law enforcement circles. The safety can be moved without shifting the shooting

SEMIAUTO PISTOLS AND THEIR CARTRIDGES

THE BOOK OF THE .45

John runs the SR1911 through its paces. The staghorn grip panels he eventually settled on look pretty good on stainless steel.

grip, but it requires some real stretching. The decocker on the P90 is for right-handers only and is easier to reach — for me — than the P85's safety lever, although it does require a goodly amount of stretching to completely operate without shifting my grip. The decocker of the P90 drops the hammer. Nothing else is required to make it ready to fire.

Sights on the Ruger P90 are the three-dot variety. The front post is pinned, the rear is drift-adjustable for windage and held in place with an Allen screw. My P90 is right on for elevation with standard .45 ACP loads.

Slide-to-frame fit of the P90 is very good, with only the slightest amount of play. The trigger is excellent. The double-action pull is better than what was found on most DA revolvers during the 1990s. The single-action pull, while somewhat creepy, is light and easy to manage. The grips are molded and grooved GE Xenoy 6123 resin; how-

ever, I've replaced them with panels of exotic wood from Hogue's.

My P90 has a very tight chamber, but all ammunition — both factory and reloads — function perfectly, except for Hornady's 230-grain flat-nosed FMJ loads. They don't seat solidly unless I push the slide forward into battery.

Because of the P90's light weight (It scales six ounces less than a 1911.), I expected more felt recoil than I actually experienced. Who purchased the P90? Not the military and not large law enforcement groups. The main buyers were the shooters who always felt anything less than a .45 was a giant step down, as well as dyed-in-the-wool Ruger fans.

If I wanted a .45 ACP semiauto for everyday hard use in every kind of weather, I would have no problem going with the P90. It is big, bulky and definitely an example of function over form. But I like it. Then the late Col. Charles Askins — who knew and understood fighting handguns — declared the P90 to be the best semiauto .45 ever produced, although due to its size, it's more difficult than most to conceal.

DOWNSIZING THE PLATFORM

Ruger certainly understood this last point as it began working to downsize the P90. There were several modifications and models along the way leading us to the next major change, the KP345. It has all the positive functioning qualities of the original P90 along with improved ergonomics. It was downsized, slimmed, given a much easier to hold grip configuration and made lighter with the use of a polymer frame. This nine-shot, double-action .45 ACP is comparatively soft-shooting. It fits well in your hand, feels good and shoots where you point it.

Targets shot at 20 yards with the SR1911 testify to the care Ruger took in putting it together.

Ruger did everything possible to make the KP345 as safe as possible. There is, of course, the warning label found on the barrels of all Ruger firearms for what seems like an eternity. Most shooters don't like it, but it is simply one of those things we have to live with. At least on the KP345 the label is smaller than usual and placed at the top of the left grip frame where it is not nearly so noticeable. A second safety feature is the loaded chamber indicator, a small bar atop the slide sitting flush when the chamber is empty and sticking up slightly to reveal a red dot on each side when a round is chambered. Personally, I do not find this objectionable at all as it may prevent negligent discharges.

The P345 also has a magazine disconnect which allows the gun to fire *only* if a magazine is inserted. Many of us dislike the feature. However, we either get used to it or contend ourselves with purchasing older used firearms.

Then there's the internal locking device. Ruger has come up with the best way I have seen yet to conceal it. It's actually almost hidden by the ambidextrous manual safety. When the manual safety is in the "on" position, a small hole behind in provides key access for locking the pistol into a "can't fire" condition.

As with all Ruger double-action semiautos, the P345's

The SR1911 comes with two magazines: seven-round and eight-round, as well as a bushing wrench.

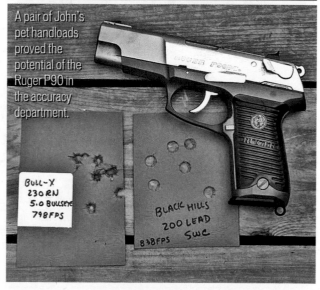

A pair of John's pet handloads proved the potential of the Ruger P90 in the accuracy department.

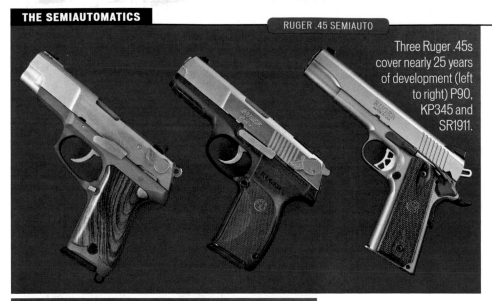

Three Ruger .45s cover nearly 25 years of development (left to right) P90, KP345 and SR1911.

The three-dot sights on the P345, as on the P90, are excellent — an easy-to-see square notch rear mated up with a post front. Both are fitted in a dovetail and adjustable for windage.

There are two versions, the standard KP345 and the KP345PR (which has an integral rail for lights and/or lasers). My KP345R has been my bedside gun since it was introduced.

RUGER'S 1911 ARRIVES

Rumors had been flying for many years about whether or not Ruger was going to actually produce a 1911. Dan Wesson had a 1911, Taurus had a 1911, Smith & Wesson had a 1911. All God's children had a 1911 — except Ruger.

The situation changed with an announcement on April 18, 2011 (making it one of the only good things about Tax Day) proclaiming Ruger had filled the gap in its lineup. The stainless SR1911 is Browning-basic all the way — it just has "Ruger" stamped on the slide.

As issued: The Ruger .45 ACP 1911 comes with cocobolo stocks and a zippered bag. The sights, magazine release, slide stop, thumb safety and beavertail are blued.

first shot is fired by a long, double-action pull. Subsequent shots are single action. Or the first shot may also be fired single-action style by manually cocking the hammer once the safety is in the "on" position.

Browning's original design was pretty near perfection, but one shortcoming involved the small sights. When I was 17 the original sights were no problem (they are now!). Thankfully, the black-with-white-dots Ruger 1911 sights are excellent. Both the front and rear are set in a dovetail and can be adjusted for windage. The rear is Novak-style with no sharp edges to hurt your hand when you're racking the slide manually to chamber a cartridge.

Second only to the importance of the sights, is the trigger. Ruger's 1911 trigger is skeletonized aluminum with an adjustable over-travel stop. The pull on mine weighs a crisp 4¾ pounds.

The Ruger P90 has a magazine capacity of seven rounds. Naturally, John replaced the original grip panels on his with a set of Hogues.

With such a sight/trigger combination, I expected the Ruger 1911 to perform well and it did.

Two other major factors involved in just how well a 1911 will perform are slide-to-frame fit and how tightly the barrel and bushing mate up. Ruger's frames are made by its sister company, Pine Tree Castings, and then CNC machines are used to provide a precise slide-to-frame fit. The stainless steel barrel and bushing are produced from the same piece of bar stock on the same machine.

What was "in" back then: Semiauto .45s of the 1990s include (from top right clockwise): Ruger P90, Glock 21, S&W 4506 and, of course, the Colt Government Model.

Other features include the now-virtually-mandatory "bite-free" beavertail with a cutout to cup the skeletonized hammer. The beavertail is not as wide as on most 1911s today; however, it performs its function without increasing felt recoil. The grip safety as well as the slightly extended thumb safety, slide lock and magazine release are all blued, providing a nice contrast to the matte stainless steel slide and frame. Ruger provides two magazines as well as a bushing wrench with each 1911. Any standard 1911 magazine will fit the Ruger 1911.

The firing pin is titanium and is matched up with a heavy firing-pin spring which mediates the need for a firing-pin block. Ruger says this offers "... an updated safety feature to the original 'Series 70' design without compromising trigger pull weight."

Ruger has stayed on the side of tradition by sticking with the old internal extractor instead of an external one. The one on my pistol has continued to work flawlessly.

Another thing I prefer is the configuration of the original 1911's flat mainspring housing. The choice is purely subjective, and I simply like the Ruger's checkered flat backstrap. Grip panels are nicely checkered with the diamond pattern and the Ruger emblem. The wood is cocobolo, but because I like personalized grip panels, my gun now wears genuine stag. They look — and feel — exceptionally nice on this stainless steel .45.

One problem inherent with fixed sights is the fact all loads do not shoot to the same point of impact. With adjustable sights, it simply requires a few clicks of the rear sight screw to compensate for this. With the SR1911, I found most loads shot 1 to 2 inches high at 20 yards. This can easily be addressed by replacing the front sight with a taller version; however, with the sights just as they are, my gun shoots right to point of aim with 230-grain RN cast bullets at 850 fps. Decisions, decisions, *decisions* ...

I've now fired my SR1911 with 21 different loads from seven manufacturers. It has never failed to feed, fire or extract. If there's anything wrong with the basic design or functioning I certainly can't find it. Ruger has done just about everything right, including placing the "lawyers label" not only in very small letters but also in an inconspicuous spot on the underneath part of the frame in front of the trigger guard.

When Ruger introduced its 1911, Ruger CEO Mike Fifer said, "We are very proud to offer a 1911 pistol, an icon of American gun design and manufacturing. In this 100-anniversary year of the introduction of the Government Model 1911 it is only fitting that such a firearm be completely manufactured in America with all American-made components."

I say "Amen" to that. ◎

THE SEMIAUTOMATICS

The latest 1911 .45s from Wesson Firearms include the full-size Specialist (top) and the Officers Model-scaled EOC (bottom).

DAN WESSON
1911s

John's Patriot Expert shoots well with just about everything he's been able to stuff into it.

CHAPTER 44

As metallic silhouette shooting began spreading across the country in the late 1970s, Dan Wesson was the company doing the most to fill the needs of long-range sixgunners. First came its heavy-barreled .357 Magnum, then other models followed in .44 Magnum, then the .357 and .375 Super Magnums. Dan Wesson stayed on the cutting-edge of firearms development with its superbly accurate revolvers.

But change is always inevitable, and it certainly happened in the silhouette game. When it did, Dan Wesson paid the price. Doors closed, doors reopened, the factory was sold and resold.

But early in the 21st-century, the company basically changed from fine revolvers to 1911s. Silhouette shooting had peaked and 1911s could be made quicker and easier than revolvers — and could command a greater profit margin.

THE EXPERT

The new Dan Wesson 1911s were given the name of Patriot and offered in two versions originally. First were the adjustable-sighted Expert and the fixed-sighted Marksman. Both were offered in either a brushed stainless finish or chrome moly blue. My first Patriot was an Expert with a deep-blue finish. Features included a Series 70-style forged frame, beavertail grip safety, Commander-style hammer, lowered and flared ejection port, external extractor, slanted cocking serrations front and rear and fully adjustable rear sight.

Many of the parts came from Chip McCormick. These included the slide stop, thumb safety, combat hammer, sear, beavertail safety, match barrel bushing, steel mainspring housing, full-length two-piece guide rod and an eight-round magazine.

All the springs came from Wolff. Custom touches included a beveled magazine well and a relief cut under the trigger guard to allow

for a more comfortable grip. The skeletonized trigger itself is lightweight alloy and is adjustable by accessing an Allen screw. Mine came set at three pounds, and I've never felt the need to change it. The frame is tastefully laser engraved with serial number and manufacturer, while the slide is marked "Dan Wesson Patriot." There are no safety warnings to detract from the classic appearance. The original factory grip panels were double-diamond checkered cocobolo. However, I am a hard sell when it comes to fac-

The Wesson Firearms compact EOC .45 utilizes a seven-round magazine.

At combat yardages, John found the Specialist to be very effective. The night sights and rail only add to its low-light utility.

REMINGTON 230 HARD BALL

tory grips with medallions. They've since been replaced with checkered cocobolo panels from Herrett's.

The Patriot looks good and it feels good, frame fit to slide is exceptional. Except for my hand-loads using the H&G #68 SWC cast 200-grain bullet (which I normally load with about ⅟₁₆ inch of the shoulder exposed), functioning was perfect. Once these bullets were seated correctly for this particular pistol, functioning was perfect. My favorite loads for this bullet are 3.5 grains of Bullseye for a mild-shooting 700 fps. My serious full-house load calls for 7.0 grains of Unique for just under 1,100 fps.

Over the past 10 years I've tested well over 20 factory loads through the Patriot with the best results coming from Cor-Bon's 185-grain +P JHP, which clocks just under 1,200 fps and cuts one ragged hole at seven yards. It is an excellent self-defense load which also happens to shoot superbly.

THE SPECIALIST

The most recent Wesson 1911 is the Specialist. When the Patriot was put together with the features the company thought most shooters would want, it took a different tack with the Specialist. This came about after police departments and special units approached Wesson to come up with a more reliable and durable 1911 than what they were carrying. So Wesson went to the drawing board to come up with the Specialist.

The first things I noticed about it were the finish and the grips. For an everyday, all-weather pistol, a bright blue finish is neither desired nor practical. The Specialist

The factory grip panels on the Specialist (left) are very aggressive. Those of the compact EOC (right) are slimmed down — befitting the concealed carry capabilities of the pistol — and feature a combined smooth/aggressive surface.

> *This is a very impressive .45, and if there's anything wrong with it — or anything else it needs — I can't find it.*

At combat yardages, this type of accuracy is above and beyond the call of duty.

REMINGTON 230 HARD BALL

reflects this thinking with a matte black duty finish — no reflection. The grips are unlike anything I've ever seen, or for that matter, felt. When my friend Denis picked up the Specialist he called them "aggressive." By that he meant the unusual pattern is such when they are grasped, they are going absolutely *nowhere*.

Wesson calls them its G10 VZ Operator II grips. They are not only attractive, their "grippability" is enhanced by the 25 LPI checkering on both the mainspring housing and front strap.

The Specialist consists of a forged slide and a tactical rail frame, which is also forged. The bottom of the frame in front of the trigger guard has a Picatinny rail with three slots to accept a laser or flashlight. The top of the slide is fully serrated lengthwise from front sight to rear sight. The sights themselves are simply superb. The rear, which is drift adjustable in a dovetail with a locking screw, is the new Wesson Ledge Sight and features an amber-colored tritium dot which matches up with a green tritium dot with a white target ring in the front sight. These sights show up beautifully in low light — appearing as a dual-colored "Figure 8."

When cocked, the skeletonized hammer fits into a deep recess in the top of the beavertail grip safety which also has a memory bump. The long trigger is not skeletonized and — by my Brownells trigger pull gauge — scales out at a smooth, creep-free 4¼ pounds. The extended thumb safety is ambidextrous and easily operated. The extended magazine release is in front of a cutout in the grip to make it easy to access. The eight-round magazine has a padded bottom and inserts easily through a two-piece flared well which is detachable. Magazine release is quick and positive.

Slide to frame fit is quite tight. The match-grade barrel — about .005 inch larger at the muzzle end — is also tightly fitted to the bushing. Total weight of the Specialist is a recoil-reducing 40 ounces. This is a very impressive .45,

The Specialist has a standard eight-round magazine and is exceptionally controllable.

and if there's anything wrong with it — or anything else it needs — I can't find it.

THE EOC

The next Wesson .45 I have on hand is also a 1911, however it's of the size normally referred to as an "Officers Model." It's called the EOC and can be looked at as the backup to the Specialist.

The EOC .45 ACP with its anodized aluminum frame

weighs in at 25 ounces with a 3½-inch barrel. The sights and finish are the same as what is on the Specialist, and the finish is also matte black. The hammer and beavertail grip safety are also the same. However, the extended thumb safety — rather than being ambidextrous — is only on the left side. Trigger pull also measures 4¼ pounds on this much smaller pistol. But even with its compact grip frame, the flush-fitting magazine holds seven rounds.

The grips are not quite as aggressive as those on the Specialist. The EOC's DW Carry G10 grips are thinner and finished in a half-smooth, "half-aggressive" pattern. They are mated up with the same 25 LPI checkering on the front strap and mainspring housing. Unlike the Specialist, the EOC does not have a barrel bushing. The muzzle end of the match-grade, target-crowned barrel fits into the end of the slide. Wesson Firearms literature says: "The recoil system is unique for this style of 1911 as we use a solid, one-piece guide rod and a flat recoil spring rated for 15,000 rounds in .45 ACP."

Take note: That's *15,000* rounds. Not 500 like most 1911 dual-recoil systems are rated for. This is unheard of in a production 1911.

The first Wesson Firearms 1911 was the Patriot Expert. John has used his heavily over the years.

Both of these Wesson .45s arrived in mid-December which is not the best time — at least for me — when it comes to test-firing outside. So the next best thing was to move to the indoor range where it is much warmer, but unfortunately has less light. (I need a *lot* of light to do my best shooting.) Fortunately, the tritium night sights helped give me a much better sight picture indoors.

I fired both of them at the normal self-defense range of seven yards with a variety of loads using FMJ, JHP and SWC bullets. No matter which bullet shape or which gun I shot, functioning was flawless. And accuracy — again for both guns — was way above adequate for self-defense. By the time this book is in print, nicer weather should be back, and hopefully I will be out shooting these newest Wesson 1911s at longer distances.

As expected, the 40-ounce Specialist was exceptionally easy to shoot; however, I was surprised to find the 25-ounce EOC was easier to handle than I expected. Felt recoil was no problem. The Specialist is easier to shoot, while the EOC is easiest to pack.

Today we are fortunate to have the finest 1911s ever offered from a variety of excellent sources. Wesson Firearms is definitely one of them. ◉

TEST-FIRE: DAN WESSON PATRIOT (5 INCH)

LOAD	MV	6 SHOTS, 20 YARDS
Black Hills 185-gr. JHP	990 fps	1 ⅜"
Black Hills 200-gr. JHP	957 fps	1 ¾
Black Hills 230-gr. JHP	850 fps	1 ¾"
CCI-Blazer 200-gr. JHP	959 fps	1 ½
CCI-Blazer 230-gr. FMJ	868 fps	1 ⅜"
Cor-Bon +P 165-gr. JHP	1,298 fps	1 ½
Cor-Bon +P 185-gr. JHP	1,183 fps	5/8"
Cor-Bon +P 200-gr. JHP	1,089 fps	1 ⅝
Cor-Bon +P 230-gr. JHP	901 fps	1 ⅜"
Cor-Bon +P 165-gr. PowRBall	1,189 fps	1 ¾
Federal 185-gr. AutoMatch	782 fps	1 ⅜
Hornady 200-gr. FMJ-FN	967 fps	2"
Hornady 200-gr. LSWC	938 fps	1 ½"
Hornady 230-gr. FMJ-FN	867 fps	1 ⅞
Remington 185-gr. JHP	1,024 fps	1 ⅝"
Remington 185-gr. +P Golden Sabre	1,117 fps	1 ¾
Speer Lawman 200-gr. JHP	1,004 fps	1 ¼"
Speer Lawman 230-gr. TMJ	748 fps	1 ¾
Speer Gold Dot 230-gr. JHP	848 fps	1 ½"
Winchester 185-gr. FMJ	771 fps	1 ⅜
H&G #68 H&G/7.0 gr. Unique	1,081 fps	1 ⅝"

THE SEMIAUTOMATICS

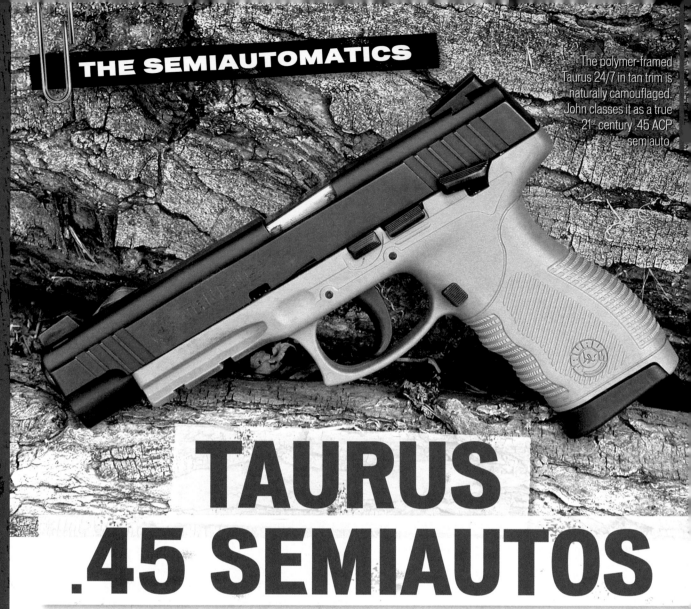

The polymer-framed Taurus 24/7 in tan trim is naturally camouflaged. John classes it as a true 21st century .45 ACP semiauto.

TAURUS .45 SEMIAUTOS

CHAPTER 45

The customizing of 1911s really began in the 1950s — mainly to satisfy bull's-eye shooters. Some of the well-known names stemming from that period include Jimmy Clark, Bob Chow and Frank Pachmayr. I feel

No accuracy complaints here! John's PT1911 is obviously fond of CCI Blazer 230-grain hardball.

particularly blessed to own a Colt Combat Commander fully customized by Jimmy Clark.

It is not difficult to spend $1,000, $2,000, even $3,000 on a customized 1911. Taurus advertised its entrance into the 1911 market, the PT1911, as having $1,600 worth of custom features on a pistol retailing for around $700. You could purchase a bare-bones 1911, add all the custom features *already* found on the PT1911, spend $2,000 and wind up with a pistol not that far removed from your original $700 Taurus.

So, just what do you get with the PT1911? The frame, slide and custom-fitted barrel are all forged steel, as are all the major components. Extras consist of an ambidextrous safety, skeletonized trigger, target hammer, serrated slide and checkering on the trigger guard, mainspring housing and front strap. On top of that, you get Heinie Straight 8 sights, a polished feed ramp, lowered and flared ejection port, custom internal extractor, beavertail grip safety with memory pad and extended magazine release. The barrel, frame and slide all carry the same serial number, ensuring every gun is hand-assembled and hand-fitted.

The only thing I could even come close to complain about is the same complaint I have about almost every handgun offered by almost every manufacturer. Grips. So I replaced the checkered black plastic panels with a pair of smooth cocobolo stocks from Herrett's. They not only feel good, they mate up beautifully with the PT1911's matte blue finish.

I found the Taurus PT1911 to be very easy to shoot. For those not acquainted with the Straight 8 sights, they are comprised of a square-notch rear matched with a slanted post front. A white dot in the front sight as well as underneath the notch in the rear sight results in a "figure 8" sight picture which lines up very quickly. The PT1911 is not a target pistol by any means and most of my 20-yard groups fired with the PT1911 are in the 2-inch neighborhood. My best results came with CCI 230-grain FMJ Blazers at just over 800 fps.

At combat yardages, the 24/7 acquitted itself well with high-performance Cor-Bon JHP's.

THE PT 24/7 OSS

We have been blessed with a nearly endless stream of polymer-framed pistols beginning with the trendsetting Glock in the 1980s. Glock still catalogs the .45 ACP Model 21, and over the past couple of years it has been joined by the Springfield's XD and the Smith & Wesson M&P, also both chambered in .45 ACP. Now the Taurus PT24/7 OSS has joined this group.

The PT24/7 OSS exhibits fine workmanship, imagina-

tion, innovation and a relatively low price tag. Shooters have four choices when it comes to choosing a 24/7 in .45 ACP. Barrel length options are 4.2 or 5.2 inches, and either version can be had in all-black or with a beige-colored frame. My pistol is the longer-barreled, tan-colored variant.

The PT24/7 has several safety features, none of which are obtrusive. If I remember correctly, Taurus was the first major manufacturer to come up with an internal safety lock. It operates with a key and is accessed by a small, round screw head above the thumb safety on the right-hand side of the slide. Thankfully, there are no external warning labels to be found. There are five other safety features on the 24/7. Two internal safeties prevent a negligent discharge if the pistol is dropped and only disengage when the trigger is pulled to the rear. One of these is a firing pin block, and the other is a trigger safety blocking the trigger bar.

External safeties include a loaded chamber indicator

High-capacity, big-bore power.
The Taurus 24/7 has a capacity
of 12+1 rounds of .45 ACP.

and a red cocking indicator at the rear of the slide. Finally we come to the three-position ambidextrous thumb safety. Even though the 24/7 is striker-fired, it can be carried cocked and locked by moving the thumb safety up from the firing position to the "safe" position. If the thumb safety is pushed all the way up, the 24/7 is decocked. When the pistol is in the cocked-and-locked mode and the safety is pushed to the "fire" position, the trigger pull is about 6½ pounds. If decocked, the pistol can still be fired after moving the lever to the firing position. However, it will require considerably more than 6½ pounds. If for some reason it fails to fire in the decocked mode, the trigger can be pulled again.

The sights are fixed, three-dot Novaks — big, bold and easy to see. Both the front and rear sight are set in a dovetail locked in place with a setscrew, and either one can be adjusted for windage. The steel slide has large serrations on both sides below the sights for easy manual operation. Magazine capacity is 12 rounds, the slide stays opened on the last round and, thankfully, there's no magazine disconnect.

The polymer frame has a very comfortable grip with a rounded back strap and minimal finger grooves on the front. Both are covered with small molded-in dots for a secure hold. My highly subjective impression is that the 24/7 has a "soft-shooting" feel to it. The magazine release is found

on the left side behind the trigger guard, is easily accessed, and the magazine releases positively when it is depressed. Although it is not ambidextrous, it can be reversed to accommodate left-handed shooters. The frame also has a molded-in accessory rail for flashlights or laser sights.

When testing any firearm, I normally chronograph and shoot for groups separately with the chronographing coming first. This serves two purposes. I have enough trouble doing one thing at a time, so once the chronographing is finished, I can concentrate on firing groups. A second and probably more important reason for doing things in this order is it allows the firearm to settle in and also expose any problems. Several times I found the last round in the 24/7's magazine would come straight up and get caught between the barrel and the slide. Whatever was causing it worked itself out by the time I was ready to group the gun. No malfunctions whatsoever occurred while using 22 different varieties of .45 ACP loads — both standard and +P. Furthermore, no malfunctions have occurred since my initial testing.

My normal procedure for testing any firearm on paper is to allow myself one throwaway round so the 24/7 was fired with six rounds with only the best five being counted. Any test-firing consists of sight alignment, trigger squeeze and, above all, concentration. Even with the 24/7's 6½-pound trigger pull, I could not imagine any problems in a defensive situation. However, the pull weight does enter into the equation when shooting for small groups on paper.

Although I found that the 24/7 will handle any quality factory ammunition flawlessly, it should not be construed to mean this — or any — pistol can be put into use without first being thoroughly tested with whatever ammunition is chosen. Every individual firearm is a law unto itself in this regard.

The most accurate load I have found was one of only two non-jacketed rounds used, namely the Black Hills 200-grain lead SWC, which clocked out at just over 850 fps and placed five shots in one inch. The most powerful loads were 200 grain +P's from Buffalo Bore and Cor-Bon (both at 1,080 fps) and Speer's 200-grain Gold Dot at 1,040 fps.

PT845

Taurus' latest entry into the 21st century .45 ACP market is the PT845, available with a blue or stainless steel slide and barrel matched up with a polymer frame. It's a dandy in every sense of the word. Whoever designed this pistol went to great lengths to incorporate everything anyone would want in this type of pistol.

Prior to World War II, it was relatively easy to make a high-capacity pistol, such as the Browning Hi-Power and Walther P38. However, to do this it was necessary to use the smaller European 9mm rather than the American .45 ACP. Before the advent of polymer frames, high-capacity .45s would simply have a grip frame too large for most folks to wrap their fingers around. The standard 1911 has a capacity of 7+1 rounds, while the polymer-framed PT845 allows a capacity of 12+1 with no more bulk than found in the 1911.

The PT845 has stippled striations over the entire front strap and halfway around both sides of the grip panel (the backstrap has this same pattern), which makes for a very secure hold.

I have large hands with rather short fingers which often makes it difficult for me to reach a double-action trigger. But the PT845 comes with three interchangeable back straps. The medium version was installed at the factory, and I found it set my hand too far back to reach the DA trigger. But the smallest back strap solved this problem. It also feels most comfortable to me when using the gun in the single-action mode. Another feature on the frame of the PT845 is an integral Picatinny rail in front of the trigger guard for a light or laser.

The PT845 is perfectly suited to any shooter, whether they are right-handed or left-handed, as all the controls are ambidextrous. This includes the magazine release and slide release.

The third control is the ambidextrous three-position safety. The PT845 is normally double action on the first shot followed by subsequent single-action pulls. This means it may be carried hammer down with a chambered round and fired just as if it were a double-action revolver.

Anyone who has shot enough has encountered at least one round that went "click" instead of "bang" when the hammer fell. This sometimes happens when the primer is not seated deeply enough. But if

The Taurus PT1911 works with a variety of factory ammunition. It shot well for John. Naturally, he replaced the factory plastic grips with smooth cocobolo panels from Herrett's.

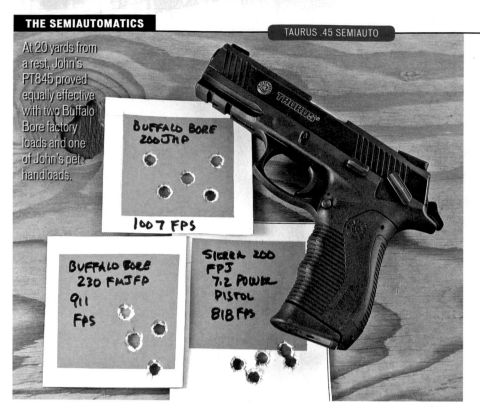

At 20 yards from a rest, John's PT845 proved equally effective with two Buffalo Bore factory loads and one of John's pet handloads.

BUFFALO BORE 200 JHP

1007 FPS

BUFFALO BORE 230 FMJFP 911 FPS

SIERRA 200 FPJ 7.2 POWER PISTOL 818 FPS

But all the well-carried-out ideas and all the special features mean nothing if they don't equate to actual performance. I look at four things to evaluate any pistol to be used for either self-defense, competition or hunting. There are things we can put up with in a pure plinkin' pistol, but in a *serious* pistol, high marks must be obtained in every category. And in some cases only perfection is acceptable.

The four things I am concerned about are sights, accuracy, function and something I will call general "feelability." Putting the PT845 through my four-point checklist tells what it will do in my hands (or yours).

it happens with the PT845, the Strike Two trigger system allows another double-action trigger pull. If it doesn't fire the second time (and it usually will), you can eject the cartridge by working the slide by hand. The feature I appreciate the most is the fact the PT845 may be carried in the traditional cocked-and-locked position.

The slide has forward slanted serrations on both sides for manual cocking, and the sights are excellent — large and easy to see. They consist of a square-notch rear with two white dots matched up with a slanting-post, white-dot front. Both sights are drift adjustable for windage and can be locked into place with a setscrew. The dots won't wear off as they are slightly recessed.

Let's look at feelability first. If a handgun feels good in my hands we are over the first hurdle. Over the past 50+ years, I have tested nearly every semiauto and revolver made. Whatever the reason, those that feel good in my hands just seem to shoot better. It may only be a mind game, but if it feels good I can do it. And the PT845 feels very good. The grip frame feels like it was tailor-made for my hands, and the single-action trigger pull measures out at just over five pounds but feels lighter to me. *Check No. 1: Positive.*

Next come the sights. Shooters in the 19th century must have had awfully good eyes, as sights then were mostly tiny and poorly shaped. Look at any antique single-action revolver and you'll see what I mean. The rear sight was usually a very shallow "V" matched up with a tiny front blade (which may explain the appeal of point-shooting back then).

However, the sights, although excellent, have to shoot to point of aim or be easily adjusted to do so. Right out of the box, this PT845 basically does so with all the loads I tried — from 185 to 230 grains in bullet weight. Of course there's always a slight variation in elevation with different weights;

Full-size .45 ACP semiautos representing two eras: Taurus' double-action, high-capacity 24/7 (top) and the single-action, single-stack PT1911 (bottom).

John's youngest grandson, Brian Panzella, shoots the Taurus PT845. Interchangeable back straps allow it to be tailored to smaller hands as well as larger ones.

12 Rounds
Winchester 230JHP
Personal Protection
843 FPS

This combat silhouette target testifies to the combat-distance potential of the PT845 using Winchester Personal Protection 230-grain JHPs.

however, at self-defense distances they can all be called "on the money." With the PT845's sights, bullets print very slightly to the right for my eyes and hold, a situation easily addressed by drifting the rear sight. *Check No. 2: Positive.*

The third thing to consider is accuracy. Accuracy is not necessarily the same in all pistols considered to be "accurate." A truly accurate match gun will consistently place shots in one inch at 50 yards. It takes a lot of special attention to make a pistol this accurate, and its price will reflect that. For a self-defense pistol, distances will be much shorter and groups of two to three inches at 20 yards are totally acceptable. In checking out the accuracy of the PT845, I found it to be in the one- to two-inch category. No problem there. *Check No. 3: Positive.*

Now we come to the most important attribute — functioning. A semiauto *must* be totally dependable. I tried both handloads and factory loads, FMJs and JHPs, and bullet weights of 185, 200 and 230 grains. Functioning was flawless. Every single round chambered perfectly with never a stutter or failure to feed. Every empty ejected perfectly. *Check No. 4: Perfection.*

The pistol comes with two magazines, two extra back straps and a magazine loader all packed in a padded polymer case. So what's not to like about it? Any regular reader knows I like beautifully finished sixguns or semiautos with exotic grips. Like other polymer-framed pistols, the PT845 does not fit into either category. Anything I do not like about it would be purely based on aesthetics. However, this is not an unattractive .45, and although I can't equip it with ivory stocks, I would feel very comfortable carrying the PT845 to protect me and mine.

When it comes to innovation, Taurus may be at the top of the heap among firearms manufacturers. When I first encountered its products a quarter-century ago, the company was basically making copies of the Smith & Wesson K-frame .38 Special. At that time I had plenty of S&Ws, so I really didn't give the Taurus second look. These pistols have made me think that maybe I made a mistake and should have given Taurus a closer look back then. ◉

THE SEMIAUTOMATICS

Hammerin' out hardball: Over a three-day period this Glock 21 fired 1,000 rounds of Black Hills 230-grain FMJ ammo without a hitch. Rugged reliability is what put Glock pistols on the map.

∞ Rapid-fire combat shooting is where the Glock 21 can really strut its stuff.

THE GLOCK .45

CHAPTER 46

A t the first Shootist Holiday in 1986, all of us up-to-date six-gunners showed up with our Colt, Ruger and Freedom Arms single actions. However, Jerry Danuser had the audacity to bring out a gun we had vaguely heard of but had yet to see — the infamous Glock "plastic gun." Even its *name* sounded sinister.

We were all fairly civil to Danuser (we did not know him well enough to be otherwise at the time), and we all shot the Glock. The following year he showed up with the Glock again, but this time he also had his newly discovered love — a single-action sixgun. We had worked our magic and he'd worked his. Over the years, it has been a long-standing joke among us sixgunners that the Glock was okay to shoot as long as no one recorded it on film!

My first real shooting sessions with several 10mm and .40 S&W Glocks came a few years after that first Shootist

The Glock 21 .45 ACP has a capacity of 14 rounds.

Holiday. I have to admit that they felt good in my hand, shot well and handled easily. After my testing was done and I sent them back, though, I didn't miss them. I still had my Colt Single Actions and Smith & Wesson N-frames. And most importantly, for serious social purposes, I still had my 1911.

I never expected this to change. Ever. I figured I could live quite well without a Glock, thank you.

Apparently I had been a rarity during the first "Glock Decade." No other handgun in history has spawned so many imitators in such a short time. Finally, I couldn't hold out any longer. So I got two of them — one in 10mm, the other in .45 ACP. It was shortly after this, Glock's Northwest District Manager, Chuck Karwan, invited me to a Glock Armorer's Class and Instructor's Workshop.

The Glock 21 (bottom) overcame competition from more conventional 1990s-era double-action .45s such as the Ruger P90 and Smith & Wesson Models 4506 and 4516.

I contacted Rob Sconce of Miniature Machine Corporation and got a pair of MMC combat night sights for the Glocks I would be shooting. And since I had little cartilage left in my wrists, I had both guns Mag-na-Ported as well to reduce torque during long strings of fire, as it is the torque more than the recoil that gives my wrist bones fits. After all, the event would call for more than 1,000 rounds in three days.

To take part in the three-day Glock Workshop, it was necessary to not only bring a Glock, proper holster, ear and eye safety equipment, but also 1,000 rounds of factory ammunition. A final request to Jeff Hoffman of Black Hills resulted in 1,000 rounds of Black Hills 230-grain .45 ACP ammo delivered to my doorstep.

THE GUN ITSELF

Before we go off to the Instructor's Workshop, let's take a look at the Glock pistol itself. Introduced in 1985, the original 9mm Glock 17 is 17 percent polymer and 83 percent steel by weight. So much for it being an "undetectable plastic gun." The magazine holds 17 rounds, but the model number comes not from the cartridge capacity, but from the fact that it represents Gaston Glock's 17th patent.

The orginal Glock 17 has 33 parts (34 for later models). The barrel twist is 1:10 (1:15¾ in the .45 ACP). The slide and barrel were originally impregnated with .003 inch of Tenifer

resulting in a hard finish that registers 69 on the Rockwell scale. (Now they employ a slightly different Nitration process.) A dull black finish is placed over it which is said by the company to be more rust resistant than stainless steel. The "plastic" frame is rated to perform at temperatures of minus 75 F to plus 400 F. It was pointed out, however, that a good-sized dog can do a real number on the polymer grip frame!

One of my concerns with the Glock has always been that of safety. We had all heard "accidental discharge" stories, including at least one of a police chief putting a round through the wall of his office. Is it really possible to fire a round when the Glock is holstered? Is the Glock more prone to ADs than other handguns? These were questions running through my mind. Although by this time I had fired the Glock in all calibers, I did not understand its operation thoroughly.

HI-TECH TRIGGERNOMETRY

The Glock is advertised as having a Safe Action trigger. After going through the Armorer's Class, I would say that there is absolutely no way to fire off a chambered round when the Glock is being holstered if the finger is off the trigger! As with any other semiautomatic, double-action or single-action sixgun, the Glock cannot fire until the trigger is pulled. It will not fire if the side of the trigger is hit or pressed. The trigger safety rides in the middle of the trigger and is a positive lock. There is no way to fire the Glock unless the trigger safety is

John shoots his Glock 21. It may not be pretty, but it always works!

Little big gun: The compact Glock 30 holds 10 rounds of .45 ACP.

pulled, and there is also no way for inertia to fire the Glock if the gun is dropped as long as the trigger safety is intact.

As the trigger safety in the center of the trigger is pressed and the trigger itself is pulled, the firing-pin safety is released, the trigger bar moves forward, and the gun fires. This means there are three safeties in total: the trigger safety, the firing-pin safety and the drop safety. Once the gun is fired, the trigger is reset and all other safeties re-engage. There are no external safeties to disengage, as everything depends upon the operation of the trigger safety. After the training I've had, I now feel perfectly safe carrying a Glock properly holstered with a round in the chamber. But any police department providing Glocks without proper training in their use is doing their officers a real disservice.

LOOKS AREN'T EVERYTHING

My main hangup with the Glock has always been one of aesthetics. They just look like ... *well*, just like they sound, *Glock*. After going through the Armorer's School, I can also now attest to the fact that the interior of the pistols mirrors the exterior. There are no finely honed parts, nothing that would indicate someone spent hours fitting beautifully machined parts. In fact, all parts are totally replaceable without any fitting of any kind. This is a handgun that is completely assembly-line friendly. Even fumble fingered as I am, I'm now qualified as an entry-level Glock armorer. I can totally strip the Glock and replace everything in the right order and place without ever losing any of the parts. I can

change the weight of the trigger pull with no tool other than the Glock punch to remove the pins that hold it all together. That alone speaks extremely well for the simplicity of the design. If I can do it, *anyone* can.

Trigger pulls are set for five pounds at the factory. Weight can be increased to eight pounds by using a connector marked "+", or decreased to 3½ pounds with a connector marked "-". Both are totally drop-in parts with no fitting necessary. Using the factory five-pound connector, the factory coil spring can be easily replaced with a New York trigger which will increase the pull to eight pounds or a New York Plus trigger (a plastic part to replace the standard coil spring) which gives a pull of 12 pounds.

During the workshop, 14 of us learned the functioning of the pistol. Two of us used .45 Glock 21s, and the rest went with 9mm's and .40 S&Ws. Early on, we learned about "resetting" the trigger. As the trigger is pulled, the gun fires, the trigger is still in its rearward position. It is not necessary to allow the trigger to return completely to the original position. It only needs to be reset. That is, the shooter can feel the trigger come forward and click into place. This allows the Glock to be fired quickly and accurately.

Weightwise, the Glock 21 — fully loaded with 13 rounds — comes in at 40 ounces, or about the same weight as an empty 1911. For three days, the Glock/Black Hills combo performed perfectly. The only malfunctions were purposely caused when we placed empty brass in the magazine for practice in clearing stoppages. We shot extensively at distances from 9 feet to 25 yards, most of which was at maximum speed (or at least *my* maximum speed). I never once pulled a bullet off target which, to me, perfectly illustrates the pointability of the Glock in general and the 21 in particular.

We learned the proper way to oil the pistol — a total of five drops on the front of the barrel, the barrel hood and lugs, inside the top of the slide, slide grooves and connector/trigger bar contact area. All this was done before the actual shooting began, and my Glock 21 was neither cleaned nor oiled at any other time until the end of the 1,000-round period. It performed perfectly, though the inside of the slide, exterior of the barrel and interior parts were coated with black soot. The breech face was streaked with soot, but the extractor was still clean. Disassembling the Glock 21 was easy using the techniques I learned during the Armorer's Class.

Highlights of the whole shooting experience included single and multiple targets, speed and tactical reloads, two-handed shooting (Weaver, Isosceles, etc.), strong- and weak-hand shooting, drawing, shooting and reloading with one arm injured and speed shooting from the holster. (I started to say "from the leather," but I was using the Glock plastic Sport/Combat holster throughout the course as the leather holster I had would not work properly.)

Of particular importance were the stoppage drills consisting of learning how to clear Phase I stoppages (slap the base of the magazine, rack the slide once) and Phase II stoppages (remove the magazine, rack the slide several times, replace the magazine). No one going through this class should freeze up if a stoppage occurs.

I found out later my particular Glock 21 really likes Hornady ammunition. And my 25-yard results prove it. The Hornady 185-grain XTP clocks out at 902 fps and places four shots in 1¼ inches. The 200-grain XTP does 872 fps and 1⅜ inches; 200-grain Match, 887 fps, 1⅛ inches; and the 230-grain XTP +P clocks out just under 1,000 fps with a most satisfying group of 1⅛ inches. My Glock 21 also

likes my handloads with the RCBS #45-201 and 6.0 grains of WW452AA clocking out over 950 fps and grouping well under 1 inch, while the Speer 185-grain GDHP over 9.0 grains of WAP clocks out at 825 fps and groups four shots in 1 inch.

WHAT I LEARNED

Before the seminar I would not have considered carrying a Glock. That has all changed. I now feel totally confident in my ability with one, as well as in the accuracy and reliability of the basic design.

But all my hardcore sixgunner friends need not worry. My personality hasn't changed totally. I don't salivate when I see a Glock as I do when a Colt Single Action Army is encountered. My heart won't do palpitations with a Glock as it does with a Smith & Wesson Triple-Lock. I won't try to fit the Glock with ivory grips or embellish it with engraving, nor will I carry it in a fancy floral-carved holster. The Glock is not built to be a piece of art. It receives an "A" for engineering and an "F" for intrinsic artistic value. It does not have one single sensuous line to its design. It is the same ugly duckling it has always been. But it becomes much more than a graceful swan when loaded for battle and strapped on for serious business. I would not hesitate to use the Glock .45 to protect me and mine. ◎

This type of 25-yard accuracy — with a good cross-section of factory ammo — is one of the main things John likes about the Glock 21.

THE SEMIAUTOMATICS

Kimber's Ultra CDP is a compact take on the "Custom Defense Package" concept.

KIMBER'S .45 1911s

CHAPTER 47

The 1911 is still Number One when it comes to full-sized semiautos, and the Number One supplier of 1911s today is Kimber. In a few short decades, Kimber has captured over 40 percent of the 1911 market. With such a large number of competitors, Kimber has to be doing something right. Recently its Stainless Steel Target Model II got my attention to the extent I ordered four of them — chambered in .45 ACP, .38 Super, 9mm Parabellum and 10mm. Kimber offers a long list of 1911s; however, my choice was made easier by the factI wanted adjustable sights, but I wanted them on a

John's "Kimber stable" includes (from the top down) the Stainless Target II, the Compact Aluminum and the CDP II.

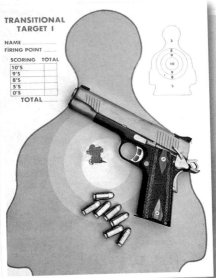

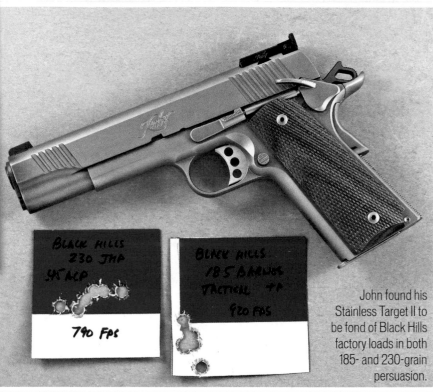

At combat yardage, the alloy-framed CDP II really showed its potential as a defensive 1911.

BLACK HILLS 230 JHP .45 ACP

790 Fps

BLACK HILLS 185 BARNES TACTICAL +P 920 FPS

John found his Stainless Target II to be fond of Black Hills factory loads in both 185- and 230-grain persuasion.

basic 1911 without such things as ambidextrous safeties, light/laser rails, beveled magazine wells and fiber-optic sights.

All of these features, of course, have their place in certain situations. But they are normally not necessary for everyday use, and the fact that none of them are found on the Stainless Target II made it even more attractive to me. After more than 100 years of "improvements" to the 1911, to me the most essential options are to be found in the sights, trigger and grip safety. On the Stainless Target II these three items are exactly as I would custom-order them. Sights are big and bold and black, with a fully adjustable rear and a post front. Both are set in a dovetail, and the serrated front post slants to the front so it won't catch in a holster. And speaking of holsters, Zach Davis, a local craftsman, came up with two beautifully constructed, high-riding rigs of exotic leather to carry any one of my four Kimbers.

ESSENTIAL ELEMENTS

On the Stainless Target II, the barrel, stainless steel bushing and trigger are all match grade. The lightweight aluminum trigger has three weight-reducing holes drilled from side to side and matches up with a Commander-style skeletonized hammer. The beavertail grip safety has a cutout to cradle the hammer, plus a very slight memory bump to make sure the grip safety is depressed when firing the pistol.

The top of the slide stop is nicely checkered as is the magazine release and flat mainspring housing. The top of the thumb safety is serrated for positive operation, and the slide has striations front and rear for ease of manipulation. As far as fit and finish goes, the slide is tightly fitted to the frame

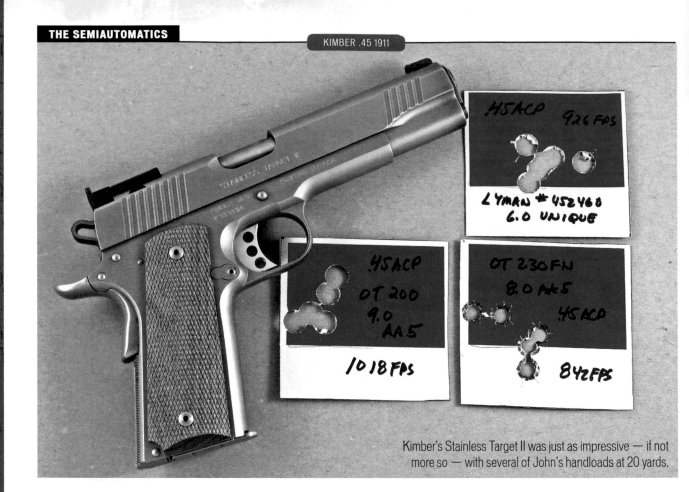

.45ACP 926 FPS

LYMAN #452460 6.0 UNIQUE

.45ACP OT 200 9.0 AA5

1018 FPS

OT 230FN 8.0 AA5 .45ACP

842 FPS

Kimber's Stainless Target II was just as impressive — if not more so — with several of John's handloads at 20 yards.

and the overall finish — except for the black sights — is matte stainless. All four pistols came with checkered rubber grips, so to tell them apart by caliber easily I replaced the grip panels with Herrett's 1911 panels of different woods.

Despite the other chamberings Kimber 1911s are available in, the most popular choice still remains the original .45 Automatic Colt Pistol.

As picky about holsters as he is about grip panels, John's Kimber .45s ride securely in leather by Zach Davis.

The 1911 .45 ACP remains the most popular self-defense/fighting handgun available. The Stainless Target II can serve for shooting bullseye competition, or it can be carried as a self-defense pistol, or simply as an everyday working gun. It's impervious to more lousy weather than I intend to spend much time in, and it has proven to be exceptionally accurate.

Thus far, I've fired mine extensively with 12 factory loads and nine cast-bullet handloads. Black Hills' 230-grain FMJs and JHPs both place five shots at 20 yards in 1⅛ inches, clocking at 781 fps and 790 fps, respectively. I get the same results with the Black Hills 185-grain Barnes Tactical +P load, which moves out at over 900 fps. The 185-grain JHP +P Black from Black Hills clocks nearly 1,000 fps and groups in 1⅜ inches. This accuracy is duplicated by my handloads with the Oregon Trail 200-grain SWC over 6.0 grains of WW452AA (965 fps).

I got a most pleasant surprise when I found a large box of reloads at the back of

Kimber's Ultra Covert II is
mission-specific indeed. It's
the embodiment of minimum size
and maximum power, all combined
with a two-tone color scheme and
Crimson Trace LaserGrips.

one of my storage shelves going back more than 25 years and consisting of Lyman's #452460SWC over 6.0 grains of Unique. This old favorite of mine clocks 926 fps and puts five shots in ⅞ inch at 20 yards .

CARRYING THE TORCH

I entered high school in 1952 and that was also the same year I first found a copy of *Gun Digest*. Most of the guns listed 60 years ago are no longer available. One that is, the Colt Government Model, was available in two versions in 1952, both blue and in .45 ACP or .38 Super. Another Colt

1911 variant had just arrived. At the time it was called the "The New Lightning Colt — The Zephyr Commander." This shorter and lighter 1911 was offered in the two standard chamberings as well as 9mm. By the time I started seriously shooting after high school, most of us had Government Models, although they were generally military surplus guns from both world wars.

I was still in grade school when Colt came out with its first Lightweight Commander .45 ACP, cutting the barrel and slide length of the standard Government Model by just under one inch and going with an alloy frame. The

SEMIAUTO PISTOLS AND THEIR CARTRIDGES

THE BOOK OF THE .45

Kimber offers specialized 1911s for virtually any purpose. This one is the aptly-named "Tactical Entry," replete with integral rail for a light/laser unit.

result was that the 26-ounce Commander is two-thirds the weight of a standard 1911. The Commander has a military name simply because it was actually designed as a possible replacement for the 1911, which had been in service for 40 years. Apparently the military was looking for something smaller and lighter. Kimber has been cataloging such a .45 for quite some time, and I have been shooting its lightweight 1911 for a couple of decades.

Kimber's alloy-framed full-sized .45 ACP 1911 is its Custom CDP II. This self-defense pistol takes everything right about the 1911 and the Commander and combines them into one pistol. The aluminum alloy frame is finished

matte black in what Kimber calls KimPro II, while the slide is brushed satin stainless. The ambidextrous thumb safety, beavertail grip safety slide stop, magazine release and grip screws are all stainless steel. It has a skeletonized, match-grade aluminum trigger and blued skeletonized steel hammer. The flat mainspring housing is also stainless steel and is finely checkered for a secure grip.

Factory stocks are double-diamond rosewood; however, I have replaced them with rosewood stocks from Herrett's. Both the front and rear sight sit low in the slide in dovetails. (The rear is adjustable for windage and can be locked in place with a setscrew.) The sight setup? Three-dot tritium.

"CDP," incidentally, stands for "Custom Defense Package." The entire pistol has been "melted." There are no sharp edges to be found anywhere — nothing to catch on clothing, hoster or hands. It's the ultimate "user-friendly" .45. At 31 ounces, the CDP is 5 ounces heavier than Colt's original Lightweight Commander, but still 8 ounces lighter than a full-size steel 1911. Yes, it is more difficult to shoot and felt recoil *is* more noticeable.

John believes his Compact Aluminum (bottom) to be the first of Kimber's series of compact 1911s. It's shown here with a 1914-vintage commercial Model 1911 (middle) and a Colt Commander (top) for comparison.

However, the more you shoot the CDP, the less obvious the difference is. Serious practice with 230-grain hardball will help you cope with the increased recoil. Self-defense pistols are certainly carried much more than they are shot, and the half-pound difference of the CDP compared to a steel 1911 makes a huge difference when carried regularly.

OTHER OPTIONS

Kimber's catalog features an extensive list of custom 1911s, a couple of which are pictured in the "Gallery of Government Models" chapter. In addition to full-sized 1911s, Kimber also offers several compact versions. I believe my Compact Aluminum is the first such model Kimber offered. As the name implies, it is both small and lightweight, quite a bit smaller than the original Colt Commander. Barrel length is 3½ inches, while the grip frame is the same size as the Colt Officers Model. Surprisingly, the weight is identical to that of the Lightweight Commander. Yes, it kicks with full-house loads, but it carries oh-so-nicely!

As the name implies the frame is an aluminum alloy finished in matte black, the slide is steel, and instead of a bushing there is a sharply tapered barrel and a full-length guide rod. Sights are excellent — basically the

same as those found on the CDP except for the lack of the tritium white dots. Both hammer and trigger are skeletonized, the thumb safety is extended, and the grip safety is of the beavertail design. The flat mainspring housing is checkered for a secure grip, which is also aided by the double-diamond checkered rosewood stocks. Even with the small grip frame, the magazine holds seven rounds.

With the CDP as my main carry pistol and the Compact Aluminum as a backup loaded with CCI Blazer 200-grain "Flying Ashtrays," I certainly feel well armed. ◎

One of John's pet carry 1911s is his Kimber Compact Aluminum, particularly when it's stoked with seven rounds of CCI Blazer 200-grain "Flying Ashtray" ammunition.

THE SEMIAUTOMATICS

Accuracy is obviously no problem with the XDM .45 ACP, whether with Hornady factory ammo or with one of John's cast-bullet handloads.

.45 ACP
H&G #68
7.0 UNIQUE
1,043 FPS

.45 ACP
HORNADY
185 XTP JHP
959 FPS

SPRINGFIELD ARMORY'S
.45 SEMIAUTOS

CHAPTER 48

After attending a Springfield Armory writers' seminar in the closing years of the last century, I asked for several models to be shipped back to me for some serious testing. We had met in Mississippi in November and, being from Idaho, I actually thought it would be warm down there. I couldn't have been more wrong. I nearly froze to death! Unfortunately, the cold weather put a hasty end to much of the shooting. I'd have to wait until I got home to do some serious range work.

MIL-SPEC DUO

Two of the guns I ordered were Springfield's military-style 1911s — Mil-Specs in both .45 ACP and .38 Super. The choice of the .45 is obvious, as this has always been the number one chambering for military style 1911s. I bought my first .45 ACP 1911 sometime around 1956, and it came complete with a flap holster for a total expenditure of less than a trip to McDonald's today.

Springfield Armory's Mil-Spec 1911s emulate — just as

Springfield Armory Mil-Specs are appropriately carried in period-style leather.

the name implies — the original military 1911. These are not accurized pistols with fully adjustable sights, but if you're looking for traditional features and quality in a no-nonsense package, the Mil-Spec is for you. Long before other companies celebrated the 100th Anniversary of the 1911 with special-issue, traditional-style pistols, Springfield Armory was already there.

Springfield's Mil-Spec deviates from the original design by having much easier-to-see, three-dot sights that are big, bold and square. Springfield calls them Hi-Viz Fixed Combat, and they are a great improvement over the originals.

My Mil-Specs have a Parkerized finish, and I made only one change to both guns, namely replaced the grip panels with exotic woods from Herrett's, fully checkered on one and diamond checkered on the other. I had originally planned to fully customize the .38 Super; however, it proved to be such a good shooter I've never touched it. The .45 ACP version has been shot a lot over the past couple of decades with the top factory load being Federal's 230-grain Hi-Shok, which clocks out at over 900 fps and groups at just over an inch.

THE TRP

The Mil-Spec .45 is strictly plain-Jane and is set up for hard use without worrying about

hurting the Parkerized finish whatsoever. At the opposite end of the spectrum is the Springfield Armory Tactical pistol, the TRP. This one has all the bells and whistles that the Mil-Spec lacks. The TRP is all stainless steel with a match-grade barrel and trigger. Sights are low-riding, three-dot Novaks. Both the post front and the rear sight slope forward to reduce glare.

The slide is tightly fitted to the frame with serrations both front and rear for easy manipulation, and the ejection port is lowered and relieved. The safety is ambidextrous. The beavertail grip safety has a memory bump and is relieved at the top to accept the skeletonized hammer when it's cocked. Both the flat mainspring housing and the front

Low-light accuracy accessorizing: The XD's utility is enhanced with a Crimson Trace LaserGrip.

strap are finely checkered. Two things I don't particularly care for are the bolt-on beveled magazine well and the bumper on the bottom of the magazine. But both are easily removed (and have been).

I can't think of anything else needed on a tactical 1911 other than what is already on the TRP, although I did add Herrett's skip-checkered grip panels which set the TRP off very nicely. This is without a doubt one of my favorite 1911s, and it shoots extremely well.

V10 ULTRA COMPACT

Another most attractive Springfield 1911 is the V10 Ultra Compact. It's basically the same size as the Colt Officers Model (and will accept Herrett's cocobolo checkered panels made for the Officers Model). The V10 gets its name from the fact it is ported with a one-inch slot on each side of the front sight, revealing five round holes. The sights are the same low riding Novak-style as found on the TRP, but they are all black (no dots). The V10 Ultra Compact has a two-tone finish with a stainless steel frame and a blued slide. The length of the tapered, bushingless barrel is 3¼ inches.

This is simply one trim little pistol for concealed carry. For my use it is loaded with Blazer "Flying Ashtray" 200-grain JHPs. With its all-steel construction, felt recoil is held to a minimum. Unfortunately, it is no longer cataloged but is certainly worth searching for in used gun outlets.

THE RANGE OFFICER

One of Springfield's latest 1911s is the Range Officer, basically an upgraded Mil-Spec. It's got black, high-visibility sights consisting of a square-notch rear and sloping-post front. The rear is fully adjustable, and the front is set in a dovetail for windage adjustment or easy replacement. Slide-to-frame fit is just about perfect. The lightweight aluminum front-serrated trigger has three holes, and the light-weight hammer is also skeletonized. The trigger pull on my pistol weighed 5¾ pounds. The beavertail grip safety has a memory bump, and the mainspring housing is of the original flat style. The whole package is reminiscent of customized military .45s from the mid-20th century.

Springfield advertises the Range Officer as being suitable for

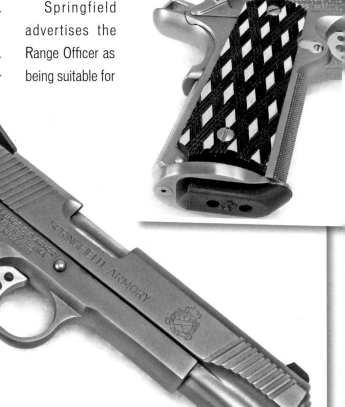

John feels the TRP is a perfectly styled fighting handgun. The beveled magazine well extension and magazine rubber bumper pad (inset) are removable.

Fourteen rounds of .45 ACP: The Springfield Armory XDM 5.25 classifies as a high-capacity, big-bore semiauto.

competition right out of the box. Shooting it was a pure pleasure. I got outstanding results with Black Hills 230-grain JHPs and FMJs. The standard-pressure JHP clocks out at 770 fps and puts five shots in ⅞ inch. The FMJ version gave me the same velocity while cutting group size to ⅝ inch. In addition, what intrigues me is the fact the Black Hills 230-grain lead RN groups at just over one inch. Winchester's 185-grain Silvertip, 230-grain JHP and 230-grain FMJ all grouped at 1¼ inches. This pistol is *definitely* a keeper.

These full-size Springfield Armory .45 ACPs pretty much cover everything to be done with a 1911. There is the Mil-Spec for heavy-duty outdoor use, the TRP for self-defense or law-enforcement and the competition-ready Range Officer. Throw in the Ultra Compact for concealment use and Springfield's got everything pretty well covered.

ENTER THE XD

The times they certainly are a-changin'! A half-century ago sixguns ruled. Today semiautos outsell revolvers by a considerable margin. Fifty years ago I couldn't afford $140 for a sixgun for which I gladly pay 10 times as much today. Anyone paying attention has seen prices rise on just about everything, in spite of the government's denial of inflation, and especially so on guns. With firearms being so expensive, the best possible solution is to have one suitable for many tasks. That brings us to the polymer-framed, striker-fired Springfield Armory XDMs. The "M" in XDM stands for "match-grade barrel," and this pistol is now also available as the XDM 5.25 and the XDS.

The Springfield Armory XDMs are designed first and foremost for competition, however they also serve well as concealed carry pistols, for home defense, for hunting (within reason), informal target shooting and for the fine, old gentlemanly sport of plinking. They will kill tin cans with

the best of them. The older I get, the more I appreciate a longer barrel and the subsequent longer sight radius. The XDM 5.25 designation comes from the fact it has a 5¼-inch barrel. This — along with the fact the rear sight is flush with the back of the slide — allows a sight radius of 7¼ inches.

A CRASH COURSE

I've often said the best thing about being a gunwriter isn't all the guns I get to test, but all the grand folks I get to meet. Two of the finest are the Leathams, father and son. For many years father Nyle was a photographer who specialized in covering shooting matches. He was a joy to be around. Nyle is gone now, but anyone who doesn't know of his son Rob is certainly out of the loop when it comes to handguns.

About 20 years ago, I attended Rob's shooting school

The Compact XDS .45, despite its small dimensions, can definitely shoot well.

Springfield's XDM line is offered with the option of a black slide or satin silver slide.

On the top of the slide is a loaded chamber indicator, and a cocking indicator protrudes from the slide's rear. There are grooves on both sides of the slide below the rear sight and also toward the front below the cutout to aid in manually working the slide. On the left side, we find cutouts on the slide for the frame-mounted takedown lever and slide stop. The barrel, which is fitted to the slide, is match grade and Melonite coated. The slide is available in black or a satin silver finish. Before this particular XDM model, the longest barrel available had been 4½ inches.

Working our way down the pistol brings us to the black polymer frame. Behind the trigger there's an ambidextrous magazine release. Two safeties are found on the frame; one in the center of the trigger must be engaged in conjunction with a grip safety before the XDM will fire. The integral grip has molded in serrations both front and rear. The XDM 5.25 comes with three interchangeable backstraps: small, medium and large. They are held in place via an easily removable pin across the bottom. (A tool for this is provided.) I went with the smallest size to give me the easiest

outside Phoenix, Arizona, and received a most warm (115 degrees F!) welcome. The only thing that saved me was regularly scheduled trips to the air-conditioned blockhouse and plenty of Gatorade. As we were shooting double taps, I kept trying to keep them close to each other. Rob said it wasn't necessary, but he made me feel awfully good when he told me, "I didn't know gunwriters could *shoot*!" That made my day.

Rob happens to be a sponsored shooter for Springfield Armory and has had a lot to do with the latest XDM. It's offered in 9mm, .40 S&W and .45 ACP, with magazine capacities of 19, 16 and 13 rounds, respectively. I requested the 9mm and .45 ACP for testing. The front sight, set in a dovetail, is a post with a red fiber optic insert. The rear sight is set low in the slide and is fully adjustable for windage and elevation. Both windage and elevation screws are clearly marked as to direction, and there are marks on the top of the rear sight assembly matched up with a scribed line on the sight itself for a setting reference.

As we look at the slide itself the first thing we notice is a cutout measuring 2 inches long by ½ inch wide behind the front sight. This performs two functions. First it cuts down on the weight of the slide, making cycling faster and reducing felt recoil. It also puts more weight to the rear of the pistol, which most shooters prefer.

Springfield Armory 1911s (from top left, clockwise): TRP, Range Officer, Mil-Spec and V10 Compact.

access to the trigger. This arrangement felt closest to giving me a 1911-type grip. The XDM also has an accessory rail molded into the underside of the frame. The front of the trigger guard is squared off, with a slight hook and serrations for those who prefer to wrap their offhand finger there.

The XDM 5.25, like all Springfield pistols, comes in a lockable plastic carrying case. Accessories include a magazine loader, a polymer holster adjustable for tension and which has a flap to fit over and behind your belt so it isn't necessary to shuck your belt to remove the holster. Each XDM also comes with three magazines, plus a polymer, tension-adjustable, double-magazine pouch.

I found the XDM — in any persuasion — to perform flawlessly. The .45 digests jacketed bullets from 185-grain JHPs to 230-grain FMJs as well as cast bullets from 200 to 230 grains. One of my favorite handloads is the H&G #68 (or RCBS #45-201 or Oregon Trail Laser Cast 200 SWC). This 200-grain SWC is loaded over 7.0 to 7.5 grains of Unique for 1,000 to 1,075 fps. The 7.5-grain load — which came from Jeff Cooper — is about as much power as one should expect from a standard .45 ACP.

Before receiving the XDM 5.25 I had been shooting the older standard XD .45 with a 4.5-inch barrel. It is still a favored pistol of mine, but I definitely prefer the longer barrel on this newer version.

Life is full of trade-offs, and there are many of them when it comes to firearms. For many years I would have preferred to have a 1911 or a .44 or .45 double-action Smith & Wesson revolver as my carry gun, but circumstances dictated something smaller. I went with a J-frame, a Smith & Wesson Chief's Special .38 with a bobbed hammer and tuned action. It went in the top of my boot. It certainly was harder to

Slim and single-stacked: The Springfield Armory V10 Compact has a magazine capacity of seven rounds.

The Range Officer comes competition ready — right out of the box.

access but virtually impossible to detect. At the time, the J-frame was not just the best choice, it was the only choice.

Today, thanks to Springfield Armory, we can literally have our cake and eat it too. Not only did the company offer the XDM 5.25, it also went the other way to shrink the size of the XD series .45 ACP. The result is the XDS. Comparing it side by side with the full-sized XD reveals just how much engineering went into this downsizing project.

At 4.4 inches in height, the XDS is 80 percent of the size of the original XD. Lengthwise at 6.3 inches, the XDS comes in at 76 percent of the original. Its 21.5-ounce weight is just barely over ⅔ that of the XD. Not much can be accomplished in the front-to-back dimensions of the grip and still stay with a .45 ACP cartridge. However, at

SPRINGFIELD ARMORY .45 SEMIAUTO

John wrings out the abbreviated XDS offhand out in the wide-open spaces. From the bench, his results were impressive (shown below).

both slide and barrel. This coating has proven to be exceptionally durable in holding up under adverse weather conditions as well as sweat or body oils. Five molded serrations are found on the slide directly in front of the rear sight providing a firm grip for operating the slide; these are also finger friendly with no sharp edges.

The sights consist of a red fiber-optic front set in a dovetail and a low-profile square notch rear with two white dots. There are no sharp edges on the rear sight to interfere with either concealment or working the slide.

The polymer frame is also black having an integral grip frame with molded-in, small-square checkered blocks providing a secure gripping surface. Interchangeable backstrap panels with the same gripping surface which allow custom tailoring to a particular hand are also included. On the bottom of the grip frame right in front of the trigger guard there is an abbreviated one-slot Picatinny rail for attaching a laser sight or flashlight type sight.

.949 inch in width, the XDS has been shrunk to 78 percent of the XD. Those are significant downsizing figures. Of course, there are still trade-offs when comparing the two pistols. The larger pistol is certainly much easier and much more comfortable to shoot; capacity is 13+1 compared to the 5+1 (or 7+1) of the XDS. If I needed a full-sized .45 ACP in a belt holster, one of my top choices would certainly be the XD. However, when it comes to *real* concealment, it would be hard to come up with anything better than the super-small XDS and still stay with the .45 ACP.

Taking a closer look at the XDS, we find many of the same features present on the full-sized XD .45; everything that is except size and weight. In this miniature 3.3-inch barreled XD, the color is all black with a Melonite finish on

The grip frame is cut high behind the trigger guard and also above the grip safety to allow the highest possible gripping which also ensures the grip safety is positively pressed when firing. There is also a trigger safety; it must be pressed simultaneously with the grip safety or the XDS will not fire. This trigger feature is known as the Ultra Safety Assurance (USA), and it locks the trigger against

I bought my first .45 ACP 1911 sometime around 1956, and it came complete with a flap holster for a total expenditure of less than a trip to McDonald's today.

accidental discharge until rearward pressure is directly applied. This trigger has a short travel and a short reset, making it very easy for follow-up shots. Trigger pull on this particular XDS weighs 7.8 pounds. On the left side of the polymer grip are two levers, the slide stop and the takedown lever; there is no thumb safety. There's also a loaded chamber indicator on top of the slide.

Disassembling the XDS (a very easy operation) reveals two recoil springs, one inside the other, which are necessarily stout to provide reliability in both feeding and firing. The disassembly lever cannot be engaged with a magazine in the pistol, nor can the magazine be reinserted when the disassembly lever is up.

The ambidextrous magazine release is directly behind the trigger guard and right above a dished-out indentation to allow a high grip. Two different magazines are available. The flush-fitting version holds five rounds and would certainly be my choice for carry, while the optional magazine holds seven rounds and comes with a fitted sleeve to extend the grip frame.

An included accessory is a polymer holster adjustable for tension which has a flap to fit over your belt. It isn't necessary to remove your belt to take off the holster. In addition to the two different backstraps, the XDS also came with three magazines plus a tension-adjustable, double-magazine pouch, also of polymer. Two of the magazines are extended seven-round versions with collared slip-on finger extensions. For my use the XDS with the five-round magazine is carried in the holster provided by Springfield Armory, or tucked

in behind the belt, or in my jacket pocket, or even possibly in the top of my boot. (In fact I have been carrying it in the top of my boot, and it is even more comfortable carried thus than the .38 Chiefs Special was. It is especially accessible when seated, making such a carry desirable when driving.) It is backed up by the two, seven-round magazines carried in the magazine pouch or in the pocket.

I tested several full-sized XD .45s including the original 5-inch version and the 5.25-inch Competition XD. Grouping was done at 20 to 25 yards, and I also did some long-range plinking at rocks. However, the XDS was test-fired at a self-defense distance of seven yards. Nine different loads were tried from four different manufacturers ranging from 185-grain JHPs to 230-grain FMJs. Four loads put four shots in ¾ inch in five instances and one inch for the other four. That is excellent performance from a wide range of ammunition choices.

I've shot literally hundreds of thousands of rounds through many types of .45s, and I've never found a better choice for maximum concealment combined with maximum effectiveness than the XDS. ◉

Polymer palette: Springfield's XD line comes in earth tones as well as utilitarian all-black.

SEMIAUTO PISTOLS AND THEIR CARTRIDGES

THE BOOK OF THE .45

THE SEMIAUTOMATICS

Here are three of Iver Johnson's Philippine-made 1911s — the Eagle, the 1911A1 and the Hawk.

FOREIGN .45s

CHAPTER 49

There's a great deal of interest in both 1911-pattern .22s as well as .22 conversion units. Some work, some don't. I walked into my local gun shop, and the boys directed my attention to a new 1911/.22. One of them had already purchased one for his own use and was quite taken with it. So on his word I bought the Umarex 1911/.22, which is manufactured by German Sporting Guns. It has proven to be an excellent rimfire.

The apple doesn't fall too far from the tree! John's grandson Brian John Panzella tries his hand with one of Iver Johnson's imported 1911s.

THE TURKISH CONNECTION

Being so satisfied with the .22 version, I was happy to see Umarex was offering a full-sized .45 known as the Regent Model 100, and I was curious enough to order one. This gun is made in Turkey with an MSRP of $499. I will say, in this case, you'll get more than you pay for. A gun at this price has no business shooting this well! Especially considering it has none of the so-called upgrades we find necessary for doing our best with a 1911.

Virtually everything about the Regent is reminiscent of a WW II-era 1911A1. The finish is matte black. The controls are the same size and configuration as those found on my 1914-manufactured commercial Colt 1911. The serrations on the arched mainspring housing and on the back of the slide are pure military style. There's no beavertail grip safety here, and the hammer is basic G.I. The sights are the same small size found on the original 1911, except they do give you a square-notch sight picture. Slide-to-frame fit, while

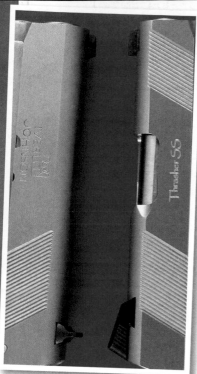

Right: Two types of fixed sights are offered, old-school (left) and a modern style (right).

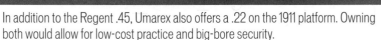

In addition to the Regent .45, Umarex also offers a .22 on the 1911 platform. Owning both would allow for low-cost practice and big-bore security.

not equivalent to a $2,000 custom gun, is much tighter than you'd expect. The takedown procedure is exactly the same as on any 1911.

One noticeable departure is in the grip area. There seems to be more metal showing on both sides of each grip panel. Removal of the magazine shows the reason for this — the grip frame of the Regent is thicker than any others I've seen. Obviously, extra strength has been built into this area. The Hogue grips supplied with the Regent are highly functional checkered rubber. However, I took the opportunity to try a new set of grips designed by my friend and fellow writer Pat Cascio. Pat spent a year working on various designs for his Code Zero grips (available from Mil-Tac). The result is an all-weather grip which basically "grabs hold" of your hand, thanks to a deeply inletted "Z" pattern on both panels surrounded by diamond checkering. There is also a scalloped area which allows easy access to the magazine release.

In testing the Regent I used six different Black Hills loads — the 185-grain JHP, plus 230-grain RNL, FMJ and three types of JHPs. Both the standard-velocity RNL and JHP grouped five shots in one inch at 20 yards. The average for all six loads combined was just 1.4 inches. I have .45s costing twice as much which won't do as well. The Turks are obviously doing *something* right.

I was surprised by the excellent performance of this

pistol, considering the small sights and its less-than-desirable trigger pull — seven pounds with a fair amount of creep, both of which can easily be corrected. Once they are, the Regent is slated to be part of the Taffin Family "Beater Gun" collection. This term came from my oldest grandson. His dad bought a used Ford 4x4 for hauling stuff and running errands. Since it was well used and could be employed for any task, my grandson called it the "Beater Truck," a term which carried over to any workhorse gun that anyone in the family can use without worrying about scratching it up or wearing it out.

BIRDS OF PREY

One of my favorite old westerns is from 1950. It's called *The Eagle and the Hawk* with John Payne and Thomas Gomez. Someone at Iver Johnson must also be a fan of old movies as they are now offering 1911s, two of which are named the Eagle and the Hawk, along with a 1911A1. I got my hands on all three. Iver Johnson has been around since 1883 and is mostly known for low-cost, double-action revolvers. Now they are part of the 1911 scene, importing semiauto .45s from the Philippines. Since they were preproduction test guns, it wasn't surprising to find a problem. All have trigger pulls which are way too heavy for my tastes, ranging from 6¾ to 8 pounds. But this is a problem that is easily fixed.

The major problem was with the sights. The problem was

Mix and match: The Thrasher series accepts Officers Model grip panels.

The Thrasher is built on an Officers Model platform and employs a tapered barrel and guide rod.

not the quality or the style, but rather how they were affixed to the Eagle and Hawk. Both rear sights, adjustable on the Eagle and fixed combat style on the Hawk, were fitted into dovetails. The first time each gun was fired, the rear sights slid right out of the dovetail. I took them to my gunsmith at Buckhorn, and he discovered the dovetail slot on the frame was not the right size. So he did a bit of welding on the slot to obtain a proper fit and also made a new, larger diameter, elevation adjustment screw for the rear sight on the Eagle. They now work perfectly.

I consider it part of my job to find problems such as this before production. In this case it worked and Iver Johnson made the necessary changes. Except for the problems I've noted, the Iver Johnson 1911 lineup seems to be very well made.

The Eagle and the Hawk are exceptional values. They come with eight-shot magazines with a padded base, a flat mainspring housing and beavertail grip safety. The slides have forward slanting grooves on both sides fore and aft for easy

slide manipulation. Any regular readers know my aversion to most factory grips, and I will equip all of these Iver Johnsons with custom stocks, simply because I prefer to personalize my pistols. However, the factory stocks are exceptionally attractive – checkered with large smooth diamonds around the grip screws and an owl head lasered into the center.

THE EAGLE

The Eagle comes with a matte or blued finish. Both the trigger and hammer are skeletonized, and the slide release and thumb safety are extended. The magazine drops easily when the release button is pushed.

The trigger pull on mine weighed seven pounds. It was originally test-fired with nine different loads with five-shot groups at 20 yards running from 1⅜ to 2¾ inches. The most accurate factory loads were the Black Hills 230-grain FMJ, Cor-Bon's 200-grain JHP+P (998 fps) and CCI Blazer 200-grain JHP (964 fps) and the CCI 230-grain FMJ (892 fps). My all-time favorite handload – the RCBS #45-201 SWC over 7.0 grains of Unique – punched a five-shot, 1⅜-inch group at 20 yards while clocking an average muzzle velocity of 972 fps. However, the same over 5.0 grains of Bullseye clocked 895 fps while grouping an amazing ⅝ inch for six shots. Needless to say, this Eagle did not go back to the factory.

THE HAWK

The Hawk is Iver Johnson's Commander-sized 1911 and, except for the sights and shorter frame and slide, it has all of the same features as the Eagle. The fixed rear sight is "melted," that is, there are no rough edges to catch on clothing.

The Regent .45 is a basic no-frills, eight-shot .45 ACP. It performs way out of proportion to its cost, as these targets show.

BLACK HILLS 230 JHP
824 FPS

BLACK HILLS 230 FMJ
802 FPS

Despite a heavier trigger pull than he would have preferred, John got excellent groups with this particular Thrasher, although there was a drop-off in velocity from the 3⅛-inch barrel.

A Turkish take on an American classic: John cuts loose with the Regent.

Mine came in the matte finish, which makes it a natural for packing in a Leather Arsenal IWB holster.

Of the three test guns, the Hawk had the worst trigger pull at eight pounds. Even so, I managed some excellent groups with it. The best factory loads for the Hawk proved to be Black Hills 230-grain JHP +P (926 fps) and the CCI Blazer 230-grain FMJ (888 fps). Both grouped into 1½ inches.

THE 1911A1

The third Iver Johnson offering is the 1911A1 — a basic matte-finished GI gun with an extended grip safety and standard hammer and trigger. The sights are fixed with a black, square-notch rear sight mated up with a slanted post front. The slide-to-frame fit is excellent with no discernible play. The trigger on the 1911A1 proved to be the best of the three pistols at 6¾ pounds. The sights are right on the money for my eyes and hold, with the best factory groups running 1⅜ inches for five shots at 20 yards. This was accomplished with both the Black Hills 230-grain FMJ (880 fps) and the Cor-Bon 200-grain JHP+P (1,016 fps).

SMALLER BIRDS

Iver Johnson's next batch of 1911-style .45s stays with the bird theme. Joining the Eagle and the Hawk is a whole flock of Thrashers. The original Iver Johnsons were full-size and Commander-size. The Thrashers are all Officers Model size (grip panels made for Officers Model Colts readily fit them). My four test Thrashers are all chambered in .45 ACP, with a barrel length of 3⅛ inches, overall length of 6⅞ inches, overall height of 4⅞ inches, and an unloaded weight

of 34 ounces. Magazine capacity is seven rounds, and each magazine has a bumper pad on the bottom.

The four finishes are polished stainless, satin stainless, polished blue and matte blue. Thrashers have Commander-style hammers and beavertail grip safeties with a memory bump. Barrels are tapered to a larger diameter at the front, and all have guide rods. Lowered ejection ports are standard.

Takedown is relatively simple. Pull the slide back until the slide stop is in line with the slide-stop notch. Push the slide-stop pin out slightly from the right side, then pull the slide stop free from the left side. Then pull the slide forward and off the frame. Finally, remove the recoil assembly from the bottom of the slide and push the barrel out through the front of the slide.

I test-fired the Thrashers with eight different 230-grain factory loads and got the following average velocities: American Eagle FMJ, 748 fps; Black Hills JHP, 711 fps; Federal FMJ, 732 fps; Herter's Nylon RN, 740 fps; Magtech FMJ, 721 fps; Remington JHP, 731 fps; Speer TMJ, 692 fps; and Winchester FMJ, 723 fps. Test-firing at 7 yards rapid fire (for me!) resulted in groups of 2 inches or less.

Except for the overly heavy trigger pulls, I found the Thrashers easy to shoot, although as expected, they do exhibit more felt recoil than standard 1911s. The shorter barrel and slightly shorter grip frame makes them somewhat easier to conceal, and although the shorter barrel length is harder to shoot (for me anyway), this presents no great handicap. They're not target pistols, but they are reliable guns with excellent sights. All I'd need for these Thrashers to fill my concealed-carry requirements would be a trigger job. ◉

THE SEMIAUTOMATICS

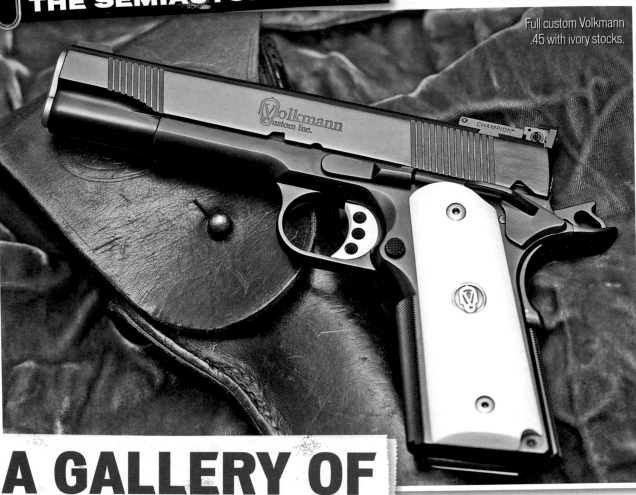

Full custom Volkmann .45 with ivory stocks.

A GALLERY OF GOVERNMENT MODELS

A fully engraved and ivory-stocked Les Baer .45.
Photo: Timothy Mullin

Diamond pattern plus: Kase Reeder's Classic .45.

Range ready: Kimber Eclipse Target II.

Kase Reeder's Condition One.

CHAPTER 50

Nothing proves a picture is worth 1,000 words quite like a fancy photo array of mouthwatering 1911s. Here you'll see specimens from Dave Lauck of DL Sports, Ed Brown, Kimber, Kase Reeder of Reeder Custom Guns, Les Baer, Jason Perkins of South Fork Arms and Luke Volkman. We've even got a classic or two from author Tim Mullin. Enjoy! ◎

Good as gold! The artistry of Dave Lauck.

Kase Reeder's Rekon Kommander.

Ed Brown Signature Edition.

Good looks, great shooting: South Fork Arms Custom .45.

HORNADY 185 GR Z-MAX 999 FPS

HORNADY 230 H&P STEEL MATCH 770 FPS

HORNADY 200 XTP 882 FPS

Dave Lauck expands on the "Barbecue Gun" concept.

Les Baer's Thunder Ranch. *Photo: Timothy Mullin*

Two-tone beauty: Another Kase Reeder Classic .45

As deadly as its namesake: Kase Reeder's Black Mamba.

Combat ready: Kimber's Desert Warrior.

Dave Lauck's "Texas Ranger" masterpiece.

Some long-ago gunfighter must've felt fully-enclosed trigger guards on a 1911 were an affectation! *Photo: Timothy Mullin*

Les Baer's Concept 2: Form and function meet match-grade accuracy.

THE SEMIAUTOMATICS

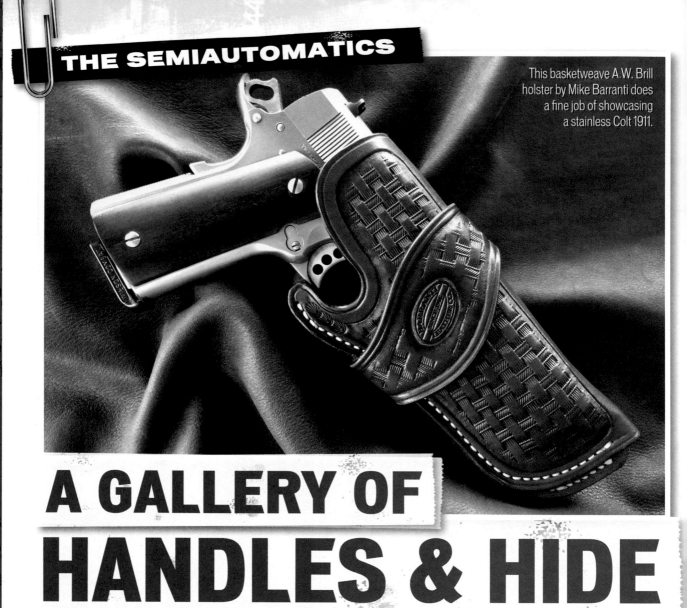

This basketweave A.W. Brill holster by Mike Barranti does a fine job of showcasing a stainless Colt 1911.

A GALLERY OF HANDLES & HIDE FOR 1911s

CHAPTER 51

Once again in keeping with my "one picture is worth 1,000 words" philosophy, I'd like to showcase some of the finest grip panels and gunleather available for the great Government Model of 1911, along with some past classics. Just as with the Colt Single Action Army, the 1911 rarely needs stocks replaced for functional considerations, but rather for aesthetics. Ivory, mother-of-pearl, stag and exotic wood really improve the looks and boost pride of ownership when it comes to John M. Browning's greatest creation. We'll also cover concealment holsters as well as traditional belt rigs of first-rate leather. So, let's get to the pictures. ◎

From pancake to belt slide, 1911 users have many choices when it comes to holsters.

Cenk Gultekin of Handmade Grips offers a personalized touch to these grip panels.

Practical minimalism: This belt slide by Black Hills Leather shows off plenty of this nickel-plated, mother-of-pearl stocked 1911.

This Texas Ranger-style Mexican-loop holster and belt were crafted by Bianchi Frontier Gunleather. *Photo: Helen Pembrook*

Herrett's skip-checkered stocks give excellent control and a unique look.

For extra control, Herrett's offers Camp Perry target stocks (bottom) and Combat Camp Perry "everyday carry" stocks (top).

SEMIAUTO PISTOLS AND THEIR CARTRIDGES — **THE BOOK OF THE .45**

Bob Mernickle captures the flavor of the Old West with this Wild Bunch rig.

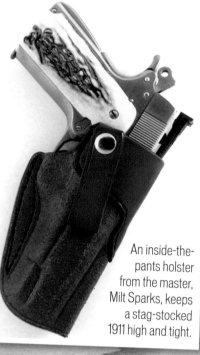

An inside-the-pants holster from the master, Milt Sparks, keeps a stag-stocked 1911 high and tight.

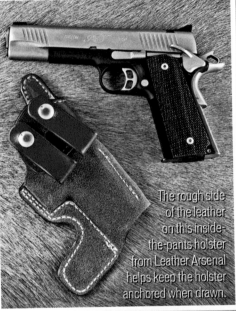

The rough side of the leather on this inside-the-pants holster from Leather Arsenal helps keep the holster anchored when drawn.

John is extremely persnickety about stocks, but he feels that the factory specimens on the Colt Combat Elite are just about perfect "as issued."

CCI BLAZER
200 COMBAT MATCH
961 FPS

Security and good looks go with this Old West Reproductions Mexican-style 1911 holster.

A 1911 with giraffe bone grips matches up well with fancy floral carved leather by El Paso Saddlery.

This quartet of Kimber 1911s all have one thing in common — exotic wood panels from Herrett's.

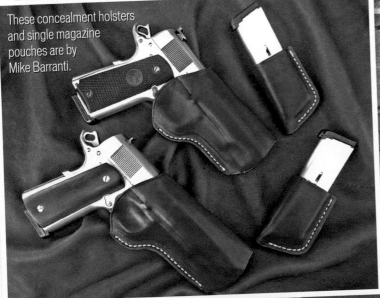

These concealment holsters and single magazine pouches are by Mike Barranti.

Legendary holstermaker Andy Anderson pioneered speed holsters for the 1911.
Photo: Bob Arganbright

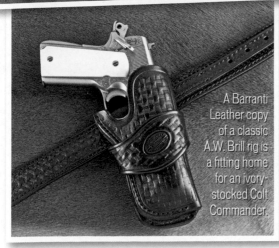

A Barranti Leather copy of a classic A.W. Brill rig is a fitting home for an ivory-stocked Colt Commander.

Old West Reproductions offers this very trim concealment holster for a 1911 — as well as a dual magazine pouch.

SEMIAUTO PISTOLS AND THEIR CARTRIDGES

THE BOOK OF THE .45

LONG

LONG GUNS
AND THEIR
CARTRIDGES

GUNS

Marlin .45-70 leverguns are handy, reliable and light years ahead of the .30-30 or .35 Remington in raw smackdown potential.

THE .45-70
THEN AND NOW

CHAPTER 52

The roots of the .45-70 run deep, going back nearly 150 years. It is as American as the flag and apple pie. When the Civil War began, the first practical lever-action rifle — the .44 Rimfire Henry — had just arrived. It was tested for use by Union troops; however, there was concern it would become a 19th-century version of the "spray and pray" philosophy. Also, the .44 Rimfire was nowhere near as powerful as the muzzleloading rifles then in use. But in 1866, shortly after the end of the Civil War, the first lever-action rifle to bear the Winchester name arrived with the Model 1866 — also chambered in .44 Rimfire.

The military was ready to move to a fixed ammunition rifle, however it would not be a rapidly firing lever-action rifle but rather a much more powerful single shot. In 1866 the

John has been a devotee of the .45-70 for almost as long as the .45 Colt! His first game with his Marlin .45-70 was this very tasty feral hog.

Forty-five caliber lever-action stalwarts from the 19th Century include (left to right): .45-75, .45-60 and .45-70.

first centerfire, cartridge-firing American rifle appeared with the 1866 Springfield chambered in .50-70. These rifles were converted muzzleloaders. Barrels were relined and actions were modified by being fitted with a swinging "trapdoor" which opened to allow the insertion of a metallic cartridge.

FROM SINGLE SHOT TO LEVER ACTION

In 1873 the Springfield Trapdoor was upgraded and chambered for a new cartridge, the .45-70. The .50-70 had featured a 450-grain bullet over 70 grains of black powder, while the .45-70 went with a longer and slimmer brass case, a smaller diameter 405-grain bullet but the same 70 grains of black powder.

The first .45-70 levergun arrived with the Model 1881 Marlin, and Winchester followed up with its Model 1886. Made for the largest and most powerful cartridges of the time, the '86 was the first Winchester whose action featured two blocks of sliding steel mated up with two slots in the receiver, resulting in a very strong rifle.

Marlin's original Model 1895 was produced from 1896 until it was removed from production in 1917. In 1972, the Marlin Model 336 was adapted to the .45-70 cartridge and became the "new" Model 1895. This modern version is much stronger than both the original 1895 and the earlier Model 1881.

The 1886 Winchester was dropped from production in 1935 and returned in a modernized version the following year with the Model 71 (chambered not in .45-70 but rather .348 Winchester). Heavy .45-70 loads must *never* be used in any of the original Marlin Models 1881 and 1895. (The heavy loads listed in chapters on the Marlin 1895 and Browning/Winchester 1886 are only for use in leverguns produced since 1972.)

The latest .45-70 from Marlin is a stainless-steel variant that has become popular among hunters who spend a lot of time in wet weather conditions. Beginning on the 100th anniversary of its introduction, the '86 Winchester has been offered at several intervals by both Browning and Winchester, including standard versions as well as takedown and lightweight versions. Whether bearing the Winchester or Browning label, all current Model 1886s are manufactured by Miroku in Japan.

ALL-AMERICAN BIG BORE

When you think of big-bore English double rifles, the image coming to mind is usually hunting the biggest game

Hornady's LeverEvolution .45-70 loads — with their flexible polymer tip — allow the use of spire-point projectiles in the tubular magazine of this stainless Marlin .45-70.

Africa has to offer. But the equivalent rifle for the largest North American game is the .45-70 levergun. However, when properly loaded, the .45-70 is also versatile enough to be just fine for black bear, feral pigs and deer. These animals are quite often found in heavy brush and timber, and the .45-70 is the perfect brush-gun cartridge. However, the term "brush gun" does not imply that it will shoot unerringly through brush and branches. There is no such thing — at least not in a hand-held firearm. A brush gun is rather a rifle/cartridge combination that is easy to carry, quick into action and powerful enough to put down game quickly.

Alaskan Jim West calls his brush gun the Co-Pilot. I sent him a used .45-70 Marlin 1895. West installed new Marlin checkered wood for both the forearm and buttstock with a Pachmayr recoil pad installed. He cut the barrel to 16½ inches, satin-chromed the entire rifle and cut a series of circular ports on both sides of the front sight to combat felt recoil. It may be noisy, but it certainly makes this little brush gun much easier to shoot with heavy loads. And for ease of travel and stowage, the Co-Pilot is also a takedown.

Some rifle shooters — especially those enamored of the new short magnums — may criticize the .45-70 as not being a long-range hunting cartridge. I do not consider this a

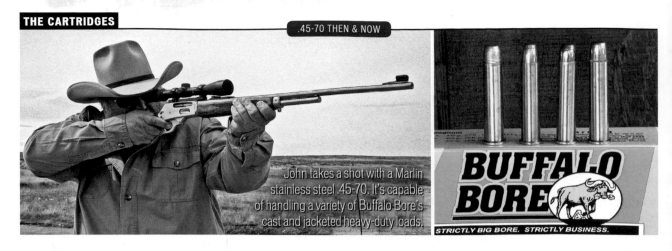

John takes a shot with a Marlin stainless steel .45-70. It's capable of handling a variety of Buffalo Bore's cast and jacketed heavy-duty loads.

BUFFALO BORE

STRICTLY BIG BORE. STRICTLY BUSINESS.

valid criticism. True, it is not for live targets 400 yards away or even 300. (I prefer to stay under 200 yards.) With the game normally hunted with the .45-70, shots are most likely to occur at 50 yards or even less. It may not be the answer for shooting across canyons, but it's exceptionally effective on animals with large, heavy muscles and tough bones capable of biting back.

A heavily loaded .45-70 in a Marlin or Browning/Winchester is more than adequate for taking anything that walks — including elk, moose, grizzly, Alaskan brown bear, elephant, rhino, African lion and even Cape buffalo.

For many years the .45-70 was loaded to black-powder levels. Today Buffalo Bore, Cor-Bon and Garrett all offer heavy-duty loadings for it. In fact, one of Garrett's customers, Vince Lupo, used the Marlin .45-70 loaded with Super Hard Cast Garrett ammunition to take all of Africa's Big Five in a very decisive manner. These Garrett heavy loads are referred to as "Hammerheads," and they really do hit like the hammer of Thor.

RELOADING TIPS

The .45-70 appears to be a straight-wall cartridge suitable for loading with a carbide sizing die, thus making the operation as easy as with sixgun cartridges like the .45 Colt. But seeing isn't always believing. In actuality, the .45-70 actually tapers to the front. If it's blown out straight, as it has been in several wildcats, it becomes a .475. Due to this taper, cases must be lubed and sized with a conventional sizing die. If I am loading just a few cartridges, I rub a lanolin-based sizing lube on the cases. However, for larger amounts it is much easier to place 50 to 75 cases in a cardboard tray large enough to hold them with some shaking room and then apply a spray-on lube.

For my use, all .45-70 cartridges are heavily crimped. Many of the Black Powder Cartridge Silhouette participants do not crimp for their single-shot rifles. But with leverguns, if the rounds are not crimped the bullets can be pushed back into the case under recoil in the magazine tube or when being chambered. The safe way to avoid this is to crimp all loads.

A few years ago it was necessary to cast your own bullets for the .45-70 for any kind of "above and beyond" performance in terms of accuracy and penetration. This is no longer the case, as there are several suppliers offering excellent hard-cast bullets for the .45-70. Some examples are Cast Performance Bullet Co.'s hard-cast, gas-checked, flatnosed, heat-treated bullets offered in weights of 405, 420, 440 and 460 grains; Oregon Trail's flatnosed line of True Shot bullets are offered in weights of 350, 405, 430 and 500 grains. The 430 grainer has a gas check, while the other three from Oregon Trail are plain-based. I have found all bullets from these manufacturers to be of excellent quality.

When it comes to jacketed bullets, I use 300-grain JHPs from Hornady and Sierra. These are recommended only for deer-sized game. For larger critters I would go with Hornady's 350-grain JSP or Speer's 400-grain JFP.

If limited to only one cast bullet/powder combination, I'd go with the RCBS #45-405-grain FNGC and Hodgdon's H322. With jacketed bullets, my one-and-only combo would be Speer's 400-grain JFP and Hodgdon's H322. For my use, the heaviest loads with these bullets would be 52.0 grains of H322 with the RCBS for just under 1,900 fps from my 18-inch barreled Marlin. For the Speer it would be 54.0 grains of H322 for just under 1,800 fps from the same Marlin. Recoil with either, of course, is heavy.

The same RCBS and Speer bulleted loads clock out at

2,025 fps and 1,900 fps, respectively, from a 26-inch barreled Marlin. For less recoil and excellent accuracy, I drop the powder charge to 47.5 grains with the Speer for 1,600 and 1,800 fps from the two barrel lengths. This load is certainly much more pleasant to shoot and will readily handle large hogs, big black bear, elk and moose. The Speer 400-grain JFP is heavier than needed for deer, so a better choice is Hornady's 300-grain JHP over 56.0 grains of H322 for 1,900 fps, or Sierra's 300-grain JHP over 44.0 grains IMR4198 for 1,700 fps (both from the easy-handling 18-inch Marlin).

My most accurate jacketed bullet load for the .45-70 is Hornady's 350-grain JSP over 44.0 grains of IMR4198 for 1,800 fps from the same little Marlin.

Hodgdon's H322 may be my most-used powder for the .45-70. But it isn't the only one. I have also had good results with Alliant's Reloder 7, Hodgdon's H4198 and H4895, IMR3031 and IMR4198 (Hodgdon is now supplying IMR powders). I've been known to use Accurate Arms AA2495 as well. For black powder-level loads without actually using black powder, an excellent choice is Accurate Arms XMR5744.

My supply of .45-70 brass includes Federal, Remington, Starline and Winchester. All is of excellent quality, with the Winchester being slightly thinner than the other three. For almost all of my loads, I use CCI #200 Rifle primers and either Pacific or RCBS dies in the RCBS Rock Chucker press. When loading black powder or black-powder substitutes, I switch to CCI's #250 Magnum Rifle primers, and instead of the standard RCBS powder measure, I switch to the Lyman #55 Black Powder measure using the 24-inch drop tube. This measure is designed to prevent any possible electric sparks when using black powder, and the long drop tube allows the black powder to settle in the case. Before seating the bullet on the black-powder loads, I also place a vegetable wad or Ox-Yoke Wonder Wad over the powder. The wad performs two functions — protecting the base of the bullet and cutting down on barrel fouling.

AN EVER-EFFECTIVE CLASSIC

Such cartridges as the .270 Winchester and .30-06 Springfield depend upon expansion in a hunting situation.

Read the label! Garrett was a pioneer in pushing the 150-year-old .45-70 into the 21st Century. These heavy-duty loads should only be used in rifles recommended for them, as the stouter ones are very close to low-end .458 Magnum territory.

However, you could say the .45-70 — with its .458-inch bullet diameter — is *already* expanded before you fire it. It kills not by expansion but by penetration. And make no doubt about it, the .45-70 — even though it is more than 140 years old and considered antiquated by many — offers, for the most part, unmatched penetration. Several tests have been conducted by Garrett Cartridges and also by shooters at the Linebaugh Seminar, and the results are impressive. A 500-grain bullet at 1,500 fps from a .45-70 will outpenetrate a 500-grain bullet at 2,100 fps from a .458 Winchester when the two rounds are fired into wet newsprint. The .458 will penetrate around 4½ feet, while the .45-70 will travel approximately 6 feet into the same media. Why? The faster rounds seem to slow down quicker.

With heavy, hard-cast bullets at +P pressures — and a modern Marlin to handle them — the awesome penetrating power of the .45-70 is truly spectacular. Nick Fadala took this Cape buffalo with a factory Buffalo Bore 430-grain Hard Cast.

I have nearly the same reverence for a .45-70 levergun as I do for a .45 Colt Single Action. If it can't be done with the .45-70, it can't be done. Or maybe I should say, if it can't be done with a .45-70, why would I want to do it?

In addition to the .45-70 there is a whole family of .45 rifle cartridges based on the same case. Winchester's Model 1876 levergun would not handle the .45-70 due to its length, so the .45-70, which has a case length of approximately 2.1 inches, was trimmed back to approximately 1.9 inches to become the .45-60 which would function in the Model 1876. Ten years later Winchester introduced the Model 1886 which would not only handle the .45-70 but also the longer, 2.4-inch .45-90. Meanwhile, there was a long line of .45 cartridges designed for single-shot rifles. This can get very confusing as sometimes cartridges with the same name had different lengths. However for our purposes here in addition to the .45-70 and the .45-90, there's also the .45-100 (2.6 inches) and the .45-110 (2.75 inches). Today there's another one some say was never chambered in any of the frontier single shots but is available today in modern manufactured single-shot "buffalo rifles." Perhaps no buffalo in the 1870s ever fell to a .45-120 Sharps with its 3.25-inch case length. (If any have, it has been in the last several decades.)

A CAUTIONARY TALE!

Not only has the .45-70 been chambered in excel-

lent rifles from Marlin/Browning/Winchester, it has also been the premier big-bore offering for the Thompson/Center Contender. I found out the hard way this is a combination to be taken *very* seriously.

I'd nestled an SSK Custom barreled Contender into the sandbags, and I was probably too occupied with concentrating on the crosshairs of the 4x Leupold Long Eye Relief scope as I took what I thought was a firm grip and squeezed the trigger. At least I intended to! Unfortunately it did not quite work out that way. Oh, the crosshairs were lined up perfectly all right and the 500-grain bullet from my full-house load landed dead center on target. But I squeezed before I had a proper grip. There was a loud *boom* and then everything went black. When I opened my eyes, everything was red. Blood red. And I immediately realized what had happened.

When the gun fired it came out of my grasp, straight up off the sandbags, hit me right at the hairline on my forehead and then fell in my lap. Luckily it did not hit the concrete floor of the shooting area. (I would heal, but a beat-up gun won't.) Fortunately, I had some ice with me and applied it to my forehead. The bleeding stopped post haste and other than a headache and a beautiful knot on my noggin, everything was okay.

My introduction to the .45-70 chambering in the Contender certainly got my attention. Right then and there I learned smooth wood grips, worn-smooth shooting gloves and heavy recoil don't mix! Now the .45-70 T/C wears Pachmayr Grippers. Felt recoil is still heavy, but it is controllable.

POWER LEVELS

Just a few years ago it was impossible to find much in the way of factory loads for the .45-70 except for a few examples suitable for deer hunting. Pressures were kept low in deference to old rifles like the original Springfield Trapdoor. This has changed dramatically. There are now several levels of loads available for .45-70 users to fit both a particular rifle and/or species of game.

All ammunition companies have greatly increased the muzzle velocities of their 300-grain JHP loads in recent years. This flattens out the trajectory, but I still do not consider these loads adequate for anything beyond deer and black bear. I had two Federal 300-grain JHPs at my disposal for testing. The first clocked out at 1,578 and 1,757 fps, respectively, from the Marlin Guide Gun and Browning 1885. But when I switched to the company's Classic load, the figures increased to 1,652 fps and 1,905 fps — both significant upgrades.

Remington has bumped up its 300-grain JHP also. In the original cast-bullet days of the .45-70, a demand arose for a faster, easier-on-the-shoulder loading with a lighter bullet. The answer back then was the 330-grain .45-70 Express load with the Gould cast HP. Today, Remington offers a modern rendition of it with the 300-grain JHP Express load. Out of the Marlin Guide Gun and the Browning Model of 1885, muzzle velocities come in at 1,652 fps and 1,911 fps.

Winchester also has two 300-grain .45-70 loads. In the same two rifles mentioned above, these loads go over the Oehler Model 35 skyscreens at 1,732 fps and 1,855 fps. I still consider this a deer/black bear load, but Winchester has a newer loading with the tougher Partition Gold 300-grain bullet that just may push it into the bigger-animal class. They certainly should be okay for elk and moose. The Partition Gold clocks out at 1,697 and 2,040 fps in the Marlin Guide Gun and Browning 1885.

Ever since I started shooting the .45-70 in an original Trapdoor back in 1957, the standard has been a 405-grain bullet at around 1,300 fps from a long barreled rifle. Today this has all changed with the introduction of truly heavy-duty loads from Garrett and Buffalo Bore.

Garrett's Hammerhead 415-grain Hard Cast .45-70 loading is rated as +P with a muzzle velocity of 1,850 fps. Each box stipulates that it is safe *only* in modern Winchester, Browning, Marlin, Ruger and Shiloh Sharps rifles. In the Marlin Guide Gun and the 24-inch Limited Edition, muzzle velocities prove to be right on the mark at 1,802 fps and 1,870 fps. This load is for the truly big, mean, want-to-hurt-

John contemplates a future hunt with the Thompson/Center Contender .45-70. His first experience in shooting a scoped one — using a serious "stomper" load — was memorable. And a bit painful!

you type animals and has been used successfully on the big bears of Alaska and the lions in Africa.

With the increased interest in the .45-70 as a hunting round, Buffalo Bore also offers high-performance loads for it. Most .45-70 brass is simply headstamped with the cartridge nomenclature and the maker's name. Buffalo Bore takes a different tack. The headstamp reads "Lever Gun .45-70 Mag." This leaves no doubt as to what you're dealing with. Buffalo Bore's brightly packaged blue and yellow boxes carry the warning: "45-70 Magnum Ammunition is intended for use in and is safe for use in only the following firearms: Browning Mod. 1885 & 1886, Marlin Mod. 1895 manufactured since 1972, Rugers No. 1 & No. 3, new-production Winchester 1886, and Shiloh Sharps rifles."

Buffalo Bore's offerings consist of a 420-grain LBT hard-cast LFNGC (Long Flat-Nose Gas Check) at 2,000 fps, a 400-grain JFN (Jacketed Flat-Nose) at 1,800 fps and a 350-grain JFN at 2,100 fps. In testing, the 420s go from a low of 1,967 fps in the Marlin Guide Gun to a high of 2,165 fps in Browning's Model 1885. The 400s do 1,774 and 2,022 in the Guide Gun and the Winchester 1886. (They will not chamber in the Browning.) The 350 loading comes in at 2,067 fps in the Guide Gun and 2,309 fps in the Browning.

With ammunition like this, the grand, old .45-70 has boldly moved into the 21st-century. ◎

Most folks automatically associate Sharps rifles with buffalo hunting, but the Remington Rolling Block was also widely used.

THE .45 SINGLE SHOTS

Not just another .45-70! John shoots his .45-110 Shiloh Sharps. Its heavy weight dampens recoil considerably, but you wouldn't want to carry it all day!

CHAPTER 53

By all standards of progress, the .45-70 should have died a natural death several generations ago. Instead, it is more popular now than ever. It is *the* choice for long-range Black Powder Cartridge Silhouette and also a favorite hunting cartridge for those who prefer rifles with a traditional flair. Today the .45-70 exists in single-shot rifles, such as the Ruger No. 1 as well as Trapdoor, Sharps and Remington Rolling Block replicas, along with several versions of the Winchester 1885 High-Wall, either offered by Browning or as an Italian import.

REMINGTON'S ROLLING BLOCK

One of the most popular single shots in the 19th century was the Remington Rolling Block. They were originally manufactured from around the end of the Civil War until after the turn of the century. In addition to .45-70, Rolling Blocks were chambered in .30 WCF, .30-40 Krag, 7mm Mauser, .40-65, .44-70 and .50-70.

To load one, cock the hammer. Then pull the small lever on the right side of the action — this unlocks the block and allows it to "roll" back, allowing access to the chamber for loading. Once you place the cartridge in the chamber, rotate the right hand lever forward to lock the block up. You're now ready to fire.

The Remington Rolling Block .45-70 — with its 30-inch octagonal barrel — weighs well over 12 pounds. It's heavy to pack but a joy to shoot. Today's Pedersoli replica has a deep blue finish, a beautiful case-colored receiver with brass trappings and very good wood and finish for the stock and forearm.

There is no lack of either commercial cast bullets or bullet molds available for the .45-70. I prefer to use RCBS molds dropping gas-check bullets weighing approximately 300, 405 and 500 grains — all three have sufficient lube grooves to make it through the barrel without leading.

Browning's 1885 High Wall Traditional Hunter shoots as good as it looks. John prefers a Weaver 4x on his.

RCBS also has a 500-grain Spire Point designed by Mike Venturino for use in single shots only.

I've rarely had great luck with the lighter weights, but the 405- and 500-grain bullets are a joy to shoot. It is easy to see hits all the way out to 600 yards, which is the farthest I've shot my Rolling Block. It would have been no problem for a frontiersman with plenty of ammunition to keep an enemy off his back by shooting the big .45 slugs at long range.

THE 1885 HIGH WALL

The original Winchester High Wall was manufactured from 1885 until 1920. Coming after the heyday of the buffalo hunters, the Model 1885 was eventually offered in both High Wall and Low Wall configurations. High Walls were for .35 WCF, .38-55, .405 Winchester, .40-65, .45-70, .45-90 and .50-110. Low Walls were for more sedate cartridges, such as the .22 Long Rifle and .25-20. All in all, more than 65 cartridges found their way into the Winchester catalog chambered in the Model 1885.

Browning has — at various times — offered three variations of the Model 1885 chambered for the .45-70. For the competitive shooter there is the BPCR (Black Powder Cartridge Rifle) complete with Badger barrel, Vernier rear sights

and a windage-adjustable globe front with spirit level. The rear sight has three interchangeable apertures, and the front sight comes with eight inserts.

Browning's Traditional Hunter variant offers a crescent buttplate, tang-mounted aperture sight and octagonal barrel. Finally we come to my favorite: the Model 1885 High Wall complete with 28-inch barrel, drilled and tapped for scope mounts and a very comfortable recoil pad to take the sting out of those heavy-duty .45-70 loads. This is a serious hunting tool, featuring a 28-inch full-octagonal barrel and checkered walnut forearm and buttstock. Sights are a windage-adjustable black front in a dovetail matched with a traditional rear on a step-adjustable ramp. (My Traditional Hunter now wears a Weaver 4x scope in Weaver mounts.)

To operate the High Wall, push down and forward on the small lever behind the trigger. This lowers the block (much like the Sharps rifle) to allow for insertion of a new cartridge or ejection of a spent one. The Model 1885 High Wall is

Either a scoped Browning Traditional Hunter (bottom) or a Ruger No. 1 with a NECG peep sight (top) will handle any hunting chore that needs doing with a .45-70.

a much trimmer and lighter design than the big Sharps. Because it sprang from the genius of John Browning, we should expect near-perfection, and we get it.

MAYER AND THE SHARPS

It was during my first year as a teenager I first heard of Frank Mayer. I was all of 13, and he was 102 and still active enough to have killed a four-point buck the year before. It was 1952, and Mayer, born in 1850, was the last surviving "buffalo runner" from the era when Wild Bill Hickok and Buffalo Bill made their footprints in the sands of history. He may also have been the oldest living Civil War veteran. (He'd lied about his age in 1863 to became a drummer boy in the Union Army.)

From 1872 through 1875, Mayer hunted buffalo. He was a dead shot but preferred to stalk within 200 to 300 yards of the shaggy beasts and set up his stand. He would then

Different rifles, different levels of .45-70 power: Garrett Cartridges of Texas offers a 405-grain load at 1,350 fps for the Trapdoor Springfield (top), a 405-grain load at 1,650 fps for the Sharps (center) and a 405-grain load at 1,850 fps for the Ruger No. 1 (bottom).

unfold the metallic bipod attached to his rifle and go to work. In the movies, a hunter might kill 100 or more buffalo, but this rarely happened.

Mayer seldom killed more than 30 buffalo a day for the simple reason his skinners could not handle any more than that. Hides brought $3 to $3.50 apiece for cows, $2 for bulls. Buffalo heads for mounting went for $10 to $20 apiece and tongues sold for all of 50¢. Most meat was left for scavengers or to rot.

Mayer started hunting in Texas and moved north with the herds. His rifles were Sharps. First came the .40-70, then the .40-90. Then Mayer got his big rifle, a 16-pound .45 that shot a 550-grain bullet and was equipped with a 10x German scope. That scope had three horizontal cross-hairs for shooting at different distances and also for esti-mating range. So much for the legend of the buffalo hunter with his tang-sighted rifle and cross sticks!

Mayer said his rifle was chambered in .45-120, but modern experts say the .45-120 did not arrive until after the Sharps Company went out of business. However, Theodore Roosevelt also said he had a .45-120 when he was in the Dakotas. Perhaps it was a .45-110 or perhaps the modern experts are mistaken. *Perhaps.* By 1875 the big herds were gone. Mayer put up his rifle and would kill only one more buffalo. That was in 1889 on Montana's Powder River, when he came upon a bull being attacked by wolves. He shot the wolves and then shot the old bull before more wolves could attack it.

EVOLUTION OF THE SHARPS

The Sharps was introduced two years before Frank Mayer was born. Christian Sharps received his patent in 1848 for a sliding-breech action on a percussion rifle. Sharps' rifle had a lever-activated breechblock that opened downward. A linen or paper cartridge consisting of a bullet and proper powder charge was inserted. Closing the breechblock tore the paper, exposing the powder. But instead of a single percussion cap, the Sharps first used a circular capper, then a roll of caps not unlike a kid's cap gun from the 1950s.

The Sharps was used in the Civil War and a trained

John's Ruger No. 1 .45-70 is trim and handy with a peep sight and capable of outstanding groups when scoped. The scope can be switched out for the peep sight in seconds, or vice versa.

shooter could get off 10 shots a minute. The first 9,000 Sharps rifles of 1859 went to the military, and the famous Berdan Sharpshooters were armed with a .52-caliber version. In all, the Union purchased over 80,000 Sharps rifles.

It was an easy step for the Sharps to go from linen or paper cartridges to the new fixed ammunition. By 1869 Christian Sharps was long gone from the company, and Richard Lawrence received a patent that year for a new rifle and started designing and chambering large brass cartridges for what became the Model 1874. But by 1881 the Sharps Rifle Company, like the buffalo, was gone. Some well-known chamberings were .40-70, .40-90, .44-77, .45-110, .50-70 and the "Big Fifty" or .50-90.

Sharps rifles were generally blued steel with a case-hardened receiver and buttplate, plus a straight-grip walnut stock. Barrel lengths were normally from 22 to 32 inches and octagonal in shape. In the 1870s, Frank Mayer's Sharps, complete with bullet mold and reloading dies, cost $225 with an extra charge of $80 for the scope, at a time when a buffalo skinner averaged $38.50 a week. Sort of puts the cost of a modern Sharps in perspective, doesn't it?

NEW BREED SHARPS

The original Sharps Rifle Company may be gone, but the void has been filled in modern times by the Shiloh Rifle Manufacturing Company of Big Timber, Montana. The "new" company goes back to 1976. It was known originally as Shiloh Products. (There would be a split in 1983 with two companies emerging — Shiloh and C. Sharps.)

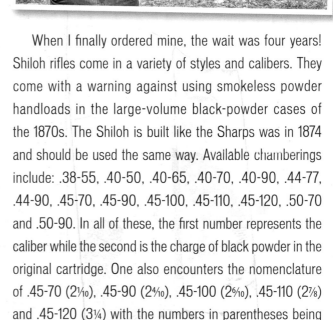

When I finally ordered mine, the wait was four years! Shiloh rifles come in a variety of styles and calibers. They come with a warning against using smokeless powder handloads in the large-volume black-powder cases of the 1870s. The Shiloh is built like the Sharps was in 1874 and should be used the same way. Available chamberings include: .38-55, .40-50, .40-65, .40-70, .40-90, .44-77, .44-90, .45-70, .45-90, .45-100, .45-110, .45-120, .50-70 and .50-90. In all of these, the first number represents the caliber while the second is the charge of black powder in the original cartridge. One also encounters the nomenclature of .45-70 (2¹⁄₁₀), .45-90 (2⁴⁄₁₀), .45-100 (2⁶⁄₁₀), .45-110 (2⅞) and .45-120 (3¼) with the numbers in parentheses being the length of the cartridge case in inches.

When I originally placed my order for a Shiloh Sharps, I went with the crowd and ordered a .45-70. With a four-year backlog, however, much time is allowed for changing one's mind about the caliber and custom touches. My good friend Tedd Adamovich of BluMagnum Grips ordered his at the same time and convinced me to go with something less

TEST-FIRE:
RUGER NO. 1
.45-70 (22-INCH BARREL)

LOAD	VELOCITY	3 SHOTS, 100 YARDS
Buffalo Bore 350-gr. JFP	2,142 fps	1 ¾"
Buffalo Bore 405-gr. JFN	2,010 fps	1 ¾"
Buffalo Bore 430-gr. LBT	1,934 fps	⅞"
Cor-Bon 350-gr. Bonded Core	1,946 fps	⅞"
Cor-Bon 350-gr. JSP	1,943 fps	⅞"
Garrett 405-gr. JSP	1,818 fps	1 ⅛"
Hornady 300-gr. JHP/55.5 gr. H322	2,056 fps	1"
Hornady 350-gr. RN/52 gr. H322	1,998 fps	1 ⅛"
Speer 350-gr. FN/52 gr. H322	1,953 fps	1"
Oregon Trail 405-gr./28.5 gr. XMP5744	1,364 fps	1"
Oregon Trail 500-gr./26 gr. XMP5744	1,237 fps	1 ⅛"

TEST-FIRE:
SHILOH SHARPS
.45-110 (30-INCH BARREL)

LOAD	MV
RCBS 525-gr. SP/90 gr. GOEX CTG	1,327 fps
RCBS 525-gr. SP/95 gr. GOEX CTG	1,380 fps
RCBS 525-gr. SP/100 gr. GOEX CTG	1,429 fps
RCBS 525-gr. SP/100 gr. GOEX FFg	1,435 fps
RCBS 525-gr. SP/100 gr. Pyrodex RS Select	1,389 fps
Lyman 400-gr. FN/100 gr. GOEX CTG	1,531 fps
Lyman 400-gr. FN/100 gr. GOEX FFg	1,535 fps

Uberti's beautiful 1885 High Wall repro in .45-70 boasts an octagonal barrel and a tang-mounted Vernier sight.

generally available. So we both wound up with rifles chambered in .45-110. I ordered the No. 3 Standard Sporter with a 30-inch heavyweight full-octagonal barrel with the Supreme Grade straight-grip military stock, Schnabel forearm, no cheekpiece and with double-set triggers. I also got two sets of sights, the standard hunting-style and an extra set of target sights consisting of rear tang and a globe front. The barrel is finished in a matte blue, the receiver, hammer and trigger guard are all casehardened, and wood-to-metal fit is absolutely excellent. Overall, the workmanship is superb!

You can't find .45-110 cases at most gunshops, However, Buffalo Arms specializes in virtually everything the black powder shooter needs, so I ordered .45-110s made from .348 Winchester for practice loads and .45-110 Bertram brass for serious use. A wad cutting punch of .45 caliber as well as vegetable fiber wad sheets were also ordered for loading the big .45. A set of .45-110 dies from RCBS, a Lyman #55 Black Powder Measure and a Hornady Single Stage Press, and I was in business. The length of the .45-110, especially with 500-grain bullets, requires a press with lots of room for longer cases, and the Hornady fills the bill nicely.

Black powder should only be metered through a measure such as the Lyman Black Powder Measure which is designed specifically for that propellant. There is danger of an electric spark igniting black powder if the wrong type of measure is utilized. Some say this can't happen; others say it can. I prefer to err on the side of caution. Stay safe! I also use the 24-inch drop tube that comes with the Lyman. This allows the powder to settle into the brass case. Once the powder is in place, I put a cardboard wad cut from the back of a legal pad, or a wad cut from vegetable fiber over the powder to protect the bullet's lead base.

Bullets must be selected with special care for black powder. Mine are cast of a lead-tin ratio of 30:1. They also need special lube for black-powder shooting. Two good ones are SPG Bullet Lube, and Lyman Black Powder Gold. These lubes help to keep fouling of the bore to a minimum, and what does occur is kept manageably soft. With the wrong lube, barrels can become so fouled it is almost impossible to get a patch through them.

Two classics that simply won't die! Both the Sharps (top) and Trapdoor .45-70 (bottom) are available in replica form.

Cartridge cases also require extra care. After firing, I decap the cases — Buffalo Arms has a special tool for handling the long .45-110 brass — drop the fired cases in a plastic gallon milk jug half full of soapy water and slosh them around between shots. When arriving home, the cases are washed in hot soapy water, rinsed and dried by laying them out on newspaper. The primer pockets are then cleaned with Q-tips®, and the cases are tumbled clean. Once they are used for black powder, brass cases are kept segregated from my smokeless brass. I prefer to clean any black-powder firearm the same day it is used. With the Sharps this is made relatively easy by the ingenious design of the Sharps. A lever on the right side of the receiver is simply moved and withdrawn and the whole breechblock drops out into the hand for easy cleaning of both block and barrel.

To operate the Shiloh Sharps, the hammer is placed at half cock, the lever is operated down and forward opening the breech, a cartridge is loaded into the chamber, the lever is brought back and up, the breechblock closes, the hammer is cocked and the Sharps is ready to fire. The first shot fired from the Shiloh Sharps .45-110 with a 500-grain bullet and I thought "That's not bad!" I felt a little less so with the second shot and by the third shot I was reaching for the Past Recoil Shield! With my favorite loading of the RCBS 515-grain roundnosed, flat-point cast bullet over 90 grains of GOEX Cartridge-Grade black powder, muzzle velocity is right at 1,300 fps, and 1- to 1½-inch groups at 100 yards for three shots are the norm. There isn't anything that walks — at least anyplace I am likely to go — that cannot be taken with a 515-grain bullet at 1,300 fps!

The Remington Rolling Block's action literally "rolls back" for loading.

AN INSTANT CLASSIC

Bill Ruger modernized the single-shot rifle with his No. 1 — one of the most accurate rifles available chambered in .45-70. One of its great attributes is its compactness — its got a shorter overall length than a lever action with a comparable barrel length. The No. 1 does not seem to be selective as it shoots all weight bullets exceptionally well with groups in the one-inch category for three shots at 100 yards. A rifleman should have no problem precisely placing shots at reasonable ranges, whether it's on a deer with 300-grain bullets or an elk or moose with heavier 400- to 500-grain bullets.

An excellent accessory for use with the No. 1 comes from New England Custom Service and is known as the N-100 Ruger Peep Sight. What's great about it is it utilizes the rear scope-mounting scallop already found on the receiver. Simply sight in with the scope, remove the scope and install this receiver sight. Once sighted in, the receiver sight can be removed and placed in your pocket or pack and the scope reinstalled. If bad weather is encountered or you find yourself in conditions where a scope would be a hindrance, all you need is a large coin to remove the scope and replace it with the peep sight. ◉

This Marlin Model 1894 menu includes (from top down): .45 Colt Trapper, .45 Colt Cowboy, .44-40 Cowboy.

.45 COLT LEVERGUNS

CHAPTER 54

The .45 Colt was a powerful sixgun loading with original rounds carrying a 250- to 255-grain bullet over 40 grains of black powder. By 1878, Colt had chambered its Single Action Army in .44 WCF. Winchester didn't reciprocate with a levergun chambered in .45 Colt, so anyone who wanted his carbine and sixgun chambered in the same caliber had to go with the .44 WCF (later known as the .44-40).

DOWN TO CASES

Why were no leverguns of the 1870s chambered in .45 Colt? A look at the .45 Colt and .44 WCF may help explain why. Until the 1950s, all brass was of the balloonhead style. A look inside such a case reveals the primer pocket sticking up above the base of the case itself. By contrast, modern brass shows a solid bottom — or "solid-head" as it is referred to now.

Balloonhead brass has a larger capacity, which is why the old-style .45 Colt and .44-40 cases held 40 grains of black powder at maximum capacity, while modern brass will normally hold somewhere around 35 grains. A little work with the micrometer is even more revealing. Using a digital caliper, I measured both balloonhead and solid-head brass in .44-40 and .45 Colt. Remington UMC .44 WCF brass measures .465 inch in diameter ahead of the rim and .516 inch at the rim. This leaves a shelf of .0255 inch for the levergun's extractor hook. The .45 Colt mea-

Winchester offered a blued version of their .45 Colt Trapper as well as a case-hardened one. The large loop lever is an aftermarket add-on.

The two bottom targets were shot with John's handloads from a Marlin Model 1894 Cowboy Competition.

sures .480 and .504 inch, respectively, leaving a very miniscule .012-inch shelf — about 50 percent the size of the .44-40s.

Going to modern Starline .44-40 brass, we find a much-altered situation. Measuring it results in numbers of .463 and .519 inch, respectively, thus allowing .028 inch for each side of the rim protrusion. Starline's .45 Colt brass comes out at .474 inch and .508 inch, respectively, allowing for .017 inch for the extractor to hold on to. In addition, modern brass has a channel running around the base just ahead of the rim. On the .44-40 this has a diameter of .448 inch, while the .45 Colt comes in at .435 inch. Couple these measurements with the rim diameters of the .44-40 and .45 Colt and we come up with differences of .071 and .073 inch — almost identical. These measurements allow rim shelves of .0355 and .0365 inch, respectively. Not only will modern .45 brass work through a levergun, but newer .44-40 brass is also better adapted to the carbine's operation.

So, more than a century after these cartridges first appeared, leverguns which never existed in the old days now do. In the early days of Cowboy Action Shooting, the most popular chambering was the .45 Colt. This has changed today as serious competitors — whose main goal is speed — have gone to smaller calibers. But before they did, Marlin and Winchester came up with leverguns chambered in .45 Colt. And so did companies who make — or import — replicas of Winchester 1860, 1866, 1873 and 1892 models.

Most replica .45 Colt Winchesters are for standard loads only. Their toggle actions are not tremendously strong. But when John Browning designed the Model 1892, he basically miniaturized his previous Model 1886, using twin locking bolts at the back of the frame. This increased the strength tremendously.

DIFFERENT STROKES

Basically, there are two groups of shooters who choose leverguns in .45 Colt. One consists of the pleasure shooters who plink, participate in CAS or hunt small game, varmints or possibly deer-sized critters up close. These same shooters look for a companion levergun to go with their Colt Single Action Army (or replica thereof). For most of my

shooting along these lines, I stay with loads in the 800- to 900-fps range and usually pick up an additional 100 to 200 fps from the longer barrel of my levergun.

The other group is looking for big-game hunting possibilities and maybe a companion carbine to go with a heavy-duty hunting sixgun such as the Ruger Blackhawk. With these sixguns, I normally use 300-grain bullets at 1,200 fps, so the long gun I need is a Winchester or replica Model 1894 or Model 1892 — or Marlin Model 1894. These leverguns easily handle my heavy-duty hunting loads.

The Winchester 1894 is basically a long action, but when chambered in .45 Colt there can be problems with feeding such a short cartridge through a long action. Personally, I have never had a problem, but perhaps I work the lever differently than others do. We have many relatively long 300-grain bullets for the .45 Colt, and these are no problem for the Model 94. However, they can be a problem in a Model 92 replica or a Marlin Model 1894.

Remember, the bullet you plan to use can be the deciding factor in which levergun to choose. With any of these stronger leverguns, the .45 Colt is certainly adequate for deer, black bear and feral hogs at any reasonable distance.

John's favorite .45 Colt bullets for use in leverguns include (left to right): The Lachmiller #45-255LC and NEI's #451.310 and #454.325. The latter two may need crimping over the front shoulder to feed through levergun actions.

THE CARTRIDGES

.45 COLT LEVERGUN

Short, handy and very much to the point:
Marlin (top) and Winchester .45 Colt Trappers.

Marlin Model 1894 Cowboy Competition in .45
Colt sits with a Ruger Bisley
and a Colt New
Frontier.

MAJOR PLAYERS

When you look back at the Marlin and Winchester lever-guns of the late 19th century, things can get a bit confusing. Winchester Model 94 chambered the .30-30 and similar length cartridges, while the Model 92 handled the .25-20, .32-20, .38-40 and .44-40 or, as they were then called, the .25 WCF, .32 WCF, .38 WCF and .44 WCF.

Over at Marlin it was the Model 1893 for the .30-30 rifle-style cartridges while *its* Model 1894 was chambered for the shorter WCF cartridges. However, Marlin did not want to stamp "Winchester" on its barrels, so instead the company used the terminology of .25-20, .32-20, .38-40 and .44-40.

Production of the original Marlin Model 1894 basically ended in about 1917, although apparently Marlin had enough parts on hand to produce leverguns into the early 1930s. Later, with the immense popularity of the .44 Magnum in both S&W and Ruger six-guns, Marlin began chambering its long-action (.30-30, .35 Remington) Model 336 for the relatively short .44 Magnum cartridge. I purchased one in the mid-1960s and never had a problem with it when I used Keith-style bullets. But there were many complaints about feeding reliability, so Marlin gave up on trying to get the Model 336 to function properly with the .44 Magnum.

MARLIN MAKES A MOVE

In 1969 the Marlin 1894 was resurrected and offered in .44 Magnum, then in subsequent years, .357 Magnum, .45 Colt, .41 Magnum, .25-20 and .32-20. The last four chamberings are gone in the standard version, with the .41 and .45 commanding premium prices at gun shows. They were replaced with the 1894 Cowboy — a 24-inch octagonal barreled levergun designed for CAS — in .45 Colt, .44 Magnum, .357 Magnum and .44-40.

In the early 1990s, Bob Baer, Brian Pearce and I met with the powers that be at Marlin to suggest some things. Two of the things we wanted were octagonal barrels and old, classic cartridges. Shortly thereafter, Marlin began introducing 24-inch octagonal barreled leverguns — in .45 Colt and .44-40 — aimed at the CAS market. Diamond Dot and I were both shooting CAS at the time and those long, heavy barrels were just a little too much of a good thing.

I measured cartridge length and magazine-tube capacity and found the barrels could be cut to 19½ inches and still hold 10 rounds of .45 Colt. The addition of tang sights completed

An open-and-shut case: John spends
a little quality shooting time afield
with his Marlin Model 1894 in .45 Colt.

the picture, giving us two excellent competition "Little Lever-guns" — a .45 Colt for me and a .44-40 for Dot.

MICRO-GROOVE® VERSUS CUT RIFLED

For many years, Marlin advertised Micro-Groove® rifling as giving a big advantage in the accuracy department. More lands and grooves were believed to produce better accuracy results with jacketed bullets as opposed to a conventionally rifled barrel. But this proved to be a problem with the loads normally used in CAS — which mandated lead bullets without gas checks at moderate velocities. Once Marlin was aware of the problem, they began to offer cut-rifled barrels on its Model 1894.

THE TRAPPERS

For years, Jim West at Wild West Guns has specialized in easy handling, short-barreled, Trapper-style .45-70s. His "Alaskan Co-Pilot" .45-70 Marlin takedown model was extremely well thought of by Col. Jeff Cooper, who even opined it was a great African lion gun. For our purposes, I'll define "Trapper" or "Little Levergun" as any levergun with a barrel under 18 inches in length.

Sometime in the 1990s, Marlin made a limited run of 16¼-inch Model 1894 Trappers in .44 Magnum and .45 Colt. I was fortunate to find both on the consignment rack at a local gun shop. These limited-edition carbines featured a full-length magazine tube holding seven or eight rounds (depending upon the nose length of the bullet), a recoil pad on a straight-gripped stock, checkering and excellent iron sights. Both were drilled and tapped for scope mounts and can easily be drilled and tapped to accept Williams or Lyman receiver sights. They're identical externally except for chambering, but carry different barrels — the .45 Colt having a cut-rifled barrel while the .44 Magnum features Marlin's proprietary old-style Micro-Groove rifling. This makes sense, because the .44 Magnum does its best work with jacketed bullets, while the most accurate loads with the .45 Colt are those I've assembled with RCBS's 300-grain hard-cast, gas-check bullet as well as Hornady's 300-grain XTP jacketed bullet.

Shooting the .45 Colt Marlin Trapper gives identical

The Marlin Trapper features side ejection to make scope mounting easier.

Winchester's later Trappers employed the Angle Eject system to allow ejected empties to clear the bottom of the scope.

TEST-FIRE: MARLIN 1984 TRAPPER .45 COLT (16½ INCH BARREL)

LOAD	VELOCITY	3 SHOTS, 50 YARDS
Ore. Trail 255-gr. SWC/9.0 gr. Unique	1,167 fps	2 ½"
Ore. Trail 250-gr. RNFP/17 gr. 5744	977 fps	1 ½"
Lyman #454424/9.3 gr. Universal	1,131 fps	1 ⅛"
Hornady 300-gr. XTP/21.7 gr. WW296	1,498 fps	1 ⅛"
Lyman 300-gr. FNGC/21.2 gr. H110	1,376 fps	1 ½"
*NEI 325-gr. KT/21.2 gr. H110	1,410 fps	2"
RCBS #45-300-gr./21.2 gr. H110	1,393 fps	1 ⅛"

*Too long for reliable feeding.

results with both cast and jacketed bullets, and with both heavy and standard weight bullets. Versatility such as this is rare, to say the least. Lyman's Keith-designed 260-grain hard-cast #454424 bullet over 9.3 grains of Universal gives a most pleasant shooting 1,130 fps load that stays right at 1 inch for three shots at 50 yards. But I prefer heavyweights for hunting with the .45 Colt and have had excellent results with both Hornady's 300-grain XTP over 21.7 grains of WW296 and RCBS's hard-cast #45-300-grain SWC gas check over 21.2 grains of H110. Both loads are in the 1,375- to 1,400-fps range and will also stay right at 1-inch at 50 yards. I like the .45 Trappers so well I've had two more made up — one in .30-30 and the other in .375 Winchester.

There's not much I can't do with one of these Trappers. ◉

A scoped Model 1895 can rival many bolt-action sporters when it comes to 100-yard accuracy. And it leaves bigger holes than most bolt guns!

HORNADY 300 JHP
50.0gr RE-7
1731 FPS
7/8"

46.0 gr RE-7
1545 FPS 3/4"

HORNADY
300 JHP
.450
MARLIN

48.0gr.
RE-7 1614 FPS
1 1/8"

THE MARLIN MODEL 1895

CHAPTER 55

The first levergun chambered for the .45-70 arrived with the Model 1881 Marlin. It gave way to the original Model of 1895, which was produced from 1896 until it was pronounced dead in 1917. But in 1972, the company took a hard look at the highly popular Model 336 chambered in .30-30 and .35 Remington and adapted it to the .45-70 cartridge. It became the new Model 1895 — and was much stronger than the original. One caveat:

Heavy loads must never be used in an original and should not even be anywhere *near* a Model 1881.

In addition to the standard Model 1895, Marlin has also offered several limited edition .45-70s such as an 18½-inch and a 24-inch LTD Model, both with full octagonal barrels, and an LTD .45-70 with a half-round/half-octagonal 24-inch barrel and an uncheckered straight-grip stock. One of the latest variants is a stain-

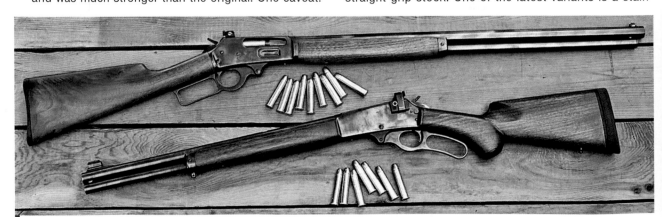

Taffin's custom .45-70 Marlin 1895s by Keith DeHart were built before the introduction of the Guide Gun series. The octagonal 24-inch barreled one at top is John's big-bore "fun gun." The handier short-barreled carbine (below) is his dedicated big-game buster.

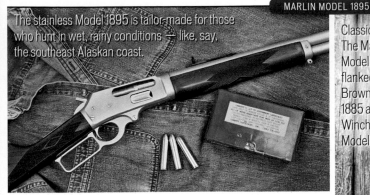

The stainless Model 1895 is tailor-made for those who hunt in wet, rainy conditions — like, say, the southeast Alaskan coast.

Classic .45-70 trio: The Marlin .45-70 Model 1895 is flanked by a Browning Model 1885 and a Winchester Model 1886.

less-steel version for hunters and outdoorsmen who spend a lot of time in bad weather conditions.

THE RIFLING QUESTION

A myth has circulated for years that Marlin's Micro-Groove barrels would not shoot cast bullets, but this is not entirely correct. Micro-Groove barrels are simply selective about which cast bullets they *will* shoot. They do exceptionally well with 400-grain (or heavier) bullets, especially those with gas checks and at muzzle velocities well above the standard 1,300 fps black powder-level load. But since 1997, this is no longer of any concern as Model 1895s now carry cut-rifled barrels.

For any Model 1895 .45-70 with Micro-Groove rifling, I have found the combination of the RCBS-designed 405-grain gas-check bullet with a maximum bearing surface driven at 1,800 fps to give excellent accuracy. It's also a great choice for heavy-boned big game. For bullet casters it is RCBS's #45-405FN mold, but if you don't cast, there are several bullet suppliers who offer the same basic design.

When the new cut-rifled barrels appeared, I wanted to try them with both cast and jacketed bullets. Using Hornady's 300-grain JHP over 52.0 grains of H322, I was pleasantly surprised with a 50-yard, three-shot ¾-inch group. Speer's 400-grain JFP over 50.0 grains of H322 yielded 1,800 fps and a 1-inch group (both were with iron sights). When I switched to the hard-cast 300-grain RCBS gas-check #45-300-grain FNGCs over 52.0 grains of H322, got a ½-inch group at 50 yards, plus a chronograph reading of 1,850 fps.

The RCBS #45-405-grain FN proved to be an exceptional performer when driven to 1,880 fps with 52.0 grains of H322, delivering 1-inch groups. If I were limited to only one load for a .45-70 levergun, this would be it.

A Marlin Model 1895 .45-70 proven to be extremely

popular with hunters, especially in Alaska and Africa, is the Guide Gun with an 18½-inch barrel, ⅔ tubular magazine, straight-grip stock and factory porting to reduce felt recoil. Sights are the standard folding rear adjustable on a sliding ramp and a bead front that is tap adjustable in a dovetail slot.

For hunting, I have equipped mine with an Ashley Emerson-designed XS Ghost Ring setup, consisting of a large-aperture rear with a broad front featuring a white stripe down the middle. This combination is *fast* for woods use as well as up-close situations with dangerous critters.

The Guide Gun's thick recoil pad plus its ported barrel is much appreciated by this shooter when using Garrett or Buffalo Bore heavy .45-70 loads. For close encounters with big stuff in tight quarters, I can't think of a better combination than a ghost-ring sighted Guide Gun with "stompin'" .45-70 ammo.

My 24-inch barreled Model 1895 LTD carries the Lyman #66 Receiver Sight. As with all Marlins, it is set up for scope mounting with a solid top strap and side ejection.

MARLIN MODEL 1895

A Wild West .45-70 Co-Pilot (top) compared to a Marlin Guide Gun Model 1895G (bottom): The takedown Co-Pilot (inset) has a capacity of six rounds .

THE CUSTOM TOUCH

The Model 1895 is a superb levergun; however, it *can* be improved. A few years back I had Jim West of Wild West Guns build me one of his take-down 16½-inch barreled .45-70 Co-Pilots. It's a very popular option in Alaska. The Co-Pilot's takedown feature allows it to be easily stowed in a bush plane or in a backpack, or for traveling anywhere you don't wish to advertise the fact you're carrying a rifle.

Jeff Cooper even took his to Africa and was quite taken with its capabilities on dangerous game. The minimum-length barrel makes it very easy to handle in close quarters. I do not believe Marlin produced a short-barreled .45-70s until after the arrival of the Co-Pilot .

A LUCKY FIND

Before Marlin started its Guide Gun series, I found not one but two Model 1895s on a used rack at "take-me-home-now" prices I couldn't resist. One was the early style with a straight-grip stock. The other had a pistol-grip stock and the later cross-bolt safety. Neither lit my fire on the basis of what they were but on what they could become.

So I decided to set one up as a short-barreled carbine strictly for hunting, while the other would satisfy my long-standing desire for a long-barreled, big-bore levergun that would probably see more black powder and cast bullets than anything else.

Gunsmith Keith DeHart and I sat down at the 1993 Shootists Holiday and discussed what we could do to turn them into more of my idea of what a great levergun should be. I did not want to get into projects that would eat up a lot of money without accomplishing anything of practical value, so it was decided to cut the original barrel to 18 inches on the later Model 1895 to make it an easy-to-carry woods rifle. Then we'd replace the original barrel on the earlier rifle with a 26-inch octagonal barrel for shooting cast bullets. The original plan called for both guns to be fitted with a receiver sight, so I found a used Lyman that worked perfectly.

From the factory, both guns came with "too much wood." The cheekpieces were higher than they needed to be. The forearms were thicker than they should be. But, ever so gently, DeHart rounded and smoothed the high spots to slick up both rifles "wood-wise." It makes a tremendous difference in shooting and handling qualities.

After DeHart started working on the rifles, he called me about a new process he could also give them called BlackStar Accurizing. It's a non-abrasive barrel polishing process to streamline the microscopic surface of the bore by removing very small amounts of metal from the existing surface. Burrs, milling marks and other machine-related

COMPARISON: MARLIN CUSTOM .45-70s

BULLET/LOAD	VELOCITY 18-INCH BARREL	VELOCITY 26-INCH BARREL
FACTORY LOADS		
Federal 300-gr. JHP	1,591 fps	1,747 fps
Winchester 300-gr. JHP	1,624 fps	1,819 fps
Garrett 405-gr. JSP	1,727 fps	1,812 fps
Garrett 415-gr. HCFP	1,686 fps	1,812 fps
CAST BULLET HANDLOADS		
Oregon Trail 405-gr./50.0 gr. AA2495	1,462 fps	1,700 fps
Oregon Trail 405-gr./34.0 gr. IMR4198	1,723 fps	1,878 fps
RCBS #45-300-gr. FN/48.0 gr. H322	1,565 fps	1,755 fps
RCBS #45-300-gr. FN/57.5 gr. H322	2,003 fps	2,195 fps
RCBS #45-300-gr. FN/34.0 gr. H4198	1,507 fps	1,651 fps
RCBS #45-300-gr. FN/38.0 gr. H4198	1,535 fps	1,663 fps
RCBS #45-300-gr. FN/42.0 gr. H4198	1,747 fps	1,811 fps
RCBS #45-300-gr. FN/49.0 gr. IMR3031	1,633 fps	1,817 fps
RCBS #45-300-gr. FN/27.0 gr. #4227	1,477 fps	1,513 fps
RCBS #45-405-gr. FN/44.0 gr. H322	1,482 fps	1,553 fps
RCBS #45-405-gr. FN/46.0 gr. H322	1,623 fps	1,761 fps
RCBS #45-405-gr. FN/52.0 gr. H322	1,876 fps	2,024 fps
RCBS #45-405-gr. FN/36.0 gr. H4198	1,508 fps	1,569 fps
RCBS #45-405-gr. FN/40.0 gr. H4198	1,626 fps	1,699 fps
RCBS #45-405-gr. FN/44.0 gr. IMR3031	1,502 fps	1,611 fps
RCBS #45-405-gr. FN/48.0 gr. IMR3031	1,678 fps	1,765 fps

ACCURACY RESULTS: WILLIAMS RECEIVER SIGHT & 18-INCH BARREL

BULLET/POWDER	VELOCITY	3 SHOTS, 50 YARDS
FACTORY LOADS		
Federal 300-gr. JHP	1,591 fps	2 ¾"
Winchester 300-gr. JHP	1,624 fps	2 ½"
Garrett 405-gr. JFP	1,727 fps	¾"
Garrett 415-gr. Cast FP	1,686 fps	1 ¼"
HANDLOADS		
Hornady 350-gr. JSP/44.0 gr. IMR4198	1,811 fps	¾"
Speer 400-gr. JFP/ 54.0 gr. H322	1,759 fps	1 ½"
Speer 400-gr. JFP/ 53.7 gr. H4895	1,438 fps	1 ⅛"

surface problems on the inside of the barrel are dramatically reduced by the BlackStar process.

Does it work? Absolutely. It also really made the long-barreled octagonal rifle much easier to clean after shooting black powder. But what it did for the short-barreled rifle's performance was even more impressive.

A SLEEPER AT THE BENCH

Here's what happened: September is a tough month to get a long-range bench at Black's Creek Rifle Range. It's when once-a-year shooters bring their deer and elk rifles out of the closet to check the zero. But I had to go, and when I did, I saw so many top-line scoped bolt guns I was almost ashamed to bring out my modest little DeHart-customized Model 1895 topped with a Weaver K2.5 scope. Well, *almost* ...

Once I settled in at the bench, I carefully squeezed off three shots at a 100-yard target. My load was 47.5 grains of H332 under a Speer 400-grain JFP, which clocked 1,600 fps out of the 18-inch barrel. It produced a cluster of two shots in one hole and the group "opened" up to 1¼ inches with the third shot. Later, the range officer looked at my group and said, "Why, half the rifles out here won't do that!"

Originally I had planned the short gun as a once-in-awhile hunting rifle and the long-barreled rifle as a fun-shootin' big bore. But I was totally taken unaware by the fact the heavier octagonal-barreled example is the most punishing. The carbine has a recoil pad that tames things, even with the heaviest loads, but the rifle picks up so much velocity over the little carbine, I pay for it at the back end. However, I just cannot bring myself to spoil the traditional lines of the octagonal-barreled rifle by adding a recoil pad. I'd rather tailor the loads than the rifle for shooting comfort.

BIG BORE FOR A BIG BOAR

Normally, all my hunting is done with a handgun. But the .45-70 carbine handled so nicely it begged to go afield. Rick

The .45-70 Marlin 24-inch LTD (top) and 1895G Guide Gun .45-70 (bottom) compared to the 1895M in .450 Marlin (center). The .450 Marlin (inset) is a belted powerhouse designed to deliver "magnumized" .45-70 performance. In this particular Buffalo-Bore loading — a 405-grain JFN at 1,940 fps — it does just that.

VonDer Heide and I found a place to hunt wild boars less that a day's drive away, so even though the temperature had been hovering around the 100-degree mark, we sallied forth to slay a big boar with the big bore. It was so hot I decided the first pig with tusks would be fair game, When we found him, one Garrett 415-grain cast-bullet load did the trick. The hog went exactly 12 inches. Straight down. The octagonal-barreled Marlin 1895 .45-70 is reminiscent of the .45-70 and .45-90 leverguns of the last century. With black-powder loads, every pull of the trigger takes me back over 125 years.

There are two reasons for customizing a firearm. One is to give it the personal touch, and the other is to make it better than the original. I do believe DeHart and I accomplished both objectives with these Model 1895s.

THE .450 MARLIN

For 28 years the only chambering available in the 1895 Marlin was the .45-70. Then in 2000, Hornady and Marlin worked together to come up with a new cartridge, the .450 Marlin.

Hornady said the reason for the cartridge was "to allow factory ammunition to take advantage of the potential of the .45-70 without loading it to pressures in excess of SAAMI maximums. We teamed up with Marlin and set out to design a cartridge that would meet performance requirements, and function reliably in Marlin's Model 1895. The belt on the .450 Marlin is similar to, but longer than, the belt on standard belted magnums, thus it will not chamber in any other firearm with the standard Magnum chamber or a standard .45-70 chamber."

If the .450 Marlin looks familiar it's because it is basically the .458x2-inch American — a cartridge developed in the early 1960s by shortening a .458 Winchester Magnum case. This allowed the building of a lightweight, short-action, big-bore bolt gun for those who wanted the caliber but not the heavy recoil of the .458.

The .458x2-inch American was a belted cartridge (just as is the .450 Marlin) and was often referred to as a belted .45-70. What happened to it? It was soon realized the

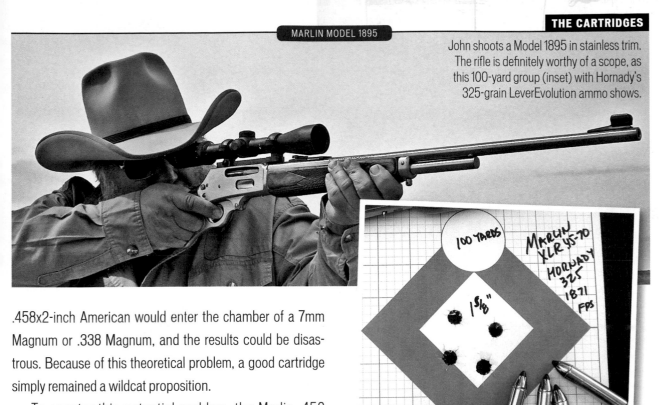

THE CARTRIDGES

John shoots a Model 1895 in stainless trim. The rifle is definitely worthy of a scope, as this 100-yard group (inset) with Hornady's 325-grain LeverEvolution ammo shows.

.458x2-inch American would enter the chamber of a 7mm Magnum or .338 Magnum, and the results could be disastrous. Because of this theoretical problem, a good cartridge simply remained a wildcat proposition.

To counter this potential problem, the Marlin .450 round has a higher belt so it cannot enter the chambers of rifles intended for other belted rounds nor will it fit in a .45-70. The .450 Marlin is an excellent round; however, as soon as it appeared we began to see strange comments from those who obviously had not done their homework. The .450 Marlin did not offer improved "smashing power" and certainly did not render the .45-70 obsolete. The original loading with a 350-grain bullet at 2,100 fps duplicated the ballistics of heavy .45-70 loads already then available from both Buffalo Bore and Cor-Bon.

The .450 Marlin, while not bearing a "magnum" label still gives magnum performance from a belted case which precludes it being inserted in any .45-70 chamber. The rifle model it's chambered in is known as the Model 1895M. It is so close to the Guide Gun (1895G) in weight, barrel length, stock configuration and barrel twist, you have to look very closely to find any difference other than the caliber marking on the barrel. In fact my .45-70 Guide Gun and my 1895M .450 Marlin are basically two peas in a pod. I like 'em both.

The 1895M chambered in the .450 Marlin may simply duplicate Heavy Duty .45-70 loads, however it is still an excellent cartridge and has proven to be exceptionally accurate in the Marlin 1895M. At 50

yards three shots group in ¾ inch, while at 100 yards in a strong wind, the three-shot group measures 1¾ inches. The .450 Marlin cartridge and the Marlin 1895M have the accuracy and power to take almost anything. ◉

TEST-FIRE: MARLIN 1895M
(18½-INCH BARREL, 4x SCOPE)

BULLET/POWDER	CHARGE	VELOCITY	3 SHOTS, 50 YARDS
.450 MARLIN HANDLOADS			
Hornady 350-gr. FN/Reloder 7	42.0 gr.	1,586 fps	7/8"
Hornady 350-gr. FN/Reloder 7	50.0 gr.	1,817 fps	1 ¼"
Hornady 350-gr. FN/H4895	56.0 gr.	1,778 fps	1¼"
Hornady 350-gr. FN/AA#2495BR	54.0 gr.	1,508 fps	7/8"
Hornady 350-gr. FN/H322	58.0 gr.	2,030 fps	3/4"
Speer 400-gr. FN/H4895	50.0 gr.	1,603 fps	5/8"
Speer 400-gr. FN/Reloder 7	47.0 gr.	1,756 fps	5/8"
RCBS #45-405-gr. FNGC/AA#2495BR	50.0 gr.	1,548 fps	7/8"

The Winchester Model 1876 chambered in .45-75 was Theodore Roosevelt's favorite rifle for hunting the Dakota Badlands. TR and the Model 1876 were featured in the January 1956 issue of *Guns*.

AS AMERICA'S 'SHOOTINGEST' PRESIDENT, T.R. PICKED BATTERY WITH EYE TO USE AS ACTIVE HUNTER IN WEST AND IN AFRICA

By WILLIAM B. EDWARDS

THE GUNS OF TEDDY ROOSEVELT

WINCHESTER'S
MODEL 1876 .45-75

John waited a spell for Cimarron to come out with the Model 1876 but was glad he did!

CHAPTER 56

One book that had a profound effect on my life was Hermann Hagedorn's *The Boy's Life of Theodore Roosevelt*. I first read it when I was in the 6th grade. Long before I ever owned my first firearm, I was reading about T.R.'s hunting expeditions and, more importantly, the type of man he was.

A few years later, in January 1956, *Guns Magazine* began its second year with Roosevelt on the front cover. He was dressed in his Dakota Badlands buckskins and holding his short-magazine Winchester Model 1876. The article within was entitled "The Guns of Teddy Roosevelt." Apparently the author was unaware Theodore did not like the nickname of "Teddy."

PRESIDENTIAL GUN GUY

Firearms were tremendously important to Roosevelt throughout his life. He was always ready to embrace the

One of the things John loves about the Model 1876 is the fact it's easy to load — no fighting with the loading gate!

newest models if they represented a definite improvement. When Winchester introduced the smokeless powder .30-30 in 1895, Roosevelt was captivated by its long-range capabilities and considered the Model 94 a fine antelope rifle. When he went on an African safari after leaving the White House, one of his rifles was the relatively new 1903 Springfield .30-06.

But earlier, as a rancher in the Dakotas, he also carried and used what he considered the best guns available at the time. His belt gun was a beautifully engraved and ivory stocked 7½-inch Colt Frontier Sixshooter, carried in an exquisitely carved leather holster. His favorite Dakota rifle was the Winchester Model 1876, which had been introduced at the Centennial Exhibition celebrating the 100th Year of American Independence.

The first Winchesters — the Model 1860, 1866 and 1873 — operated with a toggle action. This same principle was used to create the Model 1876, which is basically a larger Model 1873 capable of handling longer and more powerful cartridges. All of these rifles were designed before the advent of John M. Browning, whose lever-action designs for Winchester — the Model 1886, 1892, 1894 and 1895 — all used double locking lugs replacing the toggle action of the earlier rifles. By today's standards, the latter models are very strong rifles, but the earlier toggle-action designs are not and must only be used with black-powder loads. Today's replicas of these rifles are for black-powder (or black-powder-level) loads only.

The original Model 1876 was chambered in .40-60 .45-60, .45-75 and .50-95. The action was too short to

accommodate the .45-70; however, by going to a bottleneck design for the .45-75, Winchester was able to basically duplicate .45-70 performance with the lighter weight bullets. Roosevelt used several Winchester 1876s and considered the .40-60 a great saddle gun for deer and antelope in the Badlands. But his favorite chambering was .45-75. In his *Hunting Trips of a Ranchman*, he had this to say:

"A word as to weapons and hunting-dress. When I first came to the plains I had a heavy Sharps rifle, .45-120, (This is the second reference I have found to the .45-120 by a well-known historical figure, while others say there was no .45-120 at the time) shooting an ounce and a quarter of lead, and a 50-calibre, double-barreled English express. Both of these, especially the latter, had a vicious recoil; the former was very clumsy; and, above all, they were neither of

The .45-75 (right) was a bottlenecked attempt to approach the power level of the .45-70 (left) in a lever-action repeater.

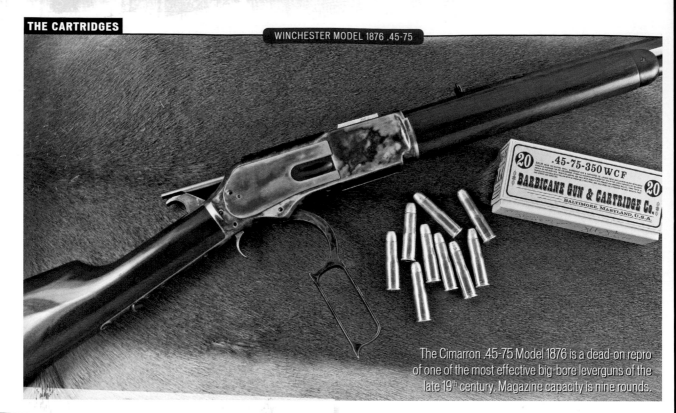

The Cimarron .45-75 Model 1876 is a dead-on repro of one of the most effective big-bore leverguns of the late 19th century. Magazine capacity is nine rounds.

> With the Model 1876, I can only find two things to object to. One is easily fixed while the other is easy to work around.

them repeaters; for a repeater or magazine-gun is as much superior to a single- or double-barreled breech-loader as the latter is to a muzzleloader. I threw them both aside and have instead a .40-90 Sharps for very long-range work; a .50-115 6-shot Ballard express, which has the velocity, shot, and low trajectory of the English gun; and better than either, a .45-75 half-magazine Winchester.

"The Winchester, which is stocked and sighted to suit myself, is by all odds the best weapon, I ever had, and I now use it almost exclusively, having killed every kind of game with it, from a grizzly bear to a bighorn. It is as handy to carry, whether on foot or on horseback, and comes up to the shoulder as readily as a shotgun; it is absolutely sure, and there is no recoil to jar and disturb the aim, while it carries adequately quite as far as a man can aim with any degree of certainty; and the bullet, weighing three quarters of an ounce, is plenty large enough for anything on this continent. For shooting the very large game (buffalo, ele-

phants, etc.) of India and South Africa, much heavier rifles are undoubtedly necessary; but the Winchester is the best gun for any game to be found in the United States, for it is as deadly, accurate, and handy as any, stands very rough usage, and is unapproachable for the rapidity of its fire and the facility with which it is loaded."

Roosevelt considered the Model 1876 to be the best rifle available at the time. However, he was not the sentimental type when it came to firearms; as better arms came about he retired the Model 1876 and used such later offerings as the Winchester Models 1894 and 1895 and the .30-06 Springfield.

TODAY'S REPLICAS

All the Winchesters — 1860, 1866, 1873 and 1892 — have long been offered in replica form while the 1886 and 1895 were offered through both Winchester and Browning, although manufactured in Japan. The legendary Model 1894 was removed from production after well over 100 years with many millions being produced, and they are still relatively easy to find in both rifle and sixgun chamberings, however it is now also available in several iterations through Winchester but manufactured by Miroku in Japan.

However, one Winchester had long been conspicuous by its absence on the replica market. More than five years

One of the best sources for factory .45-75 is Ten-X Ammunition, a company specializing in vintage calibers.

The Cimarron Model 1876 Centennial features an octagonal barrel and the traditional buckhorn-style rear sight.

ago, I talked to Mike Harvey of Cimarron Firearms about the Model 1876 which, he assured me, was in the works. It was a long time coming, however the Cimarron Centennial Model 1876 is now not only available, but it is also being offered in all four of the original chamberings: .40-60, .45-60, .45-75 and .50-95. As an extra added bonus, all of these "obsolete," cartridges are now offered by Ten-X Ammunition in both smokeless and BPC (Black Powder Cartridge) configurations. Roosevelt always looked forward, however I am quite happily traveling backwards to enjoy the rifle he used 130 years ago. Sometimes progress really does work for us!

Looking at Cimarron's Centennial Model 1876, just as Theodore Roosevelt, I find a whole lot to like about both the rifle and the .45-75 chambering. First the rifle itself: As with every Uberti-made Winchester replica I have experienced, and this includes all four of the toggle bolt-action models, this Model 1876 is beautifully crafted. The octagonal barrel, magazine tube, forend cap, sliding dust cover and buttplate are all finished in a very deep blue-black color, while the receiver, hammer, trigger, lever and tang are attractively casehardened. Both the forearm and buttstock are of nicely figured walnut although with the typical Italian reddish colored gloss finish.

The rear sight is a typical "V" shaped

Buckhorn with a square notch at the bottom of the V and is mated up with a front post of the proper size. Both sights are mounted in a dovetail for easy adjustment and also furnished with a locking screw. The rear sight is adjustable for elevation with a sliding bar with steps of varying heights as still found on even the most modern lever actions today. Behind the rear sight we find "1776 Centennial 1876," on the left side of the octagonal barrel just in front of the receiver "CAL 45-75" is inscribed, and on the top of the tang we find "Model 1876" just as on the originals. On the top of the octagonal barrel in front of the rear sight we find two lines inscribed "Cimarron's Repeating Arms Fredericksburg Texas U.S.A." and "King's Improvement Patented March 29, 1866. October 16. 1860."

John's admiration for Theodore Roosevelt adds an extra measure of pleasure to his shooting sessions with T.R.'s old standby.

CIMARRON FIREARMS MODEL 1876 .45-75 (22-INCH BARREL)

Load	Velocity	3 Shots, 50 Yards
FACTORY AMMO PERFORMANCE		
Ten-X 350-gr. FN	1,155 fps	2 ¼"
Ten-X 350-gr. FN BPC	1,253 fps	2 ¼"
HANDLOADED AMMO PERFORMANCE		
BULLET: RCBS #45-300-GR. FNGC		
27.0 gr. 5744	1,386 fps	1 ¾"
42.0 gr. 2015	1,656 fps	3 ½"
44.0 gr. H4895	1,396 fps	2 ¼"
44.0 gr. Varget	1,257 fps	2 ¼"
BULLET: LYMAN #457122 GOULD HP		
26.0 gr. 5744	1,314 fps	7/8"
40.0 gr. 2015	1,581 fps	3"
40.0 gr. H4895	1,274 fps	1 ½"
40.0 gr. Varget	1,312 fps	2 ⅜"
16.0 gr. Trail Boss	1,252 fps	7/8"
70.0 gr. GOEX Ctg.	1,231 fps	2 ⅜"
BULLET: HORNADY 300-GRAIN JFP		
27.0 gr. 5744	1,237 fps	2 ⅛"
42.0 gr. H4895	1,193 fps	1 ⅞"
BULLET: OREGON TRAIL 350-GRAIN FN		
27.0 gr. 5744	1,250 fps	2"
42.0 gr. H4895	1,240 fps	2 ⅛"

With the Model 1876, I can only find two things to object to. One is easily fixed while the other is easy to work around. According to my RCBS trigger scale, the pull weight is just over seven pounds — a fact which makes the excellent groups I acquired somewhat surprising. The other "problem" is the curved steel buttplate which is identical to the original's. Roosevelt found the recoil to be mild, which it was when compared to the more powerful single-shot rifles. However, when shooting numerous loads off the bench, I need a bit of comfort. After repeated firing, the top and bottom corners of the curved steel buttplate begin to dig into my shoulder. This was easily solved by the use of a

Pachmayr Slip-On Decelerator Pad. Of course, in a hunting situation, the pad isn't really critical, but when I'm shooting a lot of rounds, on it goes!

With a 22-inch barrel, Cimarron catalogs this particular Model 1876 as a Short Rifle (as compared to the standard 28-inch version). But even with its abbreviated length, the Short Rifle still holds nine rounds in the magazine tube. One of the problems with many lever-action rifles is the tension on the loading gate which quite often makes it difficult to insert cartridges, especially in cold weather. But this Model 1876 is the easiest-loading lever action I've ever used. Those .45-75 cartridges slide in so easily they practically load themselves. Overall feeding is as slick as anyone could ask for. It is almost a spiritual experience to work the action and feel the cartridge come straight up and chamber effortlessly as you work the lever. If the rifle is pointed slightly below horizontal, those bottlenecked .45-75s literally slide into the chamber even before the lever is closed.

Just as with the original Winchester, the Cimarron Model 1876 is available in .40-60, .45-65, .45-75 and .50-95. In his excellent book *Shooting Lever Guns of the Old West*, Mike Venturino tested all four of these cartridges in original Winchesters. He told of the ease of making the first two cartridges using .45-70 brass, the .50-95 from .348 Winchester, and the difficulty he had with .45-75 brass. Mike said:

"Unlike the .45-60 caliber, I doubt if there is any chance that the .45-75 caliber will ever be resurrected in a modern replica of the Model 1876. Its case shape is just too oddball."

I am glad Mike was wrong, and I'm sure he is too. Not only is the Cimarron Model 1876 chambered in .45-75, Ten-X Ammunition offers two loadings using 350-grain hard-cast bullets. One uses smokeless powder while the other is assembled with a special blend of Hodgdon's black-powder substitute, Triple 7. Fired from the 22-inch barrel of my Short Rifle, these clocked out at 1,155 fps and 1,253 fps, respectively. Mike's loads using the RCBS #45-300 FNGC bullet over 70 grains of Double F black powder are right at 1,440 fps from an original 1876 with a 28-inch

The Cimarron 1876 Short Rifle (top) compared to an original Winchester 1876 Centennial Model, restored and engraved, with the standard 28-inch barrel.

barrel. With the shorter barrel, my loads lost about 200 fps.

Not only is the .45-75 rifle available along with loaded ammunition and brass, but Lyman also offers excellent dies at standard prices, not with the high-dollar tag usually found on custom die sets. For reloading the .45-75, I use Ten-X brass and four bullets — Oregon Trail's 350-grain FN (a dead ringer for the bullet used in the Ten-X factory rounds), Hornady's 300-grain JFP and two home-cast bullets. The do-it-yourself ones consist of both the RCBS #45-300 FNGC and a very old design, Lyman's #457122 (known as the Gould hollowpoint).

When loading these cast bullets for use in the Model 1876, it pays to check the overall length. My friend Ray Walters has a 28-inch Cimarron 1876 and the Lyman/Gould hollowpoints will chamber when crimped in the crimping groove, but with my 1876 I have to crimp over the front shoulder or they will not chamber. Cast from wheelweights, both bullets are in the 325- to 330-grain weight range. With their softer alloy — sized to .458 inch — and with the proper powder charges, they both shot slightly tighter groups than the hard-cast 350-grain FN bullets in either the factory or handloaded versions. In fact, they even grouped better than the jacketed bullets as well.

Even with the heavy trigger pull and open iron sights, 50-yard groups in the 1 inch or less range are not unusual, and it's no problem to come up with 2-inch groups at 100 yards using the RCBS #45-300-grain FNGC bullet. My favorite handloads for this bullet are assembled with 27 grains of 5744 for 1,386 fps and 16 grains of Trail Boss for 1,246 fps. When I switch to the Lyman/Gould HP, I use the

same two powders, although with one less grain of 5744, for 1,314 fps and 1,252 fps, respectively. These results are also easily obtainable with the same-weight bullets in a 7½-inch Ruger .45 Colt Blackhawk, which should put the .45-75 in the proper perspective for hunting situations. For me, it would do for anything in the United States at 100 yards or less.

The Model 1876 from Cimarron was a long time coming but definitely worth the wait. With a cost of more than $1,500, it can scarcely be considered inexpensive. But for the price of one original Model 1876 in shooting condition, you can have Cimarron Model 1876s in all four chamberings, with the option of both smokeless and black-powder loads.

The first thing you'll see when you enter my front door is a painting of myself with Theodore Roosevelt in the Badlands. Of course the situation is purely imaginary, but thanks to Cimarron, you can bet my imagination has a field day every time I shoot T.R's favorite Dakota rifle. ◎

Two excellent bullet choices for the .45-75 are the RCBS #45-300-grain FNGC (left) and the Lyman Gould HP (right).

Doug Turnbull represents the gold standard of color casehardening. Besides beautifying Model 1886s (foreground), he will take on other models such as the Ruger No. 1.
Photo: Turnbull Manufacturing

THE
.45-70 WINCHESTER
MODEL 1886

CHAPTER 57

Way back when I started reading everything I could find about sixguns and rifles, Lucian Cary of *True* magazine had this to say in the late 1940s:

"One day a tall, gaunt, bearded man with a pack horse came along the road between our camp and the mountain stream we fished. He carried what seemed to me then to be an enormous rifle. I recognized it as a Winchester and asked what cartridge it shot. This, he said, is a forty-five-ninety. I knew even then what that meant. It was a rifle of .45 caliber shooting 90 grains of black powder. To me, who had never fired anything bigger than the .22, that .45-90 was awesome. It was a rifle to shoot grizzly bears with. It was the kind of rifle I wanted when I was big enough."

The Winchester the old man was carrying was the Model 1886, perhaps the finest lever action ever made. It came about because Winchester's son-in-law, Thomas Bennett, wanted a more powerful levergun, one that would handle the .45-70. He'd heard of a pair of brothers living in Utah who were rifle designers. So Bennett went to Ogden, met the Browning brothers and purchased two new rifle designs, one destined to be the 1885 Single-Shot, the other the levergun that would become the Model 1886.

Although Marlin had beaten Winchester to the punch with the first .45-70 levergun, John Browning eventually saved the day for Winchester by abandoning the older toggle-link action Winchester had been using in the Model 1876 for a pair of massively strong locking lugs.

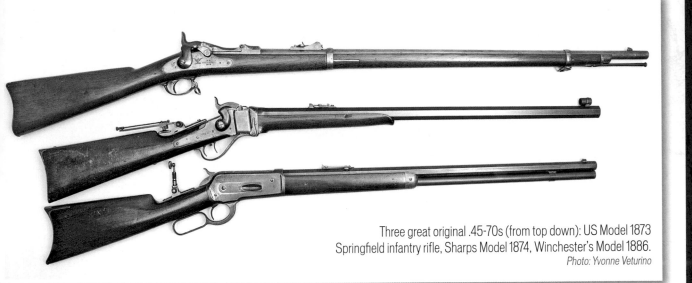

Three great original .45-70s (from top down): US Model 1873 Springfield infantry rifle, Sharps Model 1874, Winchester's Model 1886.
Photo: Yvonne Veturino

BIG MEDICINE

By today's standards the Winchester 1886 was huge, weighing about nine pounds. It also had an extremely smooth action that carried over to the "miniature 1886" that would come later — the Winchester Model 1892. Although the Model 1886 was introduced in the era of black-powder cartridges, it proved strong enough to handle the transition to smokeless. About the only change necessary was the nickel steel barrel to handle the higher velocities with jacketed bullets.

The Model 1886 was manufactured from 1886 to 1935. However, one year after It was removed from production it returned in a "modernized" version — the Model 71 in .348 Winchester. During its production run, the Model 1886 was made in several versions including full-length magazine, half-magazine, octagonal barrel, round barrel, rifle and carbine, just to name a few. Initially it was chambered in nine black-powder calibers — .45-90, .45-70, .40-82, .50-100, .50-110, .40-70, .40-60, .38-70 and .38-

56. Its last chambering before its demise in 1935 was the smokeless .33 Winchester.

REPRO OR REISSUE?

In 1986 Browning brought forth a commemorative, the Browning Centennial, a nine-shot .45-70 with a 26-inch octagonal barrel, straight-grip stock, crescent buttplate and buckhorn rear sight with a bead front. It was offered in two versions, a standard Grade I with blued finish and a High Grade with engraved receiver and select walnut. Total production was 7,000 of Grade I and 3,000 of the High Grade version. There were also 2,000 High Grade Montana Centennial rifles issued the same year.

The Browning Model 1886s were made by Miroku in Japan. In 1998, the rifle came back again under the Winchester label this time, again being made by Miroku. Each year after that a new limited-edition version was introduced, including a standard rifle, a take-down and an Extra Light model. The latter weighs slightly over seven pounds with a

Cimarron's Model 1886 features the traditional crescent steel buttplate (ouch!) as well as a 26-inch heavy octagonal barrel.

WINCHESTER
1886
45-70
50 YDS

FUSILIER
400 GC
52.0 gr H322
2027 FPS

John demonstrates a little "lever action" with his Browning/Winchester .45-70 Model 1886 Takedown (inset). At 50 yards it is a very "packable" combination of accuracy and bone-crushing power, particularly with his pet handloads.

length magazine tube. This latch lever then serves as a handle to unscrew the magazine tube to remove it. Once this is done, twist the barrel to unlock it from the receiver. The whole process takes less than a minute.

My rifle has a 26-inch full-octagonal barrel with a full-length magazine tube. The metal finish is a deep black-blue color. The wood is good quality walnut and the stock features a crescent-shaped buttplate. (It does *not* match up well with today's full-house .45-70 loads!) Magazine capacity is eight rounds.

Factory sights are a bead front and a buckhorn rear, a setup I quickly replaced with a Williams receiver sight. As your eyes get older, open rear sights become harder to see, but a receiver sight allows you to focus on the front sight while centering it automatically in the rear aperture. I am confident that I can hit at any distance I am likely to shoot live targets with this sighting arrangement. It's not a long-range combination, but neither is the .45-70 a long-range cartridge.

half magazine, 22-inch tapered barrel and shotgun style buttplate. My Browning/Winchester rifle is the 1886 Take-Down Model (original take-downs command premium prices today). This feature makes it very easy to transport without a conventional gun case advertising "Rifle Inside!" Of even greater importance to me is the fact that cleaning is made much more convenient by being able to easily remove the barrel from the action.

Simply move the lever completely forward on an unloaded gun and pull up on the latch at the end of the full-

Yes, I know it is used to 500 yards and beyond by silhouette shooters, but they are shooting at known distances, at inanimate targets, with high-quality, tang-mounted Vernier sights. A hit anywhere on the metal target counts if it knocks the steel over. But this latitude does not exist in hunting situations. I consider the .45-70 Model 1886 to be a 100- to 150-yard proposition, at least in my hands. And, truth be told, I am more than likely to stay in the 50- to 100-yard range using big bullets of 400 to 500+ grains in weight.

HEAVY-DUTY FACTORY LOADS

Specialty loads such as those offered by Buffalo Bore, Cor-Bon and Garrett Cartridges will handle anything that walks. Garrett's 530-grain Hammerhead — a hard-cast flat-nosed bullet at around 1,575 fps is particularly noteworthy.

Buffalo Bore's .45-70 offerings include a 430-grain LBT bullet at 2,000 fps, a 350-grain JFP at 2,200 fps and a 405-grain JFP at 2,050 fps. All these heavy loads shoot well in my Model 1886, with the 350-grain load being a real tack-driver. Recoil with all, of course, is stout — and is accentuated by a crescent buttplate.

Cor-Bon's .45-70 offerings consist of a 350-grain JFP Bonded Core at a little over 2,000 fps. It shoots well and is relatively easy on the shoulder. The company also has a 405-grain Penetrator load designed to do just what its name implies — penetrate from here to Sunday. Unfortunately, the throat on my Model 1886 is too tight to allow it to chamber.

The Winchester 1886 shoots many of my handloads very well. Speer's 400-grain JFP over 50.0 grains of H322 (1,830 fps), Oregon Trail's 405-grain hard cast over 48 grains of AA2495BR (1,625 fps) and the RCBS 500-grain FNGC in front of 31.0 grains of IMR4198 (1,575 fps) will all deliver 1-inch groups (or less) at 50 yards with iron sights.

Since the Model 1886 was originally a black-powder rifle, it's only natural (and a whole lot more comfortable) to use it as such. I load Lyman's 420-grain, plain-based cast bullet over both 62.5 grains of GOEX Cartridge black powder and 53.6 grains of Clean Shot, the black-powder substitute. The former load clocks out at 1,200 fps while the latter comes

in at a pleasant-shooting 1,400 fps. The best black-powder loads utilize a lot of soft lube to keep fouling to a minimum. I use Lyman's Black Powder Gold.

THE CIMARRON .45-70

Cimarron Firearms has a full range of Winchester lever-guns available, the latest being the Model 1886. It's imported

TEST-FIRE: WINCHESTER MODEL 1886 .45-70
(24-INCH BARREL, LYMAN RECEIVER SIGHT)

HANDLOADS	VELOCITY	3 SHOTS, 50 YARDS
Speer 350-gr. JFP/54.0 gr. H322	2,094 fps	1 ¾"
Speer 400-gr. JFP/50.0 gr. H322	1,831 fps	7/8"
Oregon Trail 405-gr. /48.0 gr. AA2495	1,622 fps	3/4"
RCBS #45-405-gr.FN/52.0 gr. H322	2,027 fps	2"
RCBS #45-405-gr. FN/39.0 gr. IMR4198	1,766 fps	1 ½"
RCBS #45-500-gr. FN/31.0 gr. IMR4198	1,577 fps	1 ⅛"
RCBS/#45-500-gr. FN/41.0 gr. AA2495	1,486 fps	1 ⅜"
Lyman #457193/62.5 gr. GOEX CTG	1,208 fps	1 ⅞"
Lyman #457193/53.5 gr. CleanShot	1,396 fps	1 ⅜"

TEST-FIRE: CIMARRON MODEL 1886 .45-70
(26-INCH BARREL, FACTORY OPEN SIGHTS)

FACTORY LOADS	VELOCITY	3 SHOTS, 50 YARDS
Cor-Bon 350-gr. Bonded Core	1,948 fps	1 ¾"
Federal 300-gr. Sierra Pro Hunter	1,667 fps	1 ½"
Garrett 415-gr. Hard Cast	1,844 fps	1 ¾"
Hornady 325-gr. LeverEvolution	2,164 fps	1 ¾"
Winchester 300-gr. JHP	1,905 fps	1 ¾"

by Chiappa Firearms of Dayton, Ohio, and is made by Italy's Armi Sport. The heavy octagonal barrel is 26 inches in length and the full-length magazine tube holds eight rounds. Both the barrel and tube have a deep blue/black finish while the receiver, hammer, lever, trigger, forend cap and crescent buttplate are all case-colored. Sights consist of a post front sight set in a dovetail matched up with a semi-buckhorn rear, also set in a dovetail and adjustable for elevation with an elevator bar.

Both the forearm and buttstock are nicely figured walnut, well finished and fitted. Just as with most of the originals, this replica carries a crescent steel buttplate. I've never understood why heavy recoiling rifles were ever fitted with them, but it is my understanding they were originally designed to fit the shooter's arm rather than be snugged into the shoulder. My original Winchester 1886 from the WW I era was purchased used, and long before I got it, someone fitted it with a shotgun-style buttplate complete with a heavily cushioned recoil pad.

There was a time when everything I loaded, including the .45-70, were pretty much loaded to the hilt. Those days are long gone. My powders of choice now are Trail Boss and #5744. With the latter I use a standard load of 27.0 grains with all Oregon Trail bullet weights — 350, 405, 430 and 500 grains. Muzzle velocities are right at 1,300 fps with each bullet weight with a high of approximately 1,330 fps for the lightest bullet and 1,285 fps for the heaviest. All are relatively pleasant to shoot, yet definitely powerful enough for hunting.

Hodgdon's Trail Boss is a relatively new powder originally designed to provide pleasant shooting Cowboy Action loads. It also works great for such cartridges as the .45-70 and is loaded to the base of the bullet without compression. In the .45-70 using cast bullets consisting of the 330-grain Gould HP and the RCBS #45-300-grain FNGC, this turns out to be 16.0 grains, resulting in a muzzle velocity of approximately 1,275 fps. Both should be more than adequate for hogs, black bear and deer.

The 26-inch barrel length of the Cimarron Model 1886 results in impressive muzzle velocities with heavy-duty factory loads. The Cor-Bon 350-grain Bonded Core and the Winchester 300 JHP loads both register over 1,900 fps. The Federal 300-grain Sierra Pro Hunter load clocks just under 1,700 fps, while Garrett's 415-grain hard-cast load is right at 1,850 fps.

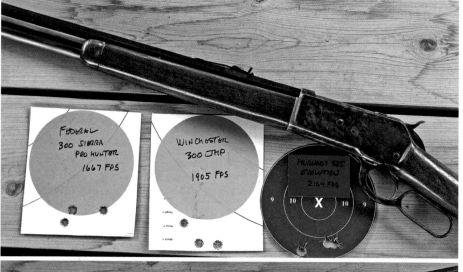

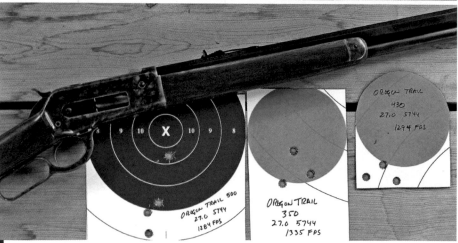

Cimarron's Model 1886 shows its potential with factory loads in the 300- to 325-grain weight range (top), as well as with John's own concoctions, featuring bullet weights from 350 to 500 grains (bottom).

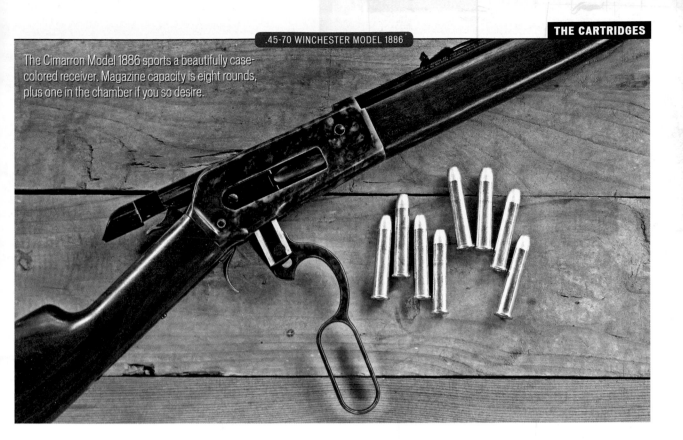

The Cimarron Model 1886 sports a beautifully case-colored receiver. Magazine capacity is eight rounds, plus one in the chamber if you so desire.

ENHANCED PERFORMER

One of the problems with lever-action rifles having a magazine tube was not being able to safely use spire-pointed bullets with their points resting against the primer of the load in front (a disaster waiting to happen!). Hornady solved this problem by using plastic-tipped bullets in its LeverEvolution line. The 325-grain .45-70 version clocks out at 2,165 fps from the long-barreled Cimarron, turning the 19th century levergun into a 21st-century hunting rifle.

With the factory iron sights, 50-yard groups for me are in the 1½- to 2-inch neighborhood, so basically this is a 100-yard hunting rifle. There have never been any malfunctions of any kind with mine, but the lever must be operated all the way to the front with authority, or the next round will not pick up and chamber. Show it who's boss and it works fine.

This is definitely the age of black plastic rifles and semi-automatic pistols. However, next to these big sellers we now have the choice of replicas of all the lever actions from the frontier period. I still think of that passage from Lucian Cary I read so long ago. Perhaps some young boy will look up from his trout stream someday as *this* grizzled old man walks by with his Model 1886 to provide him with dreams of the future. May tradition never die. ◉

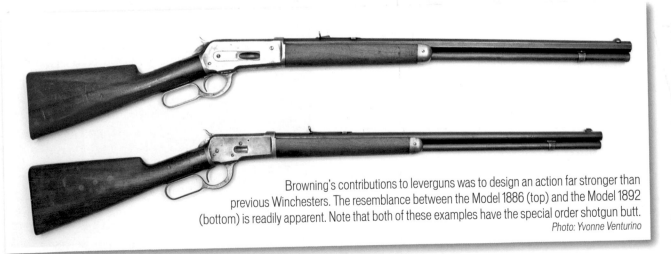

Browning's contributions to leverguns was to design an action far stronger than previous Winchesters. The resemblance between the Model 1886 (top) and the Model 1892 (bottom) is readily apparent. Note that both of these examples have the special order shotgun butt.

Photo: Yvonne Venturino

The Cowboy Action-inspired Winchester Trails End came with both the standard lever and large loop lever.

THE WINCHESTER .45 COLT MODEL 1894

CHAPTER 58

The first gun book I can ever remember reading was published the last year I was in grade school. It was Harold Williamson's classic *Winchester: The Gun That Won The West*. I checked it out of the local library so many times I'm surprised they didn't present me with my own copy. It instilled in me a lifelong love for leverguns.

Since then I've shot just about every levergun ever offered. If I had to make do with only one rifle, it would definitely have a lever on it!

ABBREVIATED BARRELS

To me the most fascinating leverguns are those with less than standard length barrels. In Sam Fadala's excellent *Legendary Sporting Rifles*, he says of the 1873 Winchester: "The early carbines carried barrels that in fact measured

Here's a lineup of easy-handling carbines (left to right): Ruger Mini-14, Ruger Mini-30, No. 5 Lee-Enfield Jungle Carbine in .303 British and Winchester's .45 Colt Trapper.

John installed a receiver sight on his 16-inch barreled Model 94 Trapper. It features the big loop lever — which really is more for "show" than "go." But big loop or standard, it's an exceptionally handy, useful tool.

19⅞ inches long, with a true 20-inch barrel appearing only later. Special-order carbines with shorter barrels were available as well — the most popular length being 15, then 16 and 18." In R.L. Wilson's *Winchester: An American Legend* is a studio picture of a cowboy with a 14-inch Trapper Model 1873. The standard Model 1892 carbine length was 20 inches; however, 325 Trapper .44-40s with barrels of 18 inches or less were manufactured with 14 inches being the most popular short length. Even John Wayne's Model 1892, which first appeared in 1939's *Stagecoach*, was shortened to allow him to easily swing it for cocking.

Just about the time I was ready to enter this world, the U.S. Congress, no doubt wishing to protect me from any evil in the future, mandated minimum barrel lengths for rifles and shotguns. It is certainly mystifying why there has to be a minimum length for long guns, but even more puzzling as to why rifle barrels can be shorter than shotgun barrels. I also wonder where the minimum 16-inch length for rifles came from. Whatever the reason, by the time I was old enough to buy a rifle, Trappers could no longer be made with 14- or 15-inch barrels.

THE MODEL 1894

Just about the time my interest in firearms began, I remember President Eisenhower being presented with the two-millionth Model 94. Winchester's lever-action classic had reached that milestone in slightly less than 60 years.

In an era when many stainless steel, synthetic-stocked bolt-action rifles feature adjustable muzzle brakes and are chambered in calibers that shoot as far as tomorrow, the ancient Model 94 with its antiquated lever-action system has passed the 7,000,000 mark. That amounts to a lot of steel and walnut being used in sensible calibers by a passel of savvy shooters.

The Winchester Model 94 stirs the heart, mind and soul as few other rifles. Even though it was not yet in existence during the time period depicted in most Hollywood westerns, the Model 94 — along with the Model 1892 — is still the rifle most of us saw in countless movies as we grew up

with Roy, Hoppy and Gene. It was indelibly printed in the mind of every kid growing up with the B movies of the 1930s and 1940s, as well as the TV westerns of the 1950s.

The .30-30 is the caliber most associated with the Model 1894, but it was not the first chambering. In 1894 John Browning's design was brought forth in the black-powder .32-40 and .38-55. Both of these cartridges (in smokeless format) were later resurrected in modern commemoratives.

During the last quarter of the 20th century, the Model 94 was given the "Trapper Treatment." Besides the inevitable .30-30 chambering, three versions were chambered for sixgun calibers. These are very handy little rifles, in spite of the fact the action is longer than necessary for them. (They actually work better in the Model 1892.) However, I have never encountered a problem with them in the Model 94, although things aren't as slick in operation as in the older models.

To make the .45 Colt Model 94 more competitive, Winchester's Trails End version has a 10-round magazine capacity.

Trappers Two: Marlin's 1894 version (top) and Winchester's Model 94 (bottom). Both are in .45 Colt, naturally.

LONG GUNS AND THEIR CARTRIDGES

THE BOOK OF THE .45

TEST-FIRE:
WINCHESTER TRAPPER
MODEL 94AE
.45 COLT (16½-INCH BARREL)

LOAD	VELOCITY	3 SHOTS, 50 YARDS
Sierra 240-gr. JHC/23.0 gr. H110	1,550 fps	1¼"
Sierra 240-gr. JHC/24.0 gr. H110	1,604 fps	2"
Sierra 240-gr. JHC/25.0 gr. H110	1,681 fps	1¼"
Hornady 250-gr. JHP/22.0 gr. H110	1,565 fps	1½"
Hornady 250-gr. JHP/23.0 gr. H110	1,598 fps	7/8"
Hornady 250-gr. JHP/25.0 gr. H110	1,741 fps	1"
Speer 260-gr. JHP/21.0 gr. WW296	1,358 fps	5/8"
Speer 260-gr. JHP/23.0 gr. H110	1,493 fps	1/2"
Speer 260-gr. JHP/25.0 gr. H110	1,591 fps	2"
Lyman #454424/22.0 gr. WW296	1,516 fps	1½"
Lyman #454424/24.0 gr. WW296	1,620 fps	2¼"
Lyman #454424/25.0 gr. WW296	1,675 fps	1½"
NEI 451.310-gr. KT/21.0 gr. WW296	1,446 fps	2"
NEI 451.310-gr. KT/22.0 gr. WW296	1,495 fps	1⅛"
NEI 451.310-gr. KT/23.0 gr. WW296	1,562 fps	1⅜"
NEI 454.325-gr. KT/23.5 gr. WW296	1,597 fps	1¾"

THE COMPANION CONCEPT

With the advent of the .44 Magnum sixgun from Smith & Wesson and Ruger in the 1950s, the demand soon rose for a companion levergun. Several gunsmiths made a comfortable living converting Model 92 Winchester .44-40s to .44 Magnum. Then in the 1960s, both Winchester and Marlin brought forth leverguns in .44 Magnum with Winchester's being on the tried and true Model 94. Since then, it's been offered in a commemorative version in .44-40, as well as .357 Magnum, .44 Magnum and .45 Colt. The Trapper versions of the Model 94 with 16½-inch barrels, full-length magazine tubes and chambered in .30-30, .44 Magnum and .45 Colt have been very popular as woods guns — easy to pack and handy in pick-ups and jeeps. Their short barrels and compact size make them infinitely more practical than a long-barreled bolt action, especially in a rancher's 4x4. The .357 Magnum chambering was eventually added to the

Winchester Trapper lineup and is, in my mind, second only to a good .22. It also makes a great choice for a "house gun" in areas where handguns are highly regulated.

THE TRAILS END VARIATION

The Winchester Trapper had been popular in some cowboy shooting matches, but competitors were at a disadvantage in those matches requiring 10 rifle shots, as the Trappers hold only nine rounds in the magazine when chambered for sixgun cartridges. Most, if not all matches adhere to the safety rule of no cartridge in the chamber at the buzzer, so it is necessary for those choosing the Trapper to load an extra round sometime during the firing sequence. This problem was addressed by Winchester with the appropriately named Trails End version designed specifically for cowboy shooters. Carrying 11 rounds, the Trails End was available in .357 Magnum, .44 Magnum and .45 Colt. All versions weigh in at 6½ pounds and were offered with the standard lever or the large loop lever.

Now, truth be told, the large loop looks good but has very little practical value. Duke and Lucas McCain could twirl their leverguns on the large loop and thus chamber a cartridge with style — a practice guaranteed to get one killed, as the bad guy simply cocked the hammer of his sixgun and fired while the levergun user was performing acrobatics. Even Cowboy Action shooters — many of whom are inclined to flamboyance — soon found the standard loop is much faster to operate than the large one. The Trails End Model 94 came equipped with a not-very-attractive cross-bolt safety which, nonetheless, performs a most worthwhile function. You and I may not need the safety, but it is most comforting to me to know everyone else out there has a safety and does not need to feel it necessary to walk around with a round in the chamber without a hammer block safety. It is easily applied and easily placed in a firing mode and should always be used anytime a round is carried in the chamber.

I have had the pleasure of shooting the Trails End Winchester for about 20 years now using it for general purpose plinking and just plain fun. Originally, Winchester supplied two test guns, both a .44 Magnum with a standard loop lever and a .45 Colt with the large loop lever. I was impressed

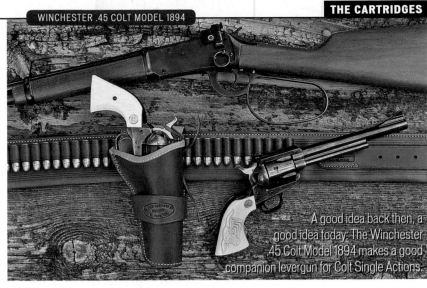

A good idea back then, a good idea today: The Winchester .45 Colt Model 1894 makes a good companion levergun for Colt Single Actions.

enough with the performance of both carbines that I bought both for my personal use, so to that end the .45 Colt large loop lever was quickly replaced with a standard loop lever.

With the Trails End one has several sight options. Standard is a rear sight with a white diamond for easy sighting and adjustable for elevation by moving up and down on a ladder mated with a post front sight. For windage, either sight can be tapped to the right or left to sight in for a particular load. A second option is the use of a scope by utilizing the drilled and tapped holes in the top of the frame for Weaver mounts. The left side of the frame is also drilled and tapped to accept receiver sights. Another option is the use of a tang-mounted peep as supplied by Lyman. It requires the drilling and tapping of a hole in the tang, but can be the answer for those who have trouble seeing the standard sights but do not want a scope.

For initial testing of the Trails End .45 Colt, I went with a 4x Weaver. Groups were fired at 50 yards with four shots being taken with each load and the best three measured. This gave me a "throwaway" shot and removed the pressure of trying to shoot a really tight group. Leverguns are mostly used for close-range hunting of such critters as deer and black bear. I generally use the .45 Colt Trails End with full-bore hunting loads as well as lighter general-purpose loads.

CARBINE-FRIENDLY .45 LOADS

While the .45 Colt Black Hills, Hornady or Winchester factory ammo will do fine as everyday loads, Federal's 225-grain lead semiwadcutter HP will serve for close range varminting, and features a muzzle velocity of 1,100 fps with a ½-inch, 50-yard capability. For a little more muzzle energy, I go to the old favorite Elmer Keith .45 Colt bullet, Lyman's #454424, a 260-grain semiwadcutter plain base. It does not seem to matter whether loads are assembled with Unique, Universal or WW231 — accuracy is excellent. This bullet crimped over the front driving band yields 960 fps with 8.0 grains of Unique, 870 with 7.5 grains of Universal and 1,150 with 7.0 grains of WW231. Average group size is 1⅛ inches for three shots at 50 yards.

My favorite hunting load in the .45 Colt for use in heavy-framed sixguns such as the Ruger Blackhawk has long been a 300-grain bullet over 21.5 grains of H110 or WW296. Using RCBS's excellent Keith-style, gas-checked 300-grain bullet #45-300SWC-GC over 21.5 grains of H110 yields a muzzle velocity of 1,400 fps from the Trails End Model 94 Colt and shoots remarkably well with groups at 1 inch. This is just the ticket for close-range deer, black bear, even elk. And the .45 Colt Trails End is a near-perfect companion to sixguns in the same chambering. ◉

Winchester's Trails End .45 Colt Model 94 works very well with standard loads — a definite plus if you're going to be working with factory Cowboy Action ammunition.

A perfect example of the "companion concept" in .45 Colt: Winchester's Model 94 with casehardened receiver and the rugged Ruger Bisley.

Mare's Leg: This "purely Hollywood" Model 92 variant was popularized in the old TV series *Wanted: Dead or Alive*. It is available in replica form from Rossi.

REPLICA .45 COLT LEVERGUNS

Rossi's Model 92 replica is available in the potent .454 Casull. It's quite accurate, but the generous recoil pad is there for a very good reason!

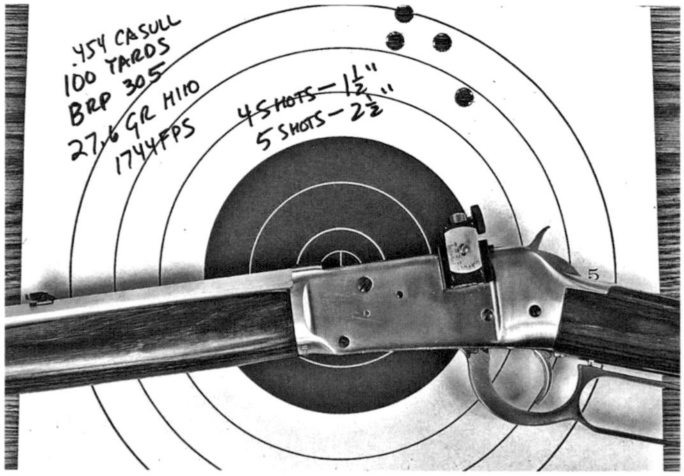

.454 CASULL
100 YARDS
BRP 305
27.6 GR H110
1744 FPS
4 SHOTS – 1½"
5 SHOTS – 2½"

CHAPTER 59

From 1860 to 1892, Winchester introduced four exceptionally handy carbines — the 1860 Henry in .44 Rimfire, the 1866 Yellow Boy (also in .44 Rimfire), the 1873 in .44 WCF and the Browning-designed 1892, also in .44 WCF. The Henry loaded much like some of today's .22 rimfire rifles, through an opening in the front of the under-barrel loading tube. With the arrival of the Model 1866, this arrangement was changed to a loading gate on the right side of the receiver. In 1873 brass gave way to iron, then quickly to steel, then from a toggle system to a pair of rear-locking steel bars — resulting in a much stronger action than in previous models.

All four of these legendary rifles are now offered in high-quality replica form, with most being available in .45 Colt as well as other chamberings. Cimarron Firearms offers 16-inch Trappers in both the 1866 and 1873 versions, chambered in .357 Magnum, .44-40 and .45 Colt. One of my favorite L'il Leverguns is the Cimarron Brush Popper, an 18-inch Model 1873 in .44-40. Anyone picking up Cimarron's Model 1866 Yellow Boy will surely feel his soul and imagination stirred if there's any feeling for our country's history whatsoever.

The toggle-link action of the 1866 Trapper, while shot as strong as later models, is unsurpassed for smoothness. Just keep it shouldered as you work the lever. In .45 Colt, John claims, "There's not a kick in a carload."

When I handle the 24-inch octagonal-barreled Model 1866, I can almost see great herds of bison grazing, rows of teepees along a riverbank, warriors on pinto ponies, transcontinental railroad workers, cowboys riding herd and a roaring campfire at the end of a long day. This is all easy for me to do as I grew up in the wonderful years BT (Before Television), when kids still had the ability to rely on their imagination.

The Model 1860 Henry was the first really successful levergun and was a tremendous step forward from the single-shot muzzleloaders of the time; however, it needed a couple of improvements. The loading operation was ingenious; however, it required the rifle be taken out of action while the end of the barrel and magazine tube were swiveled to the side to allow cartridges to be inserted base first from the front of the tube. In also lacked a forearm. Cimarron's Model 1866 is marked "King's Imported Improvement Patented March 29, 1866" signifying and paying tribute to the two great improvements transforming the Model 1860 into the Model 1866. The front-loading magazine tube was replaced by the now-traditional loading gate on the right side of the frame. As well, a wooden forearm was added to protect the support hand from a heated barrel. The frame was still brass and the cartridge was still a rimfire, both of which would be changed with the introduction of the Model 1873.

REPLICATED CLASSICS

As authentic as these replicas are, they are not in the original .44 Rimfire. (Cartridges have not been available for many decades.) Instead, Cimarron's first Model 1866 is marked ".44 WCF," or as it is most commonly known today, .44-40.

Of the two Cimarron 1866s I have, one is in .44-40, the other in .45 Colt. Each has a 24-inch octagonal barrel with a fold-down ladder sight calibrated to an optimistic 800 yards.

I normally have no reason to shoot at long distance with an iron-sighted levergun, and especially not with one chambered in .44-40 or .45 Colt. But then again, there sometimes comes a lazy summer day when I will find myself sitting under a shade tree with my Model 1866 in .45 Colt, plenty of ammunition, a jug of cool water and a dry dusty hillside several hundred yards across from me. This is simply a chance for pure shooting pleasure. For most of my shooting, however, the normal rear sight comes into play when the ladder sight is folded down. This is more than adequate for my needs.

The actions of the 1860/1866/1873 Winchesters are like no others as the cartridge feeds so easily coming straight up and then straight into the chamber as the lever is operated. Just working the action alone is an emotional experience for me.

All you need to do is sight these rifles in for standard loads — nothing else should ever be used in their old-style actions. Just loosen the locking screw on the right side of the dovetailed front sight to tap it for windage if needed. Firing both factory loads as well as my handloads with muzzle velocities well under 1,300 fps is nothing but pure pleasure. At a range of 25 yards — using eyes that are not *quite* as ancient as those old leverguns' designs — most loads hang right at 1 inch. Short range is just about the right distance for busting small rocks, pop cans and the occasional varmint. If there are any leverguns out there more enjoyable than these, please don't tell me. I couldn't stand the excitement!

As I have gotten older, the 24-inch octagonal-barreled Model 1866 in .45 Colt seemed to get heavier with each passing day. So I took it to my gunsmith to have it cut back to Trapper-style. With a barrel length of just over 16 inches, it's now still relatively heavy, thanks to the octagonal barrel, but it handles much easier. There's simply something special about a Trapper levergun.

Cimarron offers two 24-inch barreled classics, both in .45 Colt: An 1866 Yellow Boy Sporting Rifle (top) and a steel-framed Henry (bottom).

THE GREAT MODEL 92

Ringo had one. Rooster had one. Lucas had one. Josh Randall had *part* of one. Yes, all of these screen heroes had a Winchester Model 92. Who can ever forget the scene in *True Grit*, where John Wayne (as Rooster Cogburn) took a Colt .45 SAA in his left hand and a freshly twirled Winchester in his right, yells "Fill your hand you sonofabitch!" while charging Lucky Ned Pepper's gang single handedly.

Steve McQueen, as the bounty hunter Josh Randall in TV's *Wanted: Dead or Alive* also carried a bastardized Model 92 with a short barrel and shorter stock. The eye-catching loop lever was there along with someone's idea of what looked like eye-catching ammunition — as Randall's belt was filled with .45-70 cartridges that would not even come close to fitting the Model 92.

The Winchester Model 92 was made from 1892 to 1931 with some special models lasting right up to World War II with slightly over 1,000,000 units being produced. It was one of the slickest, smoothest leverguns ever made. The Model 1892 was simply a miniaturized Model 1886 chambered for the cartridges of the Model 1873. Over its long life, the '92 would be made in barrel lengths from 14 to 31 inches, however the 20-inch carbine model, holding 11 cartridges in its tubular magazine was pretty much the standard fare. None were ever made with the large loop lever. This was dreamed up in Hollywood for the Duke to use. It would appear in most of his movies over the next 30 years as well as various TV series. It has no practical value whatsoever, makes the Model 1892 harder to cock at shoulder level and, when twirled Hollywood-style, is a good way to shoot yourself.

The original Model '92 also appeared in .25-20, and .218 Bee and has been out of production for more than 80 years. Trying to find a good one is pretty tough, at least in my area. Many '92s were converted to modern cartridges in the 1950s, first to .357 Magnum (starting with a .25-20 or .32-20) and later to .44 Magnum (from a .38-40 or .44-40 as the base). The replica Rossi is a less expensive alternative to an original Model 1892 and in .45 Colt costs about half as much as the imported replica 1866 or 1873 leverguns. Sights are the standard ladder adjusting style on the rear mated up with a front post fitted into the barrel band. The rear sight can be adjusted laterally by tapping it to the right or left in its dovetail slot.

A loading gate at the right side of the receiver accepts the stubby handgun cartridges the Rossi is chambered for. Loading is easy when each round is shoved all the way into place by the next round. The last round can then be fully inserted by pushing on the base with your little finger.

Since the .45 Colt sixgun is so popular, the Rossi Model 92 .45 Colt makes an excellent companion levergun in which to utilize the same cartridge. However, the frontier sixgunner did not have the "companion .45 Colt" option.

A major asset of the .45 Colt Model 1892 Rossi (just as with the Marlin Model 1894 and the Winchester Model 94 Trapper) is the fact they will handle heavier loads than the toggle-link 1860/1866/1873 designs. These loads should be your choice for hunting deer-sized game at short ranges. My .45 Colt Rossi also works exceptionally well with mild loads — Black Hills' 250-grain flatpoint clocks out at 933 fps and drops its three shots at 50 yards into ¾ inch using the factory iron sights.

BUMPING UP THE ANTE

The Rossi Model 92 in .45 Colt is strong enough to also be chambered in .454 Casull. This, however, does not mean the .45 Colt version can be used with exceptionally heavy loads. To come up with the .454 Rossi, it was necessary to make some changes, including strengthening.

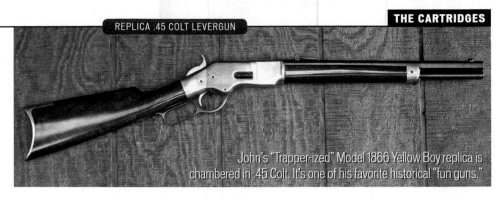

John's "Trapper-ized" Model 1866 Yellow Boy replica is chambered in .45 Colt. It's one of his favorite historical "fun guns."

Over the past nearly 30 years, I have tried several leverguns converted to .454 Casull, both the Marlin 1894 and the Winchester 1894. In both cases it did not take much shooting of full-house .454 loads for the action to start stretching. The beefed-up Model 92 Rossi seems to be able to handle it. But the shooter pays a price on the back end. Recoil, in the relatively light rifle, can be classed as "very heavy."

ANOTHER LEVERGUN REPLICA

Thus far we have talked of replica Winchester leverguns in general and, in particular, those chambered in .45 Colt. Now we'll touch on something interesting which isn't patterned after a Winchester. And although it *is* a .45, it is not the .45 Colt, but rather the .45 Smith & Wesson (aka .45 Schofield). It was introduced the same year as the 1860 Henry.

On March 6, 1860, Christopher Spencer received a patent for his levergun. The Spencer was a seven-shot rimfire, lever-action carbine with a tubular magazine in the buttstock. Pushing down and forward on the lever surrounding the trigger performs two functions. The fired case is ejected and a new round is fed into the chamber. The hammer must then be cocked manually before you can fire it. President Abraham Lincoln fired an early Spencer and was duly impressed and the United States government ordered 10,000 Spencers — the first shipment delivered in December 1862.

There is conflicting information on the chambering of the original Spencers. One source said the original cartridge was .56-56 with a 350- to 360-grain bullet over 42 to 45 grains of black powder. An earlier source cites the cartridge as .56-52 with a 410-grain bullet propelled by 40 grains of black powder. We do know nearly 95,000 Spencer carbines and 12,000 Spencer rifles had been received

by the U.S. government by 1865.

Of course, many of them went West with the expansion following the Civil War and were used by both sides at the Battle of the Little Big Horn. Custer was no stranger to the Spencer, as his Michigan cavalry unit had received Spencers in early 1863 and used them quite effectively at Gettysburg.

Original Spencers, of course, are antiques today and ammunition is difficult, if not nearly impossible, to find. Very few of us will ever have the chance to shoot one. But replica Spencers are available for anyone who wants one from Cimarron, Taylor's & Co., Inc. and other importers. As with so many other replicas, they have been modernized to the point of accepting readily available ammunition. In the case of the Spencer, that ammunition is not .45 Colt but rather the shorter, less potent .45 Schofield.

Whenever I work the Spencer's lever, cock the hammer, and fire, I swear I can hear bugles in the afternoon and the playing of "Mine Eyes Have Seen the Glory of the Coming of the Lord." As I handle it I can feel trail dust in my nostrils and even smell bacon and beans cooking over a campfire. This is something a quality historical firearm does to someone whose heart is in tune with tradition. ◉

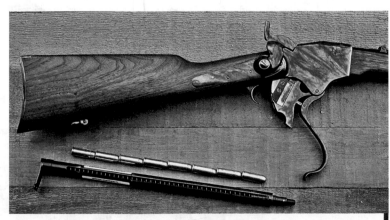

A commonly available replica .45 levergun is the Spencer, chambered in .45 Schofield. Here, the tubular magazine goes into the buttstock. The other operating difference? The hammer must be cocked manually for each shot.

His natural element: Cooper at the range (left) and in the classroom at Gunsite (right).

REMEMBERING JEFF COOPER

CHAPTER 60

'd like to end this journey with a salute to the one man who has done more than anyone else to make the .45 — specifically the .45 *ACP* — viable. We're talking, of course, about Col. John Dean "Jeff" Cooper. As a shooter

for most of my adult life, I especially identified with Cooper, who was a member of "The Greatest Generation," as well as a shooter and teacher.

Cooper entered my life through the printed word at just the right time — a time when I was just starting to become really serious about handguns. As a teenager my life-changing 75-cent purchase of his *Fighting Handguns* from a local magazine rack set everything in motion for me. That was long ago — 1958 to be exact.

I literally devoured it, and still have my original copy. It's now dog-eared and held together with masking tape. When I decided to search the Internet

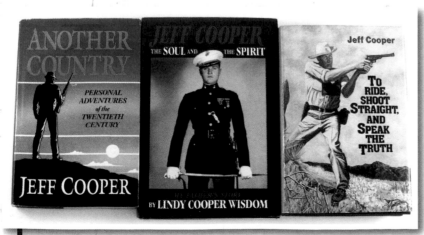

Lindy Cooper Wisdom's excellent work on her father's exploits is flanked here by two of Cooper's earlier works.

for copies to put away for my grandsons, I had to pay slightly more than the original price. About $50 more!

Shortly after *Fighting Handguns*, Cooper came out with a very small booklet entitled *Handguns Afield*. Both works gave me considerable knowledge and insight into the use of handguns, both sixguns and semiautomatics. Both have since been reprinted, and it gives me great joy to know the publisher gave me credit for calling attention to them and for my help in starting the reprinting project.

Cooper probably had more influence on handgunning and self-defense using a 1911 Government Model than anyone else during the second half of the 20th century. His thoughts on handguns, rifles (specifically the "Scout" concept), politics and life in general have had a great effect nationally and internationally. He was truly deserving of being named Outstanding American Handgunner. But when I took over as chairman of the OAH Foundation, he had yet to receive the award. My No. 1 hope was to somehow present him with it personally.

My dream was thwarted during my first meeting with him as he refused to accept the nomination. I was convinced if he were nominated, he would be voted in. But it would be several years before he could be convinced to accept. Normally the vice president of the OAH Foundation, Bill Jordan, presented the award each year. However, when Cooper won, I reserved the right to present the award personally.

I also had the privilege of spending the evening visiting with him. Every nominee received a miniature trophy and then the actual winner got the coveted bronze statue. When Cooper received the bronze, he presented me with his miniature, which now occupies a special place in my office.

A long time ago, Cooper said something I totally agree with to this day:

"The love of guns is innate in Homo sapiens. Some sociologists, some legislators, and some women deplore this, but they can't change it. The authors of the Old Testament knew it, Homer knew it, Mallory and MacCauley and Kipling and Zane Grey knew it, and we know it today. A fine personal firearm is a joyous thing and — despite the whimpering of the hoplophobes — needs no mental abnormalities for its appreciation.

"The machine age has democratically supplanted the one-of-kind gun with the production line model, and the last century or so has produced some splendid models, none of which surpasses the illustrious Colt .45 auto pistol. ... Pistols do not win wars, but they save the lives of the men who do. The noble 1911 is a mechanical marvel whose ruggedness, dependability, and ferocious power have come forward and comforted four issues of G.I.s, and which, unlike any other instrument you can name, is as much superior to its rivals in 1967 as it was in 1917. Everything considered, it is more suitable for commemoration than any firearm ever built ... I have lived intimately with the .45 auto for nearly 30 years, and I have studied its performance intensely in organized combat competition — the toughest proving ground — for over a decade."

John's initial introduction to Cooper was through these two early paperbacks, both now recognized as classics in pistolcraft.

Cooper's championing of the 1911 .45 ACP was not an overnight phenomenon. It was the result of years of open, unrestricted competition and study.

His thoughts on handguns, rifles (specifically the "Scout" concept), politics and life in general have had a great effect nationally and internationally. He was truly deserving of being named Outstanding American Handgunner.

Before Cooper came to his conclusions he had studied and experimented with just about everything else. But when it came down to combat, the obvious choice was the .45 ACP chambered in the 1911 Government Model.

Wiley Clapp — a former Marine and deputy sheriff — writes a regular column for the NRA's *Shooting Illustrated*. This is what he has to say about Cooper and the 1911:

"Even in the military, long since equipped with 9 mms, the demand for the battle-proven .45 ACP is so strong, warriors who stand a good chance of actually 'seeing the elephant' somehow end up with a 1911. This demand stems from the pioneering work of Cooper, who systematically eliminated other handgun types from consideration, developed a style of shooting and promoted both the gun and technique at Gunsite."

Another man whose work I greatly admire is my colleague at *GUNS Magazine* and *American Handgunner* Magazines, Massad Ayoob. Mas is also a recipient of the Outstanding American Handgunner award and holds Cooper in high regard:

"Hunter, traveler, connoisseur of food and wine and literature, author and race driver, John Dean Cooper was a man of many facets. He was a patriot and a quintessential Marine, whose consuming interest in what he called combat pistolcraft was born in two incidents in which he killed more heavily armed enemy personnel with his sidearm in the Pacific Theater and during his duties as an intelligence agent in Asia a few years later. Long before his distinguished service as a director of the NRA, he had proven himself one of the most persuasive spokesman for the right of the citizen to keep and bear arms ... he was never afraid to take strong positions, a trait that earned him both worshipers and enemies ... No one listed diplomacy among his attributes, and indeed, many felt his lack of it was a positive attribute."

Never in my wildest dreams as a teenager could I have ever imagine that someday I would be privileged to know such men as Jeff Cooper, Charles Askins, Rex Applegate, Elmer Keith, Bill Jordan, Skeeter Skelton and Walter Walsh. We are quickly running out of men such as these. The members of the Greatest Generation are disappearing every day. We will never see their like again. ◎

THE END